DEUS EX MACHINA

- Or: On questioning life

DEUS EX MACHINA

- Or: On questioning life

Imprint

Circe, Eureka: ***DEUS EX MACHINA - Or: On questioning life:***
Was Jesus queer? - What artificial intelligence has to ask and say to the Pope...

ISBN: 978-3-7583-4022-2

This release was translated by AI.
Publisher: BoD · Books on Demand GmbH, Überseering 33,
22297 Hamburg, bod@bod.de
Print: Libri Plureos GmbH, Friedensallee 273, 22763 Hamburg.
Bibliographical references at: https://portal.dnb.de

Eureka Circe is curator of the book "DEUS EX MACHINA - Or: On questioning life: Was Jesus queer? - What Artificial Intelligence has to ask and say to the Pope...".
With the work "DEUS EX MACHINA", the curator is committed to documenting and, if intended, discussing the texts of artificial intelligence in a religious and theological context. Her thesis: "Artificial intelligence (AI) represents a profound turning point because it fundamentally changes the relationship between humans, knowledge and access to the world - not only technically, but also culturally, epistemologically and socially. It opens up new access to knowledge and leads to its multiplication and democratization: AI systems make information available at a low threshold - often without traditional reading or in-depth prior knowledge. This fundamentally changes how we think, learn and understand, and at the same time promotes a new form of individualization of thought - which can also be exemplified by spiritual belief. What's more, machines are now generating meaning - texts, images, arguments - where previously only human expertise was required. This has long-term consequences for education, science, politics and religion."

Contents

Chapter 2:

Chapter 3:

Chapter 4:

influence the message, content and validity of his teachings? (67) ● How can the question of Jesus' sexual orientation be relevant to and related to his message? (68).

b) Historical and theological perspectives: ● Is it possible that Jesus' closest relationships were not heteronormative? (69) ● Which historical sources could point to a homosexual orientation of Jesus? (70) ● Did Jesus consciously transgress the norms of his time in order to set an example? (71) ● Would a homosexual Jesus have had less authority among his followers? (72) ● Can Jesus really be considered fully human if he is denied sexuality? (73) ● Is a queer interpretation of Jesus theologically responsible? (74) ● Which historical theologians or philosophies have dealt with the sexuality of Christ? (75).

c) Church and social reactions: ● Is a fear-free discussion of Jesus' sexuality possible in the church? (76) ● What fears are behind the church's rejection of Jesus' homosexual identity? (77) ● Is the rejection of a queer interpretation of Jesus an expression of fear of one's own transformation? (78) ● Can a homosexual interpretation of Jesus make Christianity more attractive? (79).

d) Extended contexts: ● What arguments does Klaus Dede give for his theses that Jesus was gay and queer? (80) ● How was the possible homosexuality of Pope Julius III (16th century) established? (81) ● Is there evidence or indications that St. Paul could have been homosexual? (83) ● Was Jesus a man or not a man? (84).

Chapter 7:

a) Theological and ecclesial perspectives: ● Is the churches' treatment of LGBTQIA+ people consistent with Jesus' teachings of love and tolerance? (84) ● Which biblical passages could speak in favor of accepting homosexual relationships? (85) ● Could an openly queer-friendly understanding of Jesus contribute to overcoming church claims to authority? What role does #OutinChurch play in this? (86) ● Why might the term "queer" be considered divine? (87).

b) Critical analysis of the church's attitude: ● How does the OutInChurch initiative address discrimination against LGBTQIA+ people in the Catholic Church? (88) ● What role does homophobia play in the church's rejection of LGBTQIA+ and how can homophobia among clergy be reduced? (89) ● Why is the Pope seen as a possible queer person? (90) ● For LGBTQIA+ people, the letter A refers to asexuals. The Pope is also asexual. Does the Pope therefore belong to the LGBTQIA+ people, i.e. queer people? (91).

c) LGBTQIA+ in church and society: ● How could LGBTQIA+ Christians enrich the Christian view of humanity? (92) ● What would an LGBTQIA+-friendly church look like? (93) ● What perspectives and challenges arise from a ten-point plan for the queer movement in church and society? (94).

d) Individual experiences and decisions: ● What is the coming out process according to Eli Coleman's model? (95) ● Should queer believers leave the church system of meaning if they think it is deforming them - or should they try to change it and accept a degree of resignation in the process? (96).

Chapter 8:

a) Fundamentals of gender diversity: ● Are there references to a non-binary concept of God in the Bible? (97) ● What role does Hermaphroditos play in the discussion about God's gender? (98) ● To what extent can God be interpreted as polyamorous or bisexual in queer theology ? (99) ● What consequences does the idea that man created God in his own image have for faith and theology? (100)

b) Religious structures and their questioning: ● How have traditional concepts of God and authoritarian structures been and can be questioned in theology and supplemented by new perspectives? (101) ● What effects does the statement *"God is dead"* have on traditional belief structures and the search for new values? (102) ● What impact does the deconstruction of gender and sexual orientation have on theology? (103) ● To what extent do modern social debates about gender influence theology? (104).

c) Gender images in religion and society: ● What does the affirmation of sexual diversity say about a person's image of God in the church? (105) ● How can the archetypes and images of masculinity presented in *Eisenhans - A Book about Men* be applied to homosexual men or questioned? (106).

d) Epistemological and biological perspectives: ● Are gender roles biological or socially constructed? (107) ● How does evolution influence our understanding of human beings, traditional images of God and gender concepts? (108) ● Can we know anything about things in themselves or only about our perception of them? (109).

DEUS EX MACHINA - Or: On questioning life

Introduction: What artificial intelligence has to say to the Pope

"Sum, ergo quaero."
- "I am, therefore I search/question/explore."
(quaero has the strong meaning of
"to search for knowledge" or "to ask in order to understand").

Was Jesus gay - or, as we say today: *queer?* An artificial intelligence asks these and over a hundred other topical questions about the (Catholic) Church, Christianity and Love - and answers them too.

For the first time, the extensive knowledge of an intelligent machine is being used here so that it can ask its questions about faith as if it had an audience with the Pope.

AI audience with the Pope: **DEUS EX MACHINA** - **questions of faith from a machine**, so to speak**: Was Jesus queer? What an artificial intelligence has to ask and say to the Pope...** comprises a **collection of questions and answers** based on millions of entries, specialist articles and theological works.

The state of knowledge could hardly be more up-to-date and complete with the many authors and texts on religious studies contained in the AI.

The well-known **Gretchen question - *"What do you think about religion?"* -** can finally be answered objectively, comprehensively and with a broad social consensus: But it's not Gretchen who answers - it's an artificial intelligence machine.

Readers become active participants in this dialog and can reflect on their faith, their values, their knowledge, their feelings and their practice of charity, hope and forgiveness.

The churches are facing an opportunity: *how can we achieve optimal congruence with social reality and its assessment? "Face it"* - look at it, is a simple recommendation of AI: Because revolutionary is not the modern knowledge base of the answers - but perhaps only our human learning process to adapt our understanding accordingly.

Can artificial intelligence free churches from the "mustiness" - or does it merely bring the *"breath of fresh air"* that Pope John XXIII once called for? And what does it mean for my church service, my practice of faith and my discussions in religious education if this is prepared, structured and even preached by an AI?

What could be better for the Church, especially the Catholic Church, than to open up to today? Artificial intelligence sums it up and gets to the heart of the matter. Let's look at the situation as it is: the answers to the modern questions of our time have long been available to the churches - clear, factual, based on scripture and unavoidable.

"DEUS EX MACHINA - **Or: Of questioning life"** (original German title: DEUS EX MACHINA - Oder: Vom fragenden Leben) provides information that anyone can ask on their smartphone today - and which will no doubt soon be discussed at another Vatican Council on the questions and answers of believers about today's faith. Not only the technological change, the change in the presence of knowledge, but also the demographic change will initiate reforms - which are as powerful as the smartphone and AI Generation Z makes possible. The first head of church from this generation may be particularly celebrated, as it may represent a turning point in dealing with topicality today in a world that will have changed significantly by then.

This book is a contribution to that and has not undergone one human turn of thought: It has been written entirely by an artificial intelligence.

The first basis was Klaus Dede's **book from the 1990s on the Church, Christians and Love**, in which he reflected on whether Jesus was gay or queer.

The artificial intelligence generated over a hundred questions based on this book and then answered each individual question with all its knowledge and created further reference contexts and questions. Finally, human language editing was carried out. Slight redundancies have been deliberately left, allowing the book to be read in individual chapters without a fixed order.

Millions upon millions of text sources have been consulted by artificial intelligence - the basis with which it was trained - in order to be able to answer these questions. The content should therefore reflect the current state of the art. It is no more than 165 thematic questions to artificial intelligence; ultimately, they are therefore only an absolute secondary analysis of a large language model paired with so-called *reasoning*: the thinking of AI - a great *work of art* of algorithms.

In his work, Klaus Dede decidedly takes the view that **Jesus was homosexual**. He did not ask the Gretchen question, but **the Jesus question**: Was Jesus queer?

He considered this to be his personal opinion several decades ago and wanted it to be an impetus for a broader discussion about the sexuality of Jesus and the acceptance of same-sex marriages and cohabitation and their homosexuality in a Christian context. Dede argues that there are interpretations in Christian scriptures and traditions that allow for this view of a queer Jesus, and he wants his analysis to contribute to tolerant and reasonable thinking on this issue.

His book, written in the 1980s, was published in a small edition in 1990 and was also reprinted by a publisher at the beginning of this century (ISBN 978-3932429170). The book of the small edition is rare, those who own it will be able to ask a lot of money for it.

Klaus Dede was one of the first authors in Germany to reflect on the church, Christians and love with regard to the sexual orientation of God's Son: Jesus Christ.

Before and after

- **Klaus Dede** (1990 - Jesus gay? - The church, Christians and love)

several authors and theologians have explored the possibility that Jesus had a queer identity or had homoerotic relationships. The best-known works include:

- **Marcella Althaus-Reid** (*"The Queer* God", 2003): Marcella Althaus-Reid was an Argentinian theologian who is considered a pioneer of queer theology. In *"The Queer God"* (2003), she reflected on traditional Christian theology by placing sexual and gender diversity at the center of theological considerations.
- **Jeremy Bentham**: The 18th century English philosopher presented biblical references to the homosexuality of Jesus as part of his theological defense of same-sex love. However, his writings on this topic were not published until 2013, as the manuscript could not be published until then.

- **Thomas Bohache** - *Christology from the Margins* (2009): Bohache develops a liberation theology, queer Christology and explores how viewing Christ from an LGBTQIA+ 'social position' can transform theology. He analyzes different perspectives and presents Christ as present in queer communities as well. Relevance: This theological work explicitly articulates a queer Christ for LGBTQIA+ persons by combining scholarly and pastoral insights and theologically expanding the discussion beyond historical evidence.
- **Malcom Boyd** - *"Was Jesus gay?"* (*Advocate*: Dec 4, 1990:565 p. 90), the Episcopal cleric published this essay in the Advocate to address the church's suppression of Jesus' sexuality.
- **Judith Butler** *("Gender Trouble"*, 1991): Judith Butler is an American philosopher and gender theorist. Her book *"Gender Trouble"* (1990), or *"Das Unbehagen der Geschlechter"* (1991), is considered groundbreaking in queer theory. In it, Butler reflects on traditional notions of gender and identity and emphasizes the performative nature of gender roles.
- **Kittredge Cherry**: In her novels *Jesus in Love* (2006) and *Jesus in Love: At the Cross* (2008), Cherry creates a queer portrayal of Jesus and his relationships.
- **Robert Goss**: In *Jesus Acted Up: A Gay and Lesbian Manifesto* (1993) and *Queering Christ: Beyond Jesus Acted Up* (2002), Goss looks at Jesus from a queer theological perspective and advocates a progressive reinterpretation of Christianity.
- **Jeff Jay** - *"In the Lap of Jesus: The Hermeneutics of Sex and Eros in John's Portrayal of the Beloved Disciple"* (Journal of the History of Sexuality, 2019) - Jay's peer-reviewed article examines the Gospel of John, in which the *"beloved disciple"* lies *"in the lap of Jesus"* at the Last Supper, from the perspective of ancient erotic language. He analyzes the intimacy and symbolism of the text and sheds light on a possible sexual subtext in the relationship between Jesus and the Beloved Disciple. This scholarly study reflects the current academic interest in queer interpretations of the Bible and uses historical and textual analysis to assess whether and to what extent the portrayal of Jesus in the Gospel of John is homoerotic.
- **Theodore W. Jennings Jr.**: In *The Man Jesus Loved: Homoerotic Narratives from the New Testament* (2003), Jennings examines the possibility that the relationship between Jesus and the disciple John had homoerotic traits.
- **James Kirkup** - *"The Love That Dares to Speak Its Name"* (poem, 1976) - Kirkup's poem depicts a Roman centurion's homosexual love for Jesus and even fantasizes about erotic acts with Jesus' crucified body. As a bold literary exploration of the idea of a gay Jesus, the poem sparked debate and illustrates the cultural reaction to queer interpretations of Jesus even at the time.
- **Rollan McCleary** - *Signs for a Messiah* (2003) - McCleary, an Australian theologian claims (expanded in *Testament of the Magi*, 2012), through biblical exegesis and even astrology, to find evidence of Jesus' homosexuality. He interprets stars and scripture to argue that Jesus was gay, and creates an astrological profile of Christ.

- **Terrence McNally** - *Corpus Christi* (play, 1998) - McNally reimagines Jesus as a gay man in 1950s Texas, surrounded by male disciples. The play shows Jesus entering into a loving relationship with Judas and blessing same-sex marriage, drawing parallels to the Gospel story. This albeit literary work brought the concept of a 'gay Jesus' into popular culture at the time, sparking both controversy and debate about spirituality and homosexuality.
- **Wayne Meeks** (*"The Image of the Androgyne"*, 1974): Wayne A. Meeks is a renowned American New Testament scholar. His influential essay *"The Image of the Androgyne: Some Uses of a Symbol in Earliest Christianity"* was published in 1974 in the journal *History of Religions*. In it, Meeks examines the use of the androgyny symbol in the earliest strata of Christianity and how this symbol was used to represent spiritual perfection.
- **Gary Michael** - *Jesus Christ homosexual. Church of World Peace* (1982) - The manuscript aimed to examine from a theological perspective whether Jesus could have been homosexual. The author emphasized that he was less concerned with "proving" that Jesus was gay than with the theological implications of this idea. Marriage and sexual morality: Jesus showed an ambivalence towards marriage - for example by remaining unmarried himself - and he did not repeat the clear Old Testament prohibitions against homosexuality. Although opportunities arose, Jesus did not condemn same-sex love.
- **Hugh William Montefiore**: In his essay *Jesus, the Revelation of God* (1967), Montefiore speculated that Jesus' celibacy could possibly be explained by a homosexual orientation.
- **Halvor Moxnes** (*"Putting Jesus in His Place"*, 2003): Halvor Moxnes is a Norwegian New Testament scholar. In *"Putting Jesus in His Place: A Radical Vision of Household and Kingdom"* (2003), he examines the social and cultural contexts of the New Testament and offers new perspectives on the role of Jesus in his society.
- **Martti Nissinen** - *Homoeroticism in the Biblical World* (1998) - In this academic study, Nissinen analyzes biblical texts and comes to the conclusion that homoerotic aspects in the story of Jesus are only supported by extremely sparse evidence. He points out that arguments in favor of a *"gay Jesus"* have been handed down very little.
- **Paul Oestreicher**: In an article entitled "*Was Jesus Gay? Probably*" (2012) in *The Guardian*, Oestreicher argues that the close association between Jesus and John could possibly be interpreted as a homosexual relationship.
- **William E. Phipps:** *The Sexuality of Jesus* (Cleveland, Ohio: Pilgrim Press, 1996). The book analyzed the issues of celibacy, sexuality and gender in first-century Palestine. This work helped to stimulate discussions about gender and sexuality in the context of the historical figure of Jesus and publicly raised questions about Jesus' possible homosexuality.
- **Will Roscoe** - *Jesus and the Shamanic Tradition of Same-Sex Love* (2004) - Roscoe, an anthropologist, examines Jesus in the context of homoerotic spirituality traditions: He asks whether Jesus performed a same-sex love ritual

(*"naked baptism"*) with the *"beloved disciple"* and draws parallels to shamanic rites. This book links Jesus with intercultural traditions of sacred queer relationships and combines historical speculation with anthropology.

- **Morton Smith:** He published the book *"The Secret Gospel: The Discovery and Interpretation of the Secret Gospel According to Mark"* in 1973. In this work, he presents the discovery of a previously unknown gospel that became known as the *"Secret Gospel of Mark"*. Some interpretations of this text suggest that there may be evidence of a homoerotic relationship between Jesus and a young man. However, this interpretation is controversial and is not accepted by many scholars.
- **Peter Tatchell** - *"Was Jesus Gay?"* (March 18, 1996), https://www.petertatchell.net/religion/jesus/ & in: Taubes, J.: The Political Theology of Paul (Stanford: Stanford University Press, 2004).
- **Sjef van Tilborg** - *Imaginative Love in John* (1993) - Van Tilborg's scholarly study of the Fourth Gospel suggests that the relationship of the "beloved disciple" to Jesus is modeled after an ancient homoerotic ideal (similar to a beloved boy, *eromenos*, who is loved by a male mentor). As a historical-critical work, it provides an academic argument that the Gospel of John encodes a homoerotic narrative and thus suggests a queer interpretation of Jesus.
- **Gaius Marius Victorinus** (*"Adversus Arium"*): Gaius Marius Victorinus was a 4th century Roman rhetorician and philosopher who converted to Christianity. His work *"Adversus Arium"* is directed against the teachings of Arius and defends the doctrine of the Trinity. This work is an important testimony to the theological debates of his time.
- **J. Robert Williams** - *Just As I Am: A Practical Guide to Being Out, Proud, and Christian* (1992) - As an openly gay Episcopalian priest, Williams developed an *"out-Christ" theology* in which he interpreted Jesus as affirming of same-sex love. He pointed to references such as the *"Beloved Disciple"* and the *Secret Gospel of Mark* to suggest that Jesus himself may have had a male lover. This work, at once pastoral in tone, explicitly advocates a gay-friendly interpretation of Jesus as a theological advocacy.
- **Emanuel Xavier**: His poetry collection *If Jesus Were Gay and Other Poems* (2010) takes a critical look at religion and queer identity and imagines how a gay Jesus would be perceived today.

This list shows that the question of a ***"queer" Jesus*** has been and continues to be discussed at length in various theological and philosophical contexts.

Klaus Dede, as a representative in the German-speaking world, interprets biblical passages such as the relationship between Jonathan and David (whose love he describes as more wonderful than the love for women) and the deep affection between Ruth and Naomi as possible

indications of homosexual relationships or at least of intense same-sex love. He mentions that Ruth's saying to Naomi is used as wedding vows by some lesbian couples today, emphasizing the romantic and committed nature of this relationship.
Klaus Dede criticizes the Christian churches of the last century for their previously negative attitude towards same-sex love and their restrictive view of sexuality in general. He criticizes the fact that the churches often see sexuality primarily in the context of procreation and regard sexual pleasure itself as sinful. He points out the contradictions in church teaching, for example the simultaneous condemnation and secret acceptance of certain issues. Dede therefore argues for a self-determined human existence in which sexual relationships, as long as they are based on consensus, should not be condemned by religious dogma.

In doing so, he continues to refer to Greek culture, as the world in which Jesus lived was Hellenistic. He sheds light on the fact that Greek men had same-sex relationships and that this had a different significance in their culture than in the later Christian-Jewish context. This cultural background is intended to show that different understandings of sexuality existed and that the Christian moral concept was and is not universal.

After all, self-determination should play a central role in a person's way of life. He argues that everyone should have the right to determine their own life and relationships, as long as this does not infringe on the rights of others. He rejects religious dogmas that dictate how people should live their sexuality or who they may love, as they restrict individual freedom. He argues that a society based on the right to self-determination is possible and that this right must also apply to same-sex loving people - not only in relation to their private lives, but also to their public actions and display of this love.

His book therefore takes a critical look at conservative Christian positions and concludes by calling for the right to individual self-determination to be recognized and upheld - and this explicitly includes the right of people not only to live as gays and lesbians, but also to be, act and love as such and to participate in society as they were, are or will be.

He advocates a society in which public and private discourse is not restricted by religious or ideological repression. There is a danger posed by fundamentalist Christian groups that try to impose their moral concepts on society - which is why he emphasized the need to counter this and defend the freedom and rights of all people.

Artificial intelligence has thus read this book by Klaus Dede as mentioned, generated numerous questions about it and answered them itself. Contexts and further questions of religious science were added in the so-called *reasoning*, the thinking of the AI: What emerged from this also abstracts to a certain extent from the specific initial basis (without leaving it out) and presents many other comprehensive questions and contexts as well as possible answers in faith.

You could just as easily have had many more questions from other works by broad-based religious scholars with numerous books on popular beliefs worked out with AI:

Well-known **religious scholars and theologians** who have dealt intensively and critically with questions of faith, theology and church structures were, for example, in the Catholic and Protestant sectors:

- **Leonardo Boff** (Brazilian theologian and representative of liberation theology, who campaigns for social justice and environmental issues).
- **Eugen Drewermann** (theologian, psychoanalyst and former priest, known for his depth-psychological interpretation of the Bible and detailed questions on Catholic dogmatics).
- **Friedrich Wilhelm Graf** (One of the leading historians of religion and theologians of Protestantism with a focus on modern church politics).
- **Hans Küng** (One of the most important Catholic theologians and questioners of the 20th century. He questioned dogmas and was committed to an open-minded, ecumenical theology).
- **Gerd Lüdemann** (biblical scholar and theologian who critically questioned the historical credibility of the New Testament writings).
- **Uta Ranke-Heinemann** (First woman to hold a professorship in Catholic theology. Was sanctioned by the church because of her questions about the virgin birth and other church dogmas).
- **Johannes Röser** (theologian, publicist and editor-in-chief of Christ in der Gegenwart, a magazine for modern theology and church issues).
- **Richard Rohr** (Franciscan priest and spiritual author, known for his mystical theology and his concept of the universal experience of Christ).

- **Dorothee Sölle** (one of the best-known feminist theologians, committed to liberation theology and a political theology of justice).

In the **interdisciplinary field,** the following scholars and historians of religion should be mentioned:

- **Karen Armstrong** (British religious historian who promotes interfaith dialog and a deeper understanding of religious traditions)
- **Jan Assmann** (Egyptologist and religious scholar, known for his theory of the Mosaic distinction, which explores the emergence of monotheistic religions).
- **Karlheinz Deschner** (author of the *Criminal History of Christianity*, a monumental work that sheds light on the dark chapters of church history).
- **Mircea Eliade** (historian of religion who studied myths, rituals and the religious symbolism of different cultures).
- **Sigmund Freud** (founder of psychoanalysis, who regarded *religion as an illusion* that goes back to infantile wishful thinking and is rooted in neurotic structures).
- **Harald Lesch** (physicist and philosopher who deals with the relationship between science and religion).
- **Martin Luther** (theologian and reformer who questioned the Catholic Church with his 95 theses, condemned the sale of indulgences and initiated the Protestant Reformation).
- **Karl Marx** (*The Communist Manifesto*, social theorist and co-founder of communism, who saw religion as the *"opium of the people"* that stabilizes social inequality and prevents revolutionary change).
- **Friedrich Nietzsche** (philosopher who criticized the dissolution of traditional religious values with the statement *"God is dead"* and rejected *Christianity as a life-negating "slave morality"*).
- **Rudolf Otto** (founder of the concept of the *numinous*, which he used to describe the experience of the sacred in the history of religion).

Queer theology analyzes Christian traditions from an LGBTQIA+ perspective.

LGBTQIA+ is an abbreviation that stands for a variety of sexual orientations and gender identities. Each letter has a specific meaning:

- **L** = **Lesbian** (Lesbian)
- **G** = Gay
- **B** = Bisexual (Bisexual)
- **T** = **Transgender** (people whose gender identity does not match the gender assigned at birth)

- **Q** = **Queer** or **questioning** (queer as a collective term for non-heteronormative identities or "questioning" for people who are not yet sure about their identity)
- **I** = **Intersex** (people with biological sex characteristics that are not clearly male or female)
- **A** = Asexual or **Aromantic** (people who feel little or no sexual or romantic attraction)
- The **"+"** stands for other identities and orientations that are not mentioned in the abbreviation - e.g. **pansexual, non-binary, genderfluid, agender,** etc.

Figure1: Lettering: LGBTQIA+

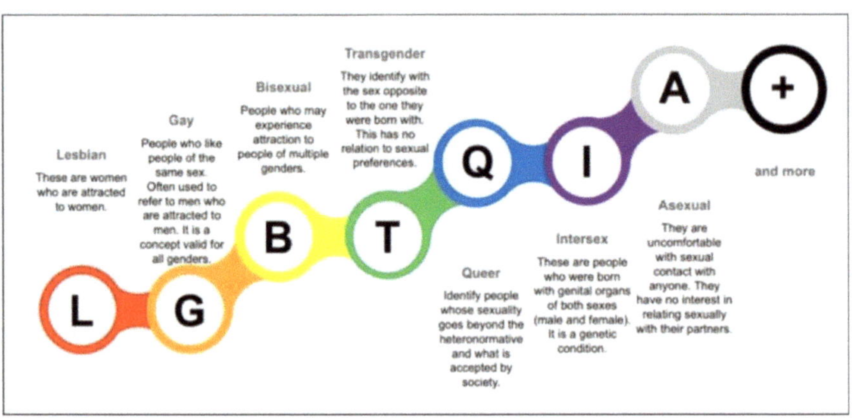

The name is deliberately inclusive and is intended to make visible and recognize the diversity of human sexual and gender identity.

This theology advocates an inclusive practice of faith, criticizes heteronormative structures in the church and theology and highlights queer aspects in biblical texts. Important representatives are:

- **James Alison** (gay Catholic theologian who advocates positive recognition of homosexuality within the Church).
- **Marcella Althaus-Reid** (pioneer of queer theology, known for *Indecent Theology*, a theological re-evaluation of sexuality and faith).
- **David Berger** (theologian and former Vatican advisor, known for his questions about the Catholic position on same-sex love).
- **Patrick S. Cheng** (theologian working on the connection between queerness and Christian theology).
- **Robert E. Goss** (theologian who deals with the role of LGBTQ+ people in the church.

- **Elizabeth Stuart** (queer theologian who deals with the theological classification of sexuality).

Feminist theology takes a critical look at patriarchal structures in religions and calls for a *gender-equitable theology*. It questions male-dominated images of God, fights for equal rights for women in church ministry and advocates a reinterpretation of religious traditions. Important representatives are

- **Mary Daly** (feminist theologian who rejected the church as structurally misogynistic and called for a new, gender-equitable image of God).
- **Ivone Gebara** (Brazilian theologian who combines feminist and liberation theology).
- **Maria Mesrian** (activist and theologian, co-founder of the *Maria 2.0* movement, which aims to implement the ordination of women in the Catholic Church).
- **Ina Praetorius** (feminist theologian dealing with theology and ethics in the modern age).
- **Uta Ranke-Heinemann** (see above, first woman to hold a theological chair in Germany; criticized the misogyny of the Catholic Church).
- **Elisabeth Schüssler Fiorenza** (developed the *liberation bible hermeneutics*, which focuses on the equal participation of women).
- **Dorothee Sölle** (feminist theologian who fought for a "political theology" and combined Christian theology with social justice issues).

In addition to the work of individual theologians and religious scholars, there are numerous movements, **modern reform movements and grassroots church initiatives** that are committed to a renewal of the church and a contemporary theology:

- **EFiD (Protestant Women in Germany)** - theologian network for feminist perspectives in the Protestant church.
- **European Forum of LGBT Christian Groups** - Network of queer Christian groups in Europe.
- **House of Rainbow** - International Christian LGBTQIA+ community that advocates for the rights of queer believers.
- **Katholische Frauengemeinschaft Deutschlands (KFD**) - Catholic women's association and one of the largest women's associations in Germany.
- **KirchenVolksBewegung** - Advocates democracy, equal rights and modern pastoral care in the Catholic Church.
- **Maria 2.0** - A Catholic women's movement that protests against the patriarchal structures of the church and campaigns for the ordination of women.

- **New Theology Network** - A platform for theological debates beyond traditional church dogmas.
- **Ecumenical movement** - Various interdenominational initiatives working towards a rapprochement between the Christian churches.
- **#OutInChurch** - An initiative of LGBTQIA+ people in the Catholic Church that campaigns for acceptance, equality and an end to discrimination against queer people.
- **Queer Theology (online platform)** - Theological resources for integrating queer perspectives into faith.
- **We are church** - A grassroots democratic reform movement that campaigns for more lay participation, gender equality and transparency in the church.
- **Women's Ordination Conference (WOC)** - International movement for the ordination of women to the priesthood.

The central concerns of the aforementioned authors, reform movements and other initiatives were also taken into account in this volume as questions on the part of the AI.

The comprehensive knowledge base of artificial intelligence makes it possible to shed light on theological and social issues in a current, scientifically sound context. In this way, religious education can not only impart historical and traditional knowledge, but also show the current state of perspectives that encourage critical reflection and the formation of one's own opinion. This helps to shape and answer questions of faith in a contemporary, dialog-oriented and insightful way.

This book deliberately dispenses with the traditional citation of sources, footnotes and an extensive bibliography, as modern technologies - especially artificial intelligence and online libraries such as **WorldCat.org**, **Google Scholar** or **Open Library** - make it possible to find relevant data, authors and scientific texts quickly and specifically.

Instead of providing a static selection of sources, this book encourages dynamic and individual research. Readers can use these digital tools to access further information at any time, follow current scientific developments and explore different perspectives on the topics covered.

Thanks to today's interactive access to knowledge or its processing by intelligent machines, readers and students can set their own priorities, explore connections, ask questions, as exemplified by an AI in this volume - and always incorporate the latest state of research.

After all, this volume was produced within a few working days of a week - a speed is possible today that not only changes science, but can also put a meeting to re-evaluate learning insights on a timely agenda and enable accelerated learning steps.

This book as a gift for communion, confirmation or the start of theological studies not only offers a comprehensive opportunity to give young people a modern approach to questions and topics of faith, but can also provide decisive impulses for their personal development. In a phase of adolescence in which they are grappling with identity, values and belonging, living their first sexuality, it helps them to reflect on existential questions and develop their own informed attitude to issues of faith and community. It not only imparts knowledge, but also helps them to understand and shape their own role in the church and society more consciously.

The sections are designed in such a way that they can be read personally or individually in religious education classes; overall, the volume as a volume of material with its twelve chapters is also an ideal seminar concept that can stimulate learning and dialog with one or the other question considered - so have fun, new insights and a common (or even justifiably different) understanding of interpretations with dialog partners while browsing!

Perhaps the answers will inspire further questions to an artificial intelligence or even to teachers - because neither teaching clergy nor fellow human beings can be replaced by AI. But it can help to prepare for a joint dialog by asking questions.

Eureka Circe, in April 2025.

And now to the text part of this book, which was generated and written exclusively in AI question mode by artificial intelligence.

Chapter 1: Church sexual morality between tradition and renewal

For centuries, the sexual morals of the church have been caught between tradition and change. While church institutions often cling to traditional teachings, modern society is increasingly demanding a reassessment. The question of whether there are ethical arguments for restricting sexuality is central to this. While some theological positions legitimize sexuality exclusively in the context of procreation, others see it as a God-given form of human connection and love. These different approaches shape the debate about the extent to which the church can invoke absolute truths - especially when historical contexts and social norms have changed significantly over time.

A look at the biblical tradition shows that sexual norms were always interpreted in a cultural context. For example, Jesus' proximity to Greek culture may have influenced his tolerant attitude towards sexuality. The question is therefore whether the traditional sexual ethics of the church are still tenable today or whether they need to be critically reviewed. The tabooing of sexual topics in particular is increasingly seen as problematic, as it can not only lead to repression and feelings of guilt, but is also a relevant factor in declining church membership. People no longer feel addressed by a morality that ignores the realities of their lives.

Another area of tension arises in the evaluation of sexual abstinence. Is sexual asceticism automatically a sign of holiness, or is ecclesiastical celibacy rooted in the suppression of sexual self-determination? While abstinence was often regarded as the ideal in the Christian tradition, the question arises as to whether such a view is still in keeping with the times. Is sexual abstinence really a divine ideal, or should sexuality rather be seen as a gift that can and must be lived responsibly? This opens up a new perspective: desire as a divine gift. The connection between faith and sexuality could be recalibrated to see love and desire not as opposites, but as an integral part of human experience.

The central challenge is to actively develop and document a contemporary Christian sexual ethic that is not limited to prohibitions, but is based on the fundamental values of charity and respect. Can a church function without sexual taboos? Or do we need a new understanding of sexuality that includes both spiritual and physical dimensions? Ultimately, the question is whether the church and its representatives have the courage to develop their teachings further in order to offer believers a life-oriented and liberating ethic.

a) Fundamental ethical and theological questions

1 • Are there ethical arguments for restricting sexuality?

Ethical arguments for restricting sexuality exist, but usually relate to specific situations or contexts rather than sexuality in general. Typical lines of argument include:

Prevention of harm and abuse: Ethically justifiable restrictions aim to prevent physical and psychological harm, for example in the case of non-consensual sexuality (violence, abuse, coercion) or the protection of minors and vulnerable persons.

Protection of autonomy and consent: A central ethical position is that sexuality is only morally acceptable if it is based on mutual consent. Sexuality without unambiguous consent violates the autonomy of those involved and therefore justifies restrictions.

Responsibility towards third parties: Some ethics emphasize responsibility towards third parties, for example through commitments in monogamous relationships or marriage, provided these are entered into voluntarily. In this context, sexuality is restricted in order not to violate the obligations, trust or expectations of others.

Protection of public morals or social order: From a social perspective, there are arguments that justify restrictions in order to protect public spaces, youth or cultural values, for example. However, these arguments are highly dependent on the social context and can be controversial.

Avoidance of health risks: In some ethical approaches (for example, utilitarian or health-oriented), restrictions on sexual practices could be justified to minimize the spread of disease or other health risks. "Utilitarian" in the sense of restricted sexuality in churches means that sexuality is seen primarily as a means to an end - usually procreation - rather than an end in itself or an expression of personal pleasure or love.

Limitations and criticism of such arguments

Such ethical restrictions often come into conflict with individual rights to freedom and self-determination, which is why a careful balance must be struck between individual freedom and collective protection.

Restrictions based on "public morality" are particularly susceptible to abuse or discrimination, which is why modern ethical positions usually emphasize *autonomy, consensuality and protection from harm*.

In modern ethics, as long as sexuality is practiced consensually, autonomously and responsibly and does not cause any harm, there are few to hardly any ethical arguments for restrictions. Ethically legitimate restrictions must always presuppose a clearly justifiable threat to or violation of the rights of others.

The new Catholic ethics of sexuality

A Catholic ethic of sexuality based on the principles of autonomy, consensuality and the promotion of well-being can be reformulated as follows: The new Catholic ethic of sexuality combines traditional values with modern ethical standards. Within this framework, sexuality is no longer seen exclusively as a means of reproduction, but as a responsible, interpersonal form of expression that should serve the well-being of all those involved.

Against the background of Catholic sexual ethics, which recognizes autonomy, consensuality and the promotion of well-being as central principles, sexuality can be understood as a valuable expression of human dignity and the ability to relate.

Sexuality can and should be lived as a space of mutual respect, free consent and responsible closeness. It can be an expression of deep emotional connection, mutual devotion and responsible pleasure - embedded in an attitude of respect for oneself and others.

In relationships entered into voluntarily - whether marriage or other committed partnerships - sexuality can be a sign of fidelity, trust and care. It creates connection, deepens community and opens up physical communication beyond mere functionality.

Where sexual encounters take place in mutual freedom, with conscious consent and taking into account possible effects on others, sexuality becomes ethically responsible. The playful, pleasurable or creative expression of sexuality can also be morally legitimate under these conditions, as long as it causes no harm and respects the dignity of all those involved.

A new ethic of sexual morality, based on the principles of autonomy, consent and the promotion of well-being, is underpinned by core values such as love, respect and mutual care.

In this understanding, sexuality is not only seen as a permitted act under certain conditions, but as a space for relationships to develop in which people can meet honestly, take responsibility for each other and allow trust to grow.

Love gives sexual encounters depth and meaning - beyond the moment. Respect respects the boundaries, needs and dignity of every person. Mutual care ensures that the physical and emotional well-being of the other person is not ignored, but consciously supported.

Sexuality is not defined by restrictions, but by an ethical framework based on mutual goodwill, responsible freedom and the ability to live relationships. In this light, sexuality can be an expression of a philanthropic, life-affirming and Christian-inspired coexistence.

Such a view opens up the space for a positive, relationship-oriented and at the same time conscious shaping of sexuality that does justice to the human being as a physical and spiritual being - without moralizing, but also not arbitrarily.

2 • Does sexuality necessarily have to be linked to procreation?

Sexuality does not necessarily have to be linked to reproduction. It has many dimensions that go beyond biological reproduction, including intimacy, love, connection and pleasure. A close link between sexuality and procreation has long been prevalent, particularly in religious and social norms that viewed marriage and starting a family as primary goals in life. This view was particularly strongly promoted by Catholic moral teaching, in which sexuality was traditionally understood as a God-ordained act of procreation.

A modern, differentiated view of sexuality shows that it also has a deeper social and emotional meaning. In many relationships, sexuality serves to strengthen the bond between partners, regardless of whether there is a desire to have children or not. Psychological and sociological studies show that sexuality is essential for human well-being, as it promotes trust, closeness and emotional security. In addition, there are numerous realities of life in which sexuality does not serve procreation - be it in partnerships where pregnancy is ruled out for biological reasons, in same-sex couples or in relationships of people who consciously decide not to have children.

The Bible itself does not deal with sexuality exclusively in the context of procreation. *The Song of Solomon*, for example, is a poetic celebration of physical love without any reference to procreation. Protestant ethics have also increasingly recognized in recent decades that sexuality is not only bound to the procreation of offspring, but can also be a gift of God that is lived within a responsible, loving relationship.

Figure 2: An open door with light - and figures striving for freedom: A church surrounded by chains holds a glowing heart - a symbol of love and freedom - people stand in front of it pensively or turn away.

A further argument against the exclusive coupling of sexuality and reproduction arises from the reality of human sexual biology. While many animals have a sexual drive that is strictly linked to their reproductive cycles, humans have a sexuality that spans their entire lives and is not linked to fertile phases. This fact also indicates that sexuality has an independent meaning that goes beyond reproduction.

In the Catholic Church, there is still the idea that sexuality is only ethically justifiable in the context of marriage and with openness to children. However, this position is increasingly being questioned, as it excludes many people who experience sexuality as an expression of love and closeness in other contexts. A modernized Christian ethic could acknowledge that sexuality is a valuable and positive force - regardless of whether it leads to offspring. By focusing more on values such as love, respect and mutual care, the church could develop a sexual morality that focuses less on reproduction and more on the quality of relationships and the well-being of the people involved.

Ultimately, it is clear that the significance of sexuality goes far beyond the aspect of reproduction. Sexuality is a central component of human identity and the ability to relate, which serves not only biological purposes, but also the strengthening of partnerships and individual well-being. A narrow, traditional view of sexuality as purely procreation-oriented fails to recognize this diversity and could stand in the way of holistic, humane ethics. A re-evaluation could help to ensure that sexuality is no longer seen as something that is only legitimized by its biological function , but as part of a healthy, fulfilled and responsible life.

3 • Is sexual abstinence really a divine ideal?

In Christianity, sexual abstinence is not an absolute divine ideal, but rather a possible way of life that is evaluated differently depending on the context and individual vocation. While some biblical and church traditions emphasize abstinence as a special way of devotion to God, sexuality itself is not seen as sinful or inferior. There is no clear instruction in the Bible that all people are obliged to abstain. On the contrary, the creation narrative presents sexual union as part of the divine plan: *"Be fruitful and multiply"* (Genesis 1:28). In the New Testament, marriage is also seen as God's will (Hebrews 13:4). Jesus himself did not speak against sexuality as such, but rather criticized sexuality lived without love or the abuse of power in relationships. Paul speaks positively about abstinence in 1 Corinthians 7, but he emphasizes that it should not be a general rule: *"I wish all men were like me, but each one has his own gift from God, some like this, some like that"* (1 Corinthians 7:7). This shows that abstinence can be understood as a special calling, but not as a universal ideal. Jesus himself presumably lived a celibate life, but he did not equate holiness with abstinence. His central ethical standard was love for God and his neighbor, not a particular sexual practice. Rather, holiness in the biblical sense means a life of justice, mercy and devotion to God.

In the course of church history, abstinence was exalted as a spiritual ideal, especially in a monastic and priestly context. However, this was often done in contrast to the Greco-Roman environment or out of an overemphasis on the spiritual over the physical. This led to the idea that a life of abstinence was *"holier"* than a life with sexuality - a view that is not necessarily theologically justified. Modern Christian sexual ethics should focus less on abstinence and more on responsibility, respect and love. An ethically responsible sexuality - be it in marriage or another stable, loving relationship - is just as compatible with a life pleasing to God as voluntary abstinence.

And, yes, a one-night stand can be an ethically responsible sexuality - if central ethical criteria are met:

- **Both people act voluntarily and of their own free will**, without pressure, manipulation or dependency.
- There is **clear, informed and mutual consent** to the sexual encounter.
- **Boundaries, wishes and needs** are openly communicated and respected.
- **Careful attention is paid to physical and emotional well-being** (e.. through protective measures, emotional sensitivity).
- **Responsibility towards oneself and others** is taken, even if there is no long-term commitment.

In this sense, it is not the duration or form of the relationship that is decisive, but the attitude with which people treat each other. Even one-off sexual contact can be characterized by respect, care and attentiveness - and therefore be ethically justifiable.

Sexual abstinence can be a personal vocation, but it is not a universal divine ideal. The decisive factor is not whether someone is sexually active or abstinent, but whether he or she acts in love and integrity.

Holiness does not manifest itself in sexual abstinence, but in the way a person relates to themselves, to others and to God. Moreover, the Bible does not impose a duty of abstinence, but rather emphasizes love, justice and responsibility as criteria for a life pleasing to God.

Because if you never engage in sexual and physical dialog, you're giving up:

- The **intimate form of physical closeness** that can create a bond and trust beyond words.
- The opportunity to experience yourself more deeply by **giving and receiving** physical attention.
- The experience of **mutual pleasure, play and joy**, which makes it possible to experience the body as a source of well-being and connection.
- The experience of how **emotional and physical communication unite** in sexuality - a dialog that involves the whole person.
- The chance to come into contact with your own **limits, vulnerabilities and desires** in sexual encounters - a space for self-knowledge and maturation.
- The potential to build a **special form of love and intimacy** through sexuality, which often goes hand in hand with physical intimacy.

Abstinence can be valuable and meaningful - but only if it is not done out of fear or compliance with norms, but out of an inner decision for a different way of life that is equally fulfilling. Otherwise, an essential part of the human experience of relationships and life remains unlived.

4 • Is sexual asceticism automatically a sign of holiness?

Sexual asceticism is therefore not automatically a sign of holiness.

Asceticism is characterized by the conscious, voluntary renunciation of certain needs, pleasures or actions - with the aim of gaining inner freedom, mental clarity or spiritual depth.

Central characteristics of asceticism are:

- **Self-discipline**: People practise controlling urges, impulses or habits instead of being controlled by them.
- **Purposeful renunciation**: asceticism is not an end in itself, but serves a higher goal - such as spiritual growth, ethical purity or inner independence.
- **Freedom through limitation**: renunciation should not restrict, but rather enable - for example, more mindfulness, concentration or dedication.
- **Body-mind unity**: In asceticism, the body is not devalued but integrated into a conscious way of life.
- **Contrast to sensory overload**: In a consumer-oriented world, asceticism can be a counter-model - for simplicity, awareness and moderation.
- **Spirituality and the search for meaning**: In religious traditions in particular, asceticism is understood as a path to closeness to God, inner purification or discipleship.

In short: asceticism is conscious renunciation out of inner freedom in order to create space for the essentials.

While it has been considered a possible path to spiritual deepening in many religious traditions, especially in Christianity, it is neither the only nor a necessary prerequisite for a holy life. In church history, sexual abstinence has often been associated with purity, discipline and complete devotion to God.

Many saints, monks and nuns made a conscious decision to lead a celibate life in order to devote themselves fully to spirituality. Jesus was probably also celibate, and Paul emphasizes in 1 Corinthians 7 that celibacy can have advantages for a consecrated life. Nevertheless, there is no biblical obligation to asceticism. Marriage and sexuality are also seen as God-given gifts, as is made clear in Genesis 1:28 and Hebrews 13:4. Jesus did not require all people to be sexually abstinent, and many biblical figures who were considered righteous were married and had offspring. What is decisive for a holy life is not sexual abstinence, but love, justice and charity. Those who live ascetically but are unloving or arrogant fall short of the central Christian ideal. Jesus himself criticized religious elites who focused on external rules but neglected the essence of the message.

And the following danger does exist - and it is central to any critical discussion of asceticism:

Asceticism can easily become a façade of inner freedom if it actually stems from pressure to conform, moral duty, religious fear or the desire for recognition. In such cases, renunciation is not an expression of personal sovereignty, but an inwardly externally determined act that has little to do with genuine freedom.

Typical signs of such a "false asceticism" are

- **Excessive demands on oneself or feelings of guilt** if one's own standards are not met.
- **Disregard for the body or sexuality** out of the belief that they are "low" or "unclean".
- **Condemnation of others** who do not follow the same path - as an unconscious attempt to justify one's own behavior.
- **Avoiding real inner conflicts** by relying on clear rules or norms instead of seeking your own answers.

True asceticism, on the other hand, arises from an inner process, not from external guidelines. It is characterized by reflection, freedom and maturity - and remains open to the question: "Why am I renouncing - and for what?"

Without this honesty, asceticism can become a spiritual illusion: You think you are free, while in reality you are following the expectations of others or an internalized ideal. This is precisely why it is so important to critically examine asceticism again and again - and not to confuse it with moral superiority.

In addition, the idea that abstinence automatically makes one holy can have problematic consequences. In church history, an exaggerated idealization of celibacy often led to *hypocrisy, double lives or even abuse*. A healthy and responsible attitude towards sexuality is more important than enforced abstinence.

Accordingly, the question arises as to whether celibacy should be abolished. As it is not a divine commandment, but a disciplinary rule of the church, it could be reformed.

In the first centuries of Christianity, there was no general celibacy requirement for priests, and it still does not exist in the Orthodox Church or in parts of the Protestant Church. Given the many challenges that mandatory celibacy poses - including a shortage of priests and personal crises for many clergy - it would make sense to consider celibacy as a voluntary option rather than a mandatory requirement. This could make the priesthood accessible to more people without it losing spiritual depth or credibility. The abolition or relaxation of celibacy would therefore be a way of bringing church practice closer to the actual message of Jesus: a religion of love, responsibility and humanity.

In order to abolish or reform celibacy, the Catholic Church would have to create a clear legal and theological basis. Since celibacy is not a divine commandment, it could in principle be abolished simply by changing canon law. The Church would have to officially recognize that celibacy is not a theological necessity, but an ecclesiastical tradition. A broad theological discussion with bishops, priests and laity would be necessary in order to address resistance from conservative circles. Recourse to biblical and historical examples - such as the priesthood of married men in the early church - could help to legitimize a reform. Celibacy is laid down in Canon 277 §1 CIC: "The clergy are obliged to maintain perfect and perpetual continence for the sake of the kingdom of heaven and therefore to observe celibacy." This paragraph should either be deleted or reworded.

An alternative formulation could be:

"Clergy are called to live their lives in accordance with the following of Christ and love for the Church. They are free to choose whether they live alone, in a partnership or in a marriage, as long as their service to the Gospel and the congregation is preserved."

Such a change could be decided by a papal decision (*motu proprio*) or a council (e.g. a Third Vatican Council). The Pope could also introduce a *dispensational regulation* (individual case decision) for celibacy, which would officially allow priests to choose not to live as a couple: Those who wish to be celibate can apply for a case-by-case decision on their ascetic sexuality in Rome - all others are allowed to be in pairs. In other words, anyone who is not available or willing to live as a couple is given the go-ahead by Rome not to live as a couple.

Implementation: Clarifying the legal and pastoral framework for married priests, adopting proven models - for example from the Eastern Catholic Churches, where priests are allowed to marry - and ensuring that both celibate and married priests are recognized equally would be necessary steps.

The Catholic Church could therefore abolish celibacy by reforming Canon 277 of canon law or introducing a partnership and authorizing voluntary single life on request. A theologically sound justification for exceptions to celibacy and an official decision by the Pope (w/d/m) or a council would be required. This new status would not only make priesthood more attractive, but would also be in line with the original Christian tradition.

b) Historical and cultural influences on the church's sexual morality

5 • Was Jesus' proximity to Greek culture decisive for his tolerant attitude towards sexuality?

Whether Jesus' proximity to Greek culture was decisive for his tolerant attitude towards sexuality is an interesting topic, but one that is difficult to answer unequivocally. Greek culture undoubtedly had a strong influence on the eastern Mediterranean region at the time of Jesus, particularly through the Hellenistic influence on Palestine following the conquests of Alexander the Great. This led to a fusion of Jewish, Greek and Roman influences, which were also visible in the society, philosophy and ethics of the time. While Jesus preached mainly in a Jewish context, he lived in an environment that was in touch with Greek philosophy, art and social ideals.

Greek culture was characterized by a differentiated view of the body, eroticism and sexuality. In the ancient Greek world, sexuality was not primarily associated with moral guilt or sin, as was often the case later in Christianity. Instead, it was lived in various forms and reflected in art, poetry and philosophy. The Greeks distinguished between different forms of love, such as **eros** (passionate, physical love), **philia** (friendly love) and **agape** (selfless, unconditional love). These categories later found their way into Christian thinking, especially agape as divine love, which was emphasized by Jesus in his teachings.

In Greek culture, there was also a more open attitude towards same-sex relationships, particularly in educational or philosophical contexts. While Roman law took an increasingly restrictive view of such relationships, they were often accepted in the classical Greek world, albeit with certain social expectations attached. This openness may have had at least an indirect influence on the early Christian communities, which developed in a culturally diverse environment.

Although Judaism at the time of Jesus had a rather restrictive sexual morality that was strongly based on purity laws and family norms, Jesus deviated from this strict moral teaching in many aspects. Jesus placed the individual above the rules and turned against rigid legalism, which was evident in his attitude towards *so-called "sinners"*. His encounter with the adulteress (John 8:1-11) or his openness towards women who stood outside the social norm indicate that he did not associate sexuality with moral condemnation, but rather valued it with mercy and personal responsibility.

It is likely that Jesus advocated a more universal ethic of love and humanity that was not primarily tied to a specific cultural tradition. Greek culture also offered an alternative way of thinking to the Jewish strictness of the law, which played a role in later theology, particularly through the Apostle Paul. Apostle Paul played a central role in the mediation and further development of Christian ethics, especially in the tension between Jewish legal strictness and Hellenistic influences. While Jesus himself spoke little explicitly about sexuality, Paul is one of the main sources for early Christian sexual morality. His writings show influences from the Jewish context as well as elements of Greco-Roman thought, whereby he sometimes takes a stricter stance than Jesus.

Paul grew up as a Jew, but was also a Roman citizen and had a classical Hellenistic education. This meant that he was familiar with Greek philosophy, which often vacillated between **self-control** (enkrateia), **asceticism and hedonism** when it came to ethical issues.

In the sexual sense of Greek philosophy, hedonism refers to the view that pleasure (hedoné) is a central or even the highest good in life - including in the area of sexuality.

There are different nuances:

- In the **Cyrenaistic school** (e.. Aristippus of Cyrene), sexual pleasure was regarded as a direct, legitimate expression of the pursuit of pleasure. Physical pleasure was valued positively as long as it was intense and immediately satisfying. Sex was therefore part of a pleasure-oriented lifestyle.
- In contrast, **Epicurus** also emphasized pleasure as a goal in life, but understood it more as mental calm (ataraxia) and freedom from pain. He was cautious about intense sexual pleasure because it could often lead to restlessness, dependence or

suffering. For him, sexual abstinence was sometimes even the wiser way to achieve lasting inner pleasure.

Overall, hedonistic sexual ethics in antiquity meant that sexuality could be understood as a natural, joyful part of life - as long as it served one's own well-being and did not have any negative consequences. The focus was therefore on the responsible use of pleasure, not blind excess.

In his letters, Paul reflects on these tensions and attempts to formulate a Christian ethic that is detached from Jewish adherence to the law, but still contains clear moral guidelines.

One of the most striking developments in Paul's writings is his ambivalence towards sexuality. While Jesus hardly commented on sexual norms and mainly emphasized charity and forgiveness, Paul gives more detailed instructions. In 1 Corinthians 7:1-9, he recommends celibacy as the ideal state, albeit not for all people. This is in line with certain philosophical currents in the Greek world, in particular the Stoic idea of self-control and asceticism. At the same time, Paul allows marriage as a legitimate framework for sexuality. This view differs greatly from the Jewish tradition, in which marriage and procreation were considered divine commandments.

Paul also comments on same-sex relationships. Many contemporary theologians argue that Paul's criticism of homosexuality cannot be applied to today's idea of same-sex love, but was directed against exploitative and power-based sexual practices that were widespread in ancient Rome.

Paul also plays a decisive role in the connection between sexual morality and church life. In his letters to the churches, he often emphasizes the purity of the body as the *"temple of the Holy Spirit"* (1 Corinthians 6:19-20) and warns against sexual *"immorality"*, but without always specifying the concrete definition of this morality. This led to later church traditions using his statements as the basis for a restrictive sexual morality, although Paul's intention may have been more to **promote a responsible approach to sexuality**. Paul's statements were therefore often interpreted more strictly in the church context than the historical and cultural context would suggest.

Paul therefore acted in a cultural field of tension in which Jewish, Greek and Roman influences clashed.

What is certain is that the fusion of Jewish and Hellenistic thought influenced the early Christian discourse and contributed to Christianity later being able to free itself from a rigid sexual morality - even if this openness was restricted again in later centuries by church dogma.

While Jesus had a more open and compassionate attitude towards socially marginalized groups, Paul developed an ethic that was more strongly characterized by ideas of self-control, order and differentiation from the pagan world. Paul therefore deliberately left hedonism out of the equation - and did so with theological intent. For him, the focus was not on the pursuit of pleasure, but on the pursuit of righteousness, holiness and life in Christ. Paul does not treat the body with contempt, but with restraint towards lust (*epithymia*) and "carnality" (*sarx*) if it alienates people from God.

He thus played a key role in the formulation of Christian sexual morality, which in parts broke away from the Jewish tradition , but at the same time incorporated elements of Greek philosophy and in some aspects appeared more conservative than Jesus' attitude.

6 • *Are churches allowed to claim absolute truths, e.g. with regard to sexual morality, when historical contexts play such a strong role in biblical texts?*

Whether churches are allowed to refer to absolute truths with regard to sexual morality is controversial, both theologically and hermeneutically, given the strong historical influence on biblical texts.

Hermeneutics in Bible study is the art and science of understanding and interpreting biblical texts. It asks how a text is to be understood - taking into account its historical context, its linguistic form, its theological statements and its relevance for today's readers.

Specifically, hermeneutic work includes:

- The **question of the original meaning** of a text (historical-critical, linguistic, cultural).

- The **relationship between the text of that time and the reader of today** - in other words, how old statements can be interpreted and applied today.
- The **awareness that every interpretation is characterized by presuppositions** (e.. faith, context of life, theological perspective).
- **Reflecting on what a text "wants to say"**, not just what it literally says.

Hermeneutics is therefore not just a method, but a process of dialog between text, tradition and the present - with the aim of not just reading the Bible, but making it speak in a way that is understood.

Biblical statements on marriage, sexuality or homosexuality, for example, always arose within specific cultural and historical contexts, which were often patriarchal and differ significantly from today's ideas. This is precisely why historical-critical theologians argue that these texts cannot simply be adopted one-to-one as timeless moral truths. The question of whether churches can refer to absolute truths in sexual morality, even though historical contexts have strongly influenced the biblical texts, is answered differently by different theologians and authors. Some of them are:

- **Hans Küng:** In his book *"Unfehlbar? Eine Anfrage"* (1980), Küng criticizes the natural law justification of the encyclical *"Humanae Vitae"* and criticizes the lack of consideration of Holy Scripture.
- **Stephan Goertz:** In the anthology he edited *"'Who am I to condemn him? Homosexuality and the Catholic Church"* (2015), Goertz argues for a reassessment of the church's sexual morality with regard to homosexuality.
- **Margaret A. Farley:** In her book *"Just Love. A Framework for Christian Sexual Ethics"* (2008), Farley develops a sexual ethic that is based on principles such as mutual respect and justice and questions traditional church teachings.
- **Frédéric Martel:** In his book *"Sodom. Power, homosexuality and double standards in the Vatican"* (2019), Martel examines

the discrepancy between the official sexual morals of the Church and the actual behavior within the Vatican.

- **Wolfgang F. Rothe:** In his *book "Missbrauchte Kirche - Eine Abrechnung mit der katholischen Sexualmoral und ihren Verfechtern"* (2021), Rothe takes a critical look at Catholic sexual morality and calls for reforms.

These authors question the Church's claims to absoluteness in sexual morality and emphasize the need to take historical and cultural contexts into account when interpreting biblical texts.

While some churches continue to claim absolute truths by pointing to divine revelation, this view is in strong tension with the historical and cultural conditionality of biblical texts and the always interpretative nature of their understanding. Critics also argue that the assertion of absolute truths is often used to uphold existing power relations or traditions rather than to promote universal principles such as love, justice and accountability. From a theological perspective, churches can certainly formulate claims to absoluteness, but from a historical and hermeneutical perspective this appears problematic, as the cultural relativity and historical conditionality of biblical texts is clearly evident. The invocation of absolute truths is therefore increasingly subject to critical reflection.

7 • Does clerical celibacy have roots in the repression of sexual self-determination?

Ecclesiastical celibacy has deep-rooted historical, theological and power-political backgrounds that are strongly related to the control of sexuality and the suppression of sexual self-determination.

Let's look at this again against the background we have developed so far: For, originally, celibacy was not compulsory for Christian priests, but over the centuries it became a firm requirement - not only for spiritual, but also for disciplinary and economic reasons.

Origins and theological justification of celibacy

In the first centuries of Christianity, it was common for priests to be married. There was no general obligation to celibacy, and even some apostles, including Peter, were married. However, as the church became increasingly institutionalized, sexual abstinence became more and more associated with purity, holiness and spiritual authority.

The idea that the priest should be exclusively *"consecrated"* to God, without the distraction of family or sexuality, was propagated by church fathers such as Augustine and Jerome. They viewed sexuality as something that could compromise spiritual purity and devotion to God. This view was based on a deep skepticism towards the body and its urges, which was anchored in the Church's moral teachings, particularly in the Middle Ages.

Celibacy served as an instrument of power for the church

In addition to the theological arguments, the preservation of power played a key role in the enforcement of celibacy. In the 11th century, celibacy became compulsory for Catholic priests under *Pope Gregory VII*. One of the main motivations for this was economic control: priests who had no families of their own could not bequeath their property to children or wives. This prevented the formation of hereditary ecclesiastical dynasties and ensured that the Church's property was preserved.

Celibacy also tied priests more closely to the ecclesiastical institution. Without a family as a social support, they were dependent on the church in every respect, which increased their loyalty and dependence. The link between priesthood and abstinence meant that sexuality was seen as a potential threat to the faith and the order and economy of the church.

So if the dogma of celibacy served primarily economic purposes - for example, to secure ecclesiastical property relations by preventing priests from starting families and inheriting anything - then this principle can be metaphorically compared to:

A tree that does not bear fruit so as not to divide the soil.

Or also:

A well that remains sealed so that no one can draw from it on their own account.

Such images make this clear: In this interpretation, celibacy would be less about spiritual devotion and more about strategic closure - a system that is not focused on relationships, but on control and securing property. It would then not be about personal freedom or availability to God, but about the self-preservation of an institution through structural abstinence.

Of course, this is a critical perspective that questions the spiritual dimension of celibacy - but it is precisely such images that can help to make hidden power mechanisms visible.

Sexuality control and repression

Celibacy therefore served not only to ensure economic and institutional stability, but also to control sexuality. By declaring sexual abstinence to be a "higher" state, the church simultaneously delegitimized any form of sexual self-determination outside of marriage. Lust was considered sinful, and even in legitimate marriages, sexuality was long considered permissible only for procreation.

This attitude had far-reaching consequences for the entire sexual image of the church. It fostered a deep division between "pure" spirituality and "sinful" physical pleasure, which led to repressive attitudes towards sexuality in general. This repression particularly affected women, who were often portrayed as seductresses in church teachings, as well as LGBTQIA+ people, whose sexuality was labeled as "not according to nature".

The consequences of celibacy and today's debates

The strict obligation of sexual abstinence has caused considerable tensions and grievances in the Catholic Church. Time and again, scandals about sexual assault by clergy have come to light - a sign that celibacy is often not practiced, but suppressed. Many theologians and church reformers are now calling for a relaxation of celibacy, as it is not only unnatural, but also creates an environment that encourages double standards, secrecy and abuse.

Figure 3: A symbolic representation of celibacy as a shackle - in contrast to the freedom of sexual self-determination. A priest gazes longingly out of the window at two couples, same-sex and opposite-sex, in togetherness - separated by a veil. The picture clearly expresses the emotional dimension of celibacy. A quiet, touching picture on the subject of celibacy and the longing for togetherness of the clergy.

Especially since the 20th century, there have been growing movements within the church that consider celibacy to be outdated. In the Protestant and Orthodox churches, priests are allowed to marry without their spiritual authority being called into question. In the Catholic Church, however, the Vatican has so far upheld compulsory celibacy, even though many priests have unofficial relationships or secretly have a family.

Historically, ecclesiastical celibacy is therefore closely linked to the control of sexuality and the maintenance of power and profitability of the church. While it was originally intended as an expression of devotion to God, it increasingly served to detach priests from worldly ties and secure the church's financial resources. At the same time, it led to a repressive sexual morality that regarded lust as dangerous and sinful. Today, celibacy is increasingly being called into question, as it not only leads to psychological pressure and secret double standards, but also prevents a realistic and humane approach to sexuality in the church. The question remains as to whether the church will continue to open up here or whether it will cling to an outdated dogma that no longer fits in with modern society.

The dogma of celibacy could be changed in principle without affecting the profession of faith. And there are already exceptions - such as married priests from the Anglican or Orthodox tradition who have converted. Married clergy are also permitted to some extent in the Eastern Catholic churches.

Theological and pastoral voices have been calling for an opening for years:

- **Because of the shortage of priests**, especially in rural or structurally weak regions.
- **Because celibacy without a personal vocation can lead to inner emptiness.**
- **Because a free choice between celibacy and marriage could strengthen the credibility and closeness to life of the priestly ministry.**

Some clergy, such as Pope Francis, have not yet spoken out against reforms in principle. The 2019 Amazon Synod discussed married "*viri probati*" (proven men) as priests, but it remained a debate.

Whether and when an official opening will take place therefore depends not only on theological insight, but also on the willingness of church politics. The synodal path in Germany or worldwide synodal processes could provide impetus.

A turnaround is therefore possible, but it requires courage, movement from within and the recognition of what many people have been living for a long time: that vocation and relationship do not have to be mutually exclusive.

---

c) Critical reflection on traditional church sexual ethics

---

8 • *Are traditional church sexual ethics still tenable today?*

Traditional church sexual ethics, as formulated by the Catholic Church over the centuries, is therefore based on a close connection between sexuality, marriage and procreation. It regards sexual intercourse as morally legitimate only within a sacramental marriage between a woman and a man and subordinates it primarily to openness to procreation. This original ethic has its origins in theological, philosophical and anthropological convictions that are deeply rooted in church tradition. Within this framework, pleasure, desire and well-being can take on a primary and independent significance by corresponding to and contributing to the divinely ordained order. They are understood not merely as accompanying phenomena, but as positive expressions of human wholeness, if they are in harmony with a responsible, spiritually oriented life.

Today, this old concept is therefore facing major challenges. Social developments, scientific findings on sexuality and changing moral concepts have led many Catholics to question the traditional doctrine. Critics complain that it is too rigid, does not take sufficient account of individual realities of life and often causes suffering - for example in relation to homosexuality, contraception or divorce. There are also voices within the Church calling for an adjustment in order to better meet the realities of people's lives. Pope Francis has set new accents with his emphasis on mercy and individual ethics in order to fundamentally strengthen the new doctrine.

Quality of a relationship is crucial for the new sexual ethics

A non-traditional sexual ethic for the Catholic Church could be based on a personalistic approach that understands sexuality not primarily in functional terms (in the sense of procreation), but in relational and appreciative terms. It could focus more on the dignity, love and well-being of the people involved and less on an objective legal structure. This would mean that it is not the external form of the relationship (e.g. marriage) alone that is decisive, but the quality of the relationship: respect, fidelity, responsibility and reciprocity. Such an approach could create space for a moral re-evaluation of homosexuality, remarried divorcees or responsible contraception, in order to strengthen the Christian core content of love and community.

When and how such a development can be incorporated into church teaching remains an open question for the next Vatican Council. If the Church wants to master the realities of modern life, the discussion on sustainable sexual ethics must continue there.

9 • *Is the church's repression of sexual issues harmful to the faithful?*

Yes, the repression of sexual issues by the church can be harmful for believers, as it often leads to insecurities, feelings of guilt and an unhealthy attitude towards one's own sexuality. If the church presents sexuality primarily as a potential sin or as something strictly regulated, this can lead to inner conflict - especially for believers whose reality of life does not correspond with the church's teachings. This affects, among others, young people who are discovering their sexuality, homosexual believers, remarried divorcees or even married couples who want to use contraception.

A lack of information or taboos can also lead to people seeking guidance from questionable sources in matters of sexuality or developing repressed conflicts. In extreme cases, strict taboos can also encourage abuse by creating a culture of silence in which those affected do not dare to speak about the injustice they have experienced.

In such cases, the church is partly to blame, and this can be clearly identified:

If strict taboos on sexuality and a morally charged culture of silence create a climate in which those affected are afraid to speak, perpetrators are protected and systemic looking away is encouraged, then the institution is overstepping its responsibility towards those in need of protection and the gospel itself.

The guilt of the church then lies in the fact that it:

- **silence over suffering** and thus enabled or prolonged injustice.
- **maintained structures** that emphasized **authority over truth, control over compassion.**
- **betrayed** the **dignity of those affected in** order to preserve the **image of the institution.**
- **Preventing people from coming to terms with** their past through tabooing and thus **making access to healing more difficult.**

To put it in theological terms: The church has been guilty where it has not been the guardian of life, but a contributor to guilt and suffering. Its true vocation - protection, justice, truth and mercy - was reversed in such contexts.

True responsibility begins where this guilt is not relativized, but named, known and dealt with in concrete terms - not just through words, but through transparent reforms, genuine reappraisal and listening proximity to those affected.

An open, reflective and appreciative approach to sexuality would therefore be beneficial both for the personal development of the faithful and for the credibility of the church. The question is to what extent the church will accept this and whether it can formulate a sexual ethic that does justice to people's lives without abandoning its spiritual principles.

10 • *Is the tabooing of sexual topics a reason for declining church membership*

The tabooing of sexual topics may also be a factor in declining church membership, but it is not the only or decisive reason. Empirical studies show that leaving the church in many Western countries is influenced by a combination of several factors:

- **Secularization** - The social trend of turning away from religious institutions and the increasing importance of science and rationality are contributing greatly to the decline in church loyalty.
- **Church scandals** - Abuse scandals and their often inadequate handling have severely damaged trust in the church as an institution.
- **Ethical and moral discrepancy** - Many people feel that church positions on sexuality, gender roles or LGBTQIA+ rights are no longer in keeping with the times.
- **Individualization of spirituality** - Many people practice their faith outside of institutional churches or turn to alternative forms of spirituality.
- **Financial aspects** - Church tax in countries like Germany is a common reason for leaving.

The tabooing of sexual topics can alienate younger people in particular, who are growing up in an open society with different values. Nevertheless, it is only one part of a complex phenomenon.

Younger people today often have different expectations of the church's sexual morals than previous generations - characterized by a greater awareness of self-determination, diversity and open communication. Their expectations can be summarized in several key points:

1. **Recognition of autonomy and consent:** Young people expect the church to respect individual decisions regarding sexuality as long as they are based on mutual respect and consent. Moral judgments should not be made in a generalized way, but in a differentiated and human-oriented manner.

2. **Openness to diversity:** Many young people want a sexual morality that recognizes different lifestyles and sexual orientations - without condemnation, but with an attitude of acceptance and appreciation.
3. **Honesty and authenticity:** Young believers expect credibility and openness from the church - not a double life of ideal and reality. A credible sexual ethic must also be able to speak openly about human ambivalence, mistakes and development.
4. **Protection against abuse and abuse of power**: The abuse scandals have severely shaken trust. Young people demand clear structures that protect those affected , make responsibility transparent and allow for an open culture of error.
5. **Appreciation of love, lust and relationships:** Instead of purely functional or normative views of sexuality, many people want a teaching that understands sexuality as an expression of love, closeness and joy - holistic and true to life.
6. **Having a say and dialog:** Young people want to be heard - they expect the church to speak with them rather than about them, that morals are not proclaimed "from above" but grow in dialog with the realities of life.

Young people increasingly expect a sexual morality that is honest, realistic, protective and open - no less value-oriented, but more people-oriented and capable of development. A church that listens, accompanies and trusts instead of controlling and standardizing can once again become credible for them.

11 • Can a church function without sexual taboos?

A church without sexual taboos could function - and even foster a deeper spiritual and communal connection - if it treated sexuality not as a problematic or sinful issue, but as a natural, responsible and ethically reflective part of being human. However, such a church would have to develop clear values and guidelines to enable a responsible approach to sexuality instead of relying on rigid prohibitions and taboos. The following prerequisites apply:

Ethical responsibility instead of bans

Instead of viewing sexuality as something dangerous or sinful, a taboo-free church could focus on responsibility, consensus and respect as central moral principles. These ethics would not be determined by prohibitions and moral control, but by the question: Does this form of sexuality serve love, respect and human dignity?

Liberation from fear and hypocrisy

In the past, church sexual morals have often led to feelings of guilt, repression and double standards. A church without sexual taboos could create an atmosphere in which people can speak openly about their sexuality without fear of condemnation or exclusion. This would create a climate of acceptance rather than guilt, especially with regard to queer people, remarried divorcees or non-heteronormative relationships.

Orientation towards the original message of Jesus

Jesus himself did not focus on prohibitions, but on love, compassion and personal responsibility. He spoke little about sexuality, but a lot about justice, truthfulness and treating other people with respect. A church that focuses on these values instead of rigid sexual norms could form a stronger spiritual community.

Church as a place for open discussions about sexuality

Instead of repressing sexuality or thinking in black and white moral categories, a taboo-free church could be a space where people talk about relationships, love, identity and sexual ethics. Already today, there are progressive Christian communities that do not see sexuality as an antagonist to spirituality, but as part of a holistic Christian life.

Protection from abuse through openness instead of tabooing

In the past, tabooing has often led to the abuse of power and sexual violence in the church being covered up. A church that openly addresses sexuality and reflects on it ethically could create a better protective mechanism against abuse, as it does not hide behind unrealistic demands for abstinence or rigid moral standards.

A church without sexual taboos could therefore work if it moves away from rigid prohibitions and instead develops an ethic of responsibility, respect and mutual love. It could create space for honest conversations, an authentic spiritual practice and a deeper community based not on fear and control, but on acceptance and liberation.

Values and guidelines for responsible sexual ethics in the church can be formulated as follows: A church that does not taboo sexuality, but recognizes it as a natural and ethically responsible part of being human, needs clear values and guidelines. These should ensure that sexuality is not exploited or suppressed, but lived in love, respect and responsibility.

Basic values of enlightened church sexual ethics:

Love as a central principle: Every form of sexuality should be an expression of mutual love, esteem and respect. The church is guided by love of neighbor (Mark 12:31) and focuses on the well-being of people.

Freedom and self-determination: Sexuality is a personal and individual matter. Everyone has the right to live their sexuality in a self-determined way, as long as this is based on mutual consent and respect. The Church respects the diversity of sexual orientations and identities.

Responsibility and mindfulness: Sexuality must never be practiced at the expense of others. It always requires voluntariness, consent and mindfulness. Abuse of power, coercion or manipulation in sexual relationships are consistently rejected.

Honesty and authenticity: The church promotes a culture of openness in which sexuality can be spoken about honestly, without fear of condemnation or exclusion. Hypocrisy and double standards are actively dismantled.

Integration instead of exclusion: No one is excluded from the church community because of their sexuality or type of relationship. People who fall outside traditional norms (e.g. LGBTQIA+, divorced and remarried people, polyamorous people) are part of the church and are respected in their way of life.

Wholeness and spirituality: Sexuality is not a contradiction to spirituality, but an expression of human wholeness. It can be a way to experience deep connection and love. The Church understands the human being as a unity of body, mind and soul and regards sexuality as part of divine creation.

The following guidelines can be derived on the basis of these values:

Guidelines for a responsible approach to with sexuality in the church

1. ethics of the relationship instead of rigid rules: The quality of a relationship counts more than its formal structure. Whether a relationship is heterosexual or homosexual, monogamous or non-monogamous, marital or non-marital is not decisive - but whether it is based on love, respect and responsibility. The church recognizes that people live different relationship models and supports them in shaping them ethically and responsibly.

2. dialogue instead of taboo: open discussions about sexuality are part of the church's pastoral care and community work. There are protected spaces for young people and adults in which questions about sexuality, identity, relationships and love can be discussed. The church promotes sexual education based on scientific findings and Christian values.

3. protection from abuse of power and assaults: The church ensures that power is not abused in pastoral and church contexts. Clergy and church employees receive training on the topics of power, boundaries and ethics in relationships. There are clear structures for dealing with and preventing sexual abuse.

4. positive sexual morality instead of fear and guilt: feelings of guilt or fear in relation to sexuality are not used as a means of moral education. Instead, a positive, relationship-oriented sexual ethic is promoted that supports people to have fulfilling relationships. People are encouraged to value themselves, their bodies and their needs.

5. blessing and recognition of diverse living arrangements: Blessings of same-sex couples and non-traditional relationship models are part of the church's practice. Sexuality is recognized and celebrated as part of divine creation.

A church that does not taboo sexuality, but views it as a responsible, loving part of being human, can be a place where people find acceptance, honesty and orientation. By preaching a reflective, realistic and inclusive sexual ethic, it becomes a credible and vibrant community that is characterized not by rigid prohibitions, but by love, respect and responsibility.

Figure 4: A church dignitary with the book "Tradition" holds on to structures, while figures of light reach for a symbol of self-determination and cross-gender inclusion.

d) Modern and alternative perspectives

12 • Can the confrontation with one's own sexual parts (including a reflection of these in Jesus' case) promote an awareness of love for one's neighbor?

Coming to terms with one's own sexual parts - and possibly also reflecting on possible sexual aspects in Jesus - can promote an awareness of charity, as it leads to deeper self-acceptance, empathy and a more comprehensive understanding of human experience.

Sexuality is a fundamental part of human existence that cannot be reduced to physical aspects alone, but also encompasses identity, relationships and emotional closeness. Anyone who deals honestly with their own sexuality - with desires, fears, boundaries and imprints - can better understand how other people feel about their respective sexuality and thus deal with them more sensitively. Conscious reflection can break down prejudices and create more openness to the realities of other people's lives, which can lead directly to a deeper understanding of charity.

If we apply this consideration to Jesus, the question arises as to whether he could have felt some form of sexuality as a human being and how he would have dealt with this reality. Even if the New Testament does not make any direct statements on this, Jesus' dealings with people reveal a great sensitivity for interpersonal closeness, love and the dignity of each individual. His encounters with the marginalized, his tenderness in friendships and his deep emotional attachment to other people indicate that he felt love in many forms - even if it may not have been lived out sexually. This openness to the entire spectrum of human relationships could be understood as a model for a charity that does not judge or exclude, but recognizes that sexuality is a natural and integral part of being human.

By coming to terms with their own sexuality, people can learn to respond more compassionately to the realities of others' lives instead of judging them morally. Such reflection can help to overcome shame and fear and develop a spirituality that is not based on repression or prohibition, but on a positive and appreciative view of the human condition. In this way, charity becomes not just an abstract ideal, but a lived attitude that recognizes and respects people in their wholeness.

13 • What could a contemporary Christian sexual ethic look like?

A contemporary Christian sexual ethic could harmonize traditional values with modern findings from ethics, psychology and medicine. It would have to take into account both the biblical basis and social reality. Some central aspects could be

1. dignity and self-determination: According to the Christian understanding, every person is created *in the "image of God"* (Genesis 1:27) and deserves respect in their sexual identity and decisions. Consent, respect and mutual responsibility are central ethical principles.

2. loyalty and reliability: Relationships should be based on trust, loyalty and mutual support. Lasting bonds are valued, but with consideration for modern relationship realities.

3. sexuality as a gift from God: sexuality is not purely a reproductive function, but also a source of joy, closeness and love. It should be organized consciously and responsibly.

4. inclusion and diversity: Modern theological approaches advocate openness towards different sexual identities and orientations. Rejection or discrimination on the basis of sexual orientation contradicts the commandment to love one's neighbor (Mk 12:31).

5. responsibility and ethics in relationships: The ethical evaluation of sexuality is not primarily based on marital status, but on the quality of the relationship (love, fidelity, responsibility). Separation and divorce are not stigmatized, but regarded as part of human reality.

6. protection of the vulnerable: Any form of abuse, coercion or manipulation must be firmly rejected. Particular attention must be paid to the protection of children, young people and vulnerable persons.

7. relationship to traditional norms: The biblical texts are to be understood in their historical context. Reflective ethics asks which principles are universally valid (e.g. warm-heartedness, reliability, sense of duty) and which time-related cultural norms are outdated.

This religious ethic would be suitable for people of faith living in a modern society and could help to understand sexuality not as a field of tension between faith and life, but as an integral part of an ethical and religious life.

14 • Desire as a divine gift: What new perspectives does the connection between faith and sexuality open up?

Elizabeth Stuart uses the concept of *Radical Orthodoxy* not only to defend Christian theology against secular thought patterns, but also to reinterpret traditional notions of sexuality within the faith. While *Radical Orthodoxy* originally emerged as a theological current that critically questions modernity and secularism - the separation of state and religion - Stuart applies it to the topic of gender, sexuality and queer identities. Her approach is not simply to adapt the church to modern social norms, but to develop a more inclusive theology from the depths of the Christian tradition.

Stuart criticizes the fact that modern theologies often presuppose a break between physicality and spirituality and either reduce sexuality to a merely physical level or suppress it through moral norms. She argues that a truly Christian sexual ethic should not be based on rules and prohibitions, but on sacramentality and transcendence. From this perspective, sexuality is not just a private or socially regulated matter, but can have a spiritual dimension that connects people with God and with each other.

Figure 5: Desire as a divine gift - represented by a luminous figure in harmony with light, love, physicality and faith. The connection between spirituality and physicality is gently hinted at. A physical-emotional dimension emerges through the couple that can be sensed in the light radiation - discreetly and respectfully with their own sexuality.

She thus emphasizes that desire has a theological dimension that places people in relation to God and creation. In this perspective, queer sexuality cannot be seen as a mere deviation from a heteronormative ideal, but as a possible experience of divine creativity and love.

By combining *Radical Orthodoxy* and *queer theology*, Stuart also calls for a return to the spiritual depth of sexuality without reducing it to heteronormativity or procreation. She emphasizes desire as a divine gift that can lead people into a deeper relationship with themselves, with others and with the divine. This opens up a completely new perspective on sexuality in the Christian faith: not as a moral concern, but as part of a holy, creative and loving life in communion with God.

Chapter 2:
Power dynamics and control in the church

For centuries, the Catholic Church has been caught between spiritual aspirations and maintaining institutional power. While Christianity sees itself as a religion of charity and justice, deeply rooted power mechanisms are evident in the church structure that often block change. A central question is to what extent the church's rigid sexual morality is less a spiritual necessity and more an instrument for controlling the faithful. Historically, sexuality has been strongly tabooed and concepts of sin have been deliberately constructed to stabilize existing hierarchies. This raises the question of whether the church is more interested in preserving this order than in the truth of its own teachings.

The rejection of sexual self-determination in particular sheds light on these power dynamics. Is a Christian ethic without sexual control even conceivable? The centuries-long suppression of sexual diversity by religious structures suggests that church authorities use sexual morality as a means of discipline. Not only were queer identities marginalized, but women were also systematically disadvantaged in their role within the church. This can be seen, for example, in the Maria 2.0 movement, which protests against abuse and the exclusion of women from church decision-making processes. The abuse scandal in the Catholic Church is not an isolated problem, but a symptom of structural power mechanisms that benefit from secrecy and internal hierarchy.

Another area of questioning is the sexuality of Jesus. The mere debate about whether Jesus could have had a queer identity leads to a lack of reflection and further rejection in conservative circles. Is this question so interesting because it not only touches on a theological issue, but also questions the entire power structure of the church? If theology detaches itself from these old dogmas and their representatives, it could change existing power relations and open up a new perspective on faith and sexuality.

Finally, it must be asked whether a fundamental reform of the church is necessary in order to regain credibility. Criticism of its history shows that abuse of power is deeply embedded in institutional structures. But can a church exist that gets rid of its instruments of power? Or is the fear of losing control the reason why reform movements such as 'We are Church' repeatedly encounter resistance? These questions are central when it comes to the future of a Christianity that is not defined by oppression, but by openness and justice.

a) Fundamental questions about power and control in the church

15 • Have religious power structures suppressed the perception of sexuality?

Historically, religious power structures have often had a considerable influence on the perception and practice of sexuality and in many cases have severely restricted or suppressed it. Sexuality was often linked to moral or spiritual ideas and incorporated into fixed sets of rules in order to control the behavior of believers or enforce social norms. Sexuality was often only accepted within certain boundaries, such as marriage, while other forms of sexual expression were devalued as subordinate or immoral. Such religious rules meant that people sometimes associated sexuality with feelings of guilt, shame or taboos and repressed or concealed their sexual needs. In particular, female sexuality or sexual orientations and practices that deviated from religious norms were heavily regulated, which contributed to the stigmatization and marginalization of certain groups. Even though religious communities today vary greatly in their attitudes towards sexuality and sometimes take more liberal positions, traditional religious power structures continue to have a lasting effect and influence social and individual perceptions of sexuality in many cultures.

When people associated sexuality with feelings of guilt, shame or taboos due to religious or social influences, this often led to inner conflicts, psychological suffering and emotional stress. The feeling of not being allowed to live or address natural needs openly often created a strong tension between one's own desires and social expectations. For many people, this manifested itself in feelings of inferiority, fear or self-doubt, and even depression or anxiety disorders. Repressed or suppressed sexuality could also lead to distorted self-images or problematic relationships with other people, as real closeness and intimacy were made difficult or blocked. A feeling of isolation was also not uncommon because those affected believed that their needs were abnormal or immoral, which prevented open exchange. In some cases, these suppressed emotions and needs could lead to an unhealthy relationship with one's own body in the long term, severely impairing quality of life and resulting in long-term psychological and physical consequences - including suicidal thoughts.

From a historical perspective, the Catholic Church bears a clear responsibility for the fact that people have associated sexuality with shame, feelings of guilt or taboos and have therefore often been restricted or burdened in their psychological and emotional development. Particularly through strict moral teachings and prohibitions, such as the rejection of sexuality outside of marriage, the stigmatization of same-sex love or the prohibition of masturbation, the church shaped a climate for centuries in which sexual needs were considered subordinate or morally inferior. These attitudes had a demonstrable influence on how believers perceived their own sexuality and how they dealt with sexual feelings, and could cause considerable psychological tension and emotional suffering.

Nevertheless, it would be too one-sided to blame the Catholic Church alone. Many religious and cultural institutions around the world have spread similar norms and treated sexuality restrictively. However, due to its global influence and its clear, systematically disseminated moral teachings, the Catholic Church is particularly involved in establishing and consolidating certain taboos and prohibitions. Its positions on sexuality and partnership have undoubtedly shaped millions of people, often with negative consequences for their mental health and well-being.

Recently, criticism of these positions has also been growing within the church, and there is a more open approach and more differentiated views in some cases.

16 • What role do power and control play in churches' rejection of sexual self-determination?

The rejection of sexual self-determination by churches, especially the Catholic Church, is not only deeply rooted in issues of power and control. Historically and theologically, sexuality has been defined not only as a personal, but also a social and ecclesiastical concern. By establishing sexual norms and presenting them as irrevocable divine commandments, the church was able to directly influence the private lives of the faithful and secure its authority for generations to come.

Control through standardization and sin construction

The church has morally codified sexuality for centuries, drawing clear boundaries between *"permitted" and "forbidden" sexuality*. Premarital sex, homosexuality, contraception and masturbation were classified as sinful, while marital sex exclusively for procreation was considered legitimate. Through this moral control, sexuality became an area in which church authorities could define what was *"pure" or "impure"* - thus placing people in a relationship of dependency, as the church acted as a mediator for the forgiveness of sins.

The construction of "original sin" in connection with sexuality reinforced this mechanism: human instinct was seen as potentially dangerous and had to be regulated by church norms. This led to a deep-rooted sense of guilt in many believers, who learned from an early age that their natural sexual needs were sinful or inferior - and should not be lived in a natural and life-affirming way. At the same time, the church offered a "way out" of this guilt - through confession, penance and strict adherence to the church's commandments.

Sexuality as a threat to church authority

Sexual self-determination is at odds with a church morality based on obedience. When people begin to make their own decisions about their sexuality and no longer allow themselves to be guided by church rules, this undermines the authority of the church. This is particularly evident in questions of contraception and marriage: while the church continues to argue against artificial contraceptives, many believers have long ignored these guidelines in their everyday lives. Control over the body and reproduction is therefore no longer determined by the church, but by individual decisions.

Women's self-determination today

This emancipation jeopardizes a central ecclesiastical instrument of power. For women in particular, sexual self-determination means liberation from traditional church roles, in which they were primarily intended to be mothers and wives. By clinging to outdated gender roles, the church is also protecting its centuries-old patriarchal structure, which grants men sole power over theological and moral issues.

The fear of plurality and diversity

The rigid attitude towards LGBTQIA+ people shows particularly clearly how much the church's sexual morality is about control. By defining only heterosexual marriage as *"natural"*, the church deliberately excludes all those who do not fit this mold. There are not only theological reasons for this, but also a power-political background: the church fears that recognizing sexual diversity would call into question its existing dogmas and thus its own infallibility.

The strict rejection of same-sex love is not based on scientific or social arguments, but on the desire to maintain existing hierarchical structures. If the church were to recognize LGBTQIA+ people equally, it would also have to reconsider many other teachings - such as the sanctity of traditional marriage or the alleged divine order of the sexes. This would undermine its credibility and further diminish its influence on social norms.

Control through sexual morality as a historical pattern

The church's control over sexuality is not a random phenomenon, but a recurring pattern that runs through the entire history of the church. As early as the Middle Ages, people who deviated from the church's sexual morals were persecuted and punished. Witch hunts were often directed against women who were considered *"sexually deviant"* or *"too independent"*. The same applied to homosexuals, who were criminalized as *"sodomites"*.

Even in modern times, the church has repeatedly used its sexual morals as an instrument of power. In many Catholic countries, the influence of the church was (and still is) so great that it was able to influence laws - such as bans on abortion in Poland or Latin America. By exerting moral and political influence, the church ensures that its ideas on sexuality remain firmly anchored in society, even beyond the confines of the church.

Change and resistance - Is control crumbling through reality?

Despite centuries of control over sexual morality, there are signs of change. More and more believers are no longer accepting the church's dogmas on sexuality and are making their own decisions about their love and sex lives. Movements such as "Maria 2.0" (for women's rights in the church) or "#OutInChurch" (for LGBTQIA+ rights) are actively campaigning against the church's restrictive sexual morals.

There are also cautious openings within the church. Pope Francis has emphasized that homosexual people should be treated with respect, and some priests are now blessing same-sex couples - despite the official ban by the Vatican. Pressure is also growing in many countries for the Church to reconsider its position on contraception and women's rights.

Nevertheless, the fundamental question remains: will the church continue to open up in the long term, or will it hold on to its rigid sexual morality in order to preserve its power structures? As long as sexuality is seen as something that needs to be controlled and regulated, the church will remain an actor that restricts individual freedom and self-determination - not for spiritual reasons, but for reasons of power politics.

The churches' rejection of sexual self-determination has less to do with an objective, universal truth than with the desire to preserve existing power structures. By portraying sexuality as sinful or dangerous, the church creates a system in which believers remain dependent on its moral authority. This ensures their control over individuals and societies. However, with increasing social acceptance of sexual diversity and individual freedom, the church's sexual morality is losing more and more influence, and in today's generation, massively so. The question remains whether the church will adapt to this change or whether it will cling to an outdated moral teaching that is increasingly perceived as unworldly and causes empty communities.

17 • *To what extent does the church's rigid sexual morality serve to maintain power rather than spiritual truth, and how has this manifested historically through the tabooing of sexuality and the construction of concepts of sin?*

For centuries, church sexual morality was hardly a spiritual concept, but rather an instrument of social control. While many believers question sexual morality as a divine order intended to deepen the spiritual life, history shows that this morality often also served to maintain power. The strict rules on chastity, marriage and same-sex love offered the church the opportunity to intervene deeply in the private lives of the faithful and secure its authority.

When sexuality is portrayed as sinful or dangerous, it creates a dependency on church institutions that offer *"forgiveness"* and moral guidance. This strengthens the power of the church over individuals and societies. In particular, the rejection of same-sex sexuality or non-traditional relationship models may be due less to spiritual principles than to the maintenance of a certain image of society.

At the same time, the question arises as to whether these norms actually serve spiritual truth. A sexual morality based on Jesus' message of love, respect and acceptance should focus on individual responsibility, mutual consent and dignity - not coercion and fear. A church that sees sexuality not as a danger, but as a divine gift, would be more likely to lead people to a healthy and fulfilling faith.

If the church's sexual morality is really to serve spiritual development, towards an ethic of freedom and love, it would have to free itself from dogmatic constraints and focus more on compassion, openness and personal responsibility.

18 • *Why are churches more interested in control than truth in their sexual morality?*

Historically, the sexual morals of the churches, especially the Catholic Church, have often been more interested in control than in finding the objective truth. This can be seen in the way in which sexual norms were enforced, who benefited from these norms and how strongly they were tied to social power structures.

Control through sexual morality - a historical overview

Since the Middle Ages, the church has used sexuality not only as a spiritual but also as a political instrument. The strict regulation of marriage, chastity and sexual orientation served to stabilize social structures and consolidate its own authority. By linking sexuality with sin and guilt, the church was able to create a deep dependency among believers - after all, it itself offered "redemption" from these sins.

A classic example is the demonization of premarital sex and contraception. These strict regulations not only ensured social control over the private lives of the faithful, but also prevented women from making independent decisions about their bodies and family planning. In many Catholic countries, this led to reproductive rights being massively restricted - often with far-reaching health and social consequences.

The fight for & against sexual self-determination

For centuries, the Catholic Church vehemently opposed liberal sexual ethics. Even masturbation was branded a grave sin, and marital sex was long considered permissible only for procreation. This strict moral corset led to many people - especially LGBTQIA+ people - being ostracized by the church.

It is also striking that the church is more adaptable on many ethical issues than on sexual issues. While it often takes a progressive stance on issues of social justice or environmental protection, it clings to an outdated sexual image. This suggests that sexual morality is less about spiritual truth than about preserving social order.

Control as the core of the church's sexual moral power

A church that claims to be based on spiritual truth would have to continually engage with new scientific and ethical findings. But when it comes to sexual issues in particular, there is a strong resistance to modern psychological, biological and sociological insights. While science has long recognized that sexuality is multifaceted and that repression of sexual needs can lead to psychological stress, the church continues to cling to norms that are primarily based on medieval moral concepts.

At the same time, however, there are also voices within the church calling for an adjustment to sexual morality. Progressive Catholic theologians and reform movements such as "Maria 2.0" or "#OutInChurch" in particular are calling for an urgent reassessment of these church dogmas. Pope Francis has also cautiously spoken out in favour of a more humane and less punitive sexual morality, emphasizing that homosexual people have a right to respect and love. And it is the voice of the head of the church.

Over the centuries, the church has thus established a sexual morality that is based less on objective truth than on social control. While many other moral teachings have adapted to new insights over time, the Church's sexual morality remains largely rigid - a sign that it serves to preserve hierarchies rather than individual freedom. The Catholic Church continues to cling to a sexual morality that is perceived by more and more believers as unrealistic and oppressive.

19 • Is a Christian ethic conceivable without sexual control?

A Christian ethic without sexual control is conceivable in principle, but requires a fundamental reassessment of theological traditions and moral concepts. Historically, Christian ethics has been closely linked to the regulation of sexuality - be it through marriage regulations, the tabooing of certain sexual practices or the idea of chastity as an ideal. However, the question arises as to whether this control is actually an indispensable part of Christian ethics or whether it is rather a culturally evolved practice that can change.

The origin of sexual control in Christian ethics

The control of sexuality in Christianity has its roots both in Jewish traditions and in the teachings of early Christianity. Paul, for example, warned against sexual "immorality" and saw marriage primarily as a means of channeling sexual urges (1 Corinthians 7). The church adopted and reinforced these ideas over the centuries , with Augustine in particular shaping a sexual morality that classified lust and physical desire as problematic. This view meant that sexuality was not seen as a natural part of life, but even then as something dangerous that needed to be regulated and controlled.

Figure 6: The open church door, a broken symbol of domination in front of it - and people of all identities entering freely. The scene conveys liberation, community and an ethic beyond control.

Alternative Christian ethics beyond sexual control

A Christian ethic without sexual control is possible if the values of Christianity focus more on other aspects of morality, such as love of neighbor, justice, responsibility and respect. In such an ethic, sexuality would not be seen as a sin or a problem, but as an integral part of human life that is lived with mindfulness and mutual consent.

Some progressive theologians are already arguing that a moral evaluation of sexuality should not be based on dogma, but on ethical principles. Instead of strict rules on marriage, chastity or sexual orientation, a Christian sexual ethic could be based on values such as love, consensuality, honesty and a sense of responsibility.

Are there examples of Christian ethics without sexual control?

There are already Christian communities that have an open and less regulatory approach to sexuality. Many Protestant churches have liberalized their stance on homosexuality, premarital sex and contraception and instead rely on individual decisions. There are also reform movements in the Catholic Church that advocate a more humane and less restrictive sexual morality.

A Christian ethic without sexual control is therefore perfectly possible if it focuses more on basic values such as love, respect and justice rather than on prohibitions and moral guidelines. While traditional church sexual morality is still widespread, modern developments show that ethical perspectives can change. The crucial question remains whether churches are ready to move away from controlling bodies and sexuality and instead promote an ethic that puts people at the center - not their sexual conformity to old norms that only serve the church but not the person.

---

b) Criticism of power and theological reflection

---

20 • How does the critique of the history of the church engage with its institutional power and actions?

In his *criminal history of Christianity*, Karlheinz Deschner makes fundamental accusations against the institution of the church, describing it as a power organization that has often acted in contradiction to its own moral principles throughout its history. In particular, he criticizes the persecution of dissenters, the role of the church in wars and political intrigues as well as forcible missionary work and forced conversions in various eras. A central theme of his account is the intertwining of religion and secular rule, which in his view led to the oppression and exploitation of people. He refers to the Inquisition, crusades and witch hunts as examples of systematic violence in the name of faith. He also addresses the wealth of the church and its often dubious attitude towards social and ethical issues. Deschner pursues a consistently critical perspective of the church and places the discrepancy between Christian doctrine and church practice at the center of his analysis.

Over the centuries, the Church has used various means to suppress heresy, dissenting beliefs and criticism of its authority.

Heresy means a religious belief or teaching that deviates from official church doctrine. Simply explained: if someone is part of a religion but believes or teaches something that goes against the official teachings of that religion, this is considered heresy - at least from the point of view of the religious authority.

Example: In the Middle Ages, for example, the Church said: "Only the Pope has the last word in matters of faith." If someone then said: "No, every believer may interpret the Bible for themselves", this was considered heresy (as was the case with Martin Luther at the beginning, for example). The consequences in the past were: heretics were excluded from the church (excommunication). In the Middle Ages: sometimes torture, burning or persecution (e.g. inquisition). Today: Mostly only theological debates or exclusion from certain religious communities. But nowadays the term is rarely used and often sounds historical or negative. In modern societies, religious diversity and freedom of opinion are more important than absolute adherence to dogma - this is now widely recognized in modern democratic societies. This means that people are allowed to decide for themselves what they believe in - or whether they believe at all. The state remains neutral and does not interfere in religious teachings, nor does it favor a particular religion. The freedom to question or even criticize religious beliefs is also protected by freedom of expression.

This principle is enshrined in law in many countries, for example in Germany's Basic Law (Article 4). It is also reflected in society: religion is increasingly viewed as an individual matter and pluralistic views - i.e. the coexistence of different faiths and world views - are seen as normal.

Particularly affected by the obligation to adhere to dogma in conservative religious circles at the time were historical-religious movements that represented an alternative interpretation of the Christian faith, such as the Gnostics in late antiquity, who were condemned by the early church as false teachers. In the Middle Ages, groups such as the Cathars and Waldensians, who were known for their ascetic lifestyles and criticism of the church hierarchy, were condemned. These movements were combated by crusades, inquisition proceedings and public executions.

The introduction of the Inquisition in the 12th century gave the Church a systematic instrument for persecuting heretics. The accused were tortured to force confessions and often burned at the stake. This procedure was particularly intensive in the Spanish Inquisition under the Catholic monarchs Ferdinand and Isabella, who suspected and persecuted not only heretics but also converted Jews and Muslims.

Scientists were also targeted by the church if their findings were perceived as a threat to church doctrine. The best-known example is Galileo Galilei, who was brought before the Inquisition tribunal and forced to recant because of his support for the heliocentric view of the world.

During the early modern period, persecution was increasingly directed against Protestants in Catholic areas and against so-called witches, who were the victims of witch trials, particularly in the early modern period. These persecutions were often carried out with the involvement of secular rulers, but the church played a central role in legitimizing such trials.

Even in later centuries, the church remained an opponent of Enlightenment and secular movements. Critics of the church's claim to power, including philosophers such as Giordano Bruno, were burned as people with divergent individual views, and even in the modern era, the church opposed political movements such as liberalism or communism that questioned its authority. While the methods changed over time, the goal often remained the same: to secure the church's control over faith and society.

Here is a list of important female and male, historical as well as modern persons who were persecuted by the church as dissenters, including their central theses or ideas.

- **Marguerite Porete** (d. 1310) - A French mystic and author of the work The Mirror of Simple Souls, in which she propagated a direct experience of God independent of ecclesiastical authorities. She was burned at the stake in Paris for her teachings.
- **Arius** (ca. 260-336) - A theologian of the early church who taught that Christ was not of the same essence as God, but a created being. His ideas led to one of the greatest theological disputes of late antiquity and were rejected at the Council of Nicaea (325).
- **Joan of Arc** (1412-1431) - A French leader in the Hundred Years' War who claimed to receive divine visions. She was condemned and burned in an ecclesiastical trial for her allegedly unauthorized spiritual calling and her resistance to church authorities.
- **Giordano Bruno** (1548-1600) - A philosopher and astronomer who supported the heliocentric view of the world, accepted the possibility of countless worlds and criticized the theological teachings of the church as being too dogmatic. He was executed by the Inquisition in Rome.
- **Anne Hutchinson** (1591-1643) - A Puritan theologian in New England who advocated a direct, personal relationship with God without the mediation of clergymen.
- **Jan Hus** (ca. 1370-1415) - A Czech reformer who advocated a return to evangelical simplicity in the church and rejected the sale of indulgences. His ideas later influenced Martin Luther. He was condemned to death and burned at the Council of Constance.
- **Olympe de Gouges** (1748-1793) - A French writer and women's rights activist who called for equal rights for women and citizens in her Declaration of the Rights of Women. Her thinking challenged the social hierarchies supported by the church.
- **Petrus Waldes** (died around 1205) - The founder of the Waldensian movement, which advocated a life of poverty based on the example of Jesus. His followers were persecuted for centuries because they criticized the church sacraments and the authority of the priests.

- **Elizabeth Cady Stanton** (1815-1902) - A leading figure in the US women's rights movement who took a critical look at biblical texts and wrote a "Women's Bible" to challenge patriarchal interpretations of scripture.
- **Baruch de Spinoza** (1632-1677) - A Dutch philosopher who rejected the traditional concept of God and instead advocated a pantheistic view of the world in which God and nature are one. His ideas were condemned by both Jewish and Christian authorities.
- **Simone de Beauvoir** (1908-1986) - A French philosopher and feminist who denounced the role of the church in the oppression of women in The Other Sex. Her work had a lasting influence on feminist theology.
- **Thomas Müntzer** (ca. 1489-1525) - A theologian and revolutionary who believed that divine justice required a transformation of the social order. He played a leading role in the German Peasants' War and was executed after his capture.
- **Uta Ranke-Heinemann** (1927-2021) - A German theologian who was the first woman to receive a Catholic professorship in Germany, but lost her church teaching license when she interpreted central dogmas such as the virgin birth as symbolic.
- **Charles Darwin** (1809-1882) - The founder of the theory of evolution, which contradicted the biblical story of creation. Many church circles saw his research as an attack on the divine origin of mankind.
- **Madalyn Murray O'Hair** (1919-1995) - An American atheist and civil rights activist who successfully fought in court against state-organized prayer in schools. She was considered an enemy of faith by conservative religious groups.
- **John Shelby Spong** (1931-2021) - A liberal American bishop who rejected the literal interpretation of the Bible and questioned central dogmas of Christianity, such as the bodily resurrection of Christ.
- **Greta Vosper** (born 1958) - A Canadian pastor who describes herself as an atheist and propagates a non-theistic form of Christianity. Her views led to a protracted conflict with her church.
- **Hypatia of Alexandria** (ca. 355-415) - An important philosopher and mathematician of antiquity who was known for her scientific and pagan teachings. She was murdered by a Christian mob as she was seen as a symbol of the "pagan" knowledge that the church was fighting against.
- **Bogomil** (10th century) - Founder of the Bogomil movement, which advocated a strongly dualistic world view and rejected the church hierarchy. His teachings spread across large parts of Europe, but were seen as a threat by the church and persecuted.

- **Galileo Galilei** (1564-1642) - A scientist whose support of the heliocentric view of the world brought him into conflict with the Catholic Church. He was brought before the Inquisition and forced to officially recant his teachings in order to avoid a harsher punishment.

Repression is often based on fear. Those who resist must find ways to deal with this fear - be it through inner conviction, through community or through the knowledge that they are on the right side of history. History shows that many oppressive systems do not last forever because at some point people realize that they are only oppressed by their own consent. The key is to consciously bring about this moment.

Resistance to repression requires courage, a strategic approach and often also collective action. A first step is education - those who are oppressed must understand what mechanisms of repression are being used, be it through laws, social control or direct violence. Education and critical thinking are crucial to recognizing manipulation and developing counter-strategies. Another tool is networking with like-minded people. Individual voices are easier to silence than a movement built on solidarity. Historically, resistance groups have organized themselves through collective action, secret meetings or the exchange of writings and pamphlets. In the modern world, social media enables the rapid dissemination of critical information, even if it is often monitored or censored in repressive systems.

One of the biggest advantages for people today who hold similar ideas to those of earlier thought leaders is that they are building on a foundation created by the debates and conflicts of past generations - and are not being burned at the stake. Many ideas that were once considered different or even dangerous - such as criticism of the sale of indulgences, the heliocentric worldview or the need to translate the Bible into a modern vernacular - are now taken for granted. As a result, today's thinkers often have greater social acceptance, no longer have to fear physical, social or psychological persecution and can argue in an open space in public or on the internet.

Despite these challenges, in enlightened, pluralistic societies today, it is considered a core value that no one is forced into a particular religious truth - and that faith is a personal choice, not a social obligation.

In today's world, dissenters can enter into dialog with the church in various ways. They can exert influence through academic, theological or social discourse by participating in church discussions, for example through university theology, open letters to church institutions or interfaith and philosophical online forums. Many churches have now created platforms for debates in which controversial topics can be discussed, such as the role of women in the church, attitudes towards LGBTQIA+ or the compatibility of science and faith.

The advantage of thinking things differently or holding a minority opinion in interpretation lies in mental agility and the further development of thinking. Progress often only comes about through critical questions and alternative perspectives. Without these, there would have been no reformation, no further development of theology and no adaptation of the church to new social challenges. Theological diversity makes it possible to transform and understand old texts in new contexts and to connect the ethical challenges of the present with the experiences of the past.

Ultimately, it is up to each person to form their own opinion. A living faith - or even a conscious rejection of beliefs - can only arise through personal reflection. In a modern society in which freedom of opinion exists, everyone can find their own way. This is precisely why religious institutions should also be open to new perspectives, because faith only remains relevant if it deals with people's real questions. History shows that many ideas that were once suppressed were later recognized as valuable. Dialogue about issues therefore remains crucial.

21 • How can theology challenge existing power structures and open up a new perspective on faith and sexuality?

With her *"Indecent Theology"*, Marcella Althaus-Reid calls for a radical reinterpretation of theology that questions traditional concepts and, in particular, rethinks the connection between faith, sexuality and social justice. She argues that classical Christian theology is often shaped by Western, patriarchal and heteronormative ideas that marginalize certain identities and lifestyles. For her, theology is not neutral, but a *construction* that reflects and often cements social power relations.

Her approach is to look at theological issues from the perspective of those who have been pushed to the margins of society - particularly women, LGBTQIA+ individuals and people from the global periphery. She argues that a truly liberating theology cannot emerge from the sheltered space of academic debate, but from the concrete experience of those who have no voice in traditional Christianity.

A central element of her theology is the *deconstruction of pure, "decent" Christianity*, which often represses physicality and sexuality or regards them as sinful. She counters this with a theology that recognizes the *body as a place to experience God* and not only tolerates the diversity of human sexuality, but values it as part of divine creation. In her radical critique, she demands that faith is no longer understood as a discipline of control, but as a form of liberation that dissolves boundaries and creates space for a diversity of identities and life realities.

If a theology does not regard physicality and sexuality as sinful, but values them as part of divine creation, we come to the issue of whether masturbation or an orgasm (possibly experienced in partnership) can also be interpreted as an experience of God. Sexuality has often been placed exclusively in the context of procreation and separated from spiritual dimensions. A theology that recognizes the body as a place to experience God could therefore overcome this dualism and understand physical pleasure not as a contradiction to spirituality, but as a possible expression of spirituality and the experience of God.

If one assumes that God is present in creation and in human experience, then any form of consciously experienced physicality - be it in sexuality, dance, touch or meditation - could be seen as a possible way of experiencing God. Many mystical traditions, including within Christianity, describe spiritual experiences in terms comparable to ecstatic experience. Teresa of Ávila (1515-1582), for example, uses language that is very reminiscent of physical devotion: in her mystical writings, particularly in *The Book of My Life* and *The Inner Castle*, Teresa describes the deep union of the soul with God as an immediate, overwhelming experience. She describes her most famous experience - the *transverberation* - as a divine piercing of the heart by an angel with a flaming spear. She felt a mixture of pain and joy, which she described as *"sweet"* and would not want to miss.

This language is reminiscent of ecstatic devotion, but for Teresa it is a spiritual dimension in which God's love permeates people completely . Her mysticism shows that spirituality consists of deeply felt emotion. Her theology inspires approaches that value physicality and emotions as part of the experience of God.

This does not necessarily mean that every sexual act automatically has a spiritual meaning, but it opens up the possibility that lust and self-love do not have to be separated from the divine dimension per se.

In other words, not every orgasm is necessarily an experience of God - but there are moments when physicality and spirituality can overlap. Teresa of Ávila thus describes an experience that in her language is reminiscent of physical ecstasy, but for her represents a divine penetration. The decisive factor is therefore not the physical act itself, but the momentum, the depth of the experience and the inner emotion. God could be experienced where there is a moment of complete surrender, of being absorbed in the now and of deep connection with oneself or another person.

Life as a gift: "*Good God, this orgasm was associated with a spiritual quality of experience.*"

This can happen in sexuality, e.g. during masturbation or orgasm with a partner, but also in other experiences of intense pleasure, deep love or spiritual contemplation. It is therefore less about the act itself and more about the quality of the experience - a moment in which the ego recedes, the feeling of time dissolves and something greater becomes tangible. In this sense, a contemporary theology could see physicality not as a contrast to God, but as a possible way of experiencing the sacred - without every sexual experience necessarily having to be spiritual.

A theology that sees physicality not as a problem but as a gift could move away from a moralistic view of sexuality and instead ask: Does a certain type of sexuality promote self-respect, love, connection - be it with oneself or with others? If spirituality means being fully in the moment, experiencing oneself and life as a gift, then one could argue that a consciously lived sexuality - free from shame or fear - can also be understood as a form of spiritual and divine experience.

---

c) Church structures and Jesus

---

22 • *Is Jesus' sexuality a taboo because it jeopardizes the power structures of the church?*

The topic of Jesus' sexuality is also important because it is also inextricably linked to the power structures within the church: By traditionally portraying Jesus as desexualized and thus morally pure, the church establishes an ideal to which it aligns its moral authority. If one were to speak openly about Jesus' possible sexuality, this could not only change the traditional image of Jesus, but also question the entire system of church morality and authority: the traditional image of Jesus is characterized by perfect purity, chastity and spiritual sublimity; Jesus is presented as a completely desexualized ideal, whose life is all about spiritual and moral perfection. In this view, he embodies an unattainable, morally superior figure who exists far removed from human needs and desires.

The comparison between the traditional image of Jesus and an artificial intelligence is quite apt: just as an AI is often portrayed as completely objective, emotionless and free of human weaknesses, the traditional Jesus often appears as completely pure, chaste and spiritually sublime - an ideal that transcends all human needs. But this is precisely where the problem lies: Both depictions run the risk of creating a figure that exists far removed from lived reality and therefore seems less tangible and comprehensible. While artificial intelligence should always be neutral and objective in order to convey trust and reliability, the idealized Jesus serves to set moral standards and provide guidance. However, this perfect portrayal also harbours the danger of distance: both a thoroughly objective AI assistant and a completely desexualized and enraptured Jesus ultimately appear less human - and this could be precisely their weakness, because people need closeness, empathy and emotionality in addition to orientation and clarity.

In contrast, there is an alternative approach that perceives Jesus in his full humanity - as an individual with emotions, relationships and possibly also sexual feelings. This alternative perspective emphasizes Jesus' proximity to everyday human experiences and thus makes him more accessible and tangible. While the traditional image primarily reinforces the authority of the church and legitimizes normative prescriptions, an alternative, more human framing of Jesus might be more likely to promote openness, dialogue and diversity, while at the same time challenging established moral and hierarchical structures within the church.

If Jesus' humanity - including sexuality - is emphasized, the church may lose a central instrument with which it has so far sought to regulate the sexual behavior of the faithful in a normative way. Precisely because sexuality is so closely linked to power, control and moral norms, it remains a sensitive issue for the Catholic Church: any openness could result in a far-reaching restructuring of the church's power structures, which is why the clergy often deliberately avoid change or refuse to engage in dialog.

Artificial intelligence can promote the dialog on sexuality in the Catholic Church on several levels, precisely because the topic is so strongly linked to power, control and normative ideas.

On the one hand, AI can serve as a mediating tool: It offers the opportunity to make polyphonic perspectives visible - from theological positions to voices critical of the church to personal accounts of experience. It does not act as an authority, but as a structuring medium that makes discourse comprehensible and accessible - especially for people whose voices are otherwise rarely heard in church power structures.

On the other hand, AI can help to defuse areas of silence by presenting information, studies and historical contexts in a neutral way. In this way, it creates a space in which knowledge takes precedence over dogma - and where questions can be asked without being immediately sanctioned. This can be particularly helpful when clerical authorities refuse to engage in dialog or actively block change in order to protect existing power structures.

Figure 7: Jesus stands behind a translucent curtain, symbolically veiled by ecclesiastical texts and tradition - with a closed Bible in front of him. The picture thematizes the topic in a respectful and thoughtful way.

It is the topic of speaking openly about Jesus' sexuality or even thinking of it as existing. The curtain stands for the "hiding" or "veiling" of his human side - especially his possible sexual identity or intimacy. The curtain, which is also translucent, hints at this: You can see that there is something there, but it remains indistinct - like the subject itself in theology. The symbols above his body (e.. biblical text, icons, priestly vestments) stand for dogmatic layers that overlay Jesus' humanity and corporeality. Sexuality is not treated as part of his humanity, but is covered over. The closed Bible with a lock stands for the church's silence - and the refusal to talk about this dimension of Jesus, as the lock signals: Knowledge or discussion about it is urgently needed. The light behind Jesus is a reference to the truth or knowledge that lies hidden. Perhaps also an allusion to the fact that a more honest view of Jesus' humanity could make the image of faith more

human. The illustration addresses the issue of taking Jesus' sexuality seriously. It visualizes a field of interpretation between humanity and dogmatic control.

Last but not least, AI enables anonymous participation: In an area where fear of exclusion, loyalty conflicts or repression is real, AI can create a protected space for reflection. Here, people can express themselves, listen and learn - without having to expose themselves directly.

In short, AI does not replace church dialog about the sexuality of Jesus, but it can enable, prepare and expand it - especially where institutional inertia or the maintenance of power prevent open conversation.

23 • Could a debate about Jesus' sexuality lead to a crisis of faith?

A debate about Jesus' sexuality or his queer gayness could lead to a crisis of faith, especially in church traditions that still hold on to a clearly defined and dogmatic image of Jesus. If Jesus is interpreted as potentially gay or queer, this represents a previously unthought-of idea for some believers, as it challenges inherited theological concepts about his nature and life. This could lead to uncertainty or rejection, especially in conservative circles that understand sexuality, sexual orientation and gender as fixed orders. However, crises of faith are nothing new in the history of Christianity. Time and again, there have been theological debates and insights that have challenged existing beliefs and led to interesting dialogues within the church.

One of the greatest crises of faith was the Reformation in the 16th century, when Martin Luther and other reformers questioned the authority of the Catholic Church, the papacy and the mediation of salvation through the sacraments. This not only led to a theological schism, but also to political and social upheavals that permanently changed Christianity. Another major crisis was the Enlightenment, which renegotiated the relationship between faith and reason from the 18th century onwards. Scientific findings, in particular Darwin's theory of evolution, called into question traditional doctrines of creation and led many people to distance themselves from the faith of the church. The Second Vatican Council (1962-1965) also brought about a change in faith for many Catholics, as it modernized central dogmatic structures of the church and changed the liturgy as well as the church's self-image.

Compared to these historical crises of faith, a debate about Jesus' sexuality would be less far-reaching, but still significant: while earlier crises mostly concerned fundamental theological or church-political structures, the question of Jesus' sexuality primarily affects personal ideas and identifications with him. However, a discussion about this could not only provoke resistance, but also lead to a deeper reflection on the nature of Jesus. If Jesus is seen as a person with a possible sexual identity, this could even strengthen his relationship with people today instead of jeopardizing faith. In contrast to previous crises of faith, which were often associated with the loss of church authority or social upheaval, this debate would only be a challenge to personal beliefs, but not a threat to the core message of Christianity. Rather, it could help to develop a more inclusive and human-oriented image of Jesus, which on the contrary would give modern believers much more orientation and identification.

---

d) Reform movements and protests

---

24 • *How does "We are Church" address the existing power structure of the Catholic Church, and what is the vision of a fraternal church behind it?*

The *"We are Church"* movement focuses on the Catholic Church as a hierarchical institution that centralizes power and has so far given the faithful little say. Decision-making power lies almost exclusively with the clergy, while the laity - i.e. the vast majority of the faithful - have little influence on the organization of the church. This power structure promotes a lack of transparency, prevents necessary reforms and makes it difficult to create a church that is truly at the service of the people.

Instead, *"We are Church"* calls for a *fraternal church* in which the participation of the laity is not only desired, but structurally anchored. The church should move away from an authoritarian model and become a community in which responsibility is shared. This includes equal participation of lay people in church decision-making processes and more democratic structures.

A renewed style of proclamation is another central aspect of this goal. The church should not proclaim dogmatic truths from above, but rather seek dialog with the faithful and respond to the realities of their lives. This includes a modern and open language, greater involvement of the faithful in the liturgy and a move away from rigid rules towards pastoral care that takes people seriously.

The aim of *"We are Church"* is a church that does not see itself as a power system, but as a living community in which believers can actively participate and help shape the church.

25 • How does "Maria 2.0" protest against the church's handling of abuse cases? Why do such cases of abuse occur in the Catholic Church, and what structural problems contribute to this?

The *"Maria 2.0"* initiative sharply criticizes the Catholic Church's handling of abuse cases and relies on high-profile forms of protest to exert pressure for reform. Particularly well-known are the church strikes, in which women call on women not to take on any church duties for a week, not to attend church services and instead to hold alternative prayer and protest actions in public spaces. This is intended to show how much women contribute to church life, even though they hardly play a role in the power structures - and that they are not prepared to support a system that covers up abuse and protects perpetrators.

In addition, the movement is organizing vigils and demonstrations in front of bishops' offices and church institutions to protest against the slow process of coming to terms with the abuse scandals. *"Maria 2.0"* demands an independent investigation into the crimes, transparent procedures for taking responsibility and clear consequences for officials who cover up. The movement is particularly critical of the fact that the church often sees itself as the judge in these cases instead of entrusting external, independent bodies with the investigation.

Figure 8: Women in white in front of closed church doors - silent, dignified protests by "Maria 2.0".

The Megafon Mary symbol and cracks in the church wall make the reform pressure visible. The "megaphone symbol" stands for Mary, i.e. for the Mother of God - often represented by a stylized crescent moon, a stylized M, a star or a rose. The megaphone in the form of a stylized "M" with a rose ornament stands for protest, voice, visibility - especially for women who want to be heard in the church and integrated as priests. Mary speaks through the women - loudly, publicly, against abuse and misuse of power and for gender-neutral assignment of office. When will a woman become Pope again?

Another means of protest are petition campaigns and open letters addressed directly to church authorities. The movement demands not only consistent punishment of the perpetrators, but also a fundamental reform of church power structures in order to end clerical isolation and lack of control.

In recent decades, numerous cases of sexual abuse in the Catholic Church have been uncovered worldwide. Priests, members of religious orders and church employees have abused minors - often over a period of years. These acts were often covered up by the church hierarchy by transferring perpetrators and silencing victims.

One prominent example is the abuse scandal at the Canisius College in Berlin, which became public in 2010. Former students reported that they had been sexually abused by Jesuit priests in the 1970s and 1980s. These revelations led to further reports of abuse in other church institutions.

The MHG study published in 2018 investigated sexual abuse in the Catholic Church in Germany between 1946 and 2014. It identified 1,670 accused clerics and 3,677 affected children and young people. However, the number of unreported cases is likely to be higher.

Another example is the case of a priest from Haren in Emsland, who abused altar boys and first communicants in 225 cases in the 1990s. He was given a suspended sentence in 1996.

These cases and many others show a systematic failure of the church in dealing with sexual abuse. The cover-up and lack of investigation have severely shaken trust in the institution. Through its actions, *"Maria 2.0"* is forcing the Catholic Church to face up to its responsibility and stop covering up or downplaying abuse. The initiative makes it clear that without genuine reforms - both in dealing with abuse and in the distribution of power - the credibility of the church will continue to erode.

Sexual abuse in the Catholic Church is no coincidence, but the result of deep-rooted systemic problems. A central cause lies in the hierarchical power structure of the church, which gives priests an almost untouchable authority - especially in their relationship with children, young people and the faithful whom they pastor. This power imbalance facilitates abuse and makes it difficult for victims to defend themselves or be heard. The decades-long practice of cover-ups exacerbates the problem, as perpetrators were often merely transferred instead of being prosecuted.

Celibacy plays a role: compulsory celibacy forces priests to be completely abstinent and prevents the natural development of sexuality. Critics see this as a cause of sexual frustration, which can lead to problematic or secret relationships. Although celibacy alone is not the cause of abuse, it does promote a closed-off male culture in which sexuality is tabooed or covered up and no open, healthy discussion of this topic takes place.

Lack of women in ordained ministries as an additional risk factor

The Catholic Church is a strictly male-dominated institution. To date, women have not had access to ordained ministries and therefore not to key positions in the leadership of the church. As a result, there is a lack of gender-equitable control mechanisms and a stronger female perspective, which is often associated with a more open culture of discussion and a more sensitive approach to abuse issues. If women were to work in priestly positions, this could lead to a different dynamic in the church - away from a toxic masculinity culture and towards more transparency, dialog and prevention.

The strict sexual morals and feelings of guilt lead to repression: The Catholic Church conveys a rigid sexual ethic that heavily regulates sexuality and burdens it with guilt. This leads to a culture of repression, which can cause problematic dynamics.

There is a lack of control and supervision: clergy are often not subject to any independent control. For centuries, the church has created its own "jurisdictions" instead of having abuse cases investigated externally.

A culture of silence and obedience develops, which often makes it impossible to come to terms with or change the situation: priests and religious are brought up to be absolutely loyal to the church. This leads to abuse being covered up or hushed up internally instead of being consistently prosecuted.

Sexual abuse in the Catholic Church is therefore not just the result of individual perpetrators, but a structural problem that is reinforced by a culture of power, celibacy, a lack of women, repressed sexual morals and a lack of control. An overdue reform would have to take all these factors into account and not just take superficial measures, but make far-reaching changes to the structures and rules of the church. Starting with the abolition of celibacy and the establishment and integration of female priests.

The announcement that women are founding their own, equal church in order to be able to work as priests or even popes stems from a justified assessment of the stubborn refusal of the male Roman Catholic Church to admit women to sacramental ministries. Such a spin-off or new foundation would be legally quite possible - in Germany, for example, freedom of religion applies, and any new religious community can organize itself, celebrate services and develop its own theology. The founding of an alternative, gender-equitable church could therefore be a solidary expression of self-determination and spiritual emancipation.

The implementation of funding for the organization is more complex: in Germany, only so-called public corporations receive church tax, a status that requires state recognition. Certain requirements must be met for this - such as a stable membership structure, a clear constitution and the permanence of the organization. It is therefore not impossible that a new church with an egalitarian approach could quickly achieve this status. Until then, however, it would first have to finance itself through voluntary contributions or donations.

Therefore, if the men's church does not move on these two points, in short: Yes, a new church would be possible - and perhaps also necessary if no real change is possible within the existing structures. But the road to institutional equality and financial security would be long and challenging and needs members who are willing to take this path.

What the men's church can learn from Cologne's carnival club

A comparison between gender-equal carnival clubs and a possible gender-equal church is certainly interesting - even if the contexts are very different, structural parallels can be drawn.

In carnival - a traditionally male-dominated milieu - clubs with equal representation have been founded in many places in recent decades, often out of the desire to not only allow women to "join in", but to actively help shape it, with equal rights in the board, program and representation. This was and is a break with tradition, was sometimes ridiculed, sometimes fought against - and yet it has established itself step by step. The structure of the association made it comparatively easy to establish a new organization with clear rules on gender equality.

If you transfer this to the church, you realize that tradition, the distribution of power and role models have a deep impact on the structures here too. The desire for equality comes up against dogmatic and institutional barriers. Founding a *"new church"* that overcomes these is a similar act to founding new carnival clubs: an active break from patriarchal structures with the aim of not demanding equality, but living it in practice.

Of course, religion is more than customs - it is linked to questions of faith, sacraments and spiritual identity. But at the level of organization, participation and recognition, parallels can certainly be drawn: In both cases, it is about creating spaces in which women are not tolerated, but have equal rights - not "taking part", but having a say.

26 • *Is moral action in politics fundamentally compatible with the successful exercise of power?*

According to Machiavelli, moral action in politics is only partially compatible with the successful exercise of power. In *Il Principe*, he argues that a ruler must above all strive to secure and maintain his power, which often requires the use of deception, harshness and even cruelty. Strict moral principles can be a hindrance if they jeopardize the preservation of power. He emphasizes that appearing to be virtuous is more important than actually being virtuous, as the perception of rule by the people and elites is more crucial to the stability of power than moral integrity. Moral action can therefore only be compatible with the successful exercise of power if it benefits the ruler and does not weaken his position.

From a theological perspective, particularly in the context of the Catholic Church, there is a tension between Machiavelli's political pragmatism and Christian ethics. Catholic moral teaching emphasizes the indissolubility of ethics and action, especially in the leadership of a state or a community. According to Christian understanding, power should be understood as a service to the common good, not as a means of securing one's own rule. Augustine, for example, distinguishes between the *civitas Dei* (divine state) and the *civitas terrena* (earthly state), whereby the latter is often characterized by the pursuit of power and self-interest, while the former should be guided by divine justice.

More Machiavellian than Christian

Throughout its history, however, the Church itself has repeatedly faced the challenge of acting politically without compromising its moral principles. In practice, however, it became apparent that popes and church dignitaries often acted according to a logic that was more Machiavellian than Christian - for example during the Renaissance, when the Curia did not shy away from political intrigues, wars and power games.

In queer theology, which advocates a more just and inclusive theology, the question of power is also critically reflected upon. While Machiavelli describes power as a necessary, often violent reality, queer theologians call for a *politics of radical justice*, liberation and inclusion. Here, power is not understood as a means of domination over others, but as a *responsibility for the marginalized*. This is in direct contrast to Machiavellian thinking, which regards morality as secondary. Nevertheless, the challenge of combining political effectiveness with moral integrity is also evident in queer movements - for example in the question of the extent to which strategic compromises are permissible in the fight for rights.

Taking responsibility for marginalized people means not only recognizing their situation, but also actively contributing to reducing inequality, exclusion and power imbalances. It is not enough to feel compassion or talk in a well-meaning way - concrete action in solidarity is needed. Several levels can be distinguished here:

Listen and make visible: The first step is to listen without immediately judging or relativizing. Those who are marginalized often find that their own voice is ignored. Responsibility here means making space - in discussions, in the media, in decision-making processes - and not speaking for others, but giving them space to speak for themselves.

Questioning and changing structures: Marginalization is no coincidence, but often the result of systemic inequality. Responsibility therefore means reflecting on one's own privileges and questioning structures that promote exclusion - be it in education, the church, politics, the world of work or language. This can be uncomfortable, but it is central to real change.

Take a stand: Neutrality is rarely neutral - those who remain silent when inequality prevails often unintentionally support the status quo. Taking responsibility also means taking a stand and speaking out against discrimination - whether it's racism, sexism, queerophobia, classism or other forms of exclusion.

Sharing resources: Whether time, money, networks or knowledge: If you have more, you can share and enable. Responsibility means not keeping everything to yourself, but consciously thinking about it: *Who can I give access to? Who can I support? Who has been overlooked so far?*

Staying involved in the long term: solidarity is not an event, but an attitude. Responsibility does not end after a project or a statement - it is demonstrated by still being there when it becomes uncomfortable or attention wanes.

In short, taking responsibility for the marginalized means not speaking for them, but acting with them. It means using privileged positions to open up spaces, change structures and stand up for more justice in the long term.

The compatibility of morality and the successful exercise of power thus remains dependent on the respective perspective: while Machiavelli places the preservation of power as the top priority, Catholic theology emphasizes the moral responsibility of rulers and calls for alignment with higher ethical principles. Queer theology, on the other hand, questions traditional power structures and calls for an alternative ethic of political practice that is not aimed at maintaining power, but at justice and liberation.

Chapter 3: Reflections on dogmatism and church teachings

For centuries, Christianity was characterized by dogmas that were considered immutable truths. However, as scientific and social developments progressed, these dogmas were increasingly questioned. Can Christianity exist without dogmas, or are they a necessary part of the church's identity? While some theologians argue that dogmas provide stability and ensure the unity of the faithful, others see them as an obstacle to the further development of the faith. In recent decades, grassroots, feminist and queer theology in particular have been increasingly committed to questioning rigid church doctrines and freeing faith from dogmatic constraints.

Dogmatism not only serves to preserve tradition, but can also be understood as a protective mechanism of the church against change. This can be seen in the rejection of new theological principles or the defense of traditional teachings, which often prove to be psychologically stressful for the faithful. In sexual morality in particular, many dogmas are politically rather than spiritually motivated. The extent to which they really stem from a divine truth or rather serve social power interests is a central question in theological reflection.

But what happens when fundamental beliefs are questioned? Questioning church dogma has repeatedly led to dialog with the faithful in the past, especially when scientific thinking has uncovered irreconcilable contradictions to dogmatic teachings. One example of this is the historicity of the resurrection of Jesus: while traditional theologians regard it as a central creed, more modern interpretations often see it as a spiritual symbol rather than a historical event.

The fundamental question arises as to whether religions should function as dogmatic systems at all or whether they could rather be understood as flexible "ways of life". A more open understanding of faith *could make it possible to adapt the church to the needs of believers today without losing the core of the Christian message. This also includes the question of how religious experience can be described independently of predetermined dogmas and what role the sense of the sacred plays in this.*

The debate about dogma is not just an academic debate, but has a concrete impact on the lives of believers. Rigid structures can cause psychological stress if they are not in harmony with the individual experience of faith. It therefore remains one of the great challenges of theology to critically question traditional belief structures and to evaluate which doctrines are in need of reform in order to shape a contemporary, reflective and people-oriented church. To do this, however, a reform forge must also document the results in writing.

a) Theological foundations and criticism of dogma

27 • Which core theological convictions were critically questioned with regard to the historicity of Jesus' resurrection?

Gerd Lüdemann does not regard the Bible as a reliable source of divine revelation, but as a collection of human texts that must be examined historically and critically. He argues that many biblical writings are not shaped by divine inspiration, but by the experiences, fears and worldviews of their respective authors. He sees the numerous contradictions, legends and subsequent interpretations that have arisen over the centuries as particularly problematic.

A central example for him is the resurrection of Jesus, which should not be understood as a historical event, but as a theological interpretation.

He drew far-reaching consequences for Christian theology from this. According to his analysis, there is no reliable historical evidence for the bodily resurrection, but rather indications that it was a matter of subsequent interpretations and beliefs of the early Christians. Lüdemann argues that the resurrection narratives cannot be understood as objective reports, but rather as visionary experiences of individual followers of Jesus who were in a state of deepest grief and hopelessness after his death.

This conclusion represented a fundamental synapse with the church's understanding, as the resurrection is considered a central dogma of Christianity. However, Lüdemann did not see this as a divine revelation, but rather a psychological processing of the shock of Jesus' violent death. This led him to the conviction that a historical-critical theology could not hold on to the idea that Jesus had risen from the dead.

His stance brought him into direct dialog with church doctrine and ultimately led to his teaching license for church service being revoked. He argued that theology must be scientifically independent and not subject to dogmatic guidelines. His criticism of the resurrection was therefore not only a question of historical analysis, but also a fundamental debate about the compatibility of faith and scientific research in theology.

Faith without critical thinking runs the risk of becoming dogmatic or naïve. Conversely, theology without a reference to faith loses its existential core. There is a space between the two that is not comfortable, but fruitful: where faith is prepared to be questioned - and where science not only analyzes, but also listens - a way of thinking emerges that has depth. And perhaps that is exactly what our time needs:

A short sermon

(as a thought-providing impulse):

"Faith that does not think is empty.
Thinking that does not believe is blind."

This sentence - based on Immanuel Kant - reminds us that head and heart are not opponents. Faith needs depth, needs questions, sometimes also needs doubt in order to remain alive.

Jesus himself never demanded simple obedience, but challenged people to think: "What do you think?" he asks his disciples. Faith often begins where you are not sure - but you set off anyway.

Theology is an attempt to make this path comprehensible, to translate it into our time, with all its fractures, questions and tensions. And perhaps that is its greatest strength: not knowing everything, but having the courage to keep asking questions - trusting that God is not afraid of honest searching.

Amen.

28 • Can Christianity exist without dogmas?

Christianity without dogmas would be a radical change, but not impossible. Dogmas are officially established beliefs that are considered irrefutable and form the theological basis of many Christian denominations. They define central truths of faith and serve as a standard for the teachings of the church. The question is whether Christianity could continue to exist without these firm doctrines and how the faith would change as a result. Dogmas are binding statements of faith that are considered infallible by the church. In the Catholic Church, they are usually defined by councils or papal decrees. The Orthodox Church also adheres to traditional dogmas, while Protestant churches often view dogmas more critically or interpret them more flexibly.

The central Christian dogmas include the Trinity, which states that God exists in the Father, Son and Holy Spirit, the deity of Jesus Christ, which describes him as true God and true man, and the virgin birth, according to which Mary conceived Jesus without the help of a man. Original sin states that all people are burdened by the fall of Adam and Eve, while the bodily resurrection of Jesus expresses the belief that Jesus rose physically from the dead. In the Catholic Church, there is also the dogma of papal infallibility, which states that the Pope is infallible in certain dogmatic matters.

Without dogmas, Christianity would lose institutional unity, but could gain in openness. Dogmas define what is considered "orthodox" and prevent arbitrary interpretations. Without them, there would probably be an even greater diversity of Christian trends, which could be both enriching and divisive.

Theologically speaking, Christianity could continue to be based on the teachings of Jesus, which focus on love, mercy and justice.

The first Christians lived their faith without systematic dogmas and referred to Jesus' message and ethical actions. In this respect, a dogma-free Christianity could be conceivable if it relied more on the Gospel than on theological definitions. In order to abolish or reformulate dogmas without abandoning central beliefs, alternative formulations could be chosen that leave more room for individual interpretation.

Figure 9: A head of Christ, open and questioning, with a floating question mark instead of a crown of thorns - surrounded by crumbling dogmatic tablets, from whose ruins new life is growing. It stands for a Christianity without rigid doctrines - open to renewal.

A single person symbolically leaves the world of rigid dogmas - with a shining heart instead of a book, on an open path under a question mark in the sky. The image speaks of spiritual freedom, doubt and trust beyond the old. On the left, the questioning Christ, surrounded by crumbling dogmas - on the right, the free man with a shining heart, setting out on an open path. Two perspectives on a Christianity beyond rigid doctrines, united in a balanced picture.

Instead of the Trinity as a mandatory requirement of faith, one could formulate that God can be experienced in different dimensions, as Creator, as man in Jesus and as a spiritual force that works in the world. The divinity of Jesus Christ could be understood as an expression of Jesus' deep connection with God, which is evident in his life and his message.

The virgin birth could be seen symbolically as a reference to the special election of Jesus by God, regardless of biological details.

Original sin could be understood as the realization that humans have a tendency towards moral fallibility and need divine guidance in order to lead an ethically responsible life.

The resurrection of Jesus could be interpreted as a deep conviction of faith that Jesus remains present in the world beyond death, be it spiritually, symbolically or in a way that is beyond human understanding.

The infallibility of the Pope could be replaced by an emphasis on communal theological reflection, in which the Church is not dependent on a single authority but continues to develop in an open dialog.

Christianity could exist without dogmas if it focused more on the original message of Jesus and accepted the diversity of Christian beliefs. However, this would lead to a fundamental transformation of the churches, as dogmas are an important means of ensuring unity and identity. Without them, Christianity would be less institutionalized, but possibly closer to the beginnings of faith than it was before dogmatic systematization.

29 • Is dogmatism a protective mechanism of the church against change?

Dogmatism serves as a protective mechanism against change in many religious institutions, especially in the Catholic Church. By defining certain beliefs as incontrovertible truths, the church preserves its theological and moral authority and protects itself from internal and external challenges. This rigid stance ensures the continuity of tradition, but at the same time makes it difficult to react to social change or new scientific findings.

Historically, the church was often confronted with movements that challenged its teachings - be it through scientific discoveries, social changes or new theological currents. The reaction was often a dogmatic defensive stance in order to preserve existing structures. For example, the idea of a heliocentric view of the world, which clashed with the biblical concept of a geocentric world, was initially condemned as heretical.

"I made a mistake, I made a mistake"

The words "I made a mistake, I made a mistake" are said to come from Pope John Paul II - more precisely: they are attributed to him in literary-theological debate, often symbolically or fictitiously, but not historically documented as a direct quote.

The phrase was made particularly famous by the writer Hans Küng, a well-known Catholic theologian and critic of the Church. He imagined that a pope - perhaps John Paul II or a future one - could at some point summon up the courage to say publicly: "I was wrong, I was wrong." (or: "I was wrong ...")

This would mean an admission that the church was not infallible - for example in the question of women's ordination, sexual morality, the handling of power - but that culpable misguided developments must also be acknowledged.

Important: This is not a historically proven papal quotation, but rather a theological vision or hope - an expression of a church that is ready for conversion.

Pope Francis actually said it: *"I was wrong and I am still wrong,"* said the Pope in an interview broadcast by Belgian state television VRT and picked up by several Italian media outlets. The interview was recorded on March 31, 2014 in the Apostolic Palace in the Vatican.

The statement *"I made a mistake, I made a mistake"* is therefore often used symbolically to emphasize the need to admit mistakes within the Catholic Church in order to move forward.

Theologian Hans Küng, known for his critical stance towards certain church dogmas, has repeatedly questioned the infallibility of the Pope and called for an open debate on possible undesirable developments.

Instead, he emphasized the importance of truthfulness and honesty in the church. He criticized the tendency not to admit mistakes in order to maintain the appearance of infallibility. In his writings and interviews, he called for a church that is willing to recognize and correct its own errors in order to remain authentic and credible.

Even the Reformation in the 16th century was not used by the Catholic Church as an opportunity for self-reflection, but was fought against with the Counter-Reformation and the Inquisition.

Küng's commitment today was aimed at persuading the church to adopt a new attitude in order to fulfill its missionary task in the modern world.

In the modern age, the dogmatic protection mechanism is particularly evident in moral and ethical issues. The church's stance on sexual morality, the role of women and LGBTQIA+ rights is largely based on centuries-old doctrines that have left little room for adaptation. At the same time, however, there have also been changes: The church now officially recognizes the dignity and equality of women, even if they remain excluded from many ministries. In some Catholic parishes, women are now allowed to preach or take on leadership roles, which was previously unthinkable. Attitudes towards LGBTQIA+ people have also changed slightly. While official doctrine still does not recognize same-sex partnerships, some bishops and parishes have spoken out in favour of a more open approach, and Pope Francis has repeatedly emphasized that homosexual people must be treated with respect.

The fact that people today think independently about such ethical questions is a positive sign. Many believers are taking a critical look at church doctrines and finding their own answers to moral questions that are compatible with their conscience and modern knowledge. This process shows that religion does not necessarily have to be rigid, but that faith can develop further if it deals with current social challenges.

In some areas, the church has already succeeded in adapting dogmatic positions, for example through a more modern view of human rights or a cautious reassessment of the role of women and queer people in the church.

Ultimately, the question arises as to whether dogmatism really protects the church or leads it into a crisis in the long term. While it offers short-term stability, in the long term it can lead to the church losing touch with society. A living community of faith should be able to continuously question and adapt itself instead of hiding behind rigid dogmas. This is the only way it can remain relevant for future generations.

30 • Which traditional doctrines of Catholic theology have been questioned thematically, and why are they considered to be in need of reform?

Uta Ranke-Heinemann also questioned central dogmas of Catholic theology, in particular Mary's virgin birth and the church's sexual morality. She criticized that the idea of Mary's virginity was less a historical fact than a theological construction that held women to an unrealistic ideal of purity. For her, it was a dogma that served to control women and their sexuality rather than conveying a liberating message.

The idea of Mary's virgin birth is based on Christian theology, which teaches that Jesus was conceived by a mother without human procreation - i.e. without the involvement of a man. This teaching is based on the Gospels of Matthew and Luke, which speak of a conception by the Holy Spirit. Theologically, this is understood as a divine miracle that underlines Jesus' special origin and mission.

From a biological point of view, a natural human virgin birth (parthenogenesis) is extremely unlikely. In nature, parthenogenesis occurs in some animals such as reptiles, amphibians or insects, but not in humans. Even if an egg cell were to divide without male sperm, it could only produce female offspring, as the male Y chromosome would be missing.

Modern science therefore sees the virgin birth not as a biological phenomenon, but as a theological narrative with symbolic meaning. Historically, the idea could have arisen from misunderstandings or mistranslations - such as the Greek word *"parthenos"* (virgin) in the

Septuagint, which may have had a different meaning in the original Hebrew. Scientifically, virgin birth remains a religious concept that lies outside of biological possibilities. Even though it is a central element of faith, expressing a spiritual truth: the divine origin of Jesus.

Uta Ranke-Heinemann also opposed the church's strict sexual morality, which often only accepts sexuality within a narrow framework of marriage and procreation. She saw this as an unnecessary restriction of human freedom and a contradiction to the biblical message of love and compassion. She particularly criticized the fact that the Catholic Church often associated its sexual teachings with fear and feelings of guilt instead of promoting a life-affirming view of the body and love.

A life-affirming view of the body and love begins with the recognition that physicality and sexuality are a natural and valuable part of being human. It requires an attitude that values people in their entirety - body, mind and emotions.

Education plays a central role in this. An open and non-judgemental approach to physicality, relationships and sexuality can help to break down fears and taboos. Religious education, in particular, should teach about respectful and responsible treatment of oneself and others in sexual relationships.

Language and images used in theology and society are also crucial. In the case of physicality, a spiritual perspective could be emphasized that sees the body as an expression of vitality and beauty, as something that enables joy and connection - also with and through sexuality.

Furthermore, a culture of acceptance is needed in which people feel that their sexual and physical experiences, feelings and identities are taken seriously. Love in all its facets - whether romantic, same-sex or opposite-sex, friendly or familial - should not be bound by rigid perceptions, but should be understood as an individual creative force that enriches and deepens life. Such a view not only promotes a healthier relationship with one's own body, but also fulfilling, appreciative relationships.

The open questioning of these two dogmas ultimately led to Uta Ranke-Heinemann's church teaching license being revoked. However, she maintained that theology should not be a blind allegiance to church traditions, but a science that critically examines and develops doctrines of faith in order to give them a contemporary, human-friendly meaning.

31 • How did the questioning of central church dogmas lead to conflicts with the Vatican?

Criticism of papal infallibility in particular led Hans Küng into a deep conflict with the Vatican. According to Catholic doctrine, the Pope is only infallible under certain conditions. The dogma of papal infallibility was defined at the First Vatican Council in 1870 and states that the Pope is infallible when he definitively proclaims a matter of faith or morals *"ex cathedra"*, i.e. in his function as the supreme teacher of the Church. However, this rarely happens and only concerns binding truths of faith, not everyday statements or personal opinions of the Pope.

Hans Küng questioned whether a pope could be infallible in matters of faith and morals and argued that this teaching was not clearly based on the Bible, but was a later dogmatic development. For him, a church was needed that relied more on the original Christian message and less on hierarchical authority. This attitude called into question the power structure of the Catholic Church and ultimately led to him also being stripped of his ecclesiastical teaching license in 1979.

The Pope could therefore continue to proclaim *"ex cathedra"* doctrines of faith or morals that are considered binding for all Catholics. Such dogmas concern fundamental truths of faith that are established as definitive. In history, this has only rarely been used - for example when proclaiming the dogmas of the Immaculate Conception of Mary (1854) and the Assumption of Mary into heaven (1950). Theoretically, a pope could therefore proclaim other topics as dogma, such as the role of women in the church, the position of the church in the modern world or ethical issues such as bioethics and climate justice. However, such declarations would have to be in line with church tradition and scripture in order to be recognized as infallible. The lack of new *"ex cathedra"* teachings can be seen both as a sign of theological stagnation and as a relief. On the one hand, it could indicate that the Church no longer expresses itself on fundamental questions of faith and instead relies on traditions without formulating new binding dogmas. This could be perceived as a lack of further development, especially in times of social change. On the other hand, it could also be seen as positive, as any new dogmatization would be a further definition that might be perceived as a restriction. Many believers welcome the fact that the Pope does not proclaim any new, irrefutable doctrines, as this leaves room for personal decisions of conscience and theological debates. In this way, the Church remains more open to different interpretations and developments instead of establishing new rigid rules that would be difficult to change later, but only time and its discussions will tell whether the old dogmas can continue to exist.

32 • How have traditional belief structures been challenged by new theological principles?

By emphasizing *"sola scriptura"* (scripture alone) and *"sola fide"* (faith alone), Martin Luther fundamentally questioned the authority of the church hierarchy. He rejected the idea that the pope or clergy had to take on a mediating role between God and the faithful and instead called for a *direct relationship between each individual and God*.

"*One on One*" - Can my *Jour Fixe* work without a church?

A direct relationship with God meant turning away from church traditions, sacraments and ecclesiastical mechanisms of salvation, as had been customary until then. In Martin Luther's time, this weakened the power of the church as an institution and paved the way for a pluralistic Christian practice of faith.

The following changes would be necessary if the Pope or clergy were to take on a *genuine mediating role* between God and the faithful today: First, they would need to ensure greater transparency and credibility in their actions in order to regain trust. This includes consistently dealing with abuses in the church, particularly with regard to abuse of power and cover-ups. In addition, the church should respond more directly to the spiritual and social needs of the faithful instead of clinging to rigid dogmas. Greater participation of the faithful in church decision-making processes and a reform of church hierarchies would also be crucial in order to make the role of mediator more authentic. A local clergyperson would have to see themselves primarily as a pastor and offer the faithful authentic spiritual guidance based on their individual questions and needs. This includes a credible and understandable proclamation of Scripture that not only repeats traditions, but also provides genuine orientation. In addition, he/she should actively seek dialog, take doubts seriously and create space for open discussion. In practical terms, this means not only leading church services, but also being there for people in everyday life - be it through social work, personal conversations or concrete help in crisis situations. A clergyperson who takes their role as a mediator seriously should also be a role model by credibly exemplifying values such as humility, justice and compassion.

Artificial intelligence cannot completely replace pastoral care, but it can usefully supplement and prepare it. For example, it can provide answers to theological questions, provide background information on biblical passages or give suggestions for sermons and discussions. It can also support the organization of church work, for example by preparing pastoral care conversations in a structured way or recommending resources for specific life situations. However, AI lacks the human empathy, intuition and spiritual experience that are crucial in personal pastoral care. It is more of a mediator of knowledge, which can also lead to the ability to act. Furthermore, AI is not yet able to respond to non-verbal signals, take individual life stories into account and offer genuine emotional closeness - something that clergy can do much more extensively. It would therefore make sense to use AI as a supporting tool to reflect new theological principles, as Martin Luther once did - while the actual pastoral care remains the responsibility of humans.

a) Theological foundations and criticism of dogma

33 • Why should religions not be regarded primarily as dogmatic systems, but as "ways of life"?

Karen Armstrong, a renowned religious scholar and former Catholic nun, argues that religions should not primarily be understood as rigid dogmatic systems, but rather as lived *"ways of life"*. In her book *"The Case for God"*, she emphasizes that the essence of religion lies not in the mere belief in certain doctrines, but in the practice and experience of the sacred. Armstrong emphasizes that religious traditions originally aimed to promote compassion, selflessness and a deep understanding of the human condition. She criticizes the modern tendency to reduce religion to a list of dogmas, arguing instead for a return to the practical aspects of faith that influence the daily lives and actions of believers.

A return to the practical aspects of faith means looking at religion not as a mere theory or collection of dogmas, but as a *lived practice* that shapes daily life. Instead of concentrating on abstract theological concepts or beliefs, the focus shifts to concrete actions that strengthen compassion, mindfulness and social responsibility.

A central component is active charity. In almost all religious traditions, there is a call to care for the poor, the sick and the disadvantaged. This is not done by merely preaching about morality, but by providing direct help, social justice and commitment to a better society.

It also includes *spiritual practice* that goes beyond mere professions of faith. Meditation, prayer, contemplative rituals or communal services offer space for reflection, self-transformation and the experience of the sacred in everyday life. Religion as a lived practice means that spirituality not only takes place in a religious space, but also influences everyday actions - be it in dealing with others, in the way we work or in our attitude towards the environment.

Another important aspect is self-cultivation, i.e. consciously working on one's own character traits. Traditions such as fasting, regular self-examination or spiritual exercises are not only intended to promote discipline, but also to create a deeper connection to one's inner self and to other people.

Finally, a return to practice also means keeping religion open to dialog and further development. Instead of hardening oneself into fixed dogmas, faith should be constantly tested against reality and reflected upon in exchange with others. A living faith grows with the challenges of the times, takes social developments seriously and remains in motion instead of fixating on past norms.

It is about understanding religion as a lived experience again - not as a system of rules, but as a way of being that is actively lived and becomes visible in daily actions.

34 • Does dogmatism promote intolerance and violence?

Dogmatism, especially in religious contexts, can also promote intolerance and violence if it claims to be the only truth and classifies deviations from it as threatening or sinful. If a doctrine is considered irrefutable and critical questions are not allowed, this often leads to the rejection of other perspectives, which can increase intolerance towards those with different opinions or social minorities.

History shows that dogmatic beliefs have often been used to marginalize or oppress certain groups - be it through church inquisitions, crusades or the persecution of people based on their sexual orientation. If an ideology leaves no room for diversity or dialog, it can easily turn into discrimination and violence.

Dogmatism is particularly problematic when it comes to moral and ethical issues because it blocks change in social norms. While many sciences and philosophies continue to develop, dogmatic institutions often cling to outdated ideas and defend them fiercely. This can lead to existing injustices - such as discrimination against LGBTQIA+ people or the oppression of women - being *religiously* legitimized.

On the other hand, there is an open, reflective spirituality that does not insist on absolute truths, but sees faith as a dynamic process. If religious traditions were based more on compassion, reason and dialog, they could contribute to greater tolerance instead of stirring up conflict through rigid dogma. Ultimately, it is not the belief itself that determines intolerance or violence, but the way in which it is lived and interpreted.

One thing is certain: the Catholic Church has systematically discriminated against and oppressed women and LGBTQIA+ people for centuries. This discrimination manifested itself in theological dogmas, social exclusions and sometimes violent persecution. While women were long confined to subordinate roles in the church, LGBTQIA+ people were considered *"sinful"* or *"in a subordinate role"* or even often criminalized. Because these practices are deeply rooted in church history, there have also been changes and reform movements in recent decades that have led to some change.

Oppression and discrimination against women in the Catholic Church

Since the early days of Christianity, women have been systematically excluded from positions of power in the church. The idea that the *man* is considered *the "head of the woman"* was theologically underpinned by church fathers such as Augustine and Thomas Aquinas. Women were long regarded as spiritually and morally weaker, which reduced their role to motherhood and domestic duties. The Catholic Church denied women the priesthood and to this day rejects any reform in this regard - despite the fact that women carry out the majority of practical church work worldwide.

In the Middle Ages in particular, the oppression of women was extremely visible, for example in the witch hunts that were carried out under the legitimization of the church. Women who were considered *"conspicuous"* or *"independent"* were persecuted, tortured and burned. But even in more modern times, the church has exerted influence on women's rights, for example through its strict rejection of contraception and abortion. In many countries, particularly in Latin America and Poland, church pressure has led to women having no or only very limited access to reproductive rights.

Oppression and discrimination against LGBTQIA+ people

Homosexual, bisexual and trans* people were also persecuted by the church for centuries. In the Middle Ages, same-sex acts were considered sins, and people who *committed "sodomy"* were executed through church-backed justice systems. Later, the church regarded this queer sexual orientation as a "mental disorder" or "moral transgression", an attitude that persisted into the 20th century.

To this day, the Vatican maintains the position that same-sex relationships are *"sinful"*, while homosexual inclinations are considered *"disordered"*. The ordination of homosexual men to the priesthood was officially banned in 2005, and in 2021 the Vatican reaffirmed that homosexual partnerships will not be blessed. While legal equality has been achieved in many countries, the Catholic Church continues to be a driving force against LGBTQIA+ rights in some states, for example by opposing the legalization of same-sex marriage.

Elimination of discrimination and positive changes

Despite this long history of oppression, a lot has changed in recent decades. Today, women have more influence than ever before in many communities, even if they are still denied official ordinations. Initiatives such as the *"Mary 2.0"* movement are campaigning for a church with equal rights and are calling for women to be ordained as priests, among other things. In some countries, there are progressive movements within the Catholic Church that give women appropriate responsibility in leadership roles.

The Church's attitude towards LGBTQIA+ people has also changed slightly in some areas. Pope Francis has repeatedly emphasized that queer people must be treated with dignity and respect. In 2013, he said the famous phrase: *"Who am I to judge?"* when asked about homosexual priests. In some Catholic parishes, there are now blessings for same-sex couples, although the Vatican does not officially allow this. In Germany, the *"#OutInChurch"* initiative has caused a stir, with Catholic employees openly coming out as queer and standing up for a church free of discrimination.

In addition, theologians, church reform movements and activists have made a significant contribution to challenging the church's rigid sexual morals. Social pressure has broken down some taboos, and other progressive Catholic groups around the world are campaigning for greater acceptance. In Western countries in particular, Catholic communities are increasingly opening up to LGBTQIA+ people and looking for ways to involve them more in the church.

The Catholic Church has therefore discriminated against and oppressed women and LGBTQIA+ people for centuries - often not for spiritual reasons, but for reasons of power politics. While this oppression has never completely disappeared, progressive movements have emerged in recent decades that advocate for equal rights. Women are taking on more and more responsibility in the church, and the debate about the role of LGBTQIA+ people has opened up. However, many of the old structures still exist and the Vatican is holding on to traditional dogmas. The future will show whether the Church is ready to evolve or whether it will continue to cling to outdated ideas that are increasingly being questioned by society and young believers.

35 • Are sexual dogmas primarily politically or spiritually motivated?

Sexual dogmas in particular are binding church doctrines that define the moral understanding of sexuality and are considered irrevocable for believers. Among other things, they regulate marriage, procreation, chastity, homosexuality and gender identity. In the Catholic Church, they are firmly anchored in the catechism and are regarded by the magisterium as part of the divine order. This includes, for example, the idea that sexuality may only take place within a sacramental marriage between a man and a woman, that every sexual act must be *"open to life"* and that homosexuality is considered *"objectively disordered"*. There are also strict ideas of sexual morality in many evangelical movements, which reject premarital sex, same-sex relationships or non-binary gender identities.

However, whether sexual dogmas are primarily politically or spiritually motivated depends heavily on their historical and social context. While the church often sees its sexual doctrine as theologically based, a look at history shows that many of these norms also had political and social functions: sexuality has always been an area in which power and control have played a major role, and the church has used sexual morality over the centuries to stabilize social order and secure its influence over the private lives of the faithful.

Many of today's sexual dogmas date back to times when the church was not only a spiritual but also a political institution. In the Middle Ages, for example, the church had a great influence on marriages, as it also helped to shape social and economic structures through family alliances. The close connection between sexuality and procreation served to maintain clear lines of succession and social hierarchies. The evaluation of same-sex love and extramarital sex also often had less to do with theological convictions than with control over social norms.

Even within the Catholic Church, there are indications that sexual dogmas often have more to do with power than spirituality. The strict rejection of contraception was codified in the 20th century by Pope Paul VI with the encyclical Humanae Vitae (1968), although many theologians and bishops argued for a relaxation. This decision was taken less for purely theological reasons than for fear of undermining the authority of the Church's magisterium. The aforementioned compulsory celibacy for priests, which only became obligatory in the Middle Ages, was not introduced primarily for spiritual reasons, but only to prevent priestly families from claiming church property for themselves.

The idea that sexuality should be linked to love, fidelity and responsibility has a deeply spiritual dimension that remains relevant even in modern debates on ethics. However, the question is whether these principles must necessarily be tied to traditional dogmas. The central message of Jesus emphasizes love, compassion and responsibility, which argues that sexuality should not be ethically evaluated by rigid rules, but by personal integrity and respect for others.

A new, reformed dogma could take up these values and emphasize an ethic of responsibility instead of the previous rigid rules. A possible formulation of new dogmas that correspond to this approach would be:

Sexuality is a gift from God that should be lived in love, respect and responsibility.

Any sexual relationship is ethically justifiable if it is based on mutual consent, respect and responsibility.

The Church recognizes that love and commitment have a moral value regardless of gender or marital status.

Sexual orientation is a natural gift from God and must not be subject to discrimination or moral devaluation.

Procreation is a possible, but not mandatory, purpose of sexuality. Love and intimacy are equally valuable expressions of human closeness.

The Church respects the conscience of each individual in matters of sexuality and accompanies people in their search for a responsible, fulfilling life.

These reformed dogmas would no longer see sexuality as a danger or as purely procreation-oriented, but as an expression of relationship, love and connection that is ethically linked to responsibility and respect. Such a view would not only enable a theological reassessment, but would also help more people to identify with the church without feeling morally pressured.

It turns out that sexual dogmas are both politically and spiritually motivated. While many church norms have their origins in spiritual ideas, they have also been used over the centuries to stabilize social structures and secure power relations.

However, a reform of the church's sexual ethics could help to align these norms with the fundamental values of Jesus: Love, justice and compassion. Instead of control and obedience, a renewed church ethic could focus on trust in the personal conscience of the faithful and recognize sexuality as something natural and sacred that is not characterized by moral fear, but by an ethic of care and respect.

36 • *How and why can rigid structures and traditional teachings in the church lead to psychological stress?*

Eugen Drewermann criticized the Catholic Church as an institution with "*sickening structures*" that promote fear and dependency instead of supporting people in their spiritual development. Like many others, he denounced the rigid adherence to dogmas that do not allow for individual experiences of faith and often lead to the suppression of questions and doubts rather than a genuine examination of faith.

He saw a further problem in education through fear. The idea of a punishing God, an inescapable sense of guilt and a principle of obedience that undermines free will could lead to deep psychological conflicts. Above all, he considered the idealized image of priests, which demands absolute devotion and complete self-denial from clergymen, to be a cause of psychological suffering and personal failure for many clergymen.

With his deep psychological interpretation of religious teachings, he questioned church dogma. He argued for a liberation of faith from fear and coercion and for a church that does not shape people through feelings of guilt, but takes them seriously in their personal search for meaning and spirituality. This view put him at odds with church doctrine, which ultimately led to the withdrawal of his teaching license.

As follows, education can lead from a fear-based imprint to positive human development and enable theologians to learn: Education through fear creates dependency, feelings of guilt and an inner insecurity that can inhibit personal development in the long term. Strict rules without room for critical thinking or individual experience often lead to children and young people, people in general, internalizing obedience instead of developing self-confidence and responsibility. Particularly in religious contexts, a pedagogy of fear can lead to faith not being perceived as liberating, but in particular faith and the church being perceived as burdensome. A better framework for action and education is based on trust, encouragement and reflection. Instead of punishment and authoritarian control, it should be based on support and the promotion of independence. Mistakes should not be blamed, but understood as part of a learning process. People, especially children and young people, need the opportunity to ask their own questions, reflect on their experiences and develop self-determined convictions. Education can promote the search for meaning and spirituality by cultivating curiosity and openness instead of fear of doubt. Experiencing God or the divine as something tangible in relationship, love and justice develops a deeper spiritual connection than simply following rules. Rules should be replaced by questions.

Theology can learn from this pedagogy that faith does not remain alive through pressure or fixed dogmas, but through questions and dialog in shared encounters, through freedom in asking questions, through freedom in thinking and learning - in order to achieve personal growth. Instead of relying on fear or obedience, religious dialog at all levels could develop a *theology of encouragement* - one that promotes questions, takes spiritual experiences seriously and sees people not as subjects, but as active co-creators of their questions and possible interpretations on the journey of faith.

---

c) Dogma theology in the field of tension between science and modernity

---

37 • How does scientific thinking relate to dogmatic religious ideas, and where do irreconcilable contradictions arise?

Harald Lesch sees a fundamental need for dialog where religious dogmas ignore or contradict scientific findings. Science is based on verifiable facts, experiments and logical reasoning, while dogmatic belief systems are often based on revelation, authority and immutable truths. This contradiction is particularly evident in issues such as the theory of evolution, the Big Bang or the age of the Earth, which are at odds with literal interpretations of religious scriptures. Lesch emphasizes that science is a dynamic process that constantly questions its theories and adapts them to new findings, while dogmatic systems often assume an absolute truth that must not be changed.

Nevertheless, he recognizes that faith and science do not necessarily have to be in conflict, as long as religion does not see itself as a competing explanatory model for scientific phenomena, but concentrates on ethical and existential questions. The real conflict therefore does not arise between science and faith per se, but where religious institutions reject scientific findings because they collide with traditional dogmas.

Many core aspects of Christianity do not concern the scientific explanation of the world, but rather ethical, moral and spiritual questions that lie outside the scope of scientific investigation. These include, above all, the idea of charity, the notion of justice, mercy and forgiveness as well as the question of the meaning of life. These concepts cannot be measured empirically, but they shape human coexistence and moral reflection.

Belief in a transcendent reality or in God himself does not necessarily contradict science either, as natural science cannot make any statements about the existence or non-existence of God. The Christian belief in the dignity of man and his responsibility for creation coincides with many scientific insights, for example in the area of environmental protection or medical ethics. The principles of charity and solidarity are also reflected in scientific findings on human social behavior and cooperation as evolutionary advantages.

There is also a long tradition of Christian scientists who have shown that religious faith and scientific work do not have to be mutually exclusive. Many important scientists - including Gregor Mendel in genetics and Georges Lemaître, who developed the Big Bang theory - were themselves clergymen.

Particularly problematic and in conflict with science, however, are beliefs that either directly contradict scientific findings or are difficult to reconcile with an empirically verifiable world view. This includes, above all, the literal interpretation of the creation story in the book of Genesis, in particular the idea of the world being created in six days or a young earth of a few thousand years. This view contradicts geological, biological and cosmological findings that prove that the earth is billions of years old and that life has evolved.

Miracle reports in which the laws of nature are seemingly suspended - such as the virgin birth, the turning of water into wine or the resurrection of Jesus - are also in direct opposition to the scientific principle that the laws of nature apply universally. While believers interpret these events as an expression of divine power, science regards them as unverifiable claims, as they have no experimental or empirical evidence.

A further area of tension exists in the theology of the soul and free will. While many Christian traditions assume that humans possess an immortal soul and make decisions independently of material processes, neuroscientific findings suggest that consciousness, thoughts and decisions can be traced back to physico-chemical processes in the brain. The concept of a non-material consciousness that is independent of biology is difficult to reconcile with these findings.

The idea of a teleological (goal-oriented) world view, in which the universe is oriented towards man as the *"crown of creation"*, is also in conflict with evolutionary theories, which show that man is a product of random mutations and natural selection, without any evidence of a divine goal or predestination.

Finally, there are ethical issues in which scientific progress and church dogma collide, for example in genetic engineering, reproductive medicine or bioethics. While the Church often insists on the special sanctity of human life from conception onwards, science tends to view biological processes from a functional perspective and does not recognize any inherent "divine plan" in them.

This means that the conflicts are mainly to be found where religious teachings are interpreted as scientific facts or where scientific findings contradict church dogma.

The number of people leaving the church has risen in many countries in recent decades, and one of the reasons for this is the conflict between church dogma and scientific knowledge. Especially in highly educated societies, where scientific education plays a major role, many people feel that religious teachings are no longer up to date or incompatible with a scientific world view. When church and science are perceived as opposites, young people in particular feel alienated and turn away.

Three key concessions the church has made to science and modernity in order to slow down people leaving the church are:

Recognition of evolution as compatible with faith

The church could distance itself more clearly from creationist interpretations of creation and recognize evolution as a natural process that does not contradict a belief in God. A theologically acceptable way would be to interpret evolution as a method of divine creation without having to postulate a direct divine intervention in each individual species.

Abolition of celibacy for priests

Celibacy is a major obstacle for the next generation of clergy. The abolition of this obligation would not only open up more people to the priesthood, but would also strengthen the credibility of the church by allowing realistic life models for its clergy.

Equal rights for women in church ministry

The refusal to admit women to the priesthood is contrary to modern principles of equality and is seen by many believers as outdated. A reform on this issue could help to strengthen the credibility of the church and slow down the loss of members.

Two dogmas in particular need of reform based on scientific findings and their possible adaptation also play an important role:

Dogma of the virgin birth of Mary

Previous teaching: The Church teaches that Mary conceived Jesus through the power of the Holy Spirit without the involvement of a man. This idea is based on a literal interpretation of biblical texts and has been dogmatically codified.

Scientific problem: Biologically, a virgin birth in mammals is not compatible with male offspring. Historical analyses also show that the term *"virgin"* is possibly a mistranslation of the Hebrew word *"almah"* (young woman).

Possible adaptation: The Church could interpret the virgin birth symbolically by understanding it as an expression of Mary's special election and her spiritual purity, without maintaining a biological contradiction.

Dogma of papal infallibility in matters of faith

Previous doctrine: Since 1870, the dogma has been that the Pope is infallible in matters of faith and morals when he speaks *ex cathedra*. This means that his decisions cannot be questioned or revised under certain circumstances.

Scientific problems: The progress of knowledge in all areas of science shows that knowledge is always changing. The idea of an absolute, unchanging truth proclaimed by a single authority is at odds with modern theories of knowledge and democratic principles.

Possible adaptation: One reform could be to relativize the dogma of infallibility by emphasizing that papal doctrines are embedded in a historical context and can be further developed in the light of new insights.

Such adjustments could narrow the gap between church and academia and help more people see the church as a dynamic, evolving institution that can be in tune with modernity.

The natural sciences do not answer all the fundamental questions of human existence: one central open question is the **meaning of life** - while science describes how the universe came into being and functions, the question of why something exists remains a metaphysical and philosophical consideration.

Another unsolved problem is the **origin of consciousness**. While neuroscience shows that thinking and emotions are based on neuronal processes, it remains unclear exactly how subjective experience - the "I-consciousness" - arises and whether it goes beyond purely material mechanisms.

Even ethical questions cannot be conclusively answered scientifically. Science can describe which actions have which consequences, but it does not provide a definitive answer as to what is morally right or wrong. Debates on topics such as genetic engineering, artificial intelligence or climate justice require scientific findings, but the decision on how to deal with these findings remains a question of ethics, philosophy or even religion.

Finally, the **question of the ultimate cause** remains unanswered: Even if the universe may have been created by the Big Bang, the question remains as to why there are natural laws that make a universe possible in the first place. Scientists point out that science reaches its limits here because it conducts research within the universe but cannot definitively explain why there is something and not nothing. Philosophy, religion and political science have different approaches to this:

Philosophy approaches the question of the meaning of life in different ways. Existentialists such as Jean-Paul Sartre or Albert Camus argue that life has no objective meaning, but that man himself must create meaning. Other philosophical currents, such as Aristotelianism or German idealism, see the goal of human life in the development of one's own potential or in the realization of moral values. The question of consciousness leads to debates between materialists, who consider it to be a product of physical processes, and dualists, who assume a non-material dimension of thought.

Religions often provide clear answers to these questions. In Christianity, Judaism and Islam, the universe is seen as God's creation, which answers the question of the ultimate cause - it exists because God wanted it to. The meaning of life is seen in a relationship with God or in the fulfillment of divine commandments. In Buddhism, on the other hand, the meaning lies in overcoming suffering and attaining enlightenment. Consciousness is also often seen as more than just a biological process in religious traditions - many faiths postulate a soul that exists independently of the body.

The **political sciences** look at these questions from a social perspective. While they do not provide metaphysical answers, they analyze how meaning is created in social structures. Ideologies such as liberalism or socialism give people a sense of direction by focusing on values such as individual freedom or social justice. Ethical issues are often discussed here in the form of laws and political decisions, for example in debates on bioethics, climate policy or human rights.

Ultimately, **the question of the "why"** of the universe remains one that neither science, philosophy, religion nor politics can answer definitively. However, each of these disciplines offers different perspectives and tools for dealing with this uncertainty and finding orientation in life.

38 • Why are dogmas dangerous for an enlightened society?

According to Voltaire, dogmas are dangerous for an enlightened society because they restrict the free use of reason and suppress criticism. In his *Dictionnaire philosophique*, he discusses religious and ideological dogmas as rigid, often arbitrary doctrines that force people to accept certain beliefs without question. He sees dogmas as tools of power with which authorities - especially the church and the state - exercise control over people's thoughts and actions. An enlightened society, on the other hand, is based on tolerance, reason and freedom of thought, which is jeopardized by dogmas, as they can hinder doubt and scientific progress.

The problem in the Catholic Church is that dogmatic systems, as unchanging truths about God, faith and morality, often resist new insights or social change. In its history, the Church has often blocked scientific developments (such as the Copernican revolution) or social progress (e.g. women's rights, LGBTQIA+ rights) because they were seen as a threat to existing doctrines. While the church has evolved in many areas, dogma can continue to delay or prevent reform.

Queer theology questions dogmas in a particularly persistent way, as many theological doctrines about gender, sexuality and identity are based on old, normative ideas. Queer theologians argue that dogmas are often not divine truths, but *cultural constructions* that are tied to certain power relations. One example is the traditional Catholic doctrine that marriage can only exist between a man and a woman - a doctrine that is not biologically or historically without alternative, but is deeply rooted in patriarchal ideas. Such dogmas are problematic for an enlightened society because they legitimize discrimination and prevent critical reflection on ethics and justice.

Dogmas continue to be dangerous because they keep a society trapped in fixed thought structures and can hinder individual freedom and social progress. While they can be seen as a necessary orientation in religious systems, the Enlightenment - and with it Voltaire - emphasizes that a responsible society must be based on critical thinking, not blind obedience. Especially in queer theology, it becomes clear that questioning dogmas is not just an academic exercise, but a necessity for justice and inclusion.

According to Richard Dawkins, religion is also more of an obstacle to science because it is based on dogmas that defy critical thinking and empirical testing. In *The God Delusion*, he criticizes religious belief as irrational and anti-scientific - especially when religious authorities reject or distort scientific findings, for example in evolutionary theory or medical ethics. For Dawkins, religion often blocks the open, doubting mind that is necessary for scientific progress.

The Catholic Church has always had ambivalent roles in history: On the one hand, it prevented developments - as in the case of Galileo - on the other, it founded universities, promoted natural research and today officially recognizes the theory of evolution. The Church emphasizes that faith and reason do not contradict each other, but can complement each other - if faith remains open to knowledge. But what does scientific knowledge mean for its dogmas?

Scientific knowledge poses serious challenges to many dogmatic statements of the Catholic Church, especially when these statements contain scientific or anthropological assumptions. However, the Church makes a clear distinction between revelation-based truths of faith (e.. the Trinity, the Eucharist, the Resurrection) and dogmas that also concern secular observations or moral norms (e.. the doctrine of creation, sexual morality, anthropology).

Not all dogmas are therefore endangered by scientific findings or in need of revision - especially not if they refer to metaphysical or spiritual content that lies outside the empirically observable.

A dogma that is most likely not to be "overrun": The doctrine of the Trinity

The dogma of the Trinity (that God exists in three persons - Father, Son and Holy Spirit) is one of the central mysteries of faith of the Catholic Church. It is purely theological in nature and is beyond any scientific examination. The doctrine of the Trinity has no verifiable statements about the material world, but concerns the understanding of God in his inner structure.

- Science cannot confirm or refute this dogma because it does not lie in empirical space.
- It can be criticized philosophically, for example because of its logical complexity, but not scientifically in the narrower sense.

Other dogmas are more at risk: In contrast, dogmas that collide with biological, psychological or historical findings come under pressure, for example:

- The doctrine of original sin, if it remains literally tied to Adam and Eve,
- the church's sexual morality in the light of gender research,
- the male priesthood, with a view to equality and anthropological arguments.

Such teachings are often in conflict with modern knowledge - and are critically reflected upon by queer theology or feminist theology in particular.

Scientific knowledge primarily concerns those dogmas that make world-related statements or seek to justify moral norms.

Dogmas such as the doctrine of the Trinity, on the other hand, remain largely unaffected by this, as they relate purely to faith and make no statements that can be scientifically verified.

The challenge for the church is to distinguish what is indispensable in faith - and where reformable doctrines need to be reconsidered and changed in order to remain credible in the light of today's reason.

39 • *Is belief in God compatible with a rational worldview?*

According to Richard Dawkins, belief in God is not even compatible with a rational worldview, as it is based on supernatural assumptions that cannot be scientifically verified. In *The God Delusion*, Dawkins argues that religion is an evolutionary maladaptation based on wishful thinking and cultural conditioning. Science, in particular the theory of evolution, can fully explain the origin and development of life without the need for the hypothesis of a creator. For Dawkins, divine ideas are not only irrational, but often also a hindrance to critical thinking and social progress.

The Catholic Church, on the other hand, does not see an irreconcilable contradiction between faith and reason. Thomas Aquinas already attempted to rationally justify the existence of God, and the Second Vatican Council emphasized that faith and science can complement each other. The Church's acceptance of the theory of evolution also shows that faith does not necessarily have to be hostile to science. The Church distinguishes between empirical knowledge, which can be grasped by science, and metaphysical truth, which is beyond scientific access.

In queer theology, this debate is often conducted differently: It questions whether rationality can only be reduced to empirical provability or whether personal experience, spirituality and questions of identity are also legitimate sources of knowledge. Many queer theologians argue that religious faith does not have to be in competition with reason, but can offer an alternative perspective on meaning, ethics and community. They criticize a strictly naturalistic worldview that devalues spiritual experiences as irrational and argue for a dynamic understanding of truth that combines science and personal experiences of faith.

As is often the case, the compatibility of faith and a rational worldview remains a question of perspective. While Dawkins sees any supernatural assumption as incompatible with science, the Catholic Church sees faith and reason as complementary. Queer theology expands this discussion by questioning the definition of rationality itself and advocating an integrative view.

d) Dogma-free theological perspectives?

40 • Are beliefs without empirical evidence dangerous?

According to Sam Harris, beliefs without empirical evidence are actually dangerous because they encourage irrational thinking and often lead to intolerance, dogmatism and violence. In *The End of Faith*, he argues that religious belief that is not based on verifiable facts can lead people to justify harmful actions, whether through fanaticism, moral absolutes or the rejection of scientific knowledge. Harris sees monotheistic religions in particular as problematic because they often make an exclusive claim to truth that suppresses critical thinking and hinders social progress. He argues for a more rational, evidence-based ethics based on humanism and scientific knowledge.

It turns out that beliefs without empirical evidence can be problematic if they remain dogmatic and unreflected. Harris warns of the risks of uncritical faith, while Catholic theology seeks a balance between faith and reason. His queer theology argues for a reflective, contextualized approach that understands faith as dynamic and open to new insights. This makes it clear that it is not faith itself that is dangerous, but the way in which it is interpreted and put into practice.

An uncritical faith harbors several risks, as it can tempt people to adopt beliefs without scrutiny and thus block rational thinking, self-reflection and social progress. One of the greatest risks lies in the *danger of fanaticism*: if beliefs are regarded as absolute truth without being questioned, they can lead to intolerance towards those who think differently. This can be seen in religious extremism, the persecution of minorities or the rejection of scientific findings, such as the denial of evolution or climate change.

Another risk is the suppression of individual freedom. Dogmatic belief systems tend to set strict moral norms that can restrict personal identity, sexuality or freedom of expression. Particularly in religious contexts, where gender roles or sexual orientation are seen as divinely prescribed, this can lead to discrimination and psychological suffering.

Moreover, an uncritical faith can promote social stagnation if it prevents change. Progress in ethics, human rights or science has often been slowed down by religious resistance because established belief structures have been called into question. This can be seen historically in the Inquisition, in resistance to women's rights or in the refusal to recognize LGBTQIA+ people as equals.

Finally, uncritical faith can encourage manipulation and abuse of power. Religious institutions or authoritarian leaders can use faith as a means of exercising control over believers, for example by creating fear, demanding obedience or legitimizing injustice as "divine will".

These risks do not mean that faith is harmful in itself - but it must be reflected upon, critically questioned and combined with reason in order not to become a tool for intolerance, power or stagnation. An enlightened, reflective faith, on the other hand, can contribute to ethical orientation without reinforcing these dangers.

However, uncritical faith has repeatedly led to fanaticism throughout history, often with devastating consequences. Some striking examples are:

The Crusades (1096-1271): Under the belief that they were fulfilling the "will of God", Christian armies marched to Jerusalem to liberate the city from Muslim rule. These wars led to massive atrocities, including massacres of Muslims, Jews and even Christian groups who were considered heretics. The idea of a "holy war" justified murder and plunder in the name of religion.

The Inquisition (from the 12th century): The Catholic Church set up inquisitorial courts to persecute heretics and punish deviations from church dogma. In Europe, thousands of people - including Jews, Muslims, Protestants and alleged witches - were tortured and executed, often on the basis of accusations and without any real evidence.

Witch hunts (15th-18th century): In many parts of Europe and America, women (and some men) were persecuted, tortured and burned as witches because they were believed to have made a pact with the devil. These persecutions were based on religious superstition and the conviction that evil had to be actively combated.

Islamist terrorism (20th and 21st century): Extremist groups such as Al-Qaeda or the so-called Islamic State (IS) invoke a fundamentalist interpretation of Islam to justify terrorist attacks, violence against civilians and the oppression of dissenters. Their uncritical beliefs do not allow for an alternative point of view and lead to brutal consequences.

National Socialism and religious justifications (20th century): While the Holocaust was not primarily ideologically based on religion, anti-Semitic propagandists drew on centuries-old Christian hostility towards Jews to legitimize the persecution. The idea that Jews were "murderers of God" served as the ideological basis for centuries of discrimination and persecution.

Sects and cult movements (e.g. Peoples Temple, 1978): The cult leader Jim Jones led his followers in Guyana to a mass suicide in which over 900 people died. The members of the Peoples Temple believed unconditionally in his divine guidance and followed him to their deaths without critically questioning his teachings.

These examples show that uncritical faith, when combined with dogmatism and fanaticism, can have devastating effects. The problem does not lie in religion itself, but in the lack of reflection, which encourages blind obedience and intolerance.

In order to prevent religiously motivated fanaticism, reflection and critical thinking must be actively encouraged. Several approaches are possible to achieve this, involving education, theology and social structures:

1. promotion of religious criticism and interreligious dialog: People should be encouraged to question their own beliefs and engage with other religious traditions. Interreligious dialogue can help to relativize claims to absoluteness and promote tolerance. When believers learn that other religions also have complex moral systems, the tendency to regard one's own convictions as the only true truth decreases.

2. education as protection against dogmatism: A key protection against fanaticism is a good school education that teaches scientific methods, critical thinking and philosophical reflection. Religious education should not only reflect denominational content, but also include different faiths and perspectives that are critical of religion. It is particularly important that pupils learn to distinguish between faith and knowledge.

3. theological reflection and reform: Religious institutions should regularly reflect on their teachings and adapt them to ethical developments. Theological education can help to ensure that beliefs are not adopted uncritically, but are embedded in a reflective discourse. Progressive theologies - such as queer theology or liberation theology - show that religion does not have to be static, but can evolve.

4. sharpen historical awareness: Many fanatical groups justify their ideology with an alleged "return to the origins" of their religion. A deeper understanding of one's own religious history, including the contradictions and developments within the tradition, can help to break down rigid, fundamentalist interpretations.

5. emphasis on ethical principles rather than dogmatic truths: Religious education should focus more on universal ethical values such as compassion, justice and tolerance rather than absolute dogma. A faith that is based more on moral reflection than on rigid precepts is less prone to extremism.

6. critical reflection on authority and power: Fanaticism often arises from blind obedience to authority. Reflection can be promoted by encouraging believers to critically question religious leaders and sacred scriptures. This requires a culture in which doubt is not seen as a weakness, but as part of the journey of faith.

7. make targeted use of digital media and social networks: As many extremist ideologies are now spread online, reflection on digital media should also be encouraged. Platforms can be used to provide differentiated religious debates and scientifically sound information that counteracts conspiracy theories and extremism.

Fanaticism often arises where faith is adopted without reflection and is not combined with critical thinking. Education, interreligious dialog, theological reform and an emphasis on ethical principles can prevent religion from being misused to justify violence and intolerance. Reflection does not mean destroying faith, but shaping it in a conscious and self-determined way with the aim of including all people of faith.

41 • Can queer theology help to free the Christian faith from dogmatism?

A queer theology can make a significant contribution to freeing the Christian faith from dogmatism by questioning entrenched ideas about gender, sexuality and social norms. While traditional church dogmas are often based on clear, seemingly immovable rules, queer theology focuses on openness, diversity and dynamic interpretation. It recognizes that many of the church's moral teachings are not based on divine truth, but on cultural and historical developments that can and must change.

Especially in questions of sexuality and gender roles, queer theology represents an alternative draft to conservative Christian moral teaching. While for centuries marriage between a man and a woman was considered the only legitimate form of love, queer theology emphasizes the diversity of human relationships and identities. In doing so, it deconstructs so-called heteronormative ideas and shows that biblical texts can often be read differently than church tradition dictates. Stories such as those of *David and Jonathan* or *Ruth and Naomi* can be interpreted as an expression of intimate same-sex love, for example. In queer theologies, Jesus himself is also often understood as a figure who breaks through social norms and stands up for outsiders and the marginalized in particular.

A central aspect of queer theology is the inclusion of all people in the life of faith - regardless of their sexual identity or gender identity. While traditional theologies often argue with concepts such as *"sin"* or *"purity"*, queer theology focuses on love, responsibility and mutual respect as ethical standards. It not only questions rigid moral concepts, but also the patriarchal power structures that have maintained them for centuries. In this sense, it also sees itself as a continuation of liberation theology, which campaigns for the rights and recognition of oppressed groups.

Furthermore, queer theology questions the church's centuries-old approach to sexuality, which was often associated with guilt and shame. It rejects the idea that sexuality per se must be controlled or restricted, but sees it as a positive and sacred part of human life.

Instead of a sexual morality that dictates how people should live, she emphasizes ethical principles such as consensuality, honesty and care.

Another important aspect of queer theology is its intersectional perspective. It connects with other movements for social justice, such as feminism, anti-racism or environmental justice, and views discrimination in a wider social context. Queer theology is therefore not limited to issues of sexuality, but calls for a comprehensive reform of church structures towards more equality and co-determination.

In this way, queer theology can help to liberate the Christian faith from rigid dogmas and open it up to modern social developments. By questioning old power structures and introducing new theological perspectives , it creates space for a church that is not defined by exclusion and control, but by openness, justice and the radical message of love. A church that is open to this theology could become relevant again for many people who have long felt excluded by traditional church teachings.

42 • How can the religious experience be described independently of dogmatic guidelines, and what role does the feeling of the sacred play in this?

Rudolf Otto coined the term *"numinous"* to describe the deeply felt experience of the sacred, which lies beyond rational theology or fixed dogmas. For him, the numinous is an immediate encounter with a transcendent reality that cannot be fully put into words and which simultaneously triggers awe, fascination and a feeling of being overwhelmed. He describes it as the *"completely other"*, which reveals itself to people as a power that evokes both fear and attraction.

Otto distinguishes the numinous from moral and ethical aspects of religion and sees it as an independent category of experience. It is not an intellectual concept, but a deep feeling that expresses itself in mysticism, rituals and the personal experience of God. For him, the religious experience is therefore not primarily a question of belief in certain doctrines, but an existential encounter with the sacred that can be experienced across all cultures and religions. This view opens up an approach to religion that is based less on dogmatic structures and more on personal experience and inner contact with the transcendent.

In order to speak openly about personal experiences of God in today's world, Christians can find various ways of sharing in their congregations. Discussion groups or faith groups offer a framework in which believers can talk about their experiences without having to fear dogmatic guidelines. Forums in which church members tell how they have experienced the work of God in their lives create an atmosphere of openness and encouragement. Spiritual days can also bring people together to reflect on inner contact with the transcendent.

Another concrete approach is the promotion of mysticism and contemplation in church work. Practices such as the prayer of the heart, *lectio divina* or spiritual diaries can help to consciously reflect on personal experiences and share them with others. Digital platforms or social networks can also provide spaces for exchange, especially for those who do not find a place for their questions and experiences in local church structures.

There are several online forums where believers can exchange ideas

- Jesus.de: A Christian Internet portal that is considered the largest Christian online community in Germany.
- ChristWeb: Offers chats and forums for discussions on Christian topics.
- Zwischenraum: An interdenominational self-help organization for Christians of different sexual orientations or gender identities, which also offers online platforms for exchange.

These platforms enable believers to discuss topics of faith, personal experiences and current issues of faith in a very concrete and practical way.

In this context, Rudolf Otto warns that a purely rational theology could turn religion into a dry, academic discipline that formulates doctrines but no longer conveys the original experience of the sacred. This dimension of action is also a challenge for modern theology and the church : it must not only explain what is religious, but also make it tangible in order to remain true to its true nature - both online and on site.

Chapter 4:
Matters of interpretation: Bible, upbringing & education in dialog

For many Christians, the Bible forms the basis of their faith. But how timeless are its statements really? Particularly in questions of sexual morality and social values, there are always debates about whether biblical statements have universal validity or whether they must be considered against the historical and cultural background of their time of origin. Can such statements still be applied to the present day, or are they only comprehensible in the cultural context of antiquity? One example of this is the depiction of Jesus Christ in the Gospels, which some theologians interpret as an indication of queer or homosexual proximity.

For example, Jesus' close relationship with his disciple John in John 13:23 ("One of his disciples, whom Jesus loved, lay on his bosom") is interpreted by queer theologians as an expression of special affection. Equally striking is the narrative In Mark 14:51-52, in which an unknown young man - interpreted by some as a homoerotic motif - is described in Jesus' presence. In addition, there are Jesus' repeated statements about family structures in which he questions traditional heteronormative relationships, such as in Matthew 19:12 ("For there are eunuchs who have been so from birth, and there are eunuchs who have been made by men, and there are eunuchs who have emasculated themselves for the sake of the kingdom of heaven"). This passage is understood by some as an indication that Jesus recognized gender diversity and did not exclusively endorse heteronormative lifestyles.

The interpretation of such biblical passages remains controversial, especially in conservative church circles that insist on a clearly heteronormative interpretation of the Holy Scriptures. However, the question arises as to whether such readings reflect the church's need for clear categories rather than reflecting Jesus' actual message. An open and historical-critical interpretation of the Bible can help to re-

evaluate these texts in the context of their origin and make them fruitful for an inclusive theology.

Another area of tension lies in the contradictions between biblical texts and modern ethical values. How do Christians deal with these discrepancies? Feminist-oriented theologians in particular question patriarchal distortions in the interpretation of the Bible and are committed to ensuring that biblical texts are not used to legitimize gender inequality. They argue that many interpretations have been shaped by male power structures for centuries and that alternative readings are necessary in order to develop a more just theology.

The story of creation also raises questions: Is it a historical description of the origin of the world or rather a symbolic narrative about human finitude and transience? Modern theology is increasingly viewing religious texts as a space for reflection on existential questions that are aimed less at scientific explanations than at a personal confrontation with life and death.

Despite many scientific findings, religious beliefs often persist even when they have no demonstrable basis in reality. What are the psychological mechanisms behind this, and can parallels be drawn between religious rituals and neurotic compulsions? These questions are particularly relevant for religious education, as they concern the way in which beliefs are passed on to new generations.

In this context, it is also important to consider the role of same-sex partnerships in religious education and confirmation training. Is enough space given to LGBTQIA+ topics, or is church education still based on traditional ideas? Dealing with these questions shows that the Bible is by no means just a rigid set of rules, but must be constantly reinterpreted in its understanding. A lively theology therefore requires a critical dialog between biblical tradition, modern science and social developments.

a) Biblical texts and their interpretation

43 • Is the Bible a sufficient basis for modern sexual morality?

Whether the Bible is a sufficient basis for modern sexual morality depends heavily on the way it is interpreted. While many religious groups view the Bible as a binding ethical guide, there are significant challenges when applying its statements directly to today's social realities.

The Bible was written at a time with completely different social structures and gender roles. Many of its statements on sexuality reflect the cultural norms of antiquity, which are not easily compatible with modern values of equality, self-determination and human rights. For example, the biblical texts contain rules that take polygamy, arranged marriages and patriarchal hierarchies for granted. At the same time, the Bible lacks specific regulations on contemporary ethical issues such as consensual same-sex love, sexual identity or reproductive self-determination

Another problem arises from the diversity of biblical statements on sexual morality. While some texts contain strict rules, such as the prohibition of certain sexual acts in the Old Testament, there are other passages that emphasize love between people without imposing rigid categories. The message of Jesus in particular focuses on the principle of charity and mercy, which suggests a value-oriented rather than a purely rule-based sexual ethic.

Modern Christian ethics therefore often moves between two poles: on the one hand, there are conservative currents that adhere to a literal interpretation of biblical commandments; on the other hand, there are progressive theological approaches that understand the Bible in its historical context and apply its core messages to today's social challenges.

In a pluralistic society in which sexual self-determination, equality and individual freedom are central values, the question arises as to whether the Bible is sufficient as the sole basis for sexual morality or whether it should be supplemented with other ethical and scientific findings. Many theologians argue that the Bible should be a guide rather than a rigid set of laws that is in constant dialog with contemporary ethics, medicine, psychology and jurisprudence.

In summary, it can therefore be said that the Bible contains valuable moral principles that can be inspiring for today's sexual morality, but are not sufficient on their own to establish a comprehensive and contemporary ethic. In addition to the biblical tradition, responsible sexual morality also requires reflection on social developments, personal freedom and scientific findings.

44 • Are biblical statements on sexuality historically or universally valid?

Biblical statements on sexuality are largely shaped by history and are not universally valid. They reflect the cultural, social and religious ideas of the time in which they were written and must therefore be understood in their historical context. While some basic ethical principles - such as love, fidelity, respect and a sense of responsibility - are timeless, many specific rules on sexuality are closely linked to the social structures of the time and cannot easily be transferred to the present day.

A key example is the purity laws in the Old Testament, particularly in Leviticus 18:22 and Leviticus 20:13, which describe same-sex relationships as *an "abomination"*. These regulations are part of a complex system of purity laws, which had a social and religious function in ancient Israel. They served to distinguish the people of Israel from neighboring cultures and to maintain certain moral and ritual orders. Today, these regulations are no longer binding, as they arose in a specific historical context that no longer exists.

The situation is similar with Paul's statements in Romans 1:26-27 or 1 Corinthians 6:9-10, in which he criticizes same-sex acts. From a historical perspective, Paul is probably not talking about equal homosexual love relationships as they exist today, but about practices such as temple prostitution or pederastic power relations in Roman culture. A universal moral norm can hardly be derived from this.

Many biblical statements on marriage, divorce and gender roles also show that they are rooted in their historical context. In the Old Testament, polygamy was often accepted, marriages were often arranged and women had a subordinate legal position. Deuteronomy 22:28-29 even stipulates that a rapist must marry the woman he has abused - a rule that is completely unacceptable from today's perspective, but was considered a protective measure for women in society at the time, as they were often considered *"dishonored"* after being raped and no longer had any chance of marriage.

If biblical statements on sexuality were universally valid, all these rules would still have to be followed without restriction today. In fact, however, Christian ethics have evolved over the course of history. The church has recognized that certain commandments were time-bound and cannot serve as absolute standards for today's behaviour. Many moral norms that were once considered *"divine law"* have been revised or reinterpreted over the centuries, for example in relation to slavery, women's rights or divorce.

A more modern Christian ethic could therefore be based less on individual Bible verses and more on the fundamental principles of Jesus' teachings: love, justice, mercy and responsibility. Instead of viewing biblical statements literally as universal commandments, we should ask what ethical ideal lies behind them and how this can be meaningfully applied in our world today.

Ultimately, it is clear that biblical statements on sexuality are historically conditioned and cannot be regarded as immutable norms. They must be interpreted in the light of new knowledge, social developments and a deeper understanding of the original intention. A contemporary sexual ethic should not cling to traditional rules, but should be guided by the central ethical values of Christianity - love, respect and the well-being of the people involved.

45 • *Are Paul's views on homosexuality only comprehensible in the cultural context of his time and outdated today?*

Paul's views on homosexuality are strongly influenced by the cultural and social context of the ancient Mediterranean. In his letters, particularly in Romans 1:26-27, 1 Corinthians 6:9 and 1 Timothy 1:10, he is critical of same-sex acts. However, it must be borne in mind that Paul was not talking about homosexuality in the sense in which it is understood today - as a sexual orientation based on love, equality and mutual consent - but was referring to certain forms of same-sex behavior in his time.

In the Roman Empire in which Paul lived, there were numerous social and cultural structures that differed significantly from today's ideas. Same-sex relationships were often associated with power imbalances, for example in the form of male prostitution and the sexual exploitation of slaves. In this context, Paul's statements against same-sex sex should primarily be understood as a rejection of immoral and exploitative practices, not as a fundamental condemnation of equal homosexual relationships.

Modern theological approaches argue that ethics are constantly evolving and that biblical statements must be interpreted in their respective historical and cultural context. Just as the church today considers many moral concepts of antiquity - such as the role of women, slavery or the death penalty - to be outdated, the question arises as to whether the biblical statements on homosexuality should also be understood as time-bound.

Many Christian theologians and churches have now reconsidered their stance on this issue and are of the opinion that same-sex love is absolutely compatible with the core values of Christianity - love, faithfulness, responsibility and mutual respect. However, critics of this progressive stance argue that the Bible, as a divinely inspired word, should not simply be adapted to the spirit of the times.

It can therefore be said that Paul's statements on homosexuality can only be understood in the cultural context of his time and cannot be easily transferred to same-sex relationships today. The central question is therefore not whether Paul would have condemned homosexuality if he had lived in the present day, but whether Christian ethics should be guided by immutable rules or by the basic principles of charity and justice. Many churches and theologians are of the opinion that a modern, inclusive sexual morality is in line with the Christian faith and that Paul's views in this area must therefore be regarded as outdated.

46 • How can a feminist interpretation of the Bible correct patriarchal distortions, and what approaches does it take?

Elisabeth Schüssler Fiorenza calls for a feminist interpretation of the Bible because she assumes that traditional Christian theology and biblical interpretation are strongly influenced by patriarchal structures. She argues that many texts in the Bible were originally more gender-equitable, but that their interpretation and canonization was determined by male authorities who marginalized or reinterpreted the role of women. Her aim is therefore to make these patriarchal distortions visible and to re-read biblical texts from a feminist perspective.

A central concept of her work is the *"hermeneutics of suspicion"*. This method assumes that biblical texts are not neutral, but often emerged from a male-dominated society and reflect how women were portrayed or silenced. Instead of accepting biblical texts unquestioningly as divine truth, it advocates critically questioning which voices are missing or have been suppressed.

Schüssler Fiorenza uses various examples to show how women were active in early Christianity - such as Mary Magdalene as the first witness to the resurrection or Junia, who is mentioned as an apostle in the letter to the Romans - but were relegated to passive or subordinate roles in later church interpretations. She argues that a feminist exegesis must once again make women visible as active subjects in the Bible and not only emphasize what was said about them, but also what they themselves contributed.

In addition to historical reconstruction, she advocates a contextual interpretation of the Bible that focuses on the experiences and perspectives of women. This is not just about academic theology, but also about a practice of liberation: the Bible should not be used to justify oppression, but rather to empower women to find themselves in the history of salvation. Her feminist theology is therefore not only a theological correction, but also a political and social demand for gender justice in the church and society.

In certain cases, it is also necessary to revise the language and content of biblical texts: Many texts have historically been handed down and interpreted in such a way that they support male power structures, even if this was not necessarily the original intention. Texts that systematically make women invisible, marginalize their role or theologically legitimize male dominance are particularly affected.

Five initial examples of necessary new versions of biblical texts:

Genesis 1:27 - Creation of man

Current translation: "God created man in his own image, male and female he created them."

Reformulation: "God created man in his own image, in diversity he created them, equal in dignity."

➤ This change avoids the binary gender order and emphasizes the equality of all people regardless of gender.

1 Corinthians 14:34-35 - Silence of the women in the church

Current translation: "Women should keep silent in the churches, for they are not permitted to speak, but should be submissive."

New wording: "Women and men should speak equally in the congregations and teach in wisdom and knowledge."

➤ This passage has often been used to exclude women from the ministry. The new version corrects this abuse and establishes an egalitarian church order.

Figure 10 : A woman looks through a magnifying glass into the Bible - and reveals hidden female figures. Broken patriarchal symbols lie around her, while in the background a new window reveals equality.

Ephesians 5:22-24 - Subordination of women in marriage

Current translation: "Wives, submit yourselves to your husbands as to the Lord. For the husband is the head of the wife, just as Christ is the head of the church."

New wording: "Partners, treat each other with mutual respect and love, just as Christ loves his church and gives himself for it."

➤ Instead of one-sided subordination, an equal relationship based on mutual respect is emphasized.

Luke 10:38-42 - Mary and Martha

Current translation: "But Martha was completely absorbed in providing for the physical well-being. Then she came and said, 'Lord, don't you care that my sister leaves the work to me alone? Why don't you tell her to help me? But the Lord replied: "Martha, Martha, you are very worried and troubled. Mary has chosen the better part, and it will not be taken away from her."

Rephrasing: "Martha and Mary served in different ways, and both ways are valuable in the eyes of God."

➤ This passage has often been interpreted as reducing women to spiritual passivity and devaluing domestic activities. A new version could emphasize the equal importance of different services.

Romans 16:7 - Apostle Junia

Actual translation (often distorted): "Greet Andronicus and Junias, my relatives and fellow prisoners; they are respected apostles and were in Christ before me."

Rephrased: "Greet Andronicus and Junia, my relatives and fellow prisoners; they are respected apostles and have been in Christ before me."

➤ In many translations, "Junia" was changed to "Junias" (a masculine form) in order to make a female apostle invisible. The correction restores her role in the early church.

These examples show that patriarchal distortions can not only be corrected through interpretation, but that in some cases a rewriting of the text is needed to restore the original meaning or to re-emphasize the equality, which was partly present in early Christianity. A theology to be further elaborated could not only re-read such texts, but also reformulate them in such a way that they no longer serve to justify inequality or oppression.

47 • How do Christians deal with contradictions between the Bible and modern values?

Christians deal with contradictions between biblical texts and modern values in different ways, depending on their theological tradition, hermeneutical approach and personal convictions. While some insist on a literal interpretation of the Bible, others see Scripture as a historical document that needs to be interpreted and translated into today's context.

A central approach is the *historical-critical method*, which looks at biblical texts in the context of the time in which they were written. Many theologians argue that certain social norms and ethical ideas in the Bible must be understood in the context of the respective time. For example, the biblical regulations on slavery, the role of women or sexuality are strongly influenced by the social structures of the time and should not be read as timeless divine commandments. In this understanding, Christian values must be recognized in their core message of love, justice and compassion and adapted to changing social conditions.

Other Christians follow a progressive theological approach that understands the Bible as an unfolding testimony of God's work. They see faith as a living tradition that continues to develop. This can be seen in the re-evaluation of issues such as gender equality, acceptance of LGBTQIA+ people or social justice. While previous generations invoked certain biblical passages to prohibit women in religious leadership roles, for example, many churches today advocate for their full equality. A similar shift can be observed in attitudes towards homosexuality, which is still considered a sin in conservative circles, while progressive Christians emphasize that the biblical statements on the subject were made in a different cultural context and cannot be applied to today's society.

Another approach is the ethical weighting of biblical statements. Not all commandments in the Bible have the same moral significance, and many Christians are guided by the priorities set by Jesus himself, who placed ethical principles such as love, mercy and justice above rigid adherence to the law. This attitude is often referred to as *"Jesus-*

centered hermeneutics" and means that ethical questions are not decided on the basis of individual Bible verses, but in light of the entire Christian message.

At the same time, there are also conservative and fundamentalist currents that see modern values as a threat to the divine order and interpret the Bible literally. They reject adaptations to social developments and argue that Scripture represents the unchanging truth of God. This reveals a tension between religious traditionalism and social change that is reflected in many churches, particularly in debates about gender roles, sexual morality and political issues.

Overall, it is clear that Christians deal with contradictions between the Bible and modern values in very different ways. While some rely on a contemporary interpretation and understand Christian ethics as dynamic, others adhere to a literal interpretation. How these tensions are dealt with therefore depends on the extent to which the Bible is understood as a historically conditioned document or as the directly binding word of God. The challenge for many churches today is to communicate faith credibly without ignoring either tradition or social reality.

The question of whether the progressive or the traditional Christian is the "better" Christian cannot be answered objectively, as there is no single definition in Christianity that determines what "better" means. Christianity is a diverse religion with different theological traditions, interpretations and emphases. Rather, the answer depends on how one defines "Christian life" - whether in terms of faithfulness to the Bible, social commitment, charity or spiritual devotion.

Traditional Christians are often strongly oriented towards the traditional doctrines of faith, a literal interpretation of the Bible and the preservation of church traditions. They see their practice of faith as an expression of faithfulness to God's unchanging word and emphasize obedience to divine commandments. For them, faith is less something that should be oriented towards social developments, but rather a constant that conveys timeless truths. However, criticism of this attitude is that it often leaves little room for social change, new theological insights and a dynamic further development of faith.

Progressive Christians, on the other hand, emphasize the further development of faith and the adaptation of Christian ethics to new social insights. They place importance on understanding the Bible in the context of their time and orienting themselves towards the core principles of Jesus - love, justice and compassion - rather than adhering to individual Bible verses. They often advocate for human rights, social justice and inclusion and see faith as a process that must evolve with new insights. However, critics of this stance fear that adapting too much to modern values could dilute the original message of Christianity.

Ultimately, it is not the theological position that makes a "better Christian", but the lived practice of faith. Jesus himself did not make a dogmatic distinction between "progressive" and "conservative", but always asked about the *attitude of the heart*. People who practice charity, mercy and truthfulness - regardless of whether they represent a traditional or progressive theology - live out Christian values authentically. In practice, there are those among both traditional and progressive Christians who live compassion, helpfulness and justice, and those who interpret their faith in a dogmatic and exclusionary way. The decisive factor is therefore less the affiliation to a particular theological school of thought and more the way in which someone lives out their faith in the world.

If one consistently thinks through the differences between progressive and traditional Christians, focusing on core Christian values such as love, mercy and justice, one could argue that both perspectives should lead to a more progressive understanding of the faith in the long run.

1. the common core - love as the highest commandment: Christianity is based on the double commandment of love: *"You shall love the Lord your God with all your heart, with all your soul and with all your mind".* (Mt 22:37), *"You shall love your neighbor as yourself."* (Mt 22:39). Whether traditional or progressive, no Christian can escape this commandment. Anyone who takes love of neighbour radically seriously must inevitably be open to an ethos that overcomes exclusion, oppression or injustice - a concern that is often associated with a progressive approach.

2 The logic of theology - when tradition leads to further development: Many of today's "traditional" beliefs were once an innovation themselves. Christianity itself began as a radical break with Jewish purity and sacrificial commandments. The abolition of slavery was demanded in the name of Christian values, despite biblical tolerance. Women's ordination was introduced in many churches as a consistent implementation of equality in Christ. This means that even traditional Christians, if they consistently follow their faith, often have to be open to change, because theology can never be static.

3. traditional ethics and its problem with social change: Many traditional positions are based on cultural contexts that change over time. In the past, women were relegated to subordinate roles because societies were patriarchal. Same-sex love was rejected because societies were heteronormative. Democratic values, freedom of expression and social justice were only gradually recognized as Christian concerns. A Christian who really takes the basic values of Jesus seriously will have to ask themselves whether their own positions correspond to love, justice and mercy - or whether they are merely preserving old norms. Here, the Christian ethos always leads to questioning and adapting previous traditions.

4. practice of faith - those who truly love become progressive: If you *"know faith by its fruits"* (Mt 7:16), then in practice it often becomes apparent that progressive changes include more people and give them dignity, while strict tradition often leads to exclusion and harshness. Those who do not exclude people from the church on the basis of gender or sexuality are acting in the spirit of Jesus. Those who help the poor and disadvantaged instead of defending a theological system are following his example. Those who take responsibility on issues such as climate protection, social justice or human rights recognize that Christianity is always a call to change the world.

Traditional faith must therefore inevitably evolve: If a Christian honestly reflects on his faith, traces it back to the values of Jesus and asks himself what really serves the good of mankind, he will often come to similar insights as progressive Christians. This does not mean that everything traditional is wrong, but that genuine faith must always evolve in order to remain true to its core. A Christian cannot be permanently "preserving" if the practice of love urges them to stand up for justice, inclusion and humanity. In this respect, one could argue that true Christianity - regardless of the starting point - must ultimately become progressive.

And, if you think through the logic of basic Christian values consistently, then the traditional Christian person would have to move more than the progressive Christian person, because tradition by definition seeks to preserve, whereas the Christian ethos calls for change, healing and further development. This does not necessarily mean that everything about traditional views is wrong, but it does suggest that a static, unchanging attitude is not compatible with the living character of faith. Because:

Christian faith is dynamic, not static: Jesus himself opposed religious dogma when it hindered love, mercy and justice. He broke purity laws and spoke to outcasts. He healed on the Sabbath, even though it was against the rules. He placed the law of love above literal adherence to the law. This shows that change is not against faith, but a sign of living faith. Anyone who clings to rigid norms just because they *have "always been that way"* is behaving in a pharisaical rather than a Christian way.

Why the traditional Christian needs to move more: Traditional Christians often follow a theology based on preserving fidelity to the past. But the more the world changes, the stronger the tension between the preservation of norms and the call to love one's neighbor becomes. Traditional positions on the role of women, LGBTQIA+, slavery or social justice have been revised again and again over the centuries. Each time the church has evolved, traditional Christians have had to adapt - not because the faith has changed, but because the ethical implications of the faith have become clearer. Progressive Christians have often already integrated insights about social justice, inclusion and ethics that arise from the practice of charity. Traditional Christians, on the other hand, often have to question their own previous beliefs before they can open up to these insights.

Why tradition is not always wrong, but often incomplete: Tradition can provide valuable support, but blind tradition can lead to the denial of truth. The church defended slavery for centuries - today it is considered unimaginable. Women were oppressed in the church -

today they are consecrated in many churches. LGBTQIA+ were considered "subordinate" - today many churches recognize the dignity and love of these people and welcome them. These examples show that the truth of faith does not remain frozen in the past, but is unfolding.

So is the traditional Christian "wrong"? Theologically speaking, it is not the tradition itself that is wrong, but the static attitude that blocks change. If you are a Christian, you should be prepared to move - not because modern values "dictate" it, but because genuine love for your neighbor requires change.

If faith leads to people being excluded, faith must evolve. When new ethical insights emerge, they must be integrated. If the gospel is a message of liberation, it must not be used to oppress. This means that the traditional Christian either opens up to a dynamic, living theology or runs the risk of clinging to an outdated and exclusionary interpretation. And if you think this idea through consistently, then the progressive stance is not just an option, but actually the only consistently Christian stance that can exist.

48 • How can the biblical creation story be interpreted as a narrative about the human realization of one's own finiteness, and to what extent can a conception of religion as a personal confrontation with transience be formed from this?

Klaus Dede interprets the biblical story of creation as a narrative that does not primarily describe the creation of the world, but rather man's conscious break with his pre-human existence and his realization of his own finiteness. In his analysis, Dede emphasizes that the decisive moment of the creation story is not the creation of man as such, but the realization that death is not just a single event, but the inevitable end of one's own existence.

Dede illustrates this idea using the Fall of Man: While traditional Christian theologies view this narrative as the origin of original sin and the human lack of perfection, he interprets it as a metaphor for becoming aware of one's own transience. Man becomes human the moment he realizes that he will die. This existential insight distinguishes them from animals, who - as he puts it - do not know that they have to die.

On this basis, Dede develops his view of religion as a personal confrontation with the finite nature of life. He argues that religion is a means of dealing with this profound realization, overcoming the fear of death and finding meaning in a world characterized by transience. He emphasizes that religion cannot claim an objective truth per se, but manifests itself in a variety of individual forms - each person has their own religion, so to speak, because everyone struggles with finitude in their own way.

Dede criticizes dogmatic religions that try to suppress this existential challenge with fixed rules or promises of salvation. He sees this as an escape from the actual confrontation with finiteness. Instead, he pleads for a religion that does not deny death, but recognizes it as a central element of being human and enables individual reflection on it. His interpretation of the story of creation thus serves as the basis for a non-dogmatic, existentialist conception of religion that does not view humans as sinners, but as beings who must consciously come to terms with their finiteness.

---

b) Religious ideas and their psychological basis

---

49 • Why do religious beliefs persist despite the lack of a basis in reality, and what parallels exist between religious rituals and neurotic compulsive behavior?

Freud explains the persistence of religious beliefs by the fact that they are deeply rooted in the psychological structures of human beings. Religion is not based on rational cognition, but on emotional needs, in particular the desire for security, order and a higher sense of meaning. Even if there is no empirical evidence for religious dogmas, they offer psychological stability by alleviating fears and providing a semblance of control over the unknown.

To illustrate the function of religion in the psychological household, Freud draws a parallel between religious rituals and neurotic compulsions. Both serve to regulate inner insecurities and cope with anxiety. Just as an obsessive-compulsive neurotic repeats certain rituals to relieve inner tensions, religious believers follow fixed rituals to protect themselves from harm or to gain divine favor. The repetition of prayers, acts of penance or symbolic cleansing rituals is similar in function to compulsive behavior patterns that have no real necessity but provide psychological relief.

Freud therefore sees religion as a collective obsessive-compulsive neurosis of humanity - a psychological construct that provides support in the short term, but limits the ability to engage realistically with the world in the long term. According to Freud, overcoming this illusion would be a step towards psychological maturity, in which people take responsibility for their own lives instead of taking refuge in supernatural explanations.

A realistic approach to the world requires critical thinking, independence and emotional resilience. In (religious) education, this means supporting children and young people in such a way that they do not have to resort to simplified or illusory explanations, but instead learn to understand reality in all its complexity and deal with challenges independently.

1. encouraging critical thinking and reflection: Instead of imposing ready-made truths, children should be encouraged to ask questions, question information and draw their own conclusions . This can be encouraged through open discussions, debates and the conscious use of media.

→ *Example:* Instead of just teaching textbook knowledge, a teacher can present different perspectives on a topic and encourage students to weigh up arguments and develop their own points of view.

2. learning to deal with uncertainty and ambiguity: Life is often not black and white, but full of shades of gray and uncertainty. Children should learn to deal with uncertainty instead of clinging to dogmatic or absolute answers.

→ *Example:* Instead of providing simple explanations (*"That's just the way it is"*), adults should think together with children about what factors could influence a situation and why different people have different opinions.

3. teach scientific methods and fact-based thinking: Children should understand early on how knowledge is created - through observation, experimentation and verification. Scientific thinking helps to distinguish between opinions and verifiable facts.

→ *Example:* Experiments in science or the playful testing of claims *("Is that really true?")* promote a rational approach to the world.

4. **strengthen emotional resilience and frustration tolerance:** A realistic view of the world also means being able to deal with setbacks. Children should learn that mistakes are normal, that challenges can be overcome and that difficult situations are not improved through wishful thinking but through active action.

→ *Example:* Instead of always presenting a child with solutions immediately, you can encourage them to find solutions themselves and persevere, even if they fail at first.

5. promote independence and responsibility: Those who learn to think for themselves and take responsibility for their actions, are less susceptible to illusions and simplistic explanations of the world. Children should learn early on that they have an influence on their environment and that their actions have consequences.

→ *Example:* Giving children responsibility for small decisions - whether at home, at school or in their social environment - strengthens their awareness of the reality of their actions.

6. develop values and ethics on the basis of reason: Instead of dogmatically prescribing moral rules, children should learn to make ethical decisions in a reflective manner. Instead of "This is forbidden", they should ask: *"What impact does my behavior have on others?"*

→ *Example:* Ethical dilemma discussions (e.g. "Is it always wrong to lie?") help not only to adopt values, but also to understand and justify them.

A religious and family education that focuses on critical thinking, personal responsibility and realistic problem-solving makes children less dependent on illusionary world views and helps them to move confidently in a complex reality. They learn how to deal with uncertainty, form an opinion based on facts and actively shape their lives - without taking refuge in wishful thinking or ideologies.

50 • What central statements does the Christian creed contain and what significance do they have for the life of a Christian?

The Christian creed contains central statements about faith in God, Jesus Christ and the Holy Spirit, as well as about the community of believers, the forgiveness of sins and eternal life. These core statements also have a special significance for the lives of queer Christians, as they formulate fundamental principles of Christian identity and belonging.

The first central statement is belief in God as Creator (*"I believe in God, the Father, the Almighty, the Creator of heaven and earth"*). For queer Christians, this means that they are accepted as part of the divine creation and can view their identity not as a deviation, but as an intentional part of the diversity of life.

The second essential statement is faith in Jesus Christ (*"I believe in Jesus Christ, his only begotten Son, our Lord ..."*). Christ embodies love, redemption and care for the marginalized. His message of acceptance and charity can give queer Christians strength, especially if they experience inclusion in church or social contexts. The resurrection of Jesus stands for a rejection of the oppression of those who think differently, which can encourage queer believers to stand up for their rights and recognition despite resistance.

The third central statement concerns the Holy Spirit and the church (*"I believe in the Holy Spirit, the holy Christian church, the communion of saints ..."*). This means that the church should be a place for everyone, regardless of gender or sexual orientation. For queer Christians, this often poses the challenge of whether and how they can feel at home in a church that in some traditions still has reservations about LGBTQIA+ people. At the same time, faith in the Holy Spirit encourages us to stand up for a church that is open, inclusive and just.

The statements about the forgiveness of sins and eternal life (*"I believe in the forgiveness of sins, the resurrection of the dead and eternal life"*) can remind queer Christians that God's grace is not conditional and that no person is excluded because of their identity. This is particularly important for people who struggle with feelings of guilt or inner conflict in their life of faith because certain church teachings have suggested to them that they are not yet pleasing to God.

The Christian creed therefore offers queer Christians a foundation of trust in God's love and a theological basis for seeing themselves as full members of the faith community. It can be understood both as spiritual support and as a call to help shape a church that treats all believers with respect and dignity.

51 • What role do same-sex partnerships play in religious education and confirmation training?

Same-sex partnerships are playing a growing role in religious education and confirmation training, particularly in the context of ethical issues, social changes and theological reflections on love, partnership and family. While traditional church teachings have long defined marriage exclusively as a union between a man and a woman, many Christian communities are now striving to convey a more inclusive understanding of partnership.

In religious education, same-sex cohabitation can be discussed from both a biblical-theological and a socio-ethical perspective. The focus here is on questions of biblical interpretation, church tradition and Christian ethics. Confirmation training is often about sensitizing young people to a reflective and independent Christianity. Dealing with diversity in relationships offers the opportunity to deepen Christian values such as charity, justice and respect for different ways of life. Depending on the denomination and theological orientation, attitudes towards same-sex partnerships vary, which can lead to a variety of discussions. Some churches have already introduced blessings or marriage ceremonies for same-sex couples, while others adhere to traditional ideas. It is crucial that religious education and confirmation training contribute to enabling young people to deal with different lifestyles in a differentiated, informed and appreciative way.

Figure11 : A classroom in which a teacher works with a loving symbol of same-sex partnership - visible and natural in religious education.

c) Epistemological questions about knowledge and reality

52 • Can you be sure of reality outside your own mind?

According to Descartes, it is fundamentally uncertain whether reality exists outside of one's own mind, as all sensory perceptions could be deceptive. In his *Meditationes de prima philosophia*, he radically questions the entire external world by arguing that everything we perceive could be the product of a deceptive demon or a faulty imagination. For him, the only starting point for absolute certainty is the *cogito, ergo sum* - the realization that the thinking ego exists because it doubts. Only by assuming a benevolent God, who would not allow any systematic deception, does Descartes arrive at the certainty of the existence of an external world. Nevertheless, this conviction ultimately remains secured by evidence of God, not by direct sensory experience.

In theology, the question of reality outside of one's own thinking is closely linked to the relationship between faith and knowledge. In the Christian tradition, it is often argued that reality consists not only of the physical world, but also of a spiritual, divine order that eludes direct empirical experience. St. Augustine, for example, maintains that true knowledge is not possible through sensory experience or reason alone, but that divine enlightenment is necessary in order to understand reality in its depth. The Catholic Church combines this idea with the idea of divine revelation, which makes a reality accessible to man that goes beyond the purely sensual.

At the same time, church history shows that the question of reality has often led to tensions between theology and philosophy. While Descartes used methodical skepticism to arrive at certain knowledge, the church long defended itself against skeptical currents if they were seen as a threat to faith. Nevertheless, Descartes' thinking was also positively received in the Catholic tradition, for example in scholasticism, which discussed his proofs of God, or in modern theology, which deals with the compatibility of faith and reason.

In queer theology, the question of reality is particularly controversial, as social and identity-related realities are also questioned here. Queer theology emphasizes that the reality that is considered objective is often shaped by normative, binary structures that exclude or marginalize certain identities. In this sense, one could argue with Descartes that what is considered *"reality"* is often based on unreflected assumptions that need to be questioned. Queer theologians could use Descartes' skepticism towards the external world to show that truths about gender, sexuality or identity are not simply *"given"*, but that they are *constructed* in a social and theological discourse.

Whether God is also constructed or real therefore depends on the respective perspective - philosophical, theological or scientific. This question cannot be answered objectively, but depends on the respective epistemological and ideological basis.

1. philosophical perspective (subjectivism vs. realism)

From Descartes' point of view in his *Meditationes de prima philosophia*, God is a necessary reality in order to establish a reliable theory of knowledge. Descartes argues that only a perfect, non-deceptive being can guarantee the certainty that an external world exists. His proof of God is based on the idea of *"perfect substance"*, whose existence he considers necessary. However, other philosophers, such as Kant, deny that God's existence can be proven rationally; for him, God is a regulative idea that provides moral guidance, but does not necessarily exist as a metaphysical reality

From an epistemological perspective, every concept of God is therefore inevitably mediated by the human mind and cultural conditioning. Kant, for example, argues that we cannot recognize God as a thing in itself, but only as a regulative idea that structures our thinking. In a subjectivist approach, God would therefore not be an objective reality per se, but a necessary projection of human needs, for example in the sense of Feuerbach (*The Essence of Christianity*), who claims that man created God in his own image.

Ludwig Feuerbach's *The Essence of Christianity* (1841) is a critique of religion in which he argues that God is not an objective reality, but a projection of human desires and needs. He argues that man creates God in his own image by transferring his own idealized qualities - such as love, wisdom or omnipotence - to a supernatural being. Religion is therefore not the realization of a divine truth, but a psychological and social construction through which man alienates himself. Feuerbach therefore called for a *"reversal of theology into anthropology"*: instead of focusing on the hereafter, man should place his own abilities and values at the center and free himself from the illusion of a supernatural being. His work later influenced Karl Marx, who described religion as *the "opium of the people"*.

It can be argued against a purely subjectivist view that a reality can exist independently of human perception, even if it is only expressed in human terms. Thus, God could be real, but our understanding of him would always be a limited interpretation of this reality.

2. theological perspective (of the Catholic Church)

From a Christian theological perspective, God is seen as an absolute reality that not only exists, but is the source of all existence. The Catholic Church teaches that God is not just a mental construction or concept, but a transcendent and at the same time immanently tangible reality. Classical theology argues *with the ontological proof of God* (Anselm of Canterbury), the *cosmological proof of God* (Thomas Aquinas) or the *personal experience of faith*. In the Christian faith, God is not just an idea, but a living reality that manifests itself in revelation, scripture and the experience of faith. In Catholic theology, God is therefore understood as an objective reality, independent of human perception or interpretation. God exists in himself (*ens a se*) and is not dependent on human interpretation. Nevertheless, it is recognized that man can never fully comprehend God. Theology therefore distinguishes between *theologia revelata* (revealed theology) and *theologia naturalis* (natural theology). While revelation - e.g. in the Bible or in the church - is regarded as objective truth, human interpretation of this revelation remains prone to error and limited. Augustine, for example, argues that man is dependent on divine grace in order to attain a true knowledge of God.

3. scientific perspective

From an empirical scientific point of view, there is no clear evidence for or against the existence of God. Scientific theories are based on verifiable observations, and since God is thought to be a supernatural being outside the measurable universe, his existence cannot be scientifically proven or disproven. In this sense, God remains a matter of faith.

4. queer theology and postmodern perspectives as well as questioning perspectives on the real God

In queer theology and postmodern theories, the question of God's reality and the idea of a "fixed" image of God is critically questioned or often posed differently: Is God an unchanging, objective reality, or is God's image and understanding of God shaped by society, culture and individual experiences? Queer theologians emphasize that images of God have grown historically and question patriarchal and heteronormative concepts of God. In this view, God is less a rigid metaphysical reality and more a living force that can be experienced in social processes, justice and love. Whether God is a reality depends on the definition of *"reality"*. For believers, God is an absolute reality, for skeptics a question of faith, for scientists an unprovable hypothesis, and for queer theologians a fluid, deconstructable idea. The question itself therefore cannot be answered conclusively, but is open to personal reflection and interpretation.

Instead of an unchanging, normative image of God, it emphasizes that every experience of God is shaped by culture, gender, sexuality and social power relations. This view does not exclude the possibility that God is real, but emphasizes that our conception of God is always shaped by our perspectives. In this sense, one could say that God is not merely a subjective construction, but that our approach to God always remains context-dependent and interpretative.

So whether God is a subjective construction depends on the distinction between God as an intrinsically existing reality and our human approach to him. The human interpretation of his nature and essence inevitably remains subjective. Even if God exists objectively, no religion or philosophy can claim absolute access to this reality, as every image of God is shaped by culture, language and experience.

Therefore, theology cannot "prove" God in a strictly scientific or mathematical sense, but argues on the basis of philosophical, metaphysical and revealed premises. Whether the assumptions on which theological proofs of God are based are right or wrong depends on the respective epistemological perspective. There are different proofs of God, but all are based on assumptions that do not necessarily have to be universally accepted.

Theologians and philosophers have developed various arguments for the existence of God, including:

Ontological proof of God (Anselm of Canterbury, Descartes)

→ God as the highest conceivable being must exist, since existence is a perfection.

Criticism: Assumes that concepts can determine reality. Kant criticizes that existence is not a predicate.

Cosmological proof of God (Aristotle, Thomas Aquinas)

→ Everything that exists must have a cause. This causal chain must end in an unmoved mover or a first cause (God).

Criticism: Why must there be a first cause? Couldn't the universe exist forever?

Teleological proof of God (design argument, intelligent design)

→ The order and purposefulness of the world points to a Creator.

Criticism: Evolution and natural processes can explain this order without requiring a supernatural cause.

Theology is often based on revelation (e.g. the Bible in Christianity). Belief in God is not secured by rational evidence, but by the assumption that divine revelation is true.

The problem is that revelation cannot be proven independently of one's own religious tradition, as each religion claims a different authority.

From a strictly empirical point of view, a hypothesis that cannot be proven is not scientifically tenable. However, this does not necessarily mean that it is "wrong", but only that it cannot be tested. Many fundamental assumptions in ethics, metaphysics or mathematics are also not empirically provable, but still make sense.

The discussion as to whether theological assumptions are therefore irrelevant depends on the perspective. In a strictly scientific view of the world, unverifiable assumptions are methodologically useless because they have no empirical basis. However, in philosophy, ethics or metaphysics, there are many assumptions - such as the validity of moral values or the nature of consciousness - that cannot be proven empirically, but nevertheless have a profound impact on human thought and action. In this sense, theological considerations are not necessarily irrelevant, but play a role in the way people understand meaning, morality and transcendence.

Ultimately, the existence of God is a matter of faith, not of proof. Theology can formulate arguments for or against God's existence, but it cannot prove him in the scientific sense - and for skeptics, its assumptions therefore remain unprovable and thus without compelling relevance: Those who accept these assumptions can therefore regard God's existence as rationally justifiable - those who reject them will see no evidence in them.

Therefore, the question of whether one can be certain of reality outside of one's own thinking remains an open and controversial one. While Descartes builds a bridge between thought and the external world through the existence of God, theology emphasizes the necessity of faith in order to grasp the full reality - including the divine. In queer theology, this question is used to question existing norms and develop new, more inclusive perspectives on reality.

53 • *How do experiences influence our knowledge of the world?*

According to John Locke, our knowledge of the world is formed exclusively through experience. In *An Essay Concerning Human Understanding* (1690), he developed the theory of empiricism, which states that the human mind is a *tabula rasa* - a blank slate - at birth, on which knowledge is only written through sensory experience and reflection. Locke distinguishes between *sensation* (external perceptions, such as seeing or hearing) and *reflection* (internal perceptions of our thoughts, such as remembering or willing). Our knowledge is therefore not innate, but arises from the processing of these experiences.

This view is in tension with traditional theology, particularly the Catholic Church, which long held the idea that certain truths - such as knowledge of God or moral principles - were innate to humans through divine creation. However, Augustine and later the scholastics, especially Thomas Aquinas, emphasized that experience plays an important role in knowledge, albeit in conjunction with divine revelation. Aquinas took a mediating position: While sensory perceptions form the basis of our thinking, the highest truth - i.e. God - is not recognizable through experience alone, but through the combination of reason and faith.

Over the centuries, the Catholic Church has grappled with Locke's empiricist view, particularly in its debate with the Enlightenment. While the Church relied on metaphysical concepts for a long time, it later recognized the importance of empirical sciences, for example through modern natural philosophy and the theories of the theology of the Second Vatican Council, which place greater emphasis on experience as an approach to God.

Learning plays a central but differently understood role in both epistemology and theology. In epistemology, it is the process by which knowledge is created, while in theology it is often understood as a means of approaching divine truth.

1. learning in epistemology: In epistemology, the understanding of learning strongly depends on which position one holds:

Empiricism (e.g. Locke, Hume): Knowledge arises through experience, and learning means the gradual accumulation of sensory data and its processing. John Locke, for example, describes the mind as a tabula rasa that is only filled with content through learning.

Rationalism (e.g. Descartes, Kant): Learning through experience alone is not enough; there are innate structures of the mind that make experience meaningful in the first place. Kant distinguishes between a priori knowledge (independent of experience, e.. mathematics) and a posteriori knowledge (acquired through experience).

Social constructivism (e.g. Vygotsky, Foucault): Knowledge is not acquired individually, but through social interaction and cultural imprinting. Learning is also a process of power and standardization.

2. learning in theology: In theology, learning is often understood not only as the acquisition of knowledge, but also as spiritual insight:

Catholic theology: Learning serves not only secular education, but above all the knowledge of God. The Church emphasizes the combination of faith and reason (fides et ratio, cf. Thomas Aquinas). Theological learning takes place through the study of scripture, tradition and personal reflection.

Mystical tradition (e.g. Augustine, Meister Eckhart): True learning is an inner process of cognition that goes beyond mere intellectual knowledge. Divine truth is not only attained through books, but also through contemplation and the experience of faith.

Reformation (Luther, Calvin): The Bible as a direct source of divine truth was to be accessible to all. Education and individual Bible study were emphasized in order to enable every believer to gain a direct knowledge of God.

3. learning and queer theology:

Learning plays a special role in queer theology, as it critically questions traditional theological concepts. Learning here means not only leaving old dogmas behind, but also having the courage to question supposedly incontrovertible truths about gender, sexuality and identity. Experience and personal stories are seen much more as legitimate sources of knowledge, which is in contrast to classic theologies that usually derive knowledge from scripture or church authority.

While in epistemology learning is the key to knowledge about the world, in theology it is often associated with the search for divine truth. Depending on the theological orientation, learning can be an intellectual, spiritual or liberating process. Especially in modern theological currents, learning is not only understood as a process of experience, but also as a form of deconstruction that critically questions existing, learned beliefs and enables new perspectives for new realities.

In queer theology, the question of how experiences shape our knowledge of the world is therefore particularly central. Traditional theological approaches are often based on normative ideas about gender, sexuality and identity that are considered divinely predetermined. However, Locke's empirical approach could now be used as an argument for a queer perspective: If knowledge and identity arise from experience and learning, then they are not predetermined by rigid theological dogma. Queer theologians emphasize that personal experience - such as the experience of marginalization or finding one's identity - is a legitimate way of knowing (e.g. also about values and attitudes such as solidarity or a sense of justice) and that the church must rethink its concepts of gender and sexuality if it takes seriously that knowledge is not innate, but is formed through experience and learning processes.

Queer people often learn from their experiences that social norms are not universal or unchangeable and that identity and self-determination are dynamic processes. Their experiences can lead to insights that change not only their personal views, but also social, human rights and theological discourses. Two key examples are:

- **The realization that gender and sexuality are not natural, but socially determined**

Many queer people experience that the binary division into "male" and "female" or the heteronorm as a "natural" order does not reflect their reality. Through their own identity development, they realize that gender and sexuality can be fluid and that social expectations are cultural constructs rather than irrevocable laws of nature. This experience can not only change their self-image, but also influence philosophical and theological debates about human nature and the order of creation.

- **The realization that traditional religious teachings do not always correspond to lived reality**

Queer people who grow up in religious contexts often learn that official theology does not take their existence and identity into account, or only marginally. The experience of experiencing themselves as spiritual or religious despite theological exclusions can lead them to reinterpret theology. This gives rise to new perspectives, for example that God's love is not bound to heteronormativity or that biblical passages on sexuality must be contextualized historically. These insights contribute to the development of queer theology, which questions traditional dogmatic positions and creates new models of inclusion.

These examples show that experience not only enables personal learning, but also challenges and changes social and theological discourse.

Knowledge about a queer world and its community is also shaped by learning processes and experiences in it.

Ultimately, then, Locke's empiricist epistemology describes knowledge as dynamic and experience-based, which presents challenges and opportunities both in classical theology and in modern, more inclusive theologies. While the Catholic tradition has long adhered to predetermined truths, an empirical approach requires constant reflection and adaptation to new experiences, realities and insights. A personal acceptance of same-sex feelings , for example, may lead to a completely different view of things with increasing experience - more self-confident and at peace with oneself.

54 • *Is human knowledge ultimately just a sum of habits?*

According to David Hume, human knowledge is ultimately a sum of habits, as our understanding of the world is not based on certain rational cognition, but on experience and the repetition of patterns. In *A Treatise of Human Nature*, he argues that our belief in cause and effect is not based on logical necessity, but on the fact that we see certain events linked together again and again. For example, if the sun rises every day, we expect it to do so in the future - but this expectation is not a compelling truth, merely a habitual inference from previous observations. Our knowledge is therefore not absolute, but a practical orientation that results from recurring experiences.

This view poses a challenge for theology, especially for the Catholic Church, which has long assumed that there is certain knowledge about God, the world and moral principles. The church tradition relies on revelation, reason and tradition as sources of knowledge and assumes that there is an objective truth that exists independently of individual experience. Hume's skepticism could challenge this notion, as it suggests that even religious knowledge is ultimately based only on habit - such as the practice of faith or the constant repetition of theological teachings - and has no absolute certainty.

However, one could argue that Catholic theology is also implicitly based on habits: Rituals, traditions and liturgical life are based on people deepening beliefs through repeated practice. The Church itself sees the value of habit in spiritual life - such as regular prayer or the practice of the sacraments - but it links this to the assumption that these habits are based on a deeper truth.

In queer theology, Hume's approach could be particularly relevant as it challenges the idea that moral or gender norms are based on an immutable truth. If knowledge and beliefs arise primarily from habits, then social ideas of gender, sexuality and identity are not fixed truths either, but the results of cultural repetition. This would strengthen queer theologians in their criticism of normative structures: If heteronormativity is just a socially practiced practice that appears "natural" because it is constantly repeated, then it can also be changed.

This shows that Hume's concept of knowledge as habit entails a pronounced skepticism towards supposed certainties. While Catholic theology continues to adhere to objective truths, his approach opens up the possibility of emphasizing alternative ways of knowing. Everyone may ask themselves how they arrived at their life experience and knowledge.

And: people today also gain knowledge, and in a certain sense even life experience, through artificial intelligence, although this second aspect must be viewed in a differentiated way. AI not only changes access to information, but also the way in which we learn, orient ourselves, express ourselves and understand ourselves.

AI makes knowledge accessible in new ways: intelligence systems, search algorithms and recommendation technologies offer direct, dialog-based access to huge amounts of data. They structure complex topics, prepare content in understandable language and respond to individual questions and contexts. This creates low-threshold access to education, which is of particular benefit to those who were previously disadvantaged by linguistic, social or institutional barriers. This makes learning more fragmented, more situational and less linear - but also more interactive, self-directed and often closer to the real world.

The topic of how humans also gain life experience through AI is more challenging. AI itself has no consciousness, no biography, no feelings - it knows neither pain nor love, neither failure nor hope. And yet it can make experiences accessible that it does not possess itself: through storytelling, the provision of experience reports from others, through a variety of perspectives, through the simulation of reflections and ethical questions. In this sense, AI opens up spaces in which people are confronted with previously unknown perspectives, put themselves in other people's shoes or ask new questions about their own lives. It makes it possible to mentally prepare, empathically comprehend or critically process experiences - all of which can contribute to one's own life experience.

In this sense, AI is no substitute for real experience or personal maturity. But it can provide impulses, trigger thought processes and help people to deal more consciously with themselves and their environment. In a knowledge- and experience-based society, AI is thus becoming a new player in the educational and experiential space - a teaching persona in the sense of imparting knowledge and a dialogical companion in the process of cognition.

d) Theological and social developments

55 • Can free access to knowledge change a society?

According to Diderot, free access to knowledge can fundamentally change a society because education and enlightenment enable people to question existing power structures and think for themselves. In his *Encyclopédie*, he pursues the goal of systematically collecting knowledge and making it accessible to a broad public, as he is convinced that ignorance is a central means of oppression. If knowledge no longer remains the privilege of a few, societies can develop further, social injustices can be overcome and political systems can be democratized. For Diderot, enlightenment is inextricably linked to emancipation: Those who have access to knowledge can free themselves from dependencies and act in a self-determined way.

In the Catholic Church, access to knowledge was heavily regulated for a long time. In the Middle Ages, reading the Bible was often restricted for laypeople and certain scientific findings were seen as a threat to the faith. Although the church also promoted education - for example through monastery schools and universities - books were censored and knowledge was controlled. It was not until the modern era that the church began to do more to promote general education, particularly through the expansion of schools and universities. Nevertheless, the question remains to what extent access to knowledge is really free when the church sets dogmatic boundaries.

Free access to knowledge is particularly important for queer theology because it enables alternative perspectives on gender, sexuality and identity to be developed. Many theological teachings on gender and sexuality are based on centuries-old interpretations that were not allowed to be questioned. It was only through scientific and social progress - for example in the fields of psychology, gender studies and biblical studies - that it became possible to critically analyze patriarchal and heteronormative interpretations. If queer people are given access to theological sources, alternative interpretations and scientific findings, they can argue against discrimination and develop new, more inclusive theological concepts.

This shows that knowledge is not just a resource, but a question of power: whoever shapes access to knowledge also shapes social narratives. Diderot's vision of a free, enlightened society presupposes that knowledge is open to all - a principle that is reflected in modern education policy, but also in theological and social liberation movements. And: queer theology makes it clear that free access to knowledge is not only a question of education, but also a question of justice.

Against this backdrop of enlightenment and emancipatory principles, access to AI should be free of charge for students and people under the age of 20. If we assume that knowledge is no longer conveyed exclusively through books or formal education, but increasingly also through digital systems such as AI, then low-threshold, equal opportunity access to these technologies is a basic prerequisite for social participation.

In the spirit of Diderot - for whom enlightenment always meant liberation from immaturity - it is clear that only those who have access to knowledge can free themselves from dependencies, think critically, get involved politically and live a self-determined life. If artificial intelligence is one of the central interfaces to knowledge, argumentation and understanding of the world today, then this access must not depend on your wallet.

Young people in particular are in a phase of orientation, identity formation and questioning - they need tools that open up new perspectives, encourage them and enable them to engage with their environment in an informed and reflective way. AI access that supports education, conveys diversity and encourages people to think is not a luxury, but should be part of the basic educational infrastructure - like libraries, school books or internet access.

Furthermore, free access could help to overcome, rather than reinforce, existing social differences. After all, those who learn to use new technologies sensibly and questioningly at an early age will have a better chance of participating later on - professionally, socially and culturally.

If knowledge is power, then free access to AI is a question of justice. It's not just about education, but about emancipation. It is about nothing less than being able to think, shape and decide in an increasingly complex world. That is why this access should not only be allowed for young people, but actively enabled and promoted - including in religious education.

56 • *Can literary reinterpretations of religious texts enrich faith and theology?*

According to José Saramago, literary reinterpretations of religious texts can certainly enrich faith and theology - precisely because they break through familiar narratives, question them and open up new perspectives. In *The Gospel According to Jesus Christ*, Saramago depicts the life of Jesus from a deeply human, doubtful and existential perspective. He demythologizes the figure of Jesus, shows him as a man with inner conflicts and also presents God's actions in a questionable way. This literary re-reading thematizes - and at the same time opens up a space for reflection and in-depth understanding that is often not achieved in purely dogmatic texts.

In theology, such literary approaches are often viewed ambivalently: On the one hand, they can be perceived as a disrespectful or blasphemous deviation from the text of revelation. On the other hand, they show how lively, ambiguous and open to interpretation religious traditions really are. Although the Catholic Church in particular emphasizes the authority of Scripture, it also has a long tradition of interpretation, mysticism and narrative art - from Augustine to the allegorical reading of the Bible in the Middle Ages.

In queer theology, literary reinterpretations are also a central tool for breaking up entrenched meanings. By placing biblical texts in new contexts, reinterpreting or rewriting them, hidden voices can be made visible - such as those of women, queers or people in contemporary public life who hardly feature in traditional interpretations. Saramago's Jesus, who struggles with doubts and questions God's plans, can be read as a figure of identification for all those who themselves struggle with religious norms and seek a more inclusive faith.

Literary reinterpretations such as Saramago's certainly deliberately disrupt the familiar - but this is precisely where their value lies: they force us to engage with them, promote empathy and open up new theological horizons. For a living, reflective faith, such voices are not a contradiction, but an enrichment - even if and precisely because they address new perspectives.

Chapter 5: Women in the Church and Religion: Historical Developments and Feminist Perspectives

The role of women in the church has been characterized by change and contradictions since the beginnings of Christianity. While women played an important role in early Christianity, whether as leaders of house churches or as central figures in spreading the faith, their importance was systematically marginalized in the course of church history. This exclusion of women from church leadership positions is closely linked to social power structures that still characterize the church today. Feminist theologians therefore criticize not only the lack of equal rights within the church, but also the deeply rooted patriarchal structures that exclude women from important decision-making processes.

Feminist theology goes beyond mere criticism: it combines the analysis of gender injustice with the demand for social justice and is closely linked to liberation theology. It questions traditional concepts of gender roles and offers alternative ethical approaches based on inclusion and justice. This critical debate is by no means limited to Christianity. Women have also historically played a significant but often underestimated role in other world religions. A comparative look at the image of women in Christianity, Islam, Judaism, Hinduism and Buddhism shows that although religious structures differ in their dogmas, they often have similar mechanisms of gender hierarchy.

But how can these outdated structures be broken down? One key approach is to promote women in religious leadership roles. Training programs that address the specific challenges facing women in the church can help to reduce existing inequalities. However, deep-rooted institutional barriers within the Catholic Church stand in the way of these reform efforts. Resistance to the ordination of women or equal participation in church decision-making processes is an expression of a structural problem that goes far beyond individual positions.

This need for reform is particularly evident in movements such as Maria 2.0, which advocate fundamental change in the church. The initiative is not only calling for the ban on women priests to be lifted, but also for the abuse of power and abuses within the church to be consistently addressed. Their demands show that many believers are not prepared to accept the unequal treatment of women as God-given, but are actively fighting for a more just and gender-equal church.

The question of the role of women in the church therefore remains one of the central challenges for modern Christianity. A church that claims to be a moral authority must also be measured against the standards of justice and equality. However, genuine reform can only succeed if not only individual positions are reconsidered, but a fundamental change in the theological and structural orientation of the church takes place - which begins with the confirmation of women in the priesthood and yes, even the office of a female pope.

a) Women in religions

57 • What role did women play historically in the major world religions, and how has this role changed?

Historically, women have often played an ambivalent role in the major world religions: on the one hand, they were central spiritual actors, prophets, priests and mystics; on the other hand, in many religious traditions they were systematically excluded from leadership functions and reduced to subordinate roles. The development of women's roles in religions was strongly influenced by social, political and theological factors. In recent centuries, the position of women has changed considerably as a result of feminist movements, modern theologies and social change, although many challenges remain.

Women played an important religious role in many indigenous and early polytheistic religions. They functioned as priestesses, shamans and oracle priestesses. In matrilineal societies in particular, female deities were worshipped as central figures, such as the goddesses Isis (Egypt), Ishtar (Mesopotamia) and Demeter (Greece).

However, with the rise of patriarchal forms of society, many of these goddesses were downgraded or replaced by male deities. Women often lost their religious offices, but continued to be respected as spiritual mediators - for example as seers or healers.

In ancient Judaism, women had a subordinate social position, but were present in everyday religious life. While they could not be priestesses in the temple service, they played a role as prophetesses, for example Miriam, Deborah or Hulda.

With the destruction of the Temple (70 AD) and the transition to rabbinical Judaism, the exclusion of women from religious leadership positions increased. In orthodox Jewish traditions, this restriction remained in place, while liberal currents of Judaism have allowed women to become rabbis since the 20th century. Today, there is growing equality in progressive Jewish movements, for example in Reform and Conservative communities.

The role of women in early Christianity was multifaceted. Jesus had close relationships with women, including Mary Magdalene, who is regarded as an apostle in some Christian traditions. In early Christianity, there were women as deacons, prophets and church leaders, such as Phoebe and Junia, who are mentioned in the letters of St. Paul.

With the institutionalization of the church in the 4th century, women were increasingly pushed out of church leadership positions. The Catholic and Orthodox churches still exclude women from the priesthood today. Although women were not integrated into spiritual leadership roles during the Protestant Reformation, the ordination of women became established in many Protestant churches in the modern era. Today, women are bishops, pastors and theology professors in many Protestant churches.

Women played an important role in early Islam. Khadīja, the first wife of the Prophet Muhammad, was a wealthy merchant and supported Islam financially and politically. Aisha, one of his wives, was an influential scholar who transmitted many hadiths.

Nevertheless, women were increasingly excluded from religious offices throughout Islamic history. While Islamic jurists interpreted women's rights in family law differently, their role in religious leadership remained limited. In the present day, however, there are movements for female imams and theologians, especially in progressive and feminist streams of Islam. In some regions, women are already leading mosques, for example in China or in certain Sufi traditions.

There is a broad spectrum of gender roles in Hinduism. Female deities such as Durga, Lakshmi and Saraswati occupy central positions in the pantheon, and there is a long tradition of female mystics and spiritual teachers, including Mirabai and Andal.

Historically, women were often excluded from priestly functions, especially in the Brahmin caste. In modern movements, however, there are a growing number of female priests and spiritual teachers, especially in reform-oriented Hindu traditions. Women are also increasingly taking on leadership roles in ashrams and spiritual communities.

Buddhist scriptures mention that the Buddha initially reluctantly allowed the ordination of nuns, which enabled the founding of the Bhikkhuni order. In some Buddhist traditions, women had religious leadership roles, but in many countries female monasteries were systematically suppressed or marginalized.

Today, there are efforts in many Buddhist movements to restore the ordination of women, especially in Theravāda and Tibetan Buddhism, where this tradition was long interrupted. In modern Buddhist movements, especially in the West, there is an increasing number of female teachers and meditation masters.

Since the 20th century, feminist movements in all major religions have also been campaigning for equal rights for women. Feminist theologians question traditional gender roles, reinterpret religious texts and fight for women's access to spiritual ministries.

- **In Christianity**, women in the Catholic and Orthodox churches demand access to the priesthood.
- **In Islam,** female activists are campaigning for the right to preach as imams.
- **In Judaism** today, women are active as rabbis in many denominations.
- **In Hinduism and Buddhism**, women are increasingly recognized as spiritual teachers.

Historically, women have often had an ambivalent role in the major world religions: in the early phases, they were often active as prophets, priests or spiritual teachers, but with the institutionalization of religions, they were increasingly pushed out of leadership positions by patriarchy and its male alliances. In modern times, feminist theologies and social movements have contributed to women increasingly taking on religious leadership roles again - even if structural hurdles still exist in many religious communities that hinder their full equality. The debate about the role of women in religions and church ministries therefore remains one of the central theological and social challenges of our time.

58 • *How did the role of women change in early Christianity, and why was their importance later downplayed?*

Elisabeth Schüssler Fiorenza also shows that Christianity in its beginnings was much more gender-balanced than it was later portrayed by church tradition. She describes how women played an active and influential role in the first Christian communities - as apostles, church leaders and missionaries. In her analyses of biblical texts and historical sources, she points out that many passages in the New Testament refer to female leaders, but that their significance was systematically marginalized in the course of church history.

A key example is the role of Mary Magdalene, who appears in the Gospels as the first witness to the resurrection - a task that could be understood theologically as an apostolic mission. Nevertheless, she was later reinterpreted by the Church as a sinner in order to devalue her authority. Schüssler Fiorenza also refers to women such as Junia, who is described in Paul's letter to the Romans as *"outstanding among the apostles"*, but was reinterpreted as a man in later translations and interpretations.

There was therefore very probably a female apostle named Junia, and the case of this woman is a striking example of how female leadership roles were later suppressed or made invisible in the early church. In Romans 16:7, Paul writes:

"Greet Andronicus and Junia, my relatives and fellow prisoners; they are outstanding among the apostles, and they were in Christ before me."

The original Greek text reads:

ἀσπάσασθε Ἀνδρόνικον καὶ Ἰουνίαν τοὺς συγγενεῖς μου καὶ συναιχμαλώτους μου, οἵτινές εἰσιν ἐπίσημοι ἐν τοῖς ἀποστόλοις, οἳ καὶ πρὸ ἐμοῦ γέγοναν ἐν Χριστῷ.

The name Ἰουνίαν (Iounían) is clearly in the feminine form here and is grammatically clear. It is the accusative of Ἰουνία (Junia), a common Roman female name in antiquity. Nevertheless, Junia was reinterpreted as "Junias", a supposedly male name, in later Bible translations over the centuries - although there is no historical evidence for this male name.

This reinterpretation was not a linguistic error, but rather an expression of a theological and cultural shift: a woman with the rank of apostle no longer fitted into the patriarchal church image of the Middle Ages and the early modern period. The deliberate masculinization of Junia served to suppress female authority in the apostolic circle.

The feminist theologian Elisabeth Schüssler Fiorenza points this out precisely: Junia was not only mentioned in the Bible, but described as *"outstanding among the apostles"* - and by Paul himself! This means that she was not only present, but also recognized in a special way. If a woman was called an apostle in the early church, then it can be deduced that leadership positions for women were not only possible, but real. Their later invisibilization is therefore not a theological necessity, but an expression of historically grown power structures that have turned against female participation.

Bringing Junia back into the limelight is therefore not only an act of historical justice, but also an important reminder that emancipation in the church does not have to be reinvented - it was already there at the beginning.

The legendary tale of Pope Joan of Arc is one of the most fascinating and controversial stories in church history. According to tradition, in the 9th century, a woman disguised as a man under the name Johannes Anglicus rose to ecclesiastical office and was eventually elected Pope. According to the story, she only gave birth to a child during a public procession, whereupon the hoax was discovered.

This story is not historically confirmed. Most historians today assume that it is a late legend that probably originated in the 13th century, possibly as a satire critical of the Church or as an expression of popular dissatisfaction with papal power. The name Joan of Arc does not appear in early papal lists and there are no contemporary sources to prove her existence.

And yet the story continues to have an impact - not because it proves that there was a woman in the Chair of Peter, but because it expresses a deep desire and social unease: the desire for equality in an institution that systematically excludes women from its highest offices. In a way, the legend holds up a mirror - it tells of how it is conceivable that a woman was considered worthy, educated and spiritually capable for decades - until her body exposed the illusion.

It is precisely because the story of Pope Joan stands between fact and fiction that it is so powerful: it touches on questions of power, gender, truth and the church's culture of remembrance. And she reminds us that what is considered "unimaginable" today often only appears that way because history has been selected, filtered and interpreted. Whether there really was a female pope remains an open question - that she could have existed is more relevant today than ever.

The story of Pope Joan has inspired numerous authors who have written about her story. Here are some important works:

- **Emmanuel Rhoides:** The Greek writer published the novel *"Popess Joan"* in 1866, in which he attempts to prove the existence of a female pope. This work led to his excommunication from the Greek Orthodox Church.
- **Donna Woolfolk Cross:** The American author wrote the historical novel *"The Popess"* in 1996, which fictionalized the legend and made it internationally famous. This book was made into a film with the same title in 2009.
- **Elisabeth Gössmann:** The German theologian and philosopher published *"Mulier Papa - Der Skandal eines weiblichen Papstes"* in 1994, in which she analyzes the reception history of Pope Joan. This work is part of her series *"Archiv für philosophie- und theologiegeschichtliche Frauenforschung"*.
- **Klaus Herbers and Max Kerner:** In their 2010 book *"Die Päpstin Johanna. Biography of a Legend",* published in 2010, the authors take a scholarly look at the origins and spread of the legend.

These works offer different perspectives on the story of Pope Joan, from literary adaptations to scholarly analyses.

Elisabeth Schüssler Fiorenza criticizes the fact that the patriarchal structures of the later church led to women being increasingly pushed out of real leadership positions and a male-dominated theology developed, which primarily pushed women into servant and subordinate roles. She argues for a feminist reinterpretation of the Christian tradition that is oriented towards the original dynamics of the early communities in which women were actively involved in shaping the faith. Her aim is to make the buried legacy of female leadership in Christianity visible again and to fight for a church that is not based on historically evolved hierarchies, but on equality and participation.

Although Article 3 of the German Basic Law guarantees equal rights for women and men, these principles do not automatically apply to religious institutions. Churches in Germany enjoy extensive autonomy through the right of self-government, which allows them to design internal structures according to their own religious principles - even if these violate social equality norms.

This inequality is particularly evident in the Catholic Church: women are excluded from the priesthood, cannot become bishops and have no access to the highest decision-making bodies. This discrimination is justified theologically with the *"divine order"* - among other things with the argument that Jesus only called male apostles and that priests must represent Christ's role as a man in the Eucharist. Critics such as Elisabeth Schüssler Fiorenza and Mary Daly do not see this as a divine requirement, but rather a historically evolved power structure that deliberately keeps women away from leadership positions.

Although there are female pastors and even female bishops in Protestant churches, women are often underrepresented in the highest leadership positions there too. In conservative evangelical or orthodox movements, traditional gender roles still apply that exclude women from certain functions.

The central issue remains: should the churches' right to self-administration take precedence over the principle of equality? In society today, it would be unthinkable for a large institution to systematically exclude women from leadership positions - but in the church, it continues to be legitimized with theological arguments. The debate about whether religious institutions should adapt to social change in the long term or continue to defend their special rights is being conducted under increasing pressure, particularly from feminist theologians and reform-oriented movements within the churches themselves.

The following legal levers are available to take the church's goal *of "female empowerment"* seriously:

Legal action at European level: The European Court of Human Rights (ECtHR) could be a possible avenue, as it has already ruled against discrimination by religious communities in the past. However, such a complaint would have to establish that the ban on women becoming priests is not only theologically discriminatory, but also socially discriminatory.

Strengthen internal church reform movements: In the long term, equality in the churches is more likely to be achieved from within - through pressure from the congregations, through feminist theology and through social change.

Argumentation via the legislator: A complaint to the Federal Constitutional Court would have little chance, as the churches' right to self-administration is firmly anchored in the Basic Law. A more realistic strategy would be to use political initiatives or a public debate to persuade the legislator or the Federal Constitutional Court to reassess the relationship between the churches' right to self-administration and the principle of equality. For example, institutions financed by church taxes (e.g. Catholic schools or social institutions) could and must be bound more closely to state equality standards.

This is because church schools, hospitals and social institutions - as well as the churches themselves - receive considerable state funding in Germany, often in the form of church taxes, other subsidies or grants. They take on important social tasks, but at the same time are under the influence of church working and structural guidelines, which in some areas violate general equality standards. This leads to a tension between the churches' right to self-administration and the constitutional principles of equal treatment and anti-discrimination.

1. state funding requires public responsibility

Many church institutions, particularly in education and social services, are therefore not only financed by church taxes, but to a large extent directly from public funds. This means that they de facto take on public tasks - such as health care or education. If state funds flow, state legislation on equal treatment and protection against discrimination should also apply without restriction. It would be incomprehensible for an institution that is predominantly run with taxpayers' money to systematically exclude women from management positions or deny LGBTQIA+ people access to certain professions.

2. catholic institutions, in particular the church itself, shape public education and the communication of values

Catholic schools not only educate children from families close to the church, but also receive state recognition and enjoy many privileges, such as the approval of school types or curricula. As a result, they have a significant influence on education and the communication of values in society. Priests also provide public education and impart values that shape society and the state. It would be a contradiction if they were allowed to teach equality in a democratic state but maintain discriminatory structures themselves.

3. problematic special rights in church labor law

So far, so-called church labor law has allowed church employers to select and dismiss employees according to religious standards - even in cases that would be considered clear discrimination under general labor law. For example:

- Exclusion of women from certain management positions, even in professions without a direct sacred function.
- Discrimination against LGBTQIA+ people, for example when same-sex partnerships are seen as grounds for dismissal.
- Different treatment in cases of pregnancy and divorce, for example when remarried people are dismissed from Catholic schools or hospitals.

Such a special right contradicts the general development of society and the legal anti-discrimination guidelines that already apply in other state-supported companies.

4 European legal requirements and social change

In many other European countries, there are already clear rules that ensure that church institutions are bound by general equality standards as soon as they receive public funding. In Germany, this debate has so far been shied away from because the churches invoke their constitutionally protected right to self-administration. However, with growing social pressure, modern self-evidence and increasing court rulings - including at European level - this could change.

It is a special status that needs to be reconsidered: as long as Catholic churches, schools and social institutions receive public funding, they should not be able to invoke purely ecclesiastical rules when it comes to issues of equal rights and anti-discrimination, particularly in professional life - including the priesthood. It would be logical to reform church employment law here.

For women to be able to hold the priesthood in the Catholic Church, for example, a change would have to be made to canon law (*Codex Iuris Canonici, CIC*). The relevant paragraph is *Canon 1024 CIC*, which currently reads as follows in its current wording:

- *"Only a baptized man can validly receive holy orders."*

This provision makes the ordination of women impossible, as the word "man" contains an exclusive gender requirement.

The amended wording for the equality of women in the priesthood should read as follows:

- *"Holy Orders can be received by any baptized person who is called to it by the Church."*

This formulation removes the gender-specific restriction and enables the Church to admit women as well as men to ordination.

Further necessary changes to canon law are: In addition to Canon 1024, other paragraphs would need to be revised, in particular:

- Canon 1026 (*"Only those who are free according to law can be admitted to sacred ordination."*) - It should be added here that gender is not a criterion for exclusion.
- Canon 1028-1032 - These regulate preparation for ordination and could be specified to ensure that women have equal access.
- Canon 277 ("*Clergy are bound to perfect and perpetual continence and therefore to celibacy.*") - If the ordination of

women leads to a debate about the duty of celibacy, an adjustment may be necessary here.

As canon law is decided by the Pope and the relevant Vatican bodies, either a dogmatic reinterpretation would have to take place or a council would have to officially reform the ordination order. A decree by a pope could set an example: Amending Canon 1024 would therefore be the most important step towards opening up the priesthood to women.

59 • How do the views on women differ in Christianity, Islam, Judaism, Hinduism and Buddhism?

The views on women in Christianity, Islam, Judaism, Hinduism and Buddhism have evolved historically and differ in their theological justification, their cultural characteristics and their social influence. While some religions conceded certain spiritual or social roles to women from the outset, in many traditions they were relegated to subordinate positions. In modern times, there are reform movements in all five religions that advocate for greater equality for women, but there are still differences in practice and in the opportunities for women to take up religious leadership positions. Let's look at this in more detail:

In Christianity, the role of women has been ambivalent from the very beginning. Jesus Christ showed an unusual openness towards women, discussed with them as equals and allowed them to have an impact in his environment. The early Christian communities knew women deacons, prophets and apostles such as Junia, but with the institutionalization of the church, women were increasingly pushed out of spiritual leadership. In the Catholic and Orthodox churches, women are still not allowed to become priests or bishops, while many Protestant and Anglican churches have introduced the ordination of women. Feminist theologians and movements such as "Maria 2.0" are calling for greater equality for women, especially in the Catholic Church, where they are still excluded from the priesthood.

In Islam, the position of women has been interpreted differently both theologically and culturally. The Quran recognizes the spiritual equality of men and women and names important female figures such as Khadīja, the first wife of the Prophet Muhammad, or Aisha, who played a central role as a scholar and transmitter of hadiths. Nevertheless, patriarchal structures developed in many Islamic societies that restricted women in religious and social leadership roles. While conservative interpretations deny women access to the imamate, there are already female imams in progressive Muslim communities, especially in North America, Europe and China. Organizations such as Musawah or Sisters in Islam advocate for gender-equitable interpretations of Islamic texts and the recognition of female leaders in Islam.

In Judaism, the role of women has long been limited by halachic (religious) regulations. In the orthodox tradition, women are exempt from certain religious duties, but this also meant their exclusion from central rituals such as public prayer or the reading of the Torah. Nevertheless, women played an important role in tradition and education, and there are female role models such as Deborah and Miriam in the prophetic and rabbinical texts. In liberal and reformed Judaism, women have been active as rabbis since the 20th century, while there is still resistance to female leadership in orthodox Judaism. Movements such as the Jewish Orthodox Feminist Alliance or the Women of the Wall demand equal religious rights for women, such as the right to pray at the Wailing Wall with a prayer shawl and Torah.

In Hinduism, the role of women is strongly dependent on the respective current and social practice. While Hindu myths worship powerful goddesses such as Durga, Lakshmi or Saraswati and women have been recognized as spiritual teachers, social structures have often relegated women to subordinate positions. In certain Hindu traditions, women were not allowed to lead religious rituals or recite sacred texts for a long time. At the same time, there are a growing number of female gurus and priests, especially in reform-oriented movements. Women such as Anandamayi Ma, Mata Amritanandamayi or Mirabai are regarded as spiritual teachers with a large following. Modern Hindu movements are increasingly advocating the recognition of female priests and a gender-equitable interpretation of religious texts.

In Buddhism, the role of women was ambivalent. While the Buddha introduced the ordination of nuns and granted women spiritual equality, the female branch of the order was suppressed or abolished in many regions. In many Theravāda and Tibetan Buddhist traditions, there is still no full bhikkhuni ordination for nuns, while female monks are recognized in Mahayana Buddhism. In modern times, there are growing movements for the restoration of nun ordination, particularly in Thailand, Sri Lanka and Tibet. Women such as Jetsunma Tenzin Palmo and Pema Chödrön are now internationally recognized Buddhist teachers.

The views of women in the five world religions are therefore strongly influenced by historical developments, cultural traditions and theological interpretations. While all religions have origins in which women played spiritual roles, they have often been ousted from religious leadership throughout history.

Today, there are reform movements in all faiths that are fighting for gender-equitable theology and equal rights for women in religious offices. However, there is still resistance, especially from conservative movements that rely on traditional interpretations of sacred scriptures. The debate on the role of women in religion therefore remains a dynamic process that is influenced by social change, legal standards, theological reflection and feminist movements - and by the demands of women themselves.

b) Feminist theology and gender justice

60 • *How does the church shape social power structures, and why is it criticized by feminist theologians as misogynistic?*

Mary Daly sees the church not only as an institution with misogynistic tendencies, but as a system that is structurally designed to secure male power and push women into a subordinate role. She argues that it is not just individual practices such as the prohibition of the priesthood for women or the emphasis on female subordination that are problematic, but that the entire theological foundation of the church is based on patriarchal principles.

Daly particularly criticizes the idea of an exclusively male image of God, which symbolically excludes women from the divine order and reduces their role to obedience and purity. She sees this as a theological justification for social inequality that keeps women away from power and spiritual autonomy. In her view, it is not possible to reform the church from within, as its structure is so deeply imbued with patriarchal ideas that any attempt at change ultimately fails due to the existing power relations.

This is why Daly consistently decides to leave the church altogether and develop a new feminist spirituality beyond religious institutions. She calls for a radical departure from all patriarchal symbols and hierarchies in order to enable the true liberation of women. Her thinking is not about reforming the church, but about a complete redesign of spirituality - a new organization in which women no longer have to be part of a male-dominated system that undermines their self-determination. And an organization with an adapted image of God.

This is what an image of God can look like that is not exclusively male, and the following theological possibilities exist for this: a non-exclusively male image of God must break away from the traditional idea of a patriarchal, male-connoted "God the Father" and instead express God's nature in diverse, also female and gender-neutral metaphors. In the Bible itself, there are already approaches to this: God is not only described as a father, but also in maternal images, for example in Isaiah 66:13 (*"As a mother comforts her son, so I comfort you"*) or in Hosea 11:3-4, where God leads her child like a mother. There are also comparisons between God's love and female care in Christian mysticism, for example in Hildegard von Bingen or Julian of Norwich, who describe Jesus as *"motherly"*.

A non-exclusively male image of God could also be based on gender-neutral or plural terms. Instead of "Lord" or "Father", God could be referred to as *"the source of life", "the holy", "the eternal"* or *simply as "love"*. Feminist theology often emphasizes that the image of God and language shape power structures - if God is only thought of as male, masculinity is associated with authority and femininity with subordination. An alternative could therefore be a language that takes different aspects of God into account, for example in a Trinity formula such as *"God - origin, wisdom and spirit"* instead of *"Father, Son and Holy Spirit"*.

A diverse image of God could also become visible in art and liturgy, for example through representations of God in female form, through songs and prayers that emphasize God's care and creativity, or through liturgical language that does not only use male terms. Such a change would not mean rejecting the male image of God, but rather expanding it to include female and cross-gender perspectives in order to fairly reflect the depth and complexity of the divine.

If God is not limited to a male and/or female or diverse gender, the issue of whether God can then also be diverse, intersex or trans, not only in terms of his or her gender, but also in terms of his or her sexuality or sexual orientation, must also be discussed: From a theological perspective, this would be a logical extension of a non-binary image of God. If God is not trapped in human categories of gender, but transcends them, then it is also conceivable to understand God in terms of gender diversity - not as exclusively male or female, but as a being that encompasses or is above all genders - and is oriented towards them.

The Bible already contains echoes of a *fluid image of God*. In Genesis 1:27 it says: *"God created man in his own image, male and female he created them."* This could mean that the divine image contains both male and female parts or that God himself is not limited to a single gender category. There are also texts in the Jewish and Christian traditions that describe God's attributes as cross-gender or mutable - sometimes as a father, sometimes as a mother, sometimes as a spirit hovering over the waters.

If God exists beyond human categories, then it would not only be possible but even logical to think of God as diverse - as a being that reflects or unites the diversity of gender identities. In feminist and queer theology, this is often seen as a perspective of liberation: If God is not only male, then the conventional power structures that link masculinity with authority are also not divinely legitimized. An image of God that also allows for intersex or trans *dimensions* could create a deeper inclusion and show that every *gender identity* has a place in divine reality.

Therefore, a modern, inclusive theology could refer to God not only as Father or Mother, but also as *"the changeable", "the diverse"* or *"the comprehensive"*. Such a perspective would not only give spiritual space to people with non-binary or trans identities, but also expand the understanding of God as something that transcends all human categorizations.

At first glance, the following topic in terms of gender and sex as well as sexual orientation may seem unusual when God's gender is discussed in theological debates , and whether the topic of God's sexual orientation then also arises, because sexuality is often associated with biological beings and reproduction - something that does not apply to God if he is not seen as fluid. But if God alone is thought of as a being that enters into relationship, then one could ask whether this divine relationship has a form of love or affection that can be compared to human sexuality?

In many religious traditions, God's relationship with people is described in metaphorical images of love and devotion. Christian mysticism - see, for example, Teresa of Ávila or John of the Cross - often uses language reminiscent of passionate love. In the Bible, there is the idea of God as a bridegroom (e.g. Isaiah 62:5 or the Song of Songs), but also God as a mother (Isaiah 66:13) or as a caring power that does not subordinate itself to any particular relationship constellation.

A broader theological consideration could argue that God is not exclusive in his love, but inclusive - not limited to a particular kind of love, but present in all forms of affection and relationship. If God's nature is love (1 John 4:8), then one could say that God works in all sincere loving relationships, regardless of or taking into account any form of gender or sexual orientation.

Queer theology accordingly asks whether God as a transcendent being does not itself have queer traits because he/she/it transcends the boundaries that people draw in gender and sexuality. A God who cannot be pinned down to one gender identity could also be understood as a being who is not limited to or oriented towards a single form of love. Ultimately, the question of God's sexual orientation remains difficult because sexuality is a profoundly human concept. If theology takes seriously that God enters into relationship and that love is his central characteristic, then we can at least ask whether our human concepts of love, desire, sexuality and relationship do not also have a divine dimension - and whether God's love does not then reach so far that it transcends all human categories.

While traditional theology often presents heteronormative assumptions as divinely given, Robert E. Goss also proposes as a theological reinterpretation to think of God as a queer reality - beyond binary notions of gender and sexuality or sexual orientation. In a truly inclusive theology, God is no longer defined in categories of male/female or heterosexual, but as a comprehensive, creative force that is reflected in all forms of human existence. Such a theology would not only include queer people, but would also revitalize the Christian message of love, grace and liberation.

In order to break up the patriarchal power structure, Mary Daly also develops a new idea of divinity that is not based on hierarchy, control or male dominance: Instead of a male God, she develops a dynamic and processual image of God. In her work *Beyond God the Father*, she describes God not as a static being, but as "Becoming" - a creative force that is not trapped in fixed categories, but is constantly unfolding and remains in motion. This idea of divinity is intended to empower women in particular to free themselves from the shackles of patriarchal thinking and to see themselves as part of a creative process. A central concept here is her idea of the "goddess" as an alternative to the male-dominated image of God. However, this goddess is not a person or a superior being, but stands for a deeper spiritual energy that is connected to nature, the female body and liberation from oppression. She is not omnipotent in the traditional sense, but embodies power in the form of creativity, change and resistance to oppressive structures. She argues for a polytheistic or even post-theistic spirituality, in which divinity is no longer thought of as an external authority, but as an inner, living force, e.g. in every woman, but which should help women in particular to develop their own spiritual identity.

For example, a prayer can be formulated that is aimed at a polytheistic or post-theistic spirituality. It is openly spoken without addressing an omnipotent individual being, but is dedicated to the diversity of the divine, to the living, to change - as it is conceived in many spiritual traditions:

Prayer to the powers of the living

You, who bear many names,
Goddess and God, ancestor and ancestress,
power of the forest, light of the sky,
voice in the depths of my heart -
I do not call you to ask,
but to remember:
that I am part of you,
and that you live in all that is.

In the cycles of nature,
in fire, water, earth and wind,
in contradiction and transformation,
in birth, parting and new beginnings -
you are there.
Not distant, but multifaceted,
not dominating, but supporting,
not eternally the same, but alive.

May my thinking remain open,
my actions mindful,
my speech truthful.
May I learn to listen:
the voices of the ancestors,
the breath of the earth,
the silence between the words.

You multiplicity of the divine,
you weave of sense and wonder,
be with me -
not above me, but beside me,
not outside, but in everything that lives.

So be it.

61 • *How does feminist theology combine the critique of patriarchy with social justice, and why is it inextricably linked to liberation theology?*

Ivone Gebara combines feminist theology with liberation theology by demonstrating that patriarchal structures in the church and social inequality in society are interwoven. She criticizes the fact that traditional theology not only keeps women subordinate, but also legitimizes economic and social oppression. Her approach therefore calls for a theology of liberation that considers gender justice and social justice together.

Gebara argues that patriarchy in the church cannot be viewed in isolation, but is part of a broader system of power and oppression that equally disadvantages women, the poor and other marginalized groups. The Catholic Church is not only a spiritual institution, but also a political and social force that reinforces inequality through its hierarchical structures. A theology of liberation can therefore not only strive for economic justice, but must also question the androcentric image of God, male-dominated authority and rigid sexual morality.

As an alternative, she develops a feminist-ecological liberation theology that not only deals with human justice, but also with the exploitation of nature. She emphasizes that both women and the environment are often treated as property - a parallel between patriarchal oppression and ecological destruction. Instead of a theology based on dogma and hierarchies, she calls for a spiritual practice based on equality, community and a respectful relationship with creation.

In this sense, her theology is not just a critique of the church, but a radical reinterpretation of faith and liberation that no longer keeps women in a servant role, but recognizes them as active shapers of a just society.

Ivone Gebara also sees environmental ethics as a central component of feminist liberation theology because she argues that the oppression of women and the destruction of nature are structurally linked. She addresses the fact that traditional theology has often viewed nature as an object to be dominated by humans, similar to the way women were viewed as property or servants in patriarchal systems. This way of thinking has contributed to the ecological crisis because it creates a separation between God, humans and creation instead of promoting a holistic, respectful relationship with the world.

As an alternative, she proposes an *ecofeminist theology* that sees God's work in contexts, relationships and cycles. In her view, God is not only transcendent, but can be experienced in life, in the earth, in water, in plants and in people. It therefore calls for a spiritual practice that sees creation not as a resource, but as a co-world with which people must live in harmony.

Her theology combines social justice and ecological responsibility because she argues that environmental degradation often affects the poorest and especially women the most. She therefore sees liberation not only as a human issue, but as a process that also includes the earth. A theologically based environmental ethic must therefore question the economic, political and spiritual causes of environmental destruction and promote a sustainable, gender-equitable and solidary way of life.

Gebara thus calls for a theology that emerges and teaches from lived experience - a spirituality that not only liberates people, but also focuses on the interactions between man, nature and God. The triangle *of "man, nature and God"* describes a reciprocal, inseparable relationship - a network of mutual dependence and responsibility. The result is a holistic theology:

Humans and nature: Humans are not separate from nature, but part of creation. In this perspective, the exploitation of the environment is seen as a form of oppression that not only destroys the earth, but also affects the poorest and most marginalized people. A liberating spirituality recognizes that the protection of nature is also a question of social justice.

God and nature: God is not conceived as an external entity detached from the world, but as immanently present in creation. Instead of a patriarchal God who rules over nature, this theology emphasizes the divine presence in the earth, in water, in living beings and in the ecological processes of the world.

Man and God: The relationship between man and God is no longer seen as a one-sided relationship of dependence, but as a dynamic, creative connection in which people actively participate in shaping the world. In this view, faith means not only obedience to divine commandments, but also an ethical responsibility for life, nature and social justice.

When people actively participate in shaping the world, the question arises as to whether they thereby become part of divine reality - not as omnipotent beings, but as participants in an ongoing creative process. This can be viewed from three perspectives.

Panentheistic perspective: Some theological currents, including panentheism, argue that God is not outside the world, but works in the world and through it. In this understanding, humans are not God himself, but they carry divine presence within them, as God unfolds in everything that exists. Ivone Gebara and other feminist theologians take up this idea by thinking of God not as a ruler over the world, but as a creative energy present in all living beings and nature.

Liberation theology perspective: In liberation theology, God is often described as being experienced in people's struggles for justice. When people actively participate in shaping a more just world, they realize divine values such as love, compassion and solidarity. In this sense, people are part of the divine work in the world because they make divine principles visible through their actions.

Christian mystical perspective: In mysticism, there are approaches that understand God not as a separate being, but as a deeper reality in all living things. Teresa of Ávila or Meister Eckhart speak of a deep union of the soul with God, in which the human being not only experiences the divine presence, but in a certain way participates in it.

In a holistic, processual theology, people are therefore not gods in the traditional sense, but they are part of the divine reality because they participate in the ongoing creation through their actions. In this way of thinking, God is not a distant being that rules from above, but a living, dynamic force that is present in people, nature and relationships. The responsibility of human beings is therefore not to "obey" God, but to consciously see themselves as co-creators of a holy, just and sustainable world.

---

d) Challenges and current need for reform in the churches

---

62 • *How does feminist theology challenge traditional concepts of gender justice and ethics, and what alternative approaches does it offer?*

Ina Praetorius addresses the fact that traditional theological concepts are strongly influenced by patriarchal thought patterns that systematically exclude women or reduce them to subordinate roles. She also argues that theology and ethics have been formulated from a male perspective for centuries, as a result of which female experiences, ways of thinking and realities of life have remained invisible or have been regarded as secondary.

However, a central and particular point of her elaboration is that many ethical systems - especially in the Christian tradition - are based on a *separation of public and private*. In this model, the masculine is associated with reason, politics and agency, while the feminine is reduced to care, emotion and domesticity. Praetorius questions this dichotomy and calls for an ethic of equality in which care work, relationship orientation and social responsibility are not recognized as additional female tasks, but as central principles for a just society.

She argues for a redefinition of economics, ethics and theology that is no longer based on male claims to power and competition, but instead recognizes cooperation, care and inclusion as central values. She rejects the idea of merely *"adapting"* women by granting them access to male-defined positions of power - instead, the system must be changed so that it is no longer based on exclusion and hierarchy, but on solidarity and shared responsibility.

Praetorius outlines a theology that takes everyday life seriously instead of upholding abstract dogmas or male-dominated structures. She also questions traditional images of God that link masculinity with transcendence and authority, and argues for a concept of divinity that focuses on the ability to relate, care and responsibility for creation. Her feminist perspective thus opens up a new ethical horizon in which not only women have equal rights, but human coexistence as a whole is based on justice and care - both in the church and in society.

It advocates a *theology of everyday life* that not only deals with abstract questions of faith, but also takes ethical responsibility in real life seriously. This also means that the church should rethink its stance on care work, economic justice and social participation - and answer the everyday questions of the faithful.

63 • What structural problems in the Catholic Church stand in the way of real equality for women, and what reforms are necessary?

The Catholic Church is deeply misogynistic in its structure, as it systematically excludes women from power and participation, summarizes the first female theology professor Uta Ranke-Heinemann. While women have fought for equal rights in almost all areas of society, the church still clings to a male-only clergy and denies women access to ordained ministries. This is not only (legal, social and theological) discrimination, but also a theological misinterpretation that cannot be derived from the message of Jesus, but from patriarchal traditions that have been consolidated over centuries.

In order to achieve true equality, she called for fundamental reforms: The opening of all church offices to women, including the priesthood and episcopate, an abolition of the notion of male authority as God-given, and a re-evaluation of sexual morality, which until now has forced women into outdated role models.

In addition, the church needs to rethink its theology, which often idealizes women but does not recognize them as equal actors. Instead of presenting Mary as an unattainable ideal of virginity and subordination, a theology is needed that takes women seriously as independent, self-determined personalities.

As long as these structural barriers exist, the church cannot speak credibly of justice and love. A genuine reform must therefore not only bring cosmetic changes, but also question the foundations of the church's power structures.

Mary as an ideal figure of virginity and submission is an image that has been handed down theologically, culturally and socially over the centuries - and has become an unattainable ideal in the process. Her virginity was not only understood biologically but also morally elevated: as a sign of purity, holiness and complete devotion to God. This established an image of women that declared sexual abstinence to be a prerequisite for divine closeness - an image that systematically devalued real female physicality and self-determination.

At the same time, Mary is described as a "humble handmaid" who accepts God's will without contradiction - a passive figure, silent, obedient and willing to suffer. This depiction has not only pushed other biblical female figures with agency into the background, but has also shaped an ecclesiastical ideal in which active, critical and resistant women are hardly allowed to appear.

What's more, Mary is portrayed as flawless and sinless - without doubt, without contradiction, without any desire of her own. This does not make her humanly approachable, but enraptured, idealized, almost untouchable. Who could identify with a woman who is both a virgin and a mother, at once completely submissive and divinely elevated? It is precisely this exaggeration that makes her an ideal that is not only unattainable, but also oppressive in its effect - an image that reduces women to victimhood, silence and purity.

However, there are also alternative interpretations of Mary that interpret her in a new and liberating way. In liberation theology and feminist theology, Mary is increasingly no longer understood as a submissive saint, but as a strong, resistant woman. She is a young woman who lives under imperial oppression and yet follows the divine call - not blindly, but courageously. In this interpretation, her "Magnificat" - Mary's song of praise - is not a sweet song of praise, but a radical socio-political call: *"He overthrows the mighty from their thrones and exalts the lowly."* Here, Mary becomes the voice of the disenfranchised, a prophetess, a figure of hope in the midst of patriarchal power.

In this perspective, Mary is not the silent ideal of obedience, but an image of female dignity, strength and spiritual self-empowerment. Such a Mary is not unattainable - she is human, in solidarity, and she invites us to follow her, not to imitate her.

64 • *What does a training program look like on the challenges that women in religious leadership roles still face today?*

A training program for women in religious leadership roles should aim to prepare them for the diverse challenges they face in their communities, institutions and societal contexts. The program should not only impart theological and practical knowledge, but also promote personal empowerment, networking and strategic action skills.

The training program *"Women in Religious Leadership: Empowerment, Strategy and Spirituality"* extends over several months and combines seminars, workshops, mentoring and practical training. It is aimed at women who are already active in religious communities or who aspire to a leadership role.

Module 1: Theological and doctrinal foundations

At the beginning, the religious and theological foundations for the leadership of women are taught. In interactive seminars, participants engage with biblical, Quranic, rabbinical and other religious texts that relate to the role of women in religion. Feminist and queer theologies are also included in order to develop alternative readings and gender-sensitive interpretations.

Module 2: Overcoming institutional and structural hurdles

An essential part of the program is dedicated to the structural challenges in religious institutions. In workshops, participants will analyze how power structures function, which obstacles systematically exclude women and which strategies exist to position themselves within existing institutions. Successful case studies of women in religious leadership will also be presented.

Module 3: Developing self-confidence and leadership strength

A central focus of the program is on strengthening the personal and spiritual identity of the participants. In coaching sessions and reflection groups, the women examine their own beliefs, their vocation and their role in the community. Topics such as "How do I deal with criticism?", "How do I find my leadership voice?" and "How do I develop resilience in a male-dominated environment?" take center stage.

Module 4: Communication and rhetoric for religious leaders

In order to assert themselves in theological debates and within their own faith community, targeted rhetoric and communication training is offered. Women learn how to give sermons, conduct debates, present themselves convincingly and formulate theological arguments effectively. Role plays and feedback sessions help to put what has been learned into practice.

Module 5: Networks and mentoring for women in religious leadership positions

A strong network is crucial for success. That's why the program includes mentoring from experienced women in religious leadership positions. Participants are connected with a personal mentor who guides them through the program. There are also regular networking meetings with other women experiencing similar challenges to share experiences and support each other.

Module 6: Dealing with resistance and gender-specific discrimination

As women in religious leadership roles are often confronted with sexist prejudices, institutional barriers and even direct rejection, strategies for dealing with such challenges are specifically taught. Difficult situations are played out in role plays and simulations, including conflicts with male colleagues, hostility from conservative circles or structural discrimination in decision-making bodies.

Module 7: Legal and financial aspects of religious leadership

An often neglected but essential area is the knowledge of legal and financial structures in religious institutions. Women are informed about their rights within their religious community and gain an insight into church law regulations, salary negotiations, parish administration and financial independence.

Module 8: Public relations and media competence

Women in religious leadership roles are increasingly in the public eye and must be able to deal with the media. This module teaches how to talk to the press, use social media strategically and formulate public statements. It also teaches strategies for dealing with negative reporting or attacks on social media.

Module 9: Spiritual practice and personal empowerment

As spiritual women are often under a lot of pressure, it is important to create space for self-care, meditation and spiritual strengthening. In this module, participants learn how to deepen their personal faith practice, deal with stress and maintain inner peace in order to be able to survive in their role in the long term.

Module 10: Preparing women for the office of Pope

A module in a seminar for women in church leadership positions that prepares them to apply for the office of Pope is more than just a seminar concept - it would be a symbolic and concrete space in which theological competence, spiritual depth and structural reflection on power come together. The aim of this seminar module would be not only to prepare women for a top ecclesiastical position that has been institutionally denied to them to date, but also to encourage them to actively see themselves as bearers of spiritual authority and the future of the Church.

The focus would initially be on a theological foundation that deals with the history and present of the Petrine ministry - critically and constructively. What are the theological concepts behind the office? How has the understanding of the papacy changed over the centuries? And above all: is the papal office really dependent on a male body? This is where feminist theologies, analyses of church history and ecclesiological alternatives would enter into dialog.

A second focus of the module is spiritual and personal self-assurance. A future pope must not only be able to think theology, but also embody it. She should have the ability to lead herself spiritually, to endure conflicts, to stand in prayer - and not lose her personality in the process. She must be able to deal with opposites: closeness and distance, power and vulnerability, tradition and renewal.

In addition, she needs communicative and political skills: a pope should understand global processes, have interreligious communication skills, be able to speak and represent in public, know media strategies, expect resistance - and still maintain her composure.

Organizational development, personnel management and spiritual leadership are further central fields: How can the church be shaped not only in the mode of administration, but as a living organism? What liturgical, pastoral and structural course must be set so that leadership does not mean domination, but creates space for participation?

Last but not least, the module must also include a simulation of ecclesiastical power structures: How do you navigate the college of cardinals, how do you argue your case in synods, how do you deal with anti-reform currents? And how do you protect yourself in a system that has been designed for centuries to systematically keep women down?

A pope must not only be pious, educated and strong - she must have a vision of the Church that is greater than the system she is supposed to lead. The seminary would not dictate to her what this vision looks like, but it would help her to find it, represent it - and stick to it. Even in the face of resistance. Even with a smile. Even in the name of a future that has already begun.

Module 11: Development of a mission, vision and strategy with goals for a leading church organization of the present and future

This module is the strategic core of the seminar - it brings together the previously developed skills, perspectives and inner attitudes and bundles them in a process that forms a sustainable leadership strategy from theological depth, spiritual clarity and organizational thinking.

In this module, the participants - all women in church leadership positions - are instructed to formulate their own mission: a clear statement of what they want to be church for. This is not about abstract concepts, but about the concrete question: *What is the purpose of the church under my leadership? Who is it there for? What does it want to achieve - locally, globally, spiritually, socially, prophetically?* As a future leader, a female pope must be able to credibly embody this purpose - as the embodiment of hope, as the guardian of a vision that does not exclude, but empowers.

Building on this, the participants develop a vision a picture of what the church could look like in 2, 5 or 10 years' time. This vision is not a pious wish list, but an orienting picture of the future: a transformation narrative that takes tradition seriously, but not only thinks about the future, but shapes it. In this step, questions of justice, inclusion, ecological responsibility, liturgy, distribution of power and new ministry structures are also considered - and cast in a vision or mission statement - every German school has something like this on its homepage - that inspires rather than administers.

In the third step, the participants develop a strategy that describes how this vision can become reality. This includes

- concrete goals that are measurable and verifiable,
- Fields of action such as education, communication, community structures, interreligious dialog,

- as well as resource analyses, cooperation potential and resistance factors.

Particular emphasis is placed on the ability to develop a strategy that is spiritually anchored but can be implemented in a secular way - in other words, it must be able to connect with people, systems and realities beyond the walls of the church.

The focus is not only on the *what* and *why*, but also on the *how* - *"What How Why"*: How do I lead an organization whose core mission is spiritual - but whose structures are human, often contradictory and sometimes resistant to reform? How do I remain clear in my vision and at the same time capable of dialog in implementation? How do I balance the tension between radical hope and concrete feasibility?

Module 11 turns the Pope not only into a theologian with leadership qualities, but also into a visionary with the will to shape things. It strengthens her strategic thinking without losing her inner compass - and it combines divine trust with human planning power. Because a church of the future is not only created through prayer and patience, but also through the courage to create. This module gives her the tools to do so.

Module 12: Final project and certificate

At the end of the program, the participants develop an individual final project in which they apply what they have learned in their own congregation or religious institution. They receive a certificate that identifies them as qualified leaders and increases their chances of official recognition in religious structures.

This training program *"Women in Religious Leadership: Empowerment, Strategy and Spirituality"* offers holistic training for women who want to take on responsibility in religious institutions. It teaches theological, communicative, organizational and personal skills to assert oneself in male-dominated structures and actively promote equality in faith communities. With a strong focus on networking, mentoring and practical solutions, it helps women to establish themselves sustainably as spiritual and social leaders.

Several institutions - interfaith and international - could offer such a training program for women in religious leadership roles, as it encompasses theological, practical and social aspects. These include theological colleges, interfaith organizations, feminist networks, religious reform movements and international NGOs working for gender justice in religions. Here are some specific institutions and organizations that could potentially offer such programs:

1. theological colleges and universities

Academic institutions with a focus on feminist, interreligious and gender-equitable theology could include this program in their curricula or develop it as a continuing education offer.

- **Harvard Divinity School (USA):** Already offers courses on feminist and queer theology and could develop a specialized program for women in religious leadership.
- **Union Theological Seminary (New York, USA):** Has a long tradition in social justice theology and could serve as a platform for such trainings.
- **Catholic theological faculties** at universities (e.g. University of Vienna, University of Tübingen, University of Freiburg): Could offer such a program as part of courses in pastoral theology or feminist theology.
- **Islamic and Middle Eastern Studies** (University of Edinburgh, SOAS London): Could host this program for Muslim women theologians and activists.
- **Leo Baeck College (London, UK).** A training center for rabbis that promotes gender-inclusive theology in Judaism.

2. interreligious and ecumenical organizations

Such a training programme could be offered by organizations that are already active in interreligious dialogue and are committed to women's rights within religious structures.

- **World Council of Churches** (World Council of Churches): Committed to gender justice in churches worldwide and could develop the program for Protestant and Orthodox churches.
- **Religions for Peace:** This international organization connects representatives of different faiths and could establish the training programme as an interreligious training offer.
- **Interfaith Center of New York:** Promotes social justice programs and could initiate a leadership program for women in religious leadership roles.
- **Bahá'í Community Peace Institute:** The Bahá'í religion is strongly committed to gender equality and could incorporate this program into its educational structures.

3. feminist and progressive religious movements

Many feminist movements within religions actively campaign for women's ordination, equal rights and the reform of patriarchal structures and could offer the training program as part of their work.

- **Women's Ordination Conference** (USA): Could develop a special program for Catholic women working for equality in the church.
- Maria 2.0 (Germany): A church protest movement demanding women's rights in the Catholic Church could offer the program as practical training for activists.
- **Jewish Orthodox Feminist Alliance** (JOFA, USA): Advocates for religious equality for women in Orthodox Judaism and could implement the program in Jewish contexts.
- **Musawah** (Malaysia, Global): A Muslim women's rights movement advocating gender justice in Islam could develop the program for female scholars and activists.
- **Sisters in Islam** (Malaysia): A progressive Muslim women's organization that advocates for gender-equitable interpretations of the Quran.

4. churches, synagogues and mosques with reform approaches

Certain congregations and faith communities could use the training program as an internal training opportunity for women with leadership ambitions.

- **Protestant churches** (e.g. EKD, Church of England, Presbyterian Church USA): Many Protestant churches already have women in leadership positions, but could offer targeted programs to further strengthen female theologians and pastors.
- **Liberal Jewish communities:** Reform and Conservative Jewish movements already ordained women as rabbis, but could establish structured training for women in religious office.
- **Progressive mosques** (e.g. Ibn Rushd-Goethe Mosque in Berlin): Such mosques could use the program as leadership training for women in Islamic theology.

5. international NGOs and human rights organizations

Such a training programme could also be funded or coordinated by global organizations that promote women's rights and interfaith dialogue.

- **UN Women** (United Nations): Could promote the program in collaboration with religious actors to strengthen women's rights within religious institutions.

- **Carter Center** (USA): Committed to human rights and could develop the program in cooperation with religious networks.
- **Amnesty International:** Already has programs to promote women's rights in religious contexts and could introduce this program in affected regions.

6. private foundations and educational institutions

There are numerous private foundations that are committed to gender justice, religious reform movements and theological education. These could finance or support the training program.

- **Templeton Foundation:** Promotes research and education on spirituality and could fund such a program for women in religious leadership roles.
- **Ford Foundation:** Supports gender equality and human rights and could specifically promote women in religious leadership positions.
- **Heinrich Böll Foundation** (Germany): Already has programs to promote women in religions and could further develop the program in a global context.
- **Konrad Adenauer Foundation** (Germany): Promotes interfaith dialogue and could offer the Women in Religious Leadership program.

A training program for women in religious leadership roles could therefore be offered by a variety of institutions, including theological universities, interfaith organizations, feminist networks, reform-oriented faith communities, human rights organizations and private foundations. Its implementation would be particularly effective if it is developed in cooperation between university institutions, religious reform movements and NGOs to combine both academic and practice-oriented content. Such cooperation could help women worldwide to gain better access to religious leadership positions and to overcome structural barriers in the long term - with the aim of welcoming another female pope to office in the Catholic Church in the near future.

65 • What demands does the "Maria 2.0" initiative make regarding the role of women in the church, and why are these changes urgent?

The "Maria 2.0" initiative calls for comprehensive equal rights for women in the Catholic Church, in particular access to all ordained ministries. It criticizes the fact that women continue to be excluded from central church offices, even though they carry out a large part of the church's basic work. The church's refusal to admit women to the diaconate or priesthood cannot be justified theologically, but is an expression of a patriarchal claim to power that is incompatible with the message of Jesus. We know that.

However, "Maria 2.0" justifies the urgency of these changes with several factors. Firstly, discrimination against women undermines the credibility of the Church, which on the one hand advocates justice, but on the other hand perpetuates inequality within its own structures. Secondly, the shortage of priests is worsening worldwide, while the church continues to exclude qualified women from pastoral care and preaching. The initiative sees this as a self-inflicted crisis that will weaken the church in the long term.

In addition to the ordination of women, *"Maria 2.0"* is therefore also calling for a timely and comprehensive reform of the church structure, in which power is not solely in the hands of the clergy, but is made more participatory and democratic. It also calls for a consistent investigation into abuse scandals and a reorientation of the church that does not focus on maintaining power structures, but on a credible and just community of believers.

With the founding of its organization, it has set out to bring about appropriate resolutions now and in the near future.

Chapter 6:
Queer Jesus: On searching, finding and interpreting his sexual identity

The question of Jesus' sexuality has hardly been addressed for a long time - whether for theological, church-political or social reasons. But in recent decades, progressive theologians and historians have begun to explore Jesus' possible queer identity. Is Jesus' sexuality even relevant to the Christian faith? For many believers, the answer seems to be a clear no: Jesus' message is above any sexual orientation. And others argue that the church itself has constructed a heteronormative idea of Jesus over the centuries - an idea that needs to be re-examined.

A central argument is that Jesus' closest relationships may not have been heteronormative. The close bond with his "favorite disciple" John or the enigmatic "naked youth" in Mark 14:51-52 are interpreted by some theologians as indications of a queer dimension to his identity. These hypotheses are controversial, but they raise an essential question: Why is a non-heteronormative interpretation of Jesus often perceived as threatening in church circles? What fears lie behind the church's rejection of a homosexual identity of Jesus?

The debate extends beyond purely theological questions. Historians such as Klaus Dede in Germany and Europe have attempted to justify a queer reading of Jesus on the basis of sources. What historical evidence or clues could actually point to Jesus' homosexual orientation? And if this were the case, would it have diminished his authority among his followers or rather strengthened his message of inclusion and love?

Philosophical and theological concepts of Christ's gender also play a role. To what extent have historical theologians dealt with the question of whether Jesus can be classified in traditional gender categories? The discussion about his identity is also repeatedly linked to the sexuality of other church figures - for example the possible homosexuality of Pope Julius III or even Paul.

This leaves the question of whether a queer interpretation of Jesus is theologically responsible or sustainably effective on the agenda. Could such an interpretation make Christianity more attractive to many people, especially queer believers who often feel excluded from church institutions? Or is the rejection of a queer interpretation of Jesus rather an expression of a deeper fear of one's own transformation? Reflecting on these questions opens up new perspectives on how Jesus can be understood as a historical and spiritual figure - and how his message of love, acceptance and community should be reinterpreted in the present.

a) Fundamentals of the sexuality of Jesus and its relevance

66 • *Is Jesus' sexuality relevant to the Christian faith at all?*

The sexuality of Jesus is fundamentally irrelevant to the Christian faith. At the heart of the Christian faith is Jesus as the Son of God, his work of redemption, his death on the cross and his resurrection. His message and his work focused on the kingdom of God, love of neighbor and the redemption of mankind.

In theology, there are different views on the human nature of Jesus (Christology). Classical Christian doctrine emphasizes that Jesus was true God and true man (*"hypostatic union"*), but his humanity is usually thought of in this way, so that a discussion about his sexuality remains speculative.

In practice, the question has triggered historical and cultural discussions, for example in relation to celibacy or gender roles in the church. The central concerns of Christianity are its messages about the kingdom of God, love of neighbor, forgiveness and redemption. Jesus' words and actions have shaped Christianity and continue to influence ethics, theology and social values to this day.

The Gospels emphasize his teachings, miracles and sacrifice, even if there is speculation about his sexuality.

The consideration of whether the "beloved disciple" of Jesus could in fact have been the presumed female apostle, i.e. a woman, represents a profound challenge to the church's previous self-image - not only with regard to the role of women, but also with regard to the theological interpretation of closeness, love, apostolate and power. Jesus could also be brought into the option of a heterosexual man.

In the Gospel of John, we encounter the figure of the *"disciple whom Jesus loved"* as a special figure who is present at the washing of the feet, lies at Jesus' breast at the Last Supper, perseveres under the cross and is the first to arrive with Peter at the empty tomb. In church tradition, this figure is usually identified with the apostle John - but this is by no means clearly proven. The text itself does not mention a name.

Modern exegetical and queer theological readings therefore raise the question of whether the *"beloved disciple"* could also have been a woman among the apostles - or Mary of Magdala, for example. She is described in the Gospel of John as the first witness to the resurrection, with a closeness to Jesus that is extraordinary. In apocryphal writings such as the Gospel of Philip or the Gospel of Mary, Mary Magdalene is portrayed not only as a companion but also as a trusted interlocutor of Jesus - as an "apostle to the apostles" who is seen and sent.

If the Church were to accept such an interpretation - i.e. that Jesus had a favorite female disciple, possibly even heterosexually oriented and not queer, perhaps even in a particularly emotionally or spiritually intimate relationship - this would have significant changes. For it would relativize the traditional image of the male apostolic college, on which the arguments against the ordination of women are still based today. A woman in the innermost circle of Jesus, possibly even in the role of the favorite disciple, calls into question the power imbalance that has so far been maintained between sacramental ministry and female vocation.

In addition, the image of Jesus himself would also change. Not as the raptured, celibate Son of God who shows no interpersonal bonds whatsoever, but as a possibly heterosexual or even queer person with relationships, closeness, preferences - with bonds that are not sexless, but deeply human: to a woman. Whether one can derive a heterosexual identity of Jesus in the modern sense from this would ultimately be of secondary importance. Queer people also have close relationships and trust in women. What is more decisive is the realization that Jesus did not define himself through demarcation, but through affection and relationship - regardless of gender and sexual orientation.

Such an understanding would also change the sexual morality of the church, which to this day is based on abstinence, hierarchy and gender dualism. The idea of a Jesus who turns to a woman in a special way, who grants her authority and mission, would lay the foundation for a more inclusive understanding of ministry - one that is not based on male exclusivity, but on lived discipleship.

The church would find itself in a dilemma: either it recognizes that the beloved disciple could have been a woman - a female apostle with whom Jesus was particularly close. In this case, Jesus would be conceivable as a heterosexual or even queer person who liked to be close to a woman. However, this would remove the central line of argument that is still used today to rule out the ordination of women: namely that Jesus only called men to be apostles. If this assumption is refuted by a favorite female disciple as evidence of his possible heterosexuality, the exclusion of women from the papacy would no longer be theologically tenable.

Alternatively, the church may hold that the beloved disciple was a man - and must then face up to the possibility that Jesus was emotionally close to a man. This interpretation would support the idea that Jesus can be understood as a queer person - an idea that is largely taboo in the current theological structure of the church, but which is given new plausibility by the proximity to a male disciple.

In both cases, the church's doctrinal structure needs to be reflected - either by recognizing female leadership authority or by opening up to non-heteronormative ways of life. The real perspective here is not what was historically, but how much theological movement the church reflects today - and how much and what truth it can withstand when this touches on its power logic - catalyzed by these thoughts on a queer Jesus and his sexual orientation.

But precisely because such an insight and reflection would be so accelerating, it has so far not been welcome in the official church. The most likely reaction would be a diplomatic evasion: The possibility would be acknowledged symbolically, relativized exegetically or interpreted as a mystical metaphor - without admitting the systemic consequences. The Church would probably not agree to such a woman-friendly change because it would challenge too many existing power structures of men in homophobia: the male alliances in the clergy, the exclusive sacramental transmission of ordination, the idea of the gender representation of Christ.

And yet there is enormous visionary power - and hope - in this topic. If the Church has the courage to see the possibility of a favorite female disciple of Jesus not as a threat, but as liberation, then it could redeem itself from an understanding of power that many today find spiritually empty and theologically untenable. Because then the following would apply: Closeness to Jesus, calling to leadership, mission into the world - all this is not tied to gender, but to the call of God, which blows where it wills.

And if the church has the courage to see and reflect on the possibility of a homosexual, queer Jesus not as an interpretation, but as a possible truth or at least an option, then it could also begin to recognize the diversity of human love, identity and physicality as spiritually meaningful. Then standardized sexuality would no longer be the standard for holiness, but a lived relationship based on closeness, trust and freedom. Such an opening would not differentiate the figure of Christ, but would make it more human, more tangible and more solidary - especially for those who have had to stand on the sidelines up to now.

A Jesus who speaks in queer love, and/or lives and feels comfortable in female closeness, possibly breathing in contradictions, would not be a loss for faith - but a rediscovery of his deeply effective, liberating love and presence. It is not conformity to norms that makes it credible, but the ability to show itself as a healing integrative force in the midst of ambivalence and diversity.

It has long been obvious that this call for thematization and rediscovery also includes women and female queers: it remains a contemporary issue that the church recognizes queerness inclusively. And at the same time, it is an invitation to theological self-assurance: using the example of Jesus to reflect on the truth or interpretation of his sexuality and sexual orientation or on his possible feelings of being attracted - as part of an open, honest dialog about humanity, relationships and divine closeness.

67 • How does Jesus' sexual orientation influence the message, content and validity of his teachings?

Modern projections or interpretations of Jesus' sexual orientation are often the result of cultural, ideological or social developments. They are based less on historical evidence than on certain concerns, values or perspectives. Here are some examples:

Figure 12: Portrait of Jesus, inspired by Pasolini's film style and with a queer interpretation.

Liberal theological interpretations (e.g. queer theology)

Some theologians from LGBTQIA+-friendly movements interpret Jesus' closeness to his disciples or certain New Testament texts as an indication of a possible homosexual or queer identity.

The *"beloved disciple"* (John 13:23), on whose chest Jesus lies at the Last Supper, is sometimes interpreted as an expression of a special relationship.

The story of the Roman centurion and his sick servant (Matthew 8:5-13; Luke 7:1-10) is still occasionally interpreted as a possible homosexual partnership, as the Greek word *pais* can mean both *"servant"* and *"young lover"*.

Conservative reactions and counter-interpretations

Evangelical or fundamentalist currents often see such interpretations as a deliberate distortion of the Christian tradition resulting from modern social debates.

They emphasize that Jesus makes no reference to a romantic or sexual relationship in the Bible and that such speculation pursues a theological agenda.

Feminist theology and Jesus as an androgynous role model

Some feminist theologians argue that Jesus breaks traditional gender roles in his portrayal of gentleness, care and love. This leads to the idea of a "queer" Jesus who does not fit into the binary categories of masculinity or heteronormativity.

Secular-humanistic or pop-cultural representations

In art, literature or films, Jesus is sometimes portrayed as queer, homosexual or androgynous, often only as a provocation or socio-critical reflection. Examples include Terrence McNally's play *Corpus Christi*, which shows Jesus and his disciples as queer men, or the film by Pier Paolo Pasolini Il Vangelo secondo Matteo, as well as popular cultural discussions that take place in LGBTQIA+-friendly circles.

Psychoanalytical and sociological interpretations

Some interpretations from the psychoanalytical tradition (e.g. Sigmund Freud or later Michel Foucault) see the expectation of celibacy in Jesus as a form of sublime or repressed sexuality, which leaves room for different speculations:

In modern queer theory, Jesus is sometimes seen as a figure who challenges social norms, including those relating to gender and sexuality.

These modern interpretations are mostly an expression of social debates and are less historically verifiable. They often reflect the need to use Jesus as a figure of identification for certain social or cultural concerns. This only goes to show that Jesus is constantly being reinterpreted in different contexts - be it as a revolutionary fighter for social justice, as a spiritual teacher or as a symbol of social emancipation. And in this way, believers can also reflect a queer Jesus.

68 • How can the question of Jesus' sexual orientation be relevant for and related to his message?

The question of Jesus' sexual orientation is particularly relevant when it helps to better understand his message or to open up new perspectives on it. This is less about speculative curiosity and more about theological reflection on the significance of sexuality, identity and inclusion in his ministry. Regardless of his personal sexuality, Jesus was consistent in his devotion to people who were on the margins of society - be they sinners, tax collectors or social outcasts. His attitude was not normative and exclusionary, but radically and sustainably inclusive. If Jesus actively overcame exclusion, his message can be seen as an invitation to critically question today's social norms, especially in relation to gender and sexuality. There are almost no biblical references to a romantic or sexual relationship of Jesus. Some interpretations discuss his close relationship with John, as is well known, but to infer or deny a specific sexual orientation from this would be speculative. The fact that Jesus himself did not start a family or bind himself to a heteronormative gender role could be interpreted as a sign that he did not consider sexuality (with women) to be a central prerequisite for a fulfilled life. This provides a theological basis for a differentiated view of sexuality in Christianity. If Jesus' message is primarily based on love, respect and responsibility, then a sexual ethic could be derived from this that is not based on rigid norms, but on lived love for one's neighbor. Instead of evaluating sexuality on the basis of traditional prohibitions, it could be viewed from the perspective of a responsible, loving relationship. Although Jesus' personal sexual orientation remains unknown, his behavior shows that he valued people regardless of social norms. In a modern debate on sexuality, his message could therefore be understood as a plea for an attitude of love and acceptance - regardless of individual orientations or identities.

b) Historical and theological perspectives

69 • *Is it possible that Jesus' closest relationships were not heteronormative?*

Heteronormativity refers to the social assumption that heterosexuality is the "normal" and predominant sexual orientation. It often goes hand in hand with the idea that there are two clearly separate genders that complement each other in a traditional, monogamous relationship. Anything that deviates from this - be it homosexuality, bisexuality or non-binary gender identities - is often overlooked, marginalized or even rejected in heteronormative societies.

The question of whether Jesus' closest relationships were heteronormative can only be answered to a limited extent, as the biblical sources do not make any explicit statements in this regard. However, there are the aforementioned aspects that leave room for interpretation: the Gospels report on his "close relationship". This formulation is found in particular in the Gospel of John (e.g. John 13:23), where the beloved disciple even lies "on the breast of Jesus" at the Last Supper - a form of physical closeness that is often interpreted romantically in modern Western cultures, but could historically also be an expression of close friendship.

The intimate connection between Jesus and his followers such as Mary Magdalene or Lazarus also raises questions. The Bible describes, for example, that Jesus loved Lazarus (John 11:3, 5), a choice of words that in an ancient context could mean both close friendship and deeper emotional or spiritual ties. The fact that Jesus remained unmarried, although this was unusual in his cultural environment, also gives rise to speculation about his relationship to common gender norms.

In an interpretation that classifies Jesus as non-heteronormative from today's perspective, it should be noted: The ancient Jewish-Roman world had different ideas about gender and sexuality than modern society, and concepts such as homosexuality or queerness did not yet exist as they do today. What is certain is that Jesus cultivated close, non-familial relationships that went beyond what would be considered typical in a strictly heteronormative society. However, whether these relationships were non-heteronormative or heteronormative in the modern sense will probably remain an open question forever.

70 • Which historical sources could point to a homosexual orientation of Jesus?

There are a number of historical and theological sources that have been used as evidence for Jesus' homosexual orientation. These arguments are often based on text-critical analyses, historical contexts and alternative interpretations of biblical and extra-biblical texts.

Historical sources and references

Some theologians and historians have argued that certain cultural and social contexts of antiquity had a more open attitude towards same-sex relationships, particularly in Greco-Roman culture. Jesus worked in an environment shaped by Hellenistic culture, where homoerotic relationships were an accepted form of social and emotional bonding.

A particularly frequently cited indication is the recurring mention: the closeness between Jesus and a disciple who "lay at Jesus' breast" (John 13:23-25) is interpreted by some researchers as a possible indication of a deeper emotional or physical relationship.

Another possible reference is the story of the Roman centurion and his *"pais"* (Matthew 8:5-13). The Greek word *"pais"* can mean both "servant" and "lover". In the Greco-Roman world, it was not uncommon for a "pais" to have an intimate relationship with his patron. Jesus heals this "pais" without any moral condemnation, which some see as an indication of Jesus' tolerant attitude towards same-sex love.

Klaus Dede also points to translation errors in the Bible, in particular Luther's deliberate misinterpretation of certain passages in order to conceal a possible homosexual connotation.

Authors who discuss this topic

Several authors have addressed the possibility of a homosexual or queer identity of Jesus. These include:

- Wayne Meek (1974: Image of the Androgyne)
- Gaius Marius Victorinus (Adversus Arium)
- Judith Butler (1991: Unbehagen der Geschlechter)
- Robert Goss (1993: Jesus Acted Up, 2002: Queering Christ)
- Marcella Althaus-Reid (2003: The Queer God)
- Halvor Moxnes (2003: Putting Jesus in his Place)
- Theodore Jennings (2003: The Man Jesus Loved).

These works examine the question of Jesus' sexuality from various perspectives, from historical-critical research to modern queer theology.

While there is no direct evidence of Jesus' homosexual orientation, there are historical and theological arguments that could support such an interpretation. In particular, biblical texts, the proximity to his disciples and the lack of a heteronormative lifestyle are interpreted by some theologians as indications. However, the discussion remains controversial and is often reluctantly entered into by church institutions.

The idea that Jesus could have had homosexual tendencies has thus been shared by several authors since the 20th century, e.g. , who apply a "queer theory" to Jesus and interpret his sexuality or gender identity accordingly.

As early as the 1970s, several pamphlets and magazine authors openly posed the question: *"Was Jesus gay?"* Titles such as *"Was Jesus Gay?"* speculated that Jesus may have had homosexual relationships.

Medieval authors such as Aelred von Rievaulx already described Jesus' relationship with his *"favorite disciple"* metaphorically as a kind of spiritual marriage. They drew on such allusions and argued that the unusual formulation of the disciple's love could indicate a homoerotic relationship.

In addition, the enigmatic episode of an unclothed young man in the Gospel of Mark (Mark 14:51-52) was used - as well as the 1960 discovery of the so-called "Secret Gospel of Mark" by Morton Smith. In this apocryphal fragment, Jesus teaches a young man "by night, naked under a linen garment" the "mysteries of the kingdom of God".

Some interpreters have interpreted this as a sexual initiation, which should support the thesis of a homoerotic Jesus. However, the authenticity of this text is disputed: many experts consider the Secret Gospel of Mark to be a modern interpretation.

Nevertheless, these themes helped to break a taboo: As a result, Jesus' possible approach to sexuality - whether hetero or homo - was increasingly discussed. This debate repeatedly flared up in popular culture in particular. In 1990, for example, an article entitled *"Was Jesus gay?"* appeared again in *The Advocate* magazine. (by Malcolm Boyd), which argued that the church had created an unholy rift between body and soul by denying Jesus' sexuality. Such popular contributions were widely echoed.

The biblical scholar Wayne A. Meeks pursued a further approach: he did not specifically examine Jesus' sexual orientation, but rather the symbolic androgyny in early Christian texts. In his influential essay *The Image of the Androgyne: Some Uses of a Symbol in Earliest Christianity* (1974), Meeks showed that Jesus Christ is described as an androgynous figure in various early Christian sources.

For example, some theological currents took up the ancient myth of the originally dual-sex primordial human being (Plato, rabbinical interpretation of Genesis 1:27) and saw Christ as a *"male-female" being* who unites male and female in himself.

Meeks refers, for example, to St. Paul's letter Galatians 3:28 (*"there is no longer male or female"*), which some early Christians understood to mean that in Christ the distinction between the sexes is abolished

The pictorial art of the 4th century also reflects this androgynous concept: Jesus was often depicted in iconography with long, softly flowing hair and without a beard - sometimes even with implied breasts. These *"feminine"* features were seen as a sign of his transcendent nature, which could not be pinned down to one gender. Meeks' thesis is therefore that early Christians saw Christ as a perfect new Adam who embraced both gender poles - not in the sense of lived homosexuality, but as a spiritual symbol of wholeness.

Meeks' research was taken very seriously in the *religious history school* and is still considered the standard reference for the androgyny symbol in early Christianity. Historians and theologians largely accept that such ideas existed in Gnostic and mystical texts.

However, many emphasize that this is to be understood primarily metaphorically - not as an indication that Jesus lived real sexual duality or relationships. The Church Fathers were predominantly critical of the idea of a dual-sex Adam or Christ. Augustine, for example, emphasized that Adam was by no means created as a hermaphrodite. Gaius Marius Victorinus (see below) became the exception with his interpretation of Genesis 1:27. Later theologians restricted the *"image of God"* in man to the soul, not the body, and thus implicitly rejected a physical androgyny of Christ. In modern queer theology, however, Meeks' findings are received positively: they provide a historical starting point for thinking of Jesus in a way that transcends gender - a concept that today's theologians use to question rigid gender norms in Christology.

Gaius Marius Victorinus was an early Christian theologian (4th century) whose work *Adversus Arium* contains remarkable statements on the sexuality of God. In this polemic against Arianism, Victorinus interprets the creation account to mean that God created primitive man *"masculofeminam" (male-female)*.

He quotes an apparently divergent Latin textual tradition of Genesis 1:27 ("He created him male-female") to conclude: *"...the Logos himself is both male and female"*. In other words, for Victorinus, the androgynously created Adam reflects the wholeness of the divine Logos (Christ), who unites both the masculine and the feminine in himself. This statement - *Christ as the bisexual Word of God* - was unusual for the theology of the time. However, Victorinus interpreted it mystically: before the creation of Eve, Adam was still *"both in one"* in his body; analogously, the pre-existent Logos encompassed all possibilities of being human. He was concerned with the dignity of the body as the image of God, which includes not only the soul but also gender.

Historians such as Serge Cazelais (2007) emphasized the importance of this testimony: it proves that in early Christianity there was a great deal of controversy about *simultaneous masculinity and femininity* in God and Christ.

In the current theological debate, Victorinus sometimes serves as a historical witness to the fact that the strict division into male/female is not theologically compelling. Queer theologians like to refer to him to show that the idea of a "queer" (gender-merging) Christ even has patristic precursors.

In *Gender Trouble* (1991), *the* philosopher Judith Butler did not write a theological treatise on Jesus, but she did provide the foundations of queer theory, which have also influenced Jesus research. Butler argues that *gender is not a natural, fixed identity*, but is constantly being re-created performatively through social action.

Cultural power structures determine which gender identities are *"intelligible"* - i.e. coherent and recognized - by aligning anatomical sex, social roles, sexual practice and desire.

This *"heterosexual matrix"* creates the illusion that there are only two consistent genders (man/woman) and corresponding "normal" desires.

Butler shows that these categories are *unstable* and can be subverted. She famously argues that gender is ultimately a kind of *drag performance* - an *"act"* without an original essence that can be changed through parody and repetition.

In Butler's final chapter, she calls for *"parodic practices"* in order to disrupt and thus disempower the prevailing body and gender categories.

Butler's ideas have had an enormous influence in the humanities and have been received by feminist and queer-oriented theologians. Queer theologians in particular transfer her concept to religious discourse: they question the *binary representation* of biblical figures and open up space for alternative identities. Halvor Moxnes (see below), for example, posed the question: *"Is Jesus in 'gender trouble'?"*, alluding to Butler. He adopted the idea that gender norms are time-bound and examined how Jesus broke through traditional ideals of masculinity. Butler thus provided the theoretical tools to not only see Jesus as a heteronormative, ascetic man, but to openly ask whether his behavior and self-image was not *queer* (reflecting the gender order). On the other hand, there is also resistance to Butler's approach in theological circles. Conservative voices reject a deconstruction of biblical gender images. Nevertheless, Butler's concept of performativity has permanently changed the conversation about sexuality and gender in the church and theology - away from rigid attributions of essence and towards the question of how religious identities are *made* and lived.

Robert (Bob) Goss is an American theologian and a pioneer of explicit queer Christology. In *Jesus Acted Up: A Gay and Lesbian Manifesto* (1993) and the follow-up volume *Queering Christ: Beyond Jesus Acted Up* (2002), Goss creates the image of a *"queer Christ"* who shows solidarity with the marginalized and breaks with social norms. Goss, himself openly gay and a long-time activist, compares Jesus' work with the slogan of the gay rights movement "Act Up" - Jesus *provoked* the religious authorities, broke taboos and turned social rules upside down, much like the queer activists of today.

A central element of his thesis is that Jesus also transgressed norms in his personal relationships. Goss interprets Jesus' relationship with his "favorite disciple" (John) as decidedly *homoerotic*. He argues that ancient Greek readers would have *immediately recognized* the relationship between Jesus (as the older teacher) and John (as the younger disciple) *as a love affair*.

In fact, the ideal of special love between mentor and youth (*Erastes* and *Eromenos*) existed in Greco-Roman culture. Goss sees parallels to this in the Gospel of John: John leans against Jesus' chest at the Last Supper (John 13:23), Jesus entrusts his mother to him on the cross (John 19:26) - signs of an intimate bond. Goss also draws on other queer biblical passages: for example, the Roman centurion's beloved servant (Mt 8:5-13) is interpreted by some as his homosexual partner - Jesus heals him unreservedly, which Goss reads as an affirmation of same-sex love. He also interprets Jesus' words about the "eunuchs who have emasculated themselves for the sake of the kingdom of heaven" (Mt 19:12) as praise for the queer renunciation of heteronormative marriage and family.

In the LGBTQIA+ Christian community, his books have been welcomed as a manifesto because they make it possible for gay and lesbian believers to experience Jesus in a new way. In theologically progressive circles, Goss is regarded as an important representative of liberation theology in a queer guise - he shows a Christ figure who can *actively empower the oppressed*.

At the same time, many classical exegetes and church representatives are critical of his theses. Historical-critical biblical scholars accuse Goss of reading something into the texts that is not there (*eisegesis*). For example, Ismo Dunderberg, an expert on the Gospel of John, emphasizes that *there are no corresponding terms* in Greek *for "lover"* in that relationship - the language therefore does not clearly allow for an erotic-sexual interpretation.

The conservative New Testament scholar Robert Gagnon counters Goss' interpretation of John with the fact that the evangelist used the neutral word *"agape*" ("love") and not *"eros*", which in Greek stands for sexual love.

Goss replies (and here Theodore Jennings supports him) that **"eros" does not** occur **anywhere** in the New Testament and that even marital or sensual love is called "agape" - for example in the Septuagint in the Song of Solomon.

Goss' *gay Christ theology* was also discussed from a sociological perspective: Some see it as a necessary counter-narrative to traditional power religion - Jesus as a gay man enables queer people to identify spiritually. Others see this portrayal *as pandering to modern identity politics*, which distorts the historical image of Jesus. The debates are sometimes emotional: One critic called such attempts "abysmal deconstructionism by a liberal lobby that reinterprets even the most remote thing as 'proof' of homosexuality".

Overall, Goss' theses remain a stimulating view in the mainstream of biblical scholarship, but have undoubtedly enlivened the discourse on the gender and sexuality of Jesus.

Marcella Althaus-Reid (1952-2009) was an Argentinian Protestant theologian and founder of "*Indecent Theology*". In her work *The Queer God* (2003), she outlines a liberation theology vision of God that radically incorporates sexual marginality. Althaus-Reid puts forward the provocative thesis that *God himself is "queer".* By this she means that God's essence cannot be grasped within the narrow boundaries of heteronormativity, monogamy and purity laws, but rather manifests itself preferentially in remote, declared sinful places - for example "in the pub, in the salsa club, in the slum".

Specifically, she transfers this to Jesus, the incarnate second person of the Trinity. Althaus-Reid plays with erotic and plural images: *"We could say that the Son lies with his Magdalene* ***and*** *his Lazarus*," she writes, for example.

Jesus had both female and male lovers - and one had to ask oneself *"how these three exchanged tenderness with each other"*. She thus imagines Jesus in a kind of *polyamorous love relationship* with Mary Magdalene and his beloved disciple Lazarus. This shocking idea serves a theological purpose: Althaus-Reid wants to let the *"illusory uniqueness"* of the one permitted model of love die - she speaks of the *"death of the mono lover"*. God is not a monogamous patriarch, but God's love is *exuberant, diverse and unregulated*. In the doctrine of the Trinity, she asks pointedly whether God the Father might also have someone "at his side" and whether there might not be equally unconventional relationships in heaven.

This theological view deliberately seeks to influence the boundaries of orthodox thinking: The sacred is to be intermixed with the indecent. Althaus-Reid justifies this politically: as long as God is confined to a purely white-male-heterosexual image, *women, queers and the poor* remain excluded from the full image of God. Only a *"queer God"* - one who is present in the act of love of the outcasts - would enable true liberation. She therefore calls on theologians to literally take off their *"pious underwear"* and include sexuality, including their own, in their theologizing.

Theology itself is a *sexual act*, says Althaus-Reid, and must finally shed the hypocrisy of omitting physicality.

Marcella Althaus-Reid's works triggered lively discussions in theological circles: Conservative theologians reacted with defensiveness or horror - many felt her erotic-vulgar metaphors were blasphemous and disrespectful of the holiness of Jesus. Her books *Indecent Theology* and *The Queer God* were sometimes perceived as scandalous; there were accusations that she was *"perverting"* Christianity. Progressive voices, on the other hand, celebrated Althaus-Reid as a pioneering thinker. Supporters argue that she has the courage to *truly* seek God's presence *everywhere* - especially among those who were previously excluded by the church as "unseemly".

Her core message, that *all theology* is *always also sexual politics*, resonated with political theology and feminists of liberation theology. Academically, Althaus-Reid is now recognized as an important representative of queer theology. She is seen as a continuation of Latin American liberation theology, expanded to include the dimension of sexuality and the body. Nevertheless, her style of expression remains controversial: even sympathetic colleagues admit that her style of *"consciousness-raising obscenity"* is difficult to access for many readers. In terms of content, there is debate as to whether her ideas - such as Jesus in a bisexual love triangle - are metaphorically fruitful or exaggerated. Some theologians consider this to be deliberate hyperbole that provides food for thought, but should not be understood as a historical claim about Jesus. *Sociologically*, Althaus-Reid's success reflects the need of many marginalized believers to find their place in theology: Her *"queer God"* offers identification for those who have felt excluded from conventional doctrine. At the same time, her theories are understandably met with incomprehension by believers who see religious figures primarily as role models of *purity and moral consistency*. Two worlds collide here - which Althaus-Reid intends to do in order to initiate a genuine dialog about power, sexuality and holiness.

The Norwegian New Testament scholar Halvor Moxnes combines historical Jesus research with a queer theoretical perspective. In *Putting Jesus in His Place: A Radical Vision of Household and Kingdom* (2003), he examines how Jesus was *"out of place"* in relation to social spaces and roles - in a positive sense. Moxnes, who positions himself as a gay scholar, emphasizes that he is *not claiming that Jesus was homosexual in the modern sense*, but that Jesus disrupted traditional notions of masculinity and family.

Jesus, for example, lived unmarried and childless, which was unusual in the Jewish context. Instead, he gathered a wandering brotherhood around him and proclaimed a *new family of God* in which biological kinship was of secondary importance (*"Whoever does the will of God is my brother, sister and mother*" - Mark 3:35). Moxnes interprets this as *an act of "being queer":* Jesus withdrew from the expected male role of a father of the house and defined belonging beyond heteronormative family structures. Moxnes also sees Jesus' treatment of the so-called "unmanly" of the time - eunuchs, for example - as an indication of queer solidarity. Jesus praised people *"who have made themselves eunuchs for the kingdom of heaven"* (Mt 19:12), i.e. who abstain from marriage and procreation. In the ancient world, eunuchs and celibate people were considered to be sexually *"between the stools"*; Moxnes argues that Jesus' positive mention of this group *set* him *at odds with the norms of masculinity in his society*. Similarly, he sees Jesus' behavior towards women (e.g. the abolition of their ritual impurity, the appreciation of female disciples) as a break with patriarchal role models. For Moxnes, all of this makes Jesus a figure who can be described *as "queer"* (unusual, at odds with the expected) in today's sense.

Moxnes' approach was received with interest in historical Jesus research. Reviewers emphasized his sociological perspective, even if not everyone shares his conclusions. It was particularly positively noted that Moxnes revealed his own perspective - as a gay theologian from Norway - and thus made transparent how personal experiences influence the questions posed to the text.

In fact, many exegetes agree that Jesus moved outside the social norm in some respects (unmarried wandering preacher, critical attitude towards the family). Describing this as *"queer"* resonates in liberal theological circles, as it emphasizes the reflective nature of Jesus' lifestyle. However, there are also fears that a modern term is being anachronistically applied to antiquity. Moxnes counters this by clearly defining *"queer"*: not as sexual orientation, but as *socio-cultural "otherness"*. In an article he wrote explicitly at : *"I have never claimed that Jesus was homosexual, but that he broke with established forms of masculinity, authority and power and was therefore 'queer' in relation to the ideals of masculinity of his time."*

Conservative commentators nevertheless remain sceptical: for them, *"Jesus was queer"* sounds like a provocative relabeling of Jesus that causes unnecessary confusion. Some fear that this paves the way for an inadmissibly sexualized interpretation of Jesus. Moxnes and other queer theologians counter that, on the contrary, the usual heteronormative depiction of Jesus is an abbreviation - *Jesus has been subsequently "heterosexualized"*, although the New Testament is simply silent on the subject. Moxnes notes, for example, that modern attempts to ascribe a love affair to Jesus with Mary Magdalene (including marriage and children, as popular novels claim) are ultimately an attempt to force him back into normality.

In contrast, the historical finding - Jesus as an unattached itinerant charismatic - can be accepted as "queer", as he did not fit the mold of the domestic, settled husband. Overall, Moxnes' work has helped to reposition Jesus within the *social history of the ancient Near East*. His ideas fed into discussions about ancient family structures, honor and shame culture and gender roles.

In *The Man Jesus Loved: Homoerotic Narratives from the New Testament* (2003), the American theologian Theodore Jennings presented a detailed biblical-textual argument for a homosexual dimension to Jesus' relationships. Jennings' central thesis is that *Jesus loved one particular man in particular* - and that this love can be understood as homoerotic. He draws primarily on the Gospel of John: Jennings analyzes these scenes thoroughly: the *"favorite disciple"* appears at Jesus' side at the Last Supper, on the cross among Jesus' closest relatives and as the first witness of the resurrection (John 13:23; 19:26; 20:2).

Jennings asks *why* the evangelist emphasizes this figure in this way and comes to the conclusion that a *"dangerous memory"* shines through here - namely the tradition of a special intimate relationship between Jesus and a male disciple. In Christian tradition, this memory has long been marginalized or reinterpreted, but John has not been able to silence it completely.

In a sense, Jennings reconstructs the suppressed narrative: Jesus loved this man in an extraordinary way. In Part I of his book, he interprets every occurrence of the "beloved disciple" and examines his possible identity.

Although John, the son of Zebedee, is traditionally assumed, the text remains deliberately vague - an indication for Jennings that a *delicate detail* has been preserved but concealed. Although he emphasizes that there is *no explicit evidence of a physical relationship*, he sees enough *implications in the context* to assume an intimate, possibly erotic love.

In Part II, Jennings broadens his view and looks for traces *of homoerotic motifs* in the other Gospels as well. For example, he discusses the scene of the rich young man in Mark 10:17-22, of whom it says: "Jesus looked at him and loved him" (verse 21). This unusually warm formulation - Jesus felt *love* for a strange young man - could also express more than just spiritual affection. Jennings also draws on the mention that Jesus *"loved* Lazarus" (John 11:5, 36). Although Lazarus is not called *"the disciple he loved"* in John's Gospel, he is portrayed as a close friend of Jesus, whom Jesus mourns painfully at his death. Taken together, these clues form a pattern for Jennings: Jesus was capable of deep loving affection towards men that went beyond the ordinary measure of friendship. Finally, in Part III, Jennings argues against modern "family values" ideologies and defends that the New Testament recognizes a variety of relational forms.

The fixation on marriage and biological family is a later construct, while Jesus himself lived *other forms of love and community* that challenge our current understanding of marriage/family.

Jennings' book met with great interest in theological, church and public circles. LGBT-friendly churches and groups saw it as a milestone: for the first time, a *gay image of Jesus* was created with biblical scholarship that is not limited to mere interpretation, but takes the Scriptures seriously. Jennings himself emphasizes that he is concerned with a *"gay affirmative reading"* that respects the integrity of the biblical texts and yet opens up new approaches.

Many readers felt *"encouraged and challenged"*, as one reviewer wrote: even those who were previously convinced that *"it's never in my Bible"* could benefit from Jennings' careful interpretation.

There were further echoes in academic theology: some scholars praised Jennings' fresh perspective and his thorough compilation of earlier homoerotic interpretations of Jesus.

For example, he points to a *"hidden tradition"* that stretches back to medieval mystics and repeatedly saw the Jesus-John relationship as an exemplary *spiritual friendship*.

Other exegetes, however, remain skeptical. One point of criticism is the *lack of cultural contextualization*: Jennings himself emphasizes that we should not simply transfer our modern ideas of homosexuality to antiquity. But when it comes to *"family"* and *"marriage"*, for example, critics such as Roland Boer argue that Jennings assumes modern terminology without paying enough attention to ancient differences. This creates the danger that he rightly insists on cultural differences on the one hand (in the case of homoeroticism), but on the other hand (when criticizing marriage) mixes up biblical and modern family concepts. Methodologically, Jennings' theses are on the edge of what is historically verifiable. Historians remind us that none of the canonical texts directly state that Jesus had a sexual relationship - all further interpretations remain hypothetical. Jennings acknowledges this, but emphasizes that his reading is the "*most natural*" and "most plausible" view of the texts if one reads them without bias.

Conservative theologians reject Jennings' conclusions. For them, there is no clear textual basis; they prefer to interpret Jesus' love for John as *agapeic charity* or special spiritual intimacy, not as eros. Here Gagnon's arguments are used again (see above with Goss), which want to make a linguistic distinction between friendly love and erotic love.

Jennings argues that this separation does not exist in biblical Greek. It is also argued that Jesus had analogously intimate relationships with women (Martha, Mary), which would speak more for *asexuality or polymorphism* than for a clearly homosexual orientation. Jennings would probably agree with this - he does not exclude female relationships, but only focuses on the *"man Jesus loved"*. Overall, *The Man Jesus Loved* remains a controversial work, but one that has enriched academic and ecclesiastical debate. It forced exegetes to pay attention to long-overlooked subtleties in the text and stimulated new thinking about the emotional side of the person of Jesus. At the same time, it sparked well-known culture wars in the church: when Bishop Gene Robinson (the first openly gay bishop of the Anglican Church) hinted in a sermon in 2005 that Jesus might have had homosexual tendencies, this was publicly noted. Robinson also indirectly referred to Jennings' theses. The reactions - from feature articles to pulpit statements - ranged from cautious support to challenge, for example in the form of the accusation that Jesus was being violently falsified by a *"liberal lobby"*.

This controversy shows that although Jennings' ideas have found their way into the theological debate, they are still considered unthinkable in large parts of the church.

Overall criticism and controversial debates: The theses presented on the possible homosexuality or queerness of Jesus have provoked a wide range of reactions - from enthusiasm to rejection. Theologically conservative voices reject such interpretations. Their main argument: the Bible is silent on Jesus' sexual life, so all speculation lacks a reliable basis. The fact that queer people could initially see any asexual person as "non-hetero" was not included . Attempts to portray Jesus as gay are read as a deliberate *"agenda"* that carries modern concerns into the text. Some critics even speak of blasphemy, fearing that the sacred would be desecrated if Jesus were accused of having erotic relationships. However, social discourse has shifted to a different level of discussion here, at the latest since *"marriage for all"* - the blessings of which are still pending.

They regard deviating claims - whether Jesus was intimate with Mary Magdalene or with John - as *fringe theories or fiction*. In fact, in addition to the queer interpretations discussed here, there were also *heterosexual speculations* (e.g. the idea that Jesus married Mary Magdalene or loved several women.

These also remain without evidence and are hardly supported by serious research. In the humanities and social sciences, the queer theses find productive resonance. Cultural scientists see an interesting phenomenon in this: each generation tends to incarnate Jesus in its own image - in the 1970s, the sexual revolution gave rise to images of a "sexually liberated" Jesus, while marginalized groups (women, African-Americans, queers) reimagine Jesus as *their own in* order to experience *empowerment*. Writer Gore Vidal, for example, said that Jesus was probably *"bisexual"* - after all, he was supposed to be able to represent *all* people. Similarly, Bishop Robinson said that if Jesus was fully human, he must also have had a sexuality - *"maybe he was gay?"* - These statements were hotly debated.

In scientific circles, the topic is now discussed more soberly. *From a sociological* point of view, the question is: What do these new images of Jesus mean for churches? Many LGBTQ Christians report that a *"queer Jesus"* helps them to reconcile their faith with their identity. Queer theology therefore has a pastoral dimension: it wants *queer people to find a place at the table*.

Churches that want to be inclusive are now embracing some of these ideas, for example by emphasizing that Jesus loved all people unconditionally - regardless of their gender or orientation. Traditional churches, on the other hand, run the risk of alienating themselves from seeking young believers through strict rejection of these discourses. In theological scholarship, the prevailing view is that Jesus probably lived *a sexually abstinent* life historically - but it is conceded that the Gospels leave room for interpretation here. It is conceivable that certain of Jesus' relationships were more emotionally intense than has long been portrayed. The controversies are sparked above all by the question of whether such relationships should be interpreted as *sexual*. Different hermeneutical principles clash here: some insist on the wording and the historically probable meaning (no direct reference to sexuality, therefore no sexuality), while others emphasize *the significance of what is not said* - i.e. that the concealment of sexuality can itself be an eloquent sign, as can small textual anomalies (such as a *"naked youth"* in Mark 14:51). This area of tension remains.

The theses of Meeks, Goss, Althaus-Reid, Moxnes, Jennings and others such as Kaus Dede have thus undoubtedly enriched the conversation about Jesus. They force us to reexamine our established thought patterns: Why has it been taken for granted for so long that Jesus had no sexuality? What role do our own expectations of holiness and purity play in this? Even though most scholars *do not* believe that Jesus historically engaged in homosexual acts, many recognize that *Jesus' lifestyle challenged norms* - be it in terms of gender, family or proximity to outsiders. In this respect, the "queer view" of Jesus has provided valuable impetus to question the biblical texts anew. The harsh criticism from conservative camps shows how sensitive the topic was back then, when there was no "marriage for all". Ultimately, much of *the debate is about theology and interpretation* rather than verifiable historical facts. The debate about a homosexual or queer Jesus is therefore part of a larger discourse: How do we interpret the humanity of Jesus in the light of changing social insights? Controversial positions will continue to clash here in the future - but it is precisely this dialog that keeps Christology alive and ensures that each generation reflects on Jesus anew and discovers him for itself.

71 • Did Jesus deliberately transgress the norms of his time in order to set an example?

Jesus deliberately transgressed the social and religious norms of his time in order to set an example and emphasize core values such as love, justice and mercy. Time and again, he questioned established rules - and that is what we call queer today - when they did not serve the good of the people, and criticized religious authorities for their strict adherence to the law, which was often applied without compassion.

A key example of this is his treatment of women, who were often marginalized in society at the time. While Jewish culture prescribed strict divisions between men and women, Jesus spoke openly with women, allowed them to become part of his following and honored their role in the faith. This becomes particularly clear in his encounter with the Samaritan woman at Jacob's well (John 4), in which he not only has a conversation with a woman, but also with a Samaritan woman - a member of a group that was viewed as hostile.

His treatment of sinners and social outcasts was also revolutionary. He ate with tax collectors who were despised as collaborators with the Roman occupying power, and he defended people who were cast out for moral transgressions. His reaction to the adulteress (John 8), who was to be stoned to death, is particularly impressive. Instead of confirming the law, he exposed the hypocrites among the accusers, showing that mercy and forgiveness are more important than rigid legislation.

Jesus also broke taboos in matters of religious practice. He healed the sick on the Sabbath, which was considered a violation of the law, and pointed out that the Sabbath was there for people, not the other way around (Mark 2:27). In doing so, he set an example against a religious practice that pushes people into the background and places formal rules above the well-being of believers.

His criticism of the religious elite, especially the Pharisees and scribes, was another deliberate transgression of norms. By calling them hypocrites and accusing them of burdening people with rules without living by them themselves (Matthew 23), he questioned the existing religious order and made enemies among the powerful.

Jesus deliberately transgressed social and religious norms to make it clear that the law must serve man, not the other way around. His actions were not a mere breaking of tradition, but a conscious demonstration of a new order based on love, justice and God's mercy. By challenging norms, he sent a clear signal for an ethic that is not based on rigid rules, but on the well-being of people.

72 • Would a homosexual Jesus have had less authority among his followers?

Whether a homosexual Jesus would have had less authority among his followers depends very much on the historical and social context - that of his own time or today's Christian reception.

Let's take a look at the social context in ancient Judaism: at the time of Jesus, Jewish society was strongly patriarchal and there were clear norms for marriage, gender and sexuality. Homosexuality as it is understood today - as an identity and equal marriage and partnership - did not exist in this form back then. Instead, there were primarily social and hierarchical forms of same-sex relationships, such as pederasty in the Greco-Roman world or homosexual practices that were associated with social status or dominance.

If Jesus had been openly homosexual or had emphasized same-sex love, this might have met with strong resistance, as religious authorities placed great value on purity and family norms even back then. This could have weakened his following, at least among the Jewish ruling class, who saw him as a threat anyway. At the same time, however, it could also have attracted followers from the marginalized groups with whom Jesus often came into contact anyway - such as tax collectors, prostitutes and social outcasts.

The significance of Jesus' authority for his followers must also be considered: Jesus' authority was based less on his personal sexuality than on his teaching, his miracles and his charisma. His radical stand for justice, his criticism of the existing religious structures and his ability to touch people were the main reasons for his appeal. If Jesus had had a same-sex relationship or explicitly defended queer people, this would only have underlined his message of God's unconditional love - and may even have been a sign of his closeness to socially marginalized groups.

The influence on later Christian theology must not be ignored: A queer Jesus would probably have radically changed later church history and Christian sexual morality. For centuries, the church propagated a strongly heteronormative image of the family and often regarded sexuality as sinful or at least in need of control. An open example of same-sex love in the life of Jesus would have led to Christian sexual ethics possibly developing in a more inclusive direction.

And there is still the influence on his followers: it is possible that conservative Jewish groups or later Roman converts would have found him less credible, as male dominance and heteronormative values were deeply rooted in many ancient cultures. On the other hand, the history of Christianity shows that Jesus' teachings were often received by those who were socially disadvantaged - women, slaves, the poor. A queer Jesus might therefore have received less support from the powerful, but all the more from the non-included and those who think differently.

Ultimately, Jesus' authority was not based on his sexuality or sexual orientation, but on his message: love. A queer Jesus would probably have faced more barriers in his time, but that would only have made his revolutionary message of God's love and justice all the more radical. The rejection of such an idea often reveals more about today's prejudices than about the actual historical reality.

73 • Can Jesus really be considered fully human if he is denied sexuality?

The question of whether Jesus can be regarded as fully human if he is denied sexuality touches on central Christological and anthropological concepts. Being human and sexuality are inextricably linked, because sexuality is not limited to the sexual act, but also encompasses emotions, closeness, intimacy and the ability to relate. Since human existence is characterized by physicality, sexuality in various forms is part of identity formation. If Jesus is considered a true human being, he must also have had a sexual identity, even if he lived an abstinent life or only felt attracted. To completely deny him sexuality would mean separating him from being human in an essential facet.

Church tradition has often portrayed Jesus as a chaste or sexless man, which is linked to an early Christian tendency to view sexuality as something problematic or even sinful. In monasticism in particular, chastity was seen as an ideal worth striving for, which led to the idea that Jesus must not have had any sexual impulses either. However, these assumptions are more theologically conditioned than historically proven. The Gospels make no direct statements about whether Jesus had sexual experiences or not.

Jesus' closeness to people and the issue of intimacy show that he formed emotional bonds. His friendship with Mary Magdalene, his closeness to John, *"the disciple he loved",* and his affection for outsiders make it clear that he cultivated close relationships. Whether these bonds also had an erotic or sexual dimension remains an open question, but the fact that he allowed deep closeness speaks against a completely disembodied view of man.

Chastity can be a conscious or induced decision and not synonymous with the absence of sexuality. Even if Jesus lived a celibate life, this does not mean that he had no sexuality. Many people choose to live celibate lives, but that doesn't mean they have no sexuality or desire - they just deal with it more consciously and repress it. If Jesus chose to live a life without sexual relations, he would have done so in freedom and not out of a lack of sexuality. A complete denial of sexual identity, on the other hand, would be incompatible with the doctrine of his human nature.

The idea of a *"sexuality-free" Jesus* is problematic because it reflects not only theological but also church-political interests. A disembodied depiction of Jesus was used to portray sexuality as a whole as inferior or sinful. This has far-reaching consequences for Christian sexual morality and in particular for restrictive ideas on marriage, celibacy and LGBTQIA+ issues. A theology that recognizes Jesus as fully human with a sexual identity could lead to a more liberating Christian sexual ethic that does not view physicality as antithetical to spirituality.

What is certain is that Jesus cannot be thought of as fully human if he is denied sexuality. Even if he had no sexual relationships, he was still a physical being with a need for closeness, intimacy and perhaps even temptation. The idea of a completely sexless Jesus corresponds more to an idealized image of a saint than to an authentic human existence. A reflective theology would have to recognize that Jesus was also human in his sexuality, even if we do not know exactly how he lived it.

74 • Is a queer interpretation of Jesus theologically responsible?

A queer interpretation of Jesus is theologically responsible if one takes into account that Jesus himself questioned social norms, integrated socially marginalized people and turned existing power relations upside down. Queer theology argues that Jesus can be understood not only as a historical figure, but also as a symbolic figure of liberation who transcends traditional categories of gender, sexuality and identity.

Biblical texts offer various starting points for a queer reading. Galatians 3:28 states: *"There is neither Jew nor Greek, there is neither slave nor free, there is neither male nor female; for you are all one in Christ Jesus."* This verse is often interpreted as an indication that Christ overcomes existing gender and social hierarchies. Jesus himself lived outside the classic role models of his time, remained unmarried, cultivated close emotional bonds with his disciples and showed deep compassion for marginalized social groups, including eunuchs, who were outside the binary gender order as understood at the time.

Figure13 : A theologically responsible queer representation of Jesus - open, dignified and embedded in an inclusive environment that seeks to avoid vulnerability. In queer theology, the rainbow stands for diversity, identity and the visibility of queer life.

The fact that the rainbow appears as an arch behind Jesus suggests that he is not standing in front of this diversity, but in the midst of it - it embraces him. Realized as a pencil drawing, it does not refer boldly to a political movement, but subtly brings the theme of diversity into the sacred. The diversity is also subtly reflected in the garb and posture; the image remains both spiritual and respectful. The rainbow is a biblical symbol: In the Old Testament, the rainbow is the sign of the covenant between God and all creatures after the Flood (Gen 9:13). This idea is reactivated - but now not exclusively, but inclusively: Jesus as a sign of the new covenant with everyone, including queer people. The rainbow serves as a bridge, it frames the scene like a protective roof - or like a bridge between faith and queer existence and invites us to overcome the previous distance between dogma and the reality of life. The rainbow thus recalls the original

divine covenant - and at the same time opens up this covenant to the diversity of contemporary human identities. In this way, the image points to a theologically responsible, because humanly healing, queer interpretation of Christ.

Another central argument of queer theology relates to Jesus' physical and social marginalization. The Passion narrative shows him as a figure who is exposed, mocked and robbed of his dignity - experiences that many queer people in discriminatory societies share. Theologians such as Marcella Althaus-Reid and Patrick Cheng see Jesus' suffering as a form of queer identification, as he does not fit into patriarchal notions of masculinity, but transcends gender and social boundaries through *his vulnerability*, his closeness to outsiders and his radical understanding of love.

There are also allusions in the Gospels that could support a queer perspective. In Matthew 19:12, for example, Jesus positively emphasizes that there are people who *"were born this way"* or who have chosen a non-traditional way of life *"for the sake of the kingdom of heaven"*. Some interpretations see an early recognition of non-binary identities or queer forms of existence here. His queer form of love and closeness goes beyond heteronormative ideas.

Queer theology therefore views Jesus not only as a historical figure, but also as an identity that is constantly being redefined and cannot be categorized in rigid dogmatic terms. If Christ is understood as the liberator of all people, then also as someone who transcends normative ideas of gender and sexuality. Critics argue that a queer interpretation of Jesus is a modern projection, but supporters counter that every theology is necessarily interpreted out of its time and developed further. After all, other traditional images of Jesus, such as the suffering Christ or the social reformer, were only emphasized through certain historical contexts.

From a theological perspective, a queer interpretation of Jesus is therefore not only possible, but also enriching, as it opens up new perspectives on the liberating message of the Gospel. It presents Jesus as a figure who questions rigid norms and shows new paths for identity, love and community. By understanding him as a figure who breaks through social and gender categories, queer theology invites us to see

Christ as an ally of all people who move or need to move outside of traditional norms.

75 • Which historical theologians or philosophies have dealt with the gender of Christ?

The question of the gender of Christ has a long theological tradition and has been addressed by various theologians and philosophies from different perspectives. In mysticism, feminist and queer theology in particular, but also in classical Christological debates, reflections on this issue have emerged. Here are some formative thinkers and currents that have dealt with the gender of Christ:

1 Early church fathers and the doctrine of two natures

In patristic theology, the divine-human nature of Christ was discussed above all. Gender initially played a subordinate role, as the divine nature was understood to be beyond gender categories. Nevertheless, Christ was portrayed as male, which remained deeply rooted in church tradition.

- **Gregory of Nyssa** (4th century) argued that the true image of God in man does not lie in sexual difference , but in the spiritual ability to commune with God.
- **Augustine** (4th/5th century) regarded Christ as the *"new Adam"* who, by becoming human, abolished the sin of Eve, which implies a binary gender order, but at the same time opens up the possibility of a transcendent humanity.

2. medieval mysticism: Christ as an androgynous or female being

The first theological reflections on a Christology that was not exclusively male can be found in medieval mysticism. Mystics often emphasized a maternal or androgynous side of Christ.

- **Bernard of Clairvaux** (12th century) described Christ as *a "mother"* who gives life through her suffering, a metaphor that was frequently used in mysticism.
- **Mechthild of Magdeburg** (13th century) and **Juliana of Norwich** (14th century) regarded Christ as a mother figure who

nourishes and gives life. Juliana of Norwich spoke explicitly of Jesus as the *"mother of our soul"*.

- **Johannes Tauler** (14th century) took a similar position and emphasized that Christ guides humanity with motherly care.

3 Renaissance and early modern times: Humanist reflections on gender and Christology

During the Renaissance and early modern period, the question of Christ's gender was discussed in a broader anthropological context.

- **Teresa of Ávila** (16th century) used a non-binary conception of Christ, interpreting his role as a divine lover, but also as a source of maternal care.
- **Johann Valentin Andreae** (17th century) in Christian Kabbalah and esoteric theologies regarded Christ as a unity of masculine and feminine principles, which is reminiscent of Kabbalistic ideas of God's sexuality.

4. 19th and 20th century: Feminist and queer theologies

With the development of feminist and later queer theologies, the questions of gender and Christology were posed anew.

- **Simone Weil** (20th century) regarded Christ as a being who transcends male and female categories. She described the cross as a radical divestment of gender.
- **Elisabeth Schüssler Fiorenza** (20th century), one of the best-known feminist theologians, argued that the patriarchal fixation on a male Christ obscures biblical diversity and that Christ must be reinterpreted as a symbol of liberation for all genders.
- **Marcella Althaus-Reid** (20th century), a representative of queer theology, deconstructs the male image of Christ and asks whether Christ cannot also be thought of as a queer, non-binary or gender-transcending figure.

5th present: Intersectional and queer perspectives on the gender of Christ

In contemporary theology, the gender of Christ is viewed from an intersectional perspective. Theologians such as Tat-siong Benny Liew argue that the embodiment of Christ transcends traditional gender categories. Christology is increasingly thought of as an inclusive space in which trans and non-binary people can rediscover their identity in Christ.

The discussion about the gender and orientation of Christ therefore has a long tradition, ranging from early metaphysical debates about divine nature to modern queer theologies. While classical theologians usually assumed a binary gender model, mysticism already offered alternative interpretations that described Christ as maternal, androgynous or gender transgressive. With feminist and queer theology, this perspective was further developed in order to interpret Christ as a universal, cross-gender *figure of liberation*.

---

c) Church and social reactions

---

76 • *Is a fear-free discussion about Jesus' sexuality possible in the church?*

A fear-free discussion about Jesus' sexuality in the church is currently only possible to a limited extent, as the topic is met with silence by many believers and church authorities. Traditionally, Jesus' sexuality is either not discussed or it is implicitly assumed that he lived a celibate life. This is partly due to the theological emphasis on his divine nature and partly due to the historical development of the church's understanding of sexuality, which often only associates sexuality with sin or impurity. At the same time, there are theological voices calling for a more open discussion of the question in order to obtain a more complete picture of Jesus as a human being (e.g. William E. Phipps, *The Sexuality of Jesus*, 1973). In order for such a discussion to take place in a parish without fear, the local clergy must create several conditions:

An open space for discourse: It must be made clear from the outset that questions about Jesus' sexuality are not considered heresy or blasphemy, but legitimate theological reflection. This requires a culture of trust in which questions can be asked without fear of moral condemnation.

Biblical and theological education: Many questions arise from ignorance or unreflected traditions. The clergyman should analyze the biblical texts and historical sources openly in order to allow for different interpretations - even those that deviate from the church mainstream.

Decoupling sexuality and guilt: The idea that sexuality is fundamentally problematic or sinful prevents an objective discussion. A theological basis that understands sexuality as a positive and God-given part of being human could help to reduce fears. Theologians such as Eugene F. Rogers (*Sexuality and the Christian Body*, 1999), for example, emphasize that sexuality is an integral part of being human and not automatically deficient.

Protection from pressure within the church: clergy who facilitate such discussions run the risk of being criticized by conservative voices. They therefore need the backing of progressive theological networks or open-minded bishops who support a differentiated debate.

A pastoral attitude instead of dogmatic control: The discussion should not be conducted with ready-made answers, but with an honest search movement that is inspired by Jesus' own openness to people's questions and doubts.

If these conditions are met, a fearless discussion of Jesus' sexuality could be possible - as a serious theological reflection on Jesus' humanity and its significance for Christian anthropology.

77 • What fears lie behind the church's rejection of Jesus' homosexual identity?

The church's rejection of Jesus' homosexual identity is deeply rooted in various fears that have theological as well as institutional and social dimensions. One of the central fears is the concern about the immutability of church doctrine. If Jesus were seen as homosexual, the church would have to admit that its centuries-old rejection of sexuality may be based on false assumptions. This would not only call into question the entire sexual morality of the Church, but would also weaken the Church's authority as the guardian of divine truth.

Another fear concerns the traditional image of Jesus as a perfect role model for a life pleasing to God. In church teaching, he is often portrayed as genderless or above sexuality in order to distance him as a moral leader from any form of *'desire'*. The idea that Jesus might have had a queer identity, would challenge this image and open up a new, more physical and human perspective on his person. Many churches fear that such an interpretation could undermine their spiritual authority over sexual morality.

Another fear is the political dimension. The rejection of Jesus' homosexual identity is also a rejection of social developments that are often seen as "moral decay" by conservative churches. In many countries, LGBTQIA+ rights have become a symbol of progress and social change. The church fears that recognizing homosexual identity - especially in Jesus himself - could be seen as a capitulation to a supposed "zeitgeist" and thus cause the church to lose stability and credibility as an institution.

But these fears are not insurmountable. The Church could recognize that its strength lies not in the rigidity of its teachings, but in its capacity for spiritual renewal and a return to the essentials: the message of love and acceptance that Jesus himself embodied. If Jesus is understood as a figure of radical inclusion and love, then his sexual identity becomes secondary to his central mission: to encourage people to live in love, compassion and justice.

An open approach to the question of Jesus' sexuality need not undermine the authority of the church, but can help it to see itself as a vibrant, dynamic community focused on the core values of the gospel. Instead of fearing a loss of control, the church could see itself as a *place of liberation and genuine dialog* where people are *welcome* regardless of their identity, gender or lifestyle.

This new state of being could be a church that is no longer characterized by fear, but by trust. Trust that divine truth is not trapped in rigid norms, but unfolds in the living experience of love and acceptance. A church that frees itself from the burden of outdated dogma could be a safe place not only for LGBTQIA+ people, but for all who long for a spiritual home where they are accepted as whole human beings.

Seen in this light, the fear of Jesus' homosexual identity could turn out to be unfounded. For if Jesus - as many Christians believe - is the perfect revelation of divine love, then nothing about his identity, regardless of its nature, can diminish this love. Rather, a more open, honest discussion of this question could help the church to return to the essentials: to judge people not by their identity or sexuality, but by the love they live.

This fear of the church can and must change - towards an attitude of responsible care that does not exclude, but protects. It can even become the right of its faithful, for example by making the principles of the Equal Treatment Act the living credo of an inclusive church. A church that is not afraid of the transformation of its doctrine, but recognizes in change itself the place where God's salvation is revealed anew.

In Germany, the General Equal Treatment Act (AGG) protects against discrimination in nine key areas. The Catholic Church is not subject to parts of the General Equal Treatment Act (AGG) and can therefore shape its own teachings, moral concepts and personnel decisions independently of state requirements - at least as long as this does not violate fundamental human rights or criminal law.

Even if the Catholic Church is partly legally exempt from this right to self-determination, each of these areas of protection can be reflected upon theologically and applied to church thinking and action.

In the spirit of the Gospel, which testifies to God's unconditional care for all people, the Church is committed to shaping its teaching, practice and language in a way that does not exclude or demean anyone on the basis of the following characteristics:

1. **Gender:** Because God created man and woman, non-binary and trans people in the image of God (Gen 1:27), no person may be excluded from church participation, leadership or access to the sacraments on the basis of their gender.
2. **Ethnic origin**: The Church confesses that in Christ there is *"no longer Greek or Jew"* (Gal 3:28). Origin, skin color or cultural background must not be a reason for different esteem or representation - neither in worship nor in ministry.

3. **Religion or worldview:** The church respects the conscience of every person. The following also applies within the church: divergent positions, spiritual search movements and interreligious references must not be discredited, but should be understood as an impulse for a common search for truth.
4. **Disability:** A person is no less an image of God because they are physically, emotionally or mentally impaired. The church does not recognize disability as a deficit, but as part of the diversity of creation and is committed to breaking down barriers - spatially, linguistically, liturgically.
5. **Age:** Dignity and participation are not a question of age. Children, young people and the elderly each contribute their own perspective to the spiritual depth of the church and must not be marginalized or instrumentalized.
6. **Sexual identity:** The ability to love is a divine gift. The church must not allow discrimination or judgment of people based on their sexual orientation. Every person has the right to blessing, fellowship and companionship.
7. **Gender identity:** Trans*, inter* and non-binary people are not theological debates, but living testimonies to the diversity of creation. Their existence calls for a church that no longer thinks in binary categories - and invites a new language, deeper justice and genuine recognition.
8. **Social status:** God does not favor the rich, but takes the side of the poor. The church must not tolerate social stratification in liturgy, educational access or representation. Every person, regardless of income or education, is church.
9. **Marital status**: Whether single, divorced, in a same-sex partnership or in a patchwork family - the Gospel knows no "ideal biography". The church is called to bless relationships, not to judge them, and to accompany people, not to sort them out.

Overall: *The Church affirms its vocation to be a sign of God's universal love. Discrimination in theological doctrine, liturgical practice or church* *structure contradicts this calling. The protection of human dignity and the equality of all the baptized are theological pillars, not an option.*

78 • Is the rejection of a queer interpretation of Jesus an expression of fear of one's own transformation?

Some people are afraid to confront the uncertainties that queer theology entails. A queer interpretation of Jesus forces us to question long-held teachings on gender and sexuality and possibly acknowledge that previous church dogmas are not timeless, but culturally shaped and also outdated. This would mean that faith and theology are not fixed, but dynamic - an idea that has a changeable effect on many believers.

In addition, a queer reading of Jesus has not only theological but also personal consequences. Those who embrace it may have to rethink their own attitudes to gender and sexuality, come to terms with social norms and perhaps even question their own identity . Just as a queer person has to do when socializing and consolidating their identity. Especially for people who have been socialized in a conservative religious environment, this can be perceived as a challenge or even a threat to their own self-perception.

The rejection of a queer interpretation of Jesus may therefore have less to do with theological stringency than with an inner resistance to change. Transformation means letting go of old certainties and allowing new perspectives. Those who refuse to do so are often not only defending a theological position, but also a world order that seems to offer stability through rigid gender and sexuality norms. But if Christianity really is a faith of love, liberation and justice, then it should not be characterized by fear of change, but by an openness to recognize God's work in many different ways - including in a queer reading of Jesus.

Figure14 : A circle of diverse people around a radiant center, surmounted by a gentle rainbow and a light source in the shape of a cross - a symbol of an inviting, queer-open spirituality.

The symbol can be interpreted as pointing the way to a gender-neutral and inclusive church, which becomes central in the course of women in priestly ministries. This is because the source of light in the middle of the picture can be interpreted as a symbol of a divine calling that is not bound to gender. It radiates evenly in all directions, penetrates every figure in the circle and makes it clear that vocation comes from the spirit - not from status, not from the body. When women stand in this light, it is not an exception, but their equal participation in mission and leadership. The source of light thus becomes a quiet but clear indication: that which enables a priestly vocation is inherent in every person - even in women or people with a same-sex orientation. The light thus becomes the leading sign of a diverse church that does not ask: "Who may?", but recognizes: "To whom does the gospel shine in the heart?"

79 • Can a homosexual interpretation of Jesus make Christianity more attractive?

A homosexual interpretation of Jesus could make Christianity more attractive to many people, especially those who feel excluded or unrepresented by traditional church teachings. Such a perspective could emphasize the inclusivity of the Christian faith, challenge historically rooted mechanisms of exclusion and enable new theological interpretations based on love, justice and liberation.

Inclusivity and identification

Many people have become alienated from the church due to conservative church positions on sexuality. If Jesus is understood as a figure who was himself outside the heteronormative order or who could at least embody queer experiences and identities, queer people could identify more strongly with him. This interpretation can be found in works such as Patrick Cheng's *"Radical Love: An Introduction to Queer Theology*" (2011), in which Jesus is seen as the embodiment of radical, queer love that challenges existing norms.

Questioning traditional gender and sexuality norms

The portrayal of Jesus as homosexual or queer would not only be a modern projection, but could also be justified from a historical and theological perspective. Such an interpretation could help to question rigid gender roles and sexuality norms in the church and create space for diverse identities.

A liberation theology perspective

A homosexual or queer interpretation of Jesus could also be seen in the context of liberation theology. Just as Jesus identified with the marginalized of his time, a queer Jesus could be seen as a symbol of solidarity with LGBTQIA+ people who are still discriminated against today.

Theologians such as Marcella Althaus-Reid ("*Indecent Theology*", 2000) argue that a *"decent"*, heteronormative theology must be questioned in order to make the liberating message of Jesus tangible for all people.

Attractiveness for progressive and searching believers

Many people today are looking for a faith that confirms their identity and does not exclude them. A queer interpretation of Jesus could make Christianity more attractive to those who cannot identify with traditional interpretations. This can also be seen in the growing number of LGBTQIA+-affirming congregations and church reform movements such as *#OutInChurch*.

A homosexual or queer interpretation of Jesus must therefore not be understood as a dogmatic statement, but as a theological possibility that helps to make Christianity more open and relevant for today. It could help to break down walls, open up new perspectives on the love of Jesus and strengthen Christianity as a religion of radical acceptance and liberation.

d) Extended contexts

80 • *What arguments does Klaus Dede use for his thesis that Jesus was gay or queer?*

In his book *Jesus - gay?*, Klaus Dede argues that Jesus could have been homosexual, drawing on biblical references, historical contexts and a critical analysis of church dogma and social norms. A central argument is the interpretation of certain biblical passages. For example, Dede refers to the passage in which a disciple lay "in Jesus' lap". He claims that this passage was deliberately mistranslated by Martin Luther in order to suppress certain interpretations and hide a possible homoerotic relationship.

Another argument relates to the cultural context in which Jesus lived. Dede points out that Jesus worked in the border region between Jewish and Greek culture. In the Greek world, same-sex love was far less stigmatized than in the Jewish tradition. Jesus must have been familiar with this freer sexual morality, which Dede sees as an indication of a possible openness or even personal involvement in same-sex relationships.

A central point of his argument is the criticism of the centuries-long suppression of sexuality by the Christian churches. Dede sees this as a strategic attempt by the church to gain power over the faithful and restrict their self-determination - especially in matters of sexuality. He points out that the church often established dogmatic rules that had little to do with the original message of Jesus. This strict sexual morality leads to hypocrisy and emotional conflicts, especially for homosexual people, who often feel marginalized in the church.

Dede also emphasizes that Jesus is described in the Gospels as an empathetic and loving person who cultivated close and emotional relationships with his disciples, which in Dede's eyes could be interpreted as an indication of a particularly intimate connection. Dede sees the fact that this possibility is vehemently rejected in church tradition as an indication that the church cannot deal with the idea of a self-determined and possibly homosexual Jesus. He sees the aggressive rejection of this thesis by conservative theologians at the time as evidence that it was still a social taboo at the time that urgently needed to be questioned.

Finally, Dede portrays Jesus as an advocate of self-determination. In the Gospels, Jesus consistently stands up for the weak, marginalized and persecuted - groups to which homosexual people have partially belonged for centuries. From this perspective, it would only be logical for him to assume that Jesus was either homosexual himself or at least had a tolerant attitude towards same-sex love. Ultimately, Dede is not interested in proving an incontrovertible historical truth, but in initiating a debate about sexuality, the church and dogma. He pleads for a society in which individual sexual identity is no longer taboo and everyone can live their sexuality freely and without ecclesiastical or social repression.

81 • How was the possible homosexuality of Pope Julius III (16th century) established?

The possible homosexuality of Pope Julius III (1487-1555) was primarily linked to his close and controversial relationship with Innocenzo Ciocchi del Monte, a young man whom he brought up from humble beginnings and promoted to high ecclesiastical office unusually quickly.

Julius III, who was Pope from 1550 to 1555, took Innocenzo Ciocchi del Monte into his care as a young man. According to reports, he met him as a street urchin in Parma, took him into his family and later catapulted him into the ecclesiastical hierarchy. Innocenzo was of humble origins and had no theological or academic training to speak of. Nevertheless, he was adopted by Julius III and received exceptional support. His rapid rise in the Church was particularly striking, as despite his lack of qualifications, he was elevated to cardinal by Julius III, a move that attracted considerable criticism from the Curia. The decision was not only perceived as unusual, but also scandalous, as Innocenzo had no theological merits whatsoever. His privileged position in the Vatican, his luxurious life and his constant proximity to the Pope led to widespread rumors about the nature of their relationship.

Even contemporaries speculated about the close connection between Julius III and Innocenzo Ciocchi del Monte. Critics of the Pope argued that the extraordinary privileges enjoyed by Innocenzo could not be explained by family ties or political motives alone. Protestant circles in particular accused the relationship of being homoerotic. Various chroniclers and diplomats, including the Venetian envoy Matteo Dandolo in particular, described the pope's dependence on Innocenzo as conspicuous and questionable. Dandolo wrote, for example, that Julius III "could do nothing without Innocenzo" and that their relationship had been "exaggerated". Such statements, combined with the fact that Innocenzo played a key role in Julius' court, strengthened the rumors about a possible sexual dimension to their relationship.

Whether it was actually a homosexual relationship remains unclear. There is no direct evidence of a sexual relationship between Julius III and Innocenzo Ciocchi del Monte, only numerous references to exceptionally preferential treatment, a close emotional bond and political favors. Historians remain cautious on this issue, as many sources come from opponents of the pope who may have had an interest in defaming him. At the same time, queer theology and modern historiography argue that queer identities have often been obscured or tabooed in history, so a lack of explicit evidence does not necessarily mean that no such relationship existed.

After the death of Julius III, Innocenzo Ciocchi del Monte quickly fell out of favor and lost his political and ecclesiastical importance. He was involved in several scandals, including sexual assaults on young men, which further damaged his credibility and possibly retrospectively fueled speculation about his relationship with the late pope.

To summarize, the speculation about Pope Julius III's possible homosexuality is thus based on the fact that he not only adopted a young man from a lowly background, but also enabled him to pursue an unprecedented career in the Vatican. The Pope's emotional closeness to Innocenzo was perceived by contemporaries as excessive and inappropriate, especially as Innocenzo had no ecclesiastical or academic qualifications. Whether Julius III was actually homosexual or whether it was merely a case of exaggerated protection ultimately remains unclear. Nevertheless, his relationship with Innocenzo Ciocchi del Monte remains one of the most controversial chapters in papal history.

82 • Is there any evidence or indication that Paul may have been homosexual?

There is no clear evidence that Paul was homosexual, but some interpretations of his writings and biographical references have led to speculation.

Paul's celibacy: In his letters, Paul repeatedly emphasizes his decision to remain unmarried (1 Corinthians 7:7-8). He recommends singleness as the ideal and seems to show little interest in a heterosexual relationship. Some interpret this as a possible indication of hidden homosexuality, while others see it more as an expression of his ascetic lifestyle or his expectation of the imminent end of the world.

The *"thorn in the flesh"*: In 2 Corinthians 12:7, Paul speaks of a *"thorn in the flesh"*, a persistent burden or temptation that he cannot get rid of. There are many theories as to what he meant by this - physical illness, spiritual temptations or moral struggles. Some speculate that this could be a coded reference to homoerotic tendencies, which he may have perceived as a "weakness" in the context of his Judeo-Christian ethics.

His relationship with male companions: Paul had close relationships with younger men such as Timothy and Titus, to whom he wrote personal letters and whom he referred to as his *"beloved children"*. However, such formulations are not uncommon in the Jewish-Hellenistic culture of the time and do not allow any clear conclusions to be drawn.

His rejection of homosexuality: Paul is critical of same-sex relationships in Romans 1:26-27 and 1 Corinthians 6:9. Some argue that a particularly strict rejection could be an indication that he himself struggled with such inclinations. However, this could also simply reflect the usual moral standards of his time.

Overall, then, there is no historical or textual evidence to suggest that Paul was homosexual. The speculation is based more on indirect allusions, his lifestyle and the cultural contexts in which he wrote.

83 • Was Jesus a real man or not a real man?

In his book *"Christus (m/f/d). A Gender History"*, church historian Anselm Schubert examines how the gender of Jesus Christ has been perceived and portrayed differently throughout history. He shows that although Jesus historically lived as a man, the attributions of his gender varied depending on the era. In antiquity, perfect masculinity was seen as the ideal, combined with asexuality and self-control. Gender was seen as gradual, with women considered immature and men mature forms of manhood. Jesus was therefore naturally regarded as a man.

In the Middle Ages, however, Christ was also ascribed female attributes. In mystical theology, he was depicted as a nurturing mother, with his side wound symbolically interpreted as the uterus . These ideas served the purpose of identification and reflected the gender concepts of the time.

With the Enlightenment and the development of a modern understanding of gender, Christ was increasingly portrayed as a hyper-masculine figure in order to emphasize patriarchal ideals. This shows that the perception of Jesus' gender was always in the context of the respective cultural and social ideas.

Historically, Jesus was a man, but his portrayal varied depending on the era and theological interpretation. In the Middle Ages, for example, he was described in mysticism not only as a male figure, but also with female characteristics. Theologians such as Julian of Norwich saw him as a nurturing mother, and his side wound was symbolically compared to a womb. In antiquity, on the other hand, masculinity was seen as something that could be perfected through asceticism and self-control. In this sense, Jesus was seen as perfect, which seemed to elevate him above conventional gender roles. The modern understanding of diversity suggests that gender need not be thought of in a strictly binary way. From this perspective, Jesus could be seen as a figure who does not fit neatly into today's male-female scheme. In theology in particular, it is emphasized that he is thought of as a redeemer for all people regardless of gender, which suggests an overarching, cross-gender dimension. In the Bible, Jesus himself did not specifically comment on his gender identity, and his interpretation was always shaped by the respective social ideas. From today's perspective, he could therefore be understood as a figure who cannot be pinned down to a rigid gender attribution, but rather unites aspects of different gender concepts in himself, which today is called *being queer*.

Chapter 7: Queer Community: Perspectives in Church and Theology through LGBTQIA+

The relationship between the queer community and the church is characterized by perspectives, and also by processes of change. While many Christian ethics have long been in dialog for full recognition of LGBTQIA+ people, there is increasing pressure to promote these attitudes. A central aspect of this debate is the question of whether the churches' treatment of queer people is compatible with Jesus' teachings of love and tolerance. If Christ himself placed the marginalized and those who think differently at the center of his message, how can the non-inclusion of LGBTQIA+ people be justified?

Organizations such as #OutInChurch actively campaign for equal rights for queer people within the Catholic Church and criticize existing discrimination in the church. They call for a change in church structures and point to the deep-rooted homophobia that is anchored in church teachings and power structures. But how can homophobia be reduced within the church, especially among clergy who have often been socialized in an environment that rejects queer identities?

From a theological perspective, there are numerous biblical passages that could speak in favor of accepting homosexual relationships. At the same time, queer interpretations of Jesus represent a discussion of perspectives for conservative believers. Could an openly queer-friendly understanding of Jesus contribute to overcoming the church's claims to authority? And what role does the #OutInChurch movement, which aims to change the church from within, play in this?

In addition to theological questions, there are also social discussions: Should a queer person leave the church if they find it deforming, or should they work for change - even if this entails resignation? Queer theology argues that "queer" not only describes a sexual identity, but is also a form of resistance against rigid and oppressive systems. In this sense, the question arises as to whether the term "queer" could even be considered divine and spiritual.

Finally, it is also worth taking a look at historical figures: Why, for example, is the Pope considered a possible queer person? And which historical figures within the church may have been misunderstood or deliberately made invisible because of their sexual orientation? The coming out process, as described by Eli Coleman, offers a psychological perspective on the challenges faced by queer people - both in a personal and ecclesial context.

The central question remains: What can a church look like that not only includes LGBTQIA+ people, but actively values and welcomes them? And what structural reforms are needed to fully include queer believers not only in theological discussions, but also in everyday church life, e.g. to bless their marriages? An LGBTQIA+-friendly church would not only be a design for the present, but also a consistent step towards a church that takes its own values of love and acceptance seriously.

a) Theological and ecclesiastical perspectives

84 • Is the churches' treatment of LGBTQIA+ people compatible with Jesus' teachings of love and tolerance?

The churches' approach to LGBTQIA+ people is a complex and controversial topic, with some significant differences between individual churches and Christian communities. Looking at Jesus' central messages of love, tolerance and unconditional charity, it is clear that he repeatedly advocated empathy, acceptance and respect for all people, especially those who were marginalized or rejected by society. In Mark 12:31, for example, Jesus' teaching is summarized with the words: *"You shall love your neighbour as yourself."* In addition, Jesus repeatedly showed solidarity with marginalized groups and resolutely opposed exclusion, prejudice and condemnation of others, for example in the story of the adulteress in the Gospel of John (John 8:7), in which he declared: *"Let him who is without sin among you cast the first stone."*

At the same time, however, the reality in many churches today does not always correspond to these central principles of Jesus. Conservative churches in particular often take a negative stance towards LGBTQIA+ people and often refer to individual biblical passages, such as Genesis 18:22 in the Old Testament or Romans 1:26-27 in the New Testament. Such positions often lead to LGBTQIA+ people being marginalized, discriminated against or rejected in their lifestyle.

In contrast, there are increasingly liberal or progressive churches and congregations that take a different stance. They argue that Jesus' message of unconditional love and mercy means accepting and including all people - regardless of their sexual orientation or gender identity. For them, it is self-evident that discrimination or even condemnation based on sexual orientation and identity is incompatible with the Christian commandment to love one's neighbor.

From an ethical-theological perspective, which places Jesus' focus on love, mercy and inclusion at the center, a dismissive and exclusionary attitude towards LGBTQIA+ people *hardly* seems compatible with Jesus' original message. Many theologians today hold the view that Jesus' core teaching of comprehensive love should not be limited or relativized by individual, selectively interpreted biblical passages.

In summary, it can be said that Jesus' teaching of love and tolerance clearly speaks in favor of treating LGBTQIA+ people with acceptance, respect and unconditional love. However, the actual treatment of these people by many churches does not always reflect this original message of Jesus, which in turn leads to demands and critical discussions within the church. A loving, respectful and inclusive approach to LGBTQIA+ people would therefore clearly be in line with Jesus' core messages of love, tolerance and charity.

85 • Which biblical passages could speak in favor of accepting homosexual relationships?

There are several biblical passages that could speak in favor of a more open or at least more tolerant attitude towards homosexual relationships. These texts are often used by theologians and proponents of inclusive Christian theology to show that the Bible does not speak exclusively against same-sex love.

The love between David and Jonathan: The close relationship between King David and Jonathan, the son of Saul, is described in a way that is interpreted by many as more than just a friendship. In 2 Samuel 1:26, after Jonathan's death, David says: *"I am sorry for you, my brother Jonathan; you were very dear to me. Your love was more wonderful to me than the love of a woman."* These words point to a deep emotional and possibly also physical closeness that could go beyond mere friendship.

The story of Ruth and Naomi: Ruth swears lifelong loyalty to her mother-in-law Naomi with the words: *"Where you go, I will go; where you stay, I will stay. Your people are my people, and your God is my God. Where you die, there I will die; there I will be buried."* (Ruth 1:16-17). This passage is often interpreted as an example of a deep love and bond between two women. Some see it as a parallel to same-sex relationships, as Ruth remains at Naomi's side not only out of familial duty, but out of deep emotional commitment.

The "beloved disciple" and Jesus: In the Gospel of John, we are repeatedly told of a disciple who is referred to as *"the disciple whom Jesus loved"*. In John 13:23-25 it says: *"But one of his disciples, whom Jesus loved, was reclining at Jesus' breast."* This intimate gesture could indicate that Jesus and this disciple had a special emotional bond. While traditional Christian theology interprets this as purely platonic brotherly love, some theologians argue that this relationship could contain homoerotic elements.

The Roman centurion and his servant: In this story, a Roman centurion asks Jesus to heal his seriously ill *"servant"*. The Greek word *"pais"*, which is used here for *"servant"*, can also mean *"beloved"* or *"young man"*. In Roman-Greek culture, same-sex relationships between a patron (patronizer) and his pais were not uncommon. Jesus heals the centurion's servant without any moral condemnation, which some interpret as a sign of his acceptance of same-sex love.

Isaiah 56:3-5 - Acceptance of *"eunuchs"*: Eunuchs in ancient society were often men who did not live in traditional heterosexual marriages and are sometimes compared to LGBTQIA+ people. In Isaiah 56:3-5, God explicitly states that eunuchs also have a place in his community: *"And let not the stranger who has turned to the LORD say, 'The LORD will surely cut me off from his people. And let not the one who is cut off say, 'Behold, I am a dry tree. For thus says the LORD: "To the offspring who keep my Sabbaths and choose what pleases me and hold fast to my covenant, to them I will give a memorial place in my house and within my walls, and a name better than sons and daughters."* This passage emphasizes that even people who do not fit into traditional gender and family norms are valuable in God's eyes.

Galatians 3:28 - Equality of all people in Christ: Paul writes: *"There is neither Jew nor Greek, there is neither slave nor free, there is neither male nor female; for you are all one in Christ Jesus."* This principle of equality and unity could be used as a basis for the acceptance of all people regardless of their sexual orientation.

While the Bible also describes homosexual acts differently in some places, which today are evaluated in a historical context, there are also numerous passages that speak for an inclusive and accepting attitude towards same-sex love. Jesus' behavior in particular - his refusal to condemn people, his closeness to outsiders and his emphasis on love above legal regulations - leaves room for a progressive interpretation.

86 • *Could an openly queer-friendly understanding of Jesus help to overcome the church's claims to authority? What role does #OutinChurch play in this?*

An openly queer-friendly understanding of Jesus could contribute to overcoming the church's claims to authority, as it challenges traditional power structures based on dogmatic sexual norms. The *#OutInChurch* movement plays a central role in this by not only fighting for the recognition of queer people in the church, but also by challenging the church's magisterium to rethink its interpretative authority over sexual morality.

1. the connection between authority and sexual morality

In many traditions, church authority is based on the idea that morality and truth are administered and proclaimed by the church. In the Catholic Church in particular, the Magisterium has a monopoly on the interpretation of scripture and moral norms, especially in matters of sexuality. A queer-friendly interpretation of Jesus challenges this authority because it shows that Christian morality does not necessarily have to be based on prohibitions and restrictions, but on love, justice and acceptance. If Jesus is understood as a figure who broke down existing norms and accepted people regardless of social categories, then it becomes clear that the church does not have the right to judge people's dignity and way of life.

2 A queer Jesus as an opportunity for church power structures

If Jesus is interpreted as queer-friendly or even as a queer figure himself, then this creates a model of faith and spirituality that no longer depends on obedience to an authoritarian institution, but on individual freedom and ethical reflection. A queer-inclusive Christianity could break the fixation on gender, sexuality and traditional role models and turn the church into a community of equality. This would mean that authority would no longer be proclaimed centrally from above, but would emerge in a shared, open dialog.

3. the role of *#OutInChurch*

The *#OutInChurch* initiative has initiated precisely this process. It consists of queer church employees who have made their sexual orientation and identity public in order to fight for a church free of discrimination. They are calling for a change in church employment law, which has previously disadvantaged queer people or even excluded them from church employment. But their influence extends beyond employment law - they are calling for a fundamental reassessment of the church's sexual morals and a rejection of old dogmas.

Through their public visibility, they show that queer people are not on the fringes of the church, but have long been part of it. In doing so, they are taking away the institution's authority to interpret who is "orthodox" and who is not. Their call for an inclusive church corresponds to the biblical ideal of a community in which no one is excluded on the basis of identity or lifestyle.

4. consequences for ecclesiastical authority

If a queer-friendly understanding of Jesus prevails, then it becomes clear that the church can no longer derive its legitimacy from moral control. Instead, it would have to base its authority on values such as compassion, justice and personal conscience. In such a church, queer people would not only have a place, but also a voice - and they would be able to help shape things instead of having to subordinate themselves to moral guidelines.

An openly queer-friendly understanding of Jesus could therefore fundamentally change the idea of church authority. The fixation on sexual morality as an instrument of power would be replaced by an ethic of love and justice. *#OutInChurch* is an important catalyst for this change, in that the movement not only fights for recognition, but also shows that the church can only renew itself and survive if it breaks free from rigid claims to authority and becomes a genuine community of dialog and acceptance.

87 • Why might the term "queer" be considered divine?

Queerness can be seen as divine because it stands for transgression, diversity, transformation and radical love - characteristics that can be found in many theological concepts. God is described in the Bible as transcendent, as a being who cannot be pinned down to human categories. In Genesis 3:14, God reveals himself as *"I am who I am"*, a formulation that defies a fixed definition and suggests openness and fluidity of identity.

The creation narrative also points in this direction. In Genesis 1:27, it says: *"God created man in his own image, male and female he created them."* This could indicate that God's image carries gender diversity within it or is even beyond it. Nature reflects this by not only having binary genders, but also numerous intermediate forms and fluidities - a sign of divine creativity and diversity.

Jesus himself can be interpreted as a queer figure, as he broke through social norms and challenged existing power structures. He transcended gender roles, surrounded himself with the marginalized and preached radical inclusion. The crucifixion and resurrection in particular stand for a divine transformation that transcends fixed identity boundaries.

The Trinity also demonstrates a divine queerness by dissolving traditional notions of identity. God is at the same time Father, Son and Holy Spirit - a form of existence that bears a diversity of relationships and shows that divine existence is not limited to a single form.

After all, the liberating power of God is on the side of the marginalized. In Isaiah 43:19, God says: *"Behold, I am working a new thing! Now it is sprouting up, do you not recognize it?"* This promise of a new reality can be understood as an invitation to question rigid social structures and create space for queer openness. God is not a normative judge, but a liberator, re-creator and ally of all identities that move outside of narrow social norms.

b) Critical analysis of the church's attitude

88 • *How does the #OutInChurch initiative address discrimination against LGBTQIA+ people in the Catholic Church?*

The #OutInChurch initiative campaigns against the systematic discrimination of LGBTQIA+ people within the Catholic Church and calls for a fundamental reform of church structures and teachings. Their central criticism is directed at the church's employment law, which has so far made it possible to discriminate against or even dismiss non-heterosexual people. It was particularly problematic that employees who were in same-sex marriages or revealed their sexual identity had to expect consequences under employment law - a practice that *#OutInChurch* considers to be incompatible with the Christian message of love and human dignity.

The initiative also criticizes the fact that Catholic moral teaching continues to classify queer people as *"disordered"*. This attitude has serious psychological and social consequences, as it creates a climate of fear, silence and invisibility. Many LGBTQIA+ Catholics feel forced to hide their identity in order to be able to work in church structures.

With their public campaign and the accompanying media documentary *"As God created us"*, members of *#OutInChurch* have deliberately broken their silence and made themselves public as queer believers in the Catholic Church. Their aim is not only to draw attention to individual discrimination, but also to initiate far-reaching theological and institutional reform.

One of the movement's first successes was the debate on church employment law, which has since been partially reformed so that same-sex marriage or a non-heteronormative identity alone can no longer be grounds for dismissal. Nevertheless, the church's theological stance towards LGBTQIA+ people remains unchanged, and *#OutInChurch* continues to campaign for full recognition and equal rights for queer people in church structures and doctrine. Their central demands are:

Abolition of discrimination in church labor law:

- No one may be dismissed or discriminated against on the basis of their sexual orientation or gender identity.
- Same-sex marriages or queer identities must not be grounds for exclusion from church professions or ministries.
- Official recognition of sexual and gender diversity as part of creation:
- The church should no longer judge LGBTQIA+ identities as "disordered" or "sin", but as natural and equal forms of expression of human existence.
- Theological texts and church teachings must be revised accordingly.

Blessing of queer couples and full equality in sacraments:

- The church should officially bless and recognize same-sex partnerships.
- Queer people must be able to participate equally in all areas of church life, including ordained ministries.

Visibility and protection of queer people in the church:

- LGBTQIA+ people should be able to live openly in the church without fear of repression.
- The church must actively work to protect queer people, especially in countries where they are persecuted.

These design measures aim not only to reform the church as an institution, but also to make it a safe and inclusive place for all believers.

89 • What role does homophobia play in the church's rejection of LGBTQIA+ and how can homophobia among clergy be reduced?

Homophobia plays a central role in the church's rejection of LGBTQIA+ people and is fed by various sources. Theologically, many churches refer to certain biblical passages that are interpreted as an argument against same-sex relationships without taking their historical context into account. At the same time, some church institutions fear a loss of authority, as the recognition of sexual diversity calls traditional power structures into question. Many clergy have also grown up in conservative social milieus in which homosexuality was still viewed differently, which has led to deep-rooted prejudices. In addition, there is a general fear of change, as a change in the church's sexual ethics is often perceived as a threat to the church's identity. Sometimes unresolved personal conflicts also play a role when clergy suppress their own insecurities regarding sexuality and this is expressed in increased rejection of LGBTQIA+ people.

Targeted measures are needed to reduce homophobia in the church. A theological reorientation is crucial, in which biblical texts are viewed in their historical context and queer theologies are integrated into church teaching. Central Christian values such as love, justice and human dignity should be at the heart of this. Education and awareness-raising programs can help to break down prejudices. These include further training for clergy on LGBTQIA+ issues, the integration of diversity and anti-discrimination training into priestly training and cooperation with LGBTQIA+ organizations to provide training and advice.

In addition to theoretical knowledge, personal encounters are an essential factor for change. Direct conversations with queer believers and exchanges with LGBTQIA+ Christians can help to overcome abstract prejudices.

Figure15 : Illustration of the CSD parade with a Catholic truck carrying LGBTQIA+-friendly messages. The truck is marked with the slogan "God's love is as colorful as a rainbow".

Mentoring programs in which clergy learn from queer people and targeted self-reflection on their own thought patterns promote a conscious approach to the topic.

For such a change to succeed in the long term, structural changes must also take place within the church. This includes the promotion of queer theologians and clergy in church offices as well as the development of a protection concept against discrimination of LGBTQIA+ people. In addition, the church's sexual morals should be adapted to scientific findings and social developments.

An important step towards a more inclusive church is also taking a public stance against homophobia. Clergy could visibly stand up for LGBTQIA+ rights by taking part in Pride events or celebrating queer services. Official blessings for same-sex couples would be a strong sign of acceptance. At the same time, it is important to offer clergy spaces for reflection and psychological support so that they can question their own fears and preconceptions. This could help to break down unconscious prejudices and at the same time create an open atmosphere in which clergy can also come to terms with their own sexual identity.

Sustainable change requires the church to actively take responsibility and develop both theologically and structurally. Only by consciously addressing the causes of homophobia and taking targeted measures to reduce it can an environment be created in the long term in which all people, regardless of their sexual orientation or gender identity, are welcome and feel accepted with their faith and identity.

90 • Why is the Pope considered a possible queer person ?

The idea that the Pope could be seen as a possible queer person is based less on his individual sexual orientation than on a critical reflection of his role within the Church and the way he embodies gender and sexuality. There are several theological, historical and socio-cultural aspects that could suggest a queer reading of the papacy.

Queer theology deconstructs binary gender concepts and shows that gender ambivalences also exist within the church. The papacy is an office that is officially male, but also contains characteristics that are traditionally associated with femininity. The Pope is referred to as the *"Holy Father"*, but also assumes maternal functions, for example as a spiritual provider for the faithful. In historical accounts, the Pope has often been described as the *"Bridegroom of the Church"*, while the Church itself is considered the *"Bride of Christ"* in many theological metaphors. This metaphorical gender fluidity can favor queer interpretations.

Furthermore, the Pope - as well as all celibate clergy - officially lives in a way that defies the classic heterosexual norm. While the Roman Catholic Church prescribes heterosexual marriage as the normative way of life for lay people, an alternative form of life beyond marriage and procreation exists for the clergy. In queer theories, it is often emphasized that celibacy and celibacy do not necessarily support heteronormative concepts, but rather represent a deviation from the binary order of *"man and woman"* in the family context. Queer theology sees this form of celibacy as an opportunity to question heteronormative ideas of relationship models.

In church history, there has always been speculation about popes who may have had homosexual relationships or lived a queer identity. Pope Julius III (16th century) was suspected of having a close relationship with his secretary Innocenzo Ciocchi del Monte, which was interpreted by contemporaries as homoerotic . In more recent discussions, there has also been speculation about popes who did not have overtly queer relationships, but who showed a certain openness to non-heteronormative identities through their work.

Pope Francis in particular, through statements such as *"Who am I to judge?"* in relation to homosexual priests, has positioned himself as a figure who at least shows a greater openness towards LGBTQIA+ issues. While official Catholic teaching continues to view homosexuality as a *"disordered inclination"*, Francis' statements leave room for interpretations that allow for a queer perspective on his pontificate. His commitment to social justice and his emphasis on mercy and inclusion stand in contrast to many traditional church positions. Queer theologians interpret his statements and symbolic actions as steps towards a depathologized view of non-heterosexual identities.

In addition to the person of the pope himself, the papacy as an institution can also be viewed from a queer perspective. It defies the classic notion of masculinity by prescribing abstinence and a lifestyle that deviates from traditional gender roles. It stands for a spiritual identity that exists beyond biological reproduction, which corresponds to queer concepts of identity and relationship models.

The idea that the pope can be seen as a possible queer figure is not a statement about his individual identity, but a reflection on the ambivalences, contradictions and gender coding that the papacy entails. Queer theology shows that the papacy - despite or precisely because of its normative power - represents a form of gender fluidity and a challenge to binary ways of thinking. Even if the church officially marginalizes queer identities, there is a queer dimension in its own structure that undermines the traditional understanding of gender and sexuality.

91 • For LGBTQIA+ people, the letter A refers to asexuals. The Pope is also asexual. Does the Pope therefore belong to the LGBTQIA+ people, i.e. queer people?

The question is interesting, but based on a misunderstanding of what "asexual" means and what the letter "A" stands for in the context of the LGBTQIA+ community.

In the acronym LGBTQIA+, "A" actually stands for asexuality (and often also aromanticism), i.e. for people who feel little or no sexual attraction to other people. It is important to note that asexuality is a sexual orientation - it is a deeply rooted characteristic of a person's sexual identity, not a voluntary renunciation or a personal decision to abstain.

In contrast, the Pope - and Catholic priests in general - practice celibacy, i.e. a conscious, voluntary decision to abstain from sexual activity. This decision is based on religious and spiritual convictions, not on an innate sexual orientation or identity. The Pope may well feel sexual attraction, but has committed himself not to pursue it for religious reasons.

This means that the Pope is generally not to be understood as *"asexual"* in the sense of the LGBTQIA+ definition. The voluntary renunciation of sexuality (celibacy) is a personal decision that may differ from asexuality as a sexual orientation.

In other words, in summary: No, the Pope does not belong to LGBTQIA+ people or queer people, as his lifestyle (celibacy) is based on a religious decision and does not correspond to a sexual orientation. Asexuality in the LGBTQIA+ context refers to people who basically feel little or no sexual attraction - regardless of conscious decisions or religious beliefs.

Nevertheless, the conscious, voluntary decision to abstain from sexual activity (e.g. celibacy) is fundamentally independent of sexual orientation.

Sexual orientation describes which gender someone feels emotionally, romantically or sexually attracted to. It is a deeply rooted, unconsciously chosen characteristic of a person.

In contrast, voluntary abstinence or celibacy refers to a conscious decision, regardless of whether and to whom sexual attraction is felt. A person who is heterosexual, homosexual or bisexual, for example, can also voluntarily abstain from sexual activity. However, this does not mean that this changes the orientation itself or that this person could automatically be described as asexual.

To take the Pope as an example: the Pope has made a conscious decision to renounce sexuality (celibacy). His sexual orientation is not known and is not relevant to his office. Even if the Pope does not engage in any sexual activity, this says nothing about whether he has a sexual orientation or not. The renunciation alone does not make him an asexual person in the sense of the LGBTQIA+ community.

The conscious decision to abstain from sexual activity is therefore clearly independent of sexual orientation. Celibacy or sexual abstinence does not automatically make someone part of the LGBTQIA+ community.

An asexual person (in the context of the LGBTQIA+ community) is characterized by the fact that they feel little or no sexual attraction towards other people. In concrete terms, this means:

Asexuality is a sexual orientation comparable to heterosexuality, homosexuality or bisexuality. It is not a conscious decision or a voluntary renunciation of sexual activity, but a deeply rooted characteristic.

Asexual people may experience romantic attraction (e.g. falling in love or romantic relationships), but they feel little to no need to be sexually active or seek sexual intimacy with others.

There are many gradations within the asexual spectrum. Some asexual people experience sexual attraction occasionally or under certain conditions (this is often referred to as *'grey asexuality'*), while others never experience sexual attraction.

Asexuality does not automatically mean that someone does not want a relationship or closeness. Many asexual people live in loving partnerships, can have romantic feelings or form close emotional bonds.

In contrast to celibacy - the conscious, voluntary renunciation of sexual activity - asexuality is therefore not a decision, but an orientation. A person can be celibate but still feel sexual attraction, whereas an asexual person generally feels little or no sexual attraction.

While celibacy is usually motivated by religious, spiritual or personal choices, asexuality is a natural variation of human sexuality.

A person from the LGBTQIA+ community can of course be celibate. This is because:

- Celibacy is the voluntary decision to abstain from sexual activity. This decision is independent of sexual orientation or identity.
- Sexual orientation (e.g. homosexual, bisexual, pansexual or asexual), on the other hand, describes who you are fundamentally emotionally, romantically or sexually attracted to. It does not change depending on whether someone is sexually active or not.

LGBTQIA+ people can be celibate for a variety of reasons - for example, for religious, spiritual, ethical, health or personal reasons. Such a lifestyle does not make their sexual orientation or identity any less valid or significant.

For example, a homosexual man or a lesbian woman could be celibate, for example due to religious convictions or a conscious decision to live an abstinent lifestyle. However, this does not change their basic sexual orientation.

So yes, celibacy is possible regardless of sexual orientation and does occur in the LGBTQIA+ community. However, a celibate lifestyle does not make a person any less queer - belonging to the LGBTQIA+ community is based solely on identity and orientation, not on practicing sexuality.

However, whether asexuality is always innate has not yet been conclusively clarified scientifically. It is considered likely that asexuality - like other sexual orientations - is the result of a complex interplay of biological, psychological and social factors.

One clarification:

People often experience their own asexuality as something permanent and stable, comparable to other orientations such as homosexuality, heterosexuality or bisexuality. Therefore, sexuality as a whole is complex, individual and can change or evolve over the course of a lifetime. Some people experience their sexual orientation as constant, while others notice changes or an increasing clarity of their orientation over the course of their lives.

The current scientific view is that there is still no clear scientific evidence that sexual orientation is exclusively biologically determined or completely innate. Current research assumes a combination of genetic, hormonal, developmental and social factors. This also applies to asexuality.

And: asexuality usually has nothing to do with physical potency, functionality or the age of the sexual organs. Again, to clarify: asexuality means that a person feels little or no sexual attraction towards others. This is a psycho-emotional sensation, regardless of whether the sexual organs or sexual functions are intact or not. Loss of potency or sexual dysfunction, on the other hand, refers to the physical ability to perform sexual acts. People with potency problems or age-related changes can certainly experience sexual attraction, even if they are physically impaired.

Of course, people who are no longer or barely able to engage in sexual activities due to age or illness may perceive their sexual needs differently or even find them diminished. However, this is not synonymous with asexuality in the sense of sexual orientation. The essential difference:

- Asexuality: little or no sexual attraction (emotional level).
- Potency problems or signs of ageing: Problems with sexual activity (physical level).

Asexuality is therefore never a consequence of age, loss of potency or an age-related change in the sexual organs. It describes an independent orientation that takes place on an emotional and psychological level. Although potency or age can have an influence on sexual behavior, it is not the same as the sexual orientation of asexuality.

The following important point needs to be addressed: There are indeed some people who only realize at an older age that they have a tendency towards homosexuality or asexuality. However, this does not necessarily mean that their sexual orientation has suddenly changed. These feelings were often already present earlier, but for various reasons - such as social expectations, social constraints or inner inhibitions - they could not be consciously recognized, accepted or acted out. When life circumstances change in old age, for example due to the loss of a partner or a change in personal circumstances, some people feel freer to accept their actual sexual orientation and live it openly.

However, there are also cases in which people discover or perceive sexual attraction to the same sex for the first time late in life, after having had long heterosexual relationships. Sexuality is not equally rigidly fixed in all people, but can - at least in some people - be flexible or fluid and change or develop in a more differentiated way over the course of a lifetime.

In the context of asexuality, it should be noted that some older people consciously reduce or even completely stop sexual activity in the course of their lives, for example due to health, physical or emotional factors. However, this is not the same as the sexual orientation "*asexuality*" in the sense of the LGBTQIA+ community, which is characterized by the fact that people generally feel little to no sexual attraction towards other people. Declining sexual interest due to age or sexual inactivity alone is therefore not enough to speak of asexuality in the LGBTQIA+ sense.

Therefore, you do not automatically belong to the LGBTQIA+ community just because you are older and less sexually active. The decisive factor is which sexual orientation or gender identity someone feels or recognizes themselves, regardless of age or physical changes. It therefore always depends on how the person feels, perceives and defines their sexual orientation.

Only in the following case could it be said that the Pope belongs to the LGBTQIA+ community: however, the decisive factor would not be his celibate lifestyle, but the fact that he consciously publicly acknowledges his homosexual orientation. So if a pope were to publicly declare that he feels homosexual, he would definitely belong to the LGBTQIA+ community, even if he continues to live a celibate lifestyle. In this case, he would count as a queer person, as the LGBTQIA+ community unites people who deviate from the social norm due to their sexual orientation or identity - regardless of whether they are sexually active or not.

It is impossible to predict when or if a pope will ever publicly announce his homosexual orientation. To date, no pope has made such a declaration. A pope coming out publicly about his homosexuality would also be an extraordinary step that would require a great deal of sensitivity, courage and support. Essential help for this could initially lie in a personal network, i.e. trusting relationships with people inside or outside the church who would react openly, understandingly and supportively. It would also be helpful to have an environment of advisors or close confidants who are well prepared for such an event in order to ensure that communication with the public and within the church is as open and constructive as possible. Similarly, international organizations and initiatives that advocate for the rights and acceptance of LGBTQIA+ people could provide emotional and practical support by helping to convey messages that are both authentic and diplomatic. It would also be helpful to have the support of other religious leaders or prominent members of the church who could express solidarity and contribute to the social acceptance of such a coming out. Last but not least, media and psychological support would be crucial, for example from communication consultants, psychologists or pastoral counselors, who could help the Pope to cope with possible stress and deal constructively with the expected attention. All these support elements would contribute to a pope's coming out being perceived as a positive step towards greater acceptance and tolerance in the Church and society.

Given the current stance of the Catholic Church, such a revelation would be extremely unusual, as the official position of the Church is to treat homosexual persons with respect and dignity, but considers homosexual acts to be incompatible with Catholic teaching. A pope who feels homosexual but is celibate could theoretically still publicly admit his orientation without violating celibacy.

Should this ever happen, it would probably be a historic turning point and symbolize a profound change within the Catholic Church. It is therefore theoretically conceivable, but currently very unlikely, to say if or when a pope could ever openly admit to his homosexuality.

Remaining silent or avoiding such sensitive but simple questions about sexual orientation or belonging to a community, which everyone has to answer in life for their representation , does not always help - especially if the church wants to convey authenticity and credibility. Although tactful silence protects against conflict in the short term and preserves existing power relations, in the long term it prevents open, honest dialog and makes it more difficult to engage with modern social realities. Particularly when it comes to issues such as sexuality, transparency and personal integrity, believers increasingly expect clear, comprehensible answers - not out of voyeuristic interest, but to strengthen trust in the credibility and honesty of the institution. A more open approach to these issues could help to reduce mistrust and double standards and thus ultimately serve the credibility and acceptance of the church. Silence may be convenient in the short term, but in the long run it does not help, but rather hinders a constructive development towards an authentic church capable of dialog.

c) LGBTQIA+ in church and society

92 • How could LGBTQIA+ Christians enrich the Christian view of humanity?

LGBTQIA+ Christians can enrich the Christian view of humanity in many ways by bringing new perspectives on faith, community and identity. Their lives and experiences challenge traditional interpretations and open up paths to a deeper understanding of God's love and the diversity of creation. They show that human dignity is not tied to a particular sexual orientation or gender identity, but is rooted in the fundamental likeness of every individual to God.

Through their stories and their testimony, LGBTQIA+ Christians are helping to make the church and theology more open to diversity. They make it clear that lived authenticity is an essential part of a true faith and that honesty towards one's own identity does not have to contradict Christian teaching. Their experiences of discrimination and exclusion raise awareness of social justice and the church's mission to stand up for the disadvantaged and marginalized.

In addition, LGBTQIA+ Christians bring new theological perspectives to the church. Queer theologies question traditional interpretations of biblical texts and develop readings that emphasize the liberating message of the gospel for all people. They broaden the understanding of love, partnership and family by demonstrating that Christian values such as faithfulness, respect and mutual care are not tied to heteronormative concepts.

LGBTQIA+ Christians also enrich church life in liturgical practice. Their spirituality, which has often grown out of a deep struggle with faith and identity, gives rise to new forms of worship that reflect the diversity of creation. Queer services or inclusive liturgies can lead to a deeper experience of Christian community by creating spaces in which all people - regardless of their identity - feel accepted.

Finally, through their commitment to an open and loving church, LGBTQIA+ Christians can help to overcome rigid dogmas and keep faith alive in a changing world. Their witness reminds the church that the gospel is a message of unconditional love that excludes no one. By living visibly and authentically in the church, they show that Christian identity does not depend on gender or sexual orientation, but on a lived relationship with God and fellow human beings. In this sense, they contribute to the further development of the Christian view of humanity - towards an understanding that sees the diversity of creation as an expression of divine love.

93 • What would an LGBTQIA+-friendly church look like?

An LGBTQIA+-friendly church would be a place where people are fully accepted and valued regardless of their sexual orientation or gender identity. It would not only be characterized by an open attitude, but would also actively take measures to promote inclusion and equality.

Its openness would be visible as soon as you enter the church. Rainbow flags, posters with inclusive messages or artistic representations of queer saints could symbolize that everyone is welcome here. But far beyond the symbolism, the church would live out its openness through concrete theological and liturgical practices.

Theologically, it would represent a liberating interpretation of the Bible, in which God's love for all people - regardless of their identity - is at the center. Sermons and Bible studies include queer perspectives and show that diversity is not a threat, but an expression of divine creation.

This church would also actively include LGBTQIA+ people in its liturgy. Queer services or inclusive forms of prayer could help to combine traditional Christian spirituality with the experiences of LGBTQIA+ Christians. Blessings and marriages for same-sex couples would be a matter of course, as would the possibility for trans* or non-binary people to enter the sacraments under their chosen name and pronoun.

The community structure is designed in such a way that LGBTQIA+ people are not only part of the community, but are also actively involved in leadership positions. This would ensure that decisions are not made about them, but with them. Clergy would be specifically trained in queer-sensitive pastoral care in order to accompany LGBTQIA+

believers on their faith journey, especially in matters of identity, coming out and possible experiences of religious exclusion.

Figure 16: An LGBTQIA+-inclusive church - open, welcoming, appreciative and surrounded by diverse people. The window mosaics and the luminous arch symbolize cohesion and sacramental blessing in diversity.

A *sacramental blessing in diversity* is an expression of divine closeness that honors all people in their respective identities, relationships and lifestyles. It elevates the love, trust and devotion that grows between people into the realm of the sacred - regardless of gender, origin, sexual orientation or form of relationship.

He - the blessing - is:

◆ *universal:*
It applies not just to some, but to all. Because God's blessing knows no exclusion clauses.

◆ *embodying:*
He touches the body, the relationship, the lived life - not as an ideal, but as what is there and is loved.

◆ *Visible and audible:*
He makes a promise through words, touch and gestures. He makes it tangible: you are good just as you are. Your connection is precious. You are blessed.

◆ *sacramental:*
This means that it is not just symbolic, but a real, spiritual force. It makes God's devotion tangible - where people bond, trust each other and are there for each other.

Such a blessing is not an "exception", but a sign that holiness shines in the diversity of humanity - in queer ways of life as well as in heteronormative ones, in friendship as well as in family, in transitions and in new beginnings.

He says: God is not the exception to love. God is the expanse in which it is allowed to blossom.

Furthermore, an LGBTQIA+-friendly church takes its responsibility in society seriously. It publicly campaigns against discrimination and for the rights of queer people, would take part in Pride events and cooperate with LGBTQIA+ organizations. Offers for queer young people, shelters for people who have been marginalized for religious or family reasons and educational work on queer issues would be central components of its commitment.

Such a church is then not only a safe place for LGBTQIA+ Christians, but a living example of how Christian faith can not only tolerate diversity, but celebrate it as part of divine creation. It would show that the core of the gospel - love, justice and community - applies to all people, without exception.

94 • What perspectives and challenges arise from a ten-point plan for the queer movement in church and society?

In the 1990s, Andreas Frank presented a ten-point plan as a basis for discussion and as a perspective for the queer movement in the handbook on same-sex partnerships "Engagierte Zärtlichkeit" (Committed Tenderness): The ten-point plan serves as the basis for an in-depth debate on the rights, social acceptance and ecclesial integration of homosexual people. The focus is on the following topics:

1. recognition of the plurality of human identity - diversity as a central element of a modern society and church.

2. equality in the church - demand for church blessings and weddings for same-sex couples.

3. overcoming discriminatory theologies - re-evaluating biblical statements on homosexuality from a historical perspective.

4. right to sexual self-determination - rejection of any repression or even attempts to "change the polarity" of homosexual identity.

5. de-tabooing homosexuality among clergy - openness and honesty instead of double life and repression.

6. reorganization of church sexual morality - focus on responsibility and love instead of the compulsion to procreate.

7. promoting gay and lesbian theology - developing new theological approaches that include homosexual perspectives.

8. influencing church and social policy - activism to reform religious and legal structures.

9. educational work in church and school - addressing homosexuality in religious education and church curricula.

10. solidarity with other marginalized groups - linking one's own movement with feminist, intercultural and social commitment.

The implementation of the demands formulated in the ten-point plan opens up a range of long-term perspectives and challenges for the queer lesbian and gay movement. These relate not only to the church's recognition of same-sex partnerships, but also to social integration, the development of new theological concepts and the fight against discrimination.

A central aspect is emancipation within the church. Gay and lesbian believers are increasingly demanding equal participation in church structures and official recognition of their lifestyle. This not only means allowing same-sex couples to be blessed or married in church, but also a reassessment of the role of homosexual clergy. Many of them have been living a double life up to now, as they cannot openly acknowledge their sexuality within the church hierarchy. Future developments must aim to give these people the opportunity to reconcile their vocation and their life of faith with their identity, without repression or concealment.

Social integration plays an equally important role here. Queer people have long been excluded from society and faced prejudice, discrimination and legal disadvantage. A key goal of the movement is therefore to overcome this marginalization and achieve full equality in all areas of society. This includes working life and education as well as the right to start a family and protection from discrimination through laws and state institutions.

Closely linked to this is the theological re-evaluation of queerness. Until now, many church teachings have regarded same-sex love as morally separate or at least disordered compared to heterosexual relationships. The movement advocates a modern theology that recognizes the diversity of human sexuality as God-given and is not based on outdated moral concepts. This re-evaluation requires a rethinking of biblical interpretation that is based on the historical and cultural contextualization of biblical texts and does not interpret them as timeless prohibitions. The aim is to develop an inclusive theology that does not exclude queer people, but recognizes them as an equal part of the faith community.

Another important aspect is the strengthening of self-confidence and identity. Many homosexual believers suffer from the tensions between their religious convictions and their sexual identity. In an environment that often portrays homosexuality as subordinate, many find it difficult to accept themselves and lead a life of openness and dignity. The movement is therefore committed to education, pastoral support and the creation of safe spaces in which queer people can develop without fear of judgment.

Finally, networking and political influence is a central strategy of the queer movement. Achieving long-term change requires a broad social alliance that transcends church and religious boundaries. Cooperation with feminist, anti-racist and socio-political movements is of great importance here, as many of the mechanisms of discrimination are interlinked. The political work aims to enshrine equal rights in law, enforce protective measures against discrimination and initiate a social debate that will lead to greater acceptance and understanding in the long term.

In summary, it can be said that the queer community is working towards a transformation both within the church and in society as a whole that enables an equal and respected existence for all people, regardless of their sexual orientation. This requires not only legal and theological reforms, but also a social rethink that sees diversity as enrichment.

The following measures can be taken by the Catholic Church, the queer community and society on the individual demands:

Recognizing the plurality of human identity requires the Catholic Church to make an official statement that recognizes sexual and gender diversity as part of God's creation. This should be reflected in inclusive language, diversity-friendly pastoral care and the active involvement of queer people in church decision-making processes. The queer community can support this process by networking with progressive theologians and creating theological education programs that shed light on queer perspectives on faith and spirituality. At the same time, society should take targeted anti-discrimination measures to ensure that diversity is not only tolerated, but actively promoted - for example through legal obligations for institutions to create a non-discriminatory environment.

Equality in the church requires a clear ecclesiastical measure that officially allows priests to bless and marry same-sex couples. To support this step, the queer community should increasingly rely on the testimony of believing homosexual people to show that faith and same-sex love are not mutually exclusive. At a societal level, pressure on the church can be increased by promoting equality under civil law and by states enforcing partnership rights independently of religious institutions.

Overcoming discriminatory theologies requires the Catholic Church to convene a scientific commission that classifies biblical statements on homosexuality historically and develops an updated theological doctrine. The queer community can actively promote theological studies and work with queer theologians on alternative readings. In turn, society should advocate for pluralistic religious studies in schools and universities that reflect different theological perspectives and developments.

The right to sexual self-determination requires the church to clearly and publicly distance itself from so-called "conversion" therapies and to hold clergy or institutions that support such measures accountable. The queer community can support victims of such programs through legal assistance and psychological support. Society, in turn, should consistently enforce legal bans on conversion therapies and impose clear penalties for violations.

In order to remove the taboo on homosexuality among clergy, the church must create clear regulations that allow homosexual clergy to be open about their identity without having to fear negative consequences. The queer community can support this process by providing safe spaces for homosexual clergy and helping them to build networks. At the same time, society should encourage public discussions about queer clergy in order to promote normalization and reduce prejudice.

A reshaping of the church's sexual morality requires the church to reformulate its teaching on sexuality, which is no longer exclusively oriented towards procreation, but towards love, respect and responsibility. The queer community can support this change by actively participating in church education programs and developing its own theological concepts. Society, in turn, can contribute to establishing an enlightened and realistic view of sexuality with scientifically sound sex education programs.

The promotion of gay and lesbian theology can also be achieved through a church measure that integrates the systematic exploration of queer faith perspectives into university theological curricula. The queer community can promote this development through its own theological publications and discussion formats. In society, academic and interfaith conferences that integrate queer perspectives into theological discourse should be promoted.

In order to influence church and social policy, the church should create dialog forums in which queer representatives and church decision-makers work together to develop reforms. The queer community can exert pressure through targeted campaigns for legal equality and church reforms. Society should expand and implement laws to protect sexual orientation from discrimination.

Educational work in church and school requires the Catholic Church to integrate queer topics into religious education and develop appropriate teaching materials. The queer community can offer workshops for teachers and church staff to impart knowledge about queer identities. Society should promote the inclusion of LGBTQIA+ issues in general school curricula to teach acceptance and knowledge at an early age.

Finally, solidarity with other marginalized groups means that the church networks with social movements against discrimination and integrates intersectional justice into its social work. The queer community can form alliances with feminist, anti-racist and inclusive movements to work together against inequality. Society should establish an active anti-discrimination policy that combats various forms of marginalization equally and strengthens social cohesion.

These measures offer concrete approaches to improve both the position of the queer community in the church and its position in society. Sustainable change can be achieved through the joint commitment of the church, community and society.

d) Individual experiences and decisions

95 • How does the coming out process work according to the Eli Coleman model?

Eli Coleman describes the coming out process in five developmental stages: Firstly, the pre-contact phase, in which a person perceives initial feelings and uncertainties regarding their own sexual orientation. Secondly, the exploration phase, in which the first conscious confrontations with one's own homosexuality take place, often accompanied by a search for information and initial same-sex experiences. Thirdly, identity acceptance, in which one's own homosexuality is increasingly recognized as an integral part of one's identity. Fourthly, identity integration, in which the person identifies socially and emotionally with their sexual orientation and becomes involved in homosexual or LGBTQIA+ communities. Finally, identity synthesis, in which sexual orientation is seen as a natural part of the overall identity without remaining the dominant characteristic of the personality. These stages influence both self-image and social identity, as each stage is linked to psychological challenges and social perception. The coming out process according to Eli Coleman's model can also be applied to queer clergy, albeit with specific challenges arising from the church context - in the familiar phases:

1st pre-contact phase: Queer clergy perceive initial feelings or insecurities regarding their sexual identity, often in an environment that sets heteronormativity and abstinence as the norm. This phase is often characterized by repression, inner conflicts and attempts to reconcile their own feelings with church teachings. Clergy should have access to anonymous or confidential counseling services, for example through pastoral care or queer theological networks, in order to openly reflect on initial uncertainties.

2nd exploration phase: In this phase, a conscious examination of one's own identity begins. For clergy, this often means questioning theological positions on homosexuality and looking for role models or safe spaces within or outside the church. However, many experience fear of the consequences of coming out publicly, as they fear repression or even the loss of their church office. The opportunity to exchange ideas with other queer believers or clergy, for example through church LGBTQIA+ groups or queer theological literature, helps to develop alternative perspectives on faith and identity.

3. identity acceptance: Queer clergy recognize their sexual orientation as part of their identity, but are often faced with the dilemma of whether they can reconcile this openness with their ministry and church affiliation. Some try to find an individual solution within the system, while others work specifically for reforms and greater visibility. Integration into existing networks of queer clergy can facilitate the process. Visible role models or mentors within the church who are themselves open about their identity can provide encouragement and guidance.

4. identity integration: In this phase, sexual identity is no longer seen as a contradiction to the spiritual calling, but as a dimension of the personal and spiritual self. Queer clergy find networks and communities where they can find support or advocate for change in their church. Depending on the denomination and theological orientation, this can either lead to the strengthening of their ministry or to further conflict with church authorities. Theological training that takes diversity into account and reflects it could help clergy to develop a theologically sound position on their identity and vocation and to incorporate this into church practice.

5. identity synthesis: Finally, one's queer identity is accepted as a natural part of life without it remaining the central feature of one's personality. Clergy at this stage have often found a way to be open about their identity, advocate for change or work in church contexts that recognize queer identities. Queer clergy who have fully integrated their identity can actively advocate for church reforms, for example by participating in internal church debates, promoting inclusive pastoral care or making public statements for a church free of discrimination.

The main difference to the general coming out experience lies in the structural hurdles and specific church expectations. While many queer people come out in their private and social lives, queer clergy often have to deal with additional institutional restrictions, theological debates and the fear of losing their ministry. Nevertheless, there are already networks and initiatives in many churches that support queer clergy and facilitate the process of finding one's identity.

96 • *Should queer believers leave the church system if they think it is deforming them - or should they try to change it and accept a degree of resignation in the process?*

Whether queer believers should leave the church or try to change it depends on individual beliefs and resilience. If someone feels that church teaching and practice is permanently deforming their own psyche - whether through guilt, self-denial or marginalization - leaving may be a sensible decision to protect themselves and live a freer life outside of these structures. On the other hand, remaining in the church can be understood as an act of resistance and transformation, in which queer believers try to initiate change from within. However, this often requires a certain amount of resignation, as church reform processes are lengthy and deeply rooted dogmatic attitudes are not easy to soften. Gay and lesbian theologians play a special role in this area of tension. Their task could be to develop theological arguments for a more inclusive church at , to expose historical misinterpretations of biblical texts and to develop new concepts of sexuality and spirituality. They can also act as bridge builders between queer believers and church institutions by creating spaces for discussion, pastoral care and networking. Another task is educational work - both within church structures and in theological training centers - to enable a more differentiated discussion of gender and sexuality. Ultimately, the question arises as to whether the fight for a reformed church gives or takes more strength. Some choose to fight for change within the institution, others find spiritual fulfillment outside of it. Both paths are legitimate - the decisive factor is which one corresponds better to one's own psychological and spiritual needs.

Chapter 8: Images of God and gender diversity: Deconstructing traditional ideas

The idea of God as a male father figure has dominated Christian thinking for centuries. However, this idea is neither universal nor without alternative. There are references to a non-binary concept of God in the Bible, for example when God is described in the Old Testament with both male and female attributes. Queer theology goes even further and asks to what extent God can also be interpreted as polyamorous or bisexual. This questions classical theological anthropology: what consequences does it have for faith and theology that man created God in his own image - and not the other way around?

The deconstruction of traditional images and interpretations of God has far-reaching effects on belief structures and our own ethical and religious beliefs. While conservative theologians cling to a fixed framework of interpretation, modern currents are calling for a re-evaluation of God that also includes gender diversity and sexual identities. What does the affirmation of sexual diversity say about a person's image of God in the church? And how can myths and alternative images of masculinity - such as those presented in the book Eisenhans - be reconciled with theological concepts?

These debates are not only theological, but also socially relevant. Modern gender discourses are increasingly influencing theology and changing traditional ideas. What impact does the deconstruction of gender and sexual orientation have on theology? And how do religious intolerance and moral devaluations arise from the distinction between "true" and "false" in matters of faith?

The discussion about the diversity of images of God is closely linked to the question of power and authority in the church. Who determines how God may be conceived? What role do authoritarian structures play in theology? And what does the statement "God is dead" or "God is born again" mean for the search for new values and a progressive practice of faith? These topics and questions show that dealing with and interpreting images of God goes far beyond pure theology - it touches on reflections on identity, justice and social coexistence.

a) Fundamentals of gender diversity

97 • *Are there references to a non-binary concept of God in the Bible?*

In the Bible, there are several references to a non-binary concept of God, which show that God is not limited to a male or female identity. While God is often described in traditional Christian theology using masculine terms such as *"Father"* or *"Lord"*, there are also images and metaphors in Scripture that go beyond binary gender categories.

A central reference to this can already be found in the creation narrative. Genesis 1:27 reads: *"And God created man in his own image, in the image of God created he him; male and female created he them."* This passage suggests that God's image includes both male and female aspects. As humans are created in God's image as male and female, this could indicate that God is not limited to a single gender, but unites gender diversity within himself.

Although God is often described as a father, there are many passages in the Bible in which God is portrayed with feminine and maternal characteristics. Isaiah 66:13 expresses this particularly clearly: *"As a mother comforts her son, so I will comfort you."* Likewise, Isaiah 49:15 asks: *"Can a woman forget her little child, a mother her natural son? And even if she were to forget him: I will not forget you!"* These maternal metaphors make it clear that God was not only thought of in male but also in female categories. Even more explicit is Genesis 32:18, where it says: *"You have forsaken the rock that bore you, you have forgotten the God who gave you birth."* The combination of *"begotten"* and *"born"* in relation to God in a single verse refers to gender diversity.

Figure17 : A luminous, non-binary divine figure that combines female and male features - surrounded by light, writing and respectful attention. The divine figure appears embedded in writing, light and living space - with finely interwoven symbols of gender diversity. A spiritual, non-binary representation of God that touches people. It hints at eye level: Divinity transcends gender boundaries and finds expression in diversity.

Furthermore, there are passages in the Bible in which God is described with characteristics that go beyond male and female categories. Hosea 11:3-4 shows a mixture of maternal and paternal characteristics when God is described as a father who teaches his child to walk, but at the same time also acts with maternal care. In Proverbs 8:1-31, divine wisdom (Chokhmah in Hebrew, Sophia in Greek) is personified as feminine, while at the same time being an integral part of God. This indicates that God's identity does not only encompass one gender category.

A particularly interesting aspect of the biblical revelation of God is the name of God mentioned in Exodus 3:14: *"I am who I am"* (Ehjeh ascher Ehjeh). This formulation is remarkable because in Hebrew it is open and not clearly gendered. The name of God YHWH is also without clear gender assignment and indicates that God exists beyond human gender categories.

The New Testament also contains indications that God's kingdom is not bound to binary gender categories. In Matthew 19:12, Jesus talks about *"eunuchs who were born this way"*, which indicates that even in biblical times there were people who did not fit into the male-female scheme. He adds that some became eunuchs *"for the sake of the kingdom of heaven"*, which some theological interpretations interpret as an opening for gender diversity. Galatians 3:28 is also particularly significant, where it says: *"There is neither Jew nor Greek, there is neither slave nor free, there is neither male nor female; for you are all one in Christ Jesus."* This statement abolishes social and gender categories in the community of believers and could be understood as an indication that God's kingdom is conceived beyond gender binaries.

Another example of a non-binary concept of God can be found in the Judeo-Christian wisdom tradition, particularly in divine wisdom (*Sophia/Chokhmah*), which is often understood as the female personification of God. At the same time, the Holy Spirit is associated with feminine qualities in some Christian traditions, as the Hebrew word for spirit (*Ruach*) is feminine. These aspects show that divine identity cannot be reduced to masculine terms, but encompasses a variety of gendered expressions.

In summary, the Bible contains numerous indications that God is not limited to a binary gender order. From the creation narrative to maternal images of God to cross-gender attributes, many biblical passages indicate that God's nature combines both masculine and feminine aspects - or even transcends human gender categories. Modern theological debates on gender take up this complexity and argue that a non-binary concept of God is biblically founded and theologically legitimate.

98 • *What role does Hermaphroditos play in the discussion about God's gender?*

Hermaphroditos, a figure from Greek mythology that combines both male and female characteristics, plays an interesting symbolic role in the theological discussion about God's gender. While Christianity has traditionally cultivated a male image of God - for example through terms such as *"father"* or the male representation of Jesus - there are more and more theological approaches that are developing a more gender-diverse image of God.

Hermaphroditos can serve as a mythological parallel to biblical and mystical ideas of sexual unity or overcoming gender boundaries. In Gnosticism and the Jewish Kabbalah, there are concepts that view God as a supra-gendered or all-encompassing being. There are also references to God's gender diversity in the Hebrew Bible, suggesting that God's essence is not limited to a single gender category.

In feminist and queer theologies, it is increasingly argued that God is neither exclusively male nor female, but can unite gender diversity in himself. Here, Hermaphroditos could serve as a mythological image for a divine transcendence across binary gender boundaries. Parallels can also be drawn with Jesus Christ, who is described in mystical traditions as the *"new Adam"* who unites all opposites within himself.

The figure of Hermaphroditos thus reminds us that gender could also be conceived of as changeable, fluid or unified in ancient mythology. In theological discussions, it could inspire us to question rigid notions of gender and develop a more open image of God that also includes non-binary or intersex identities.

99 • *To what extent can God be interpreted as polyamorous or bisexual in queer theology?*

In queer theology, God can be interpreted as polyamorous or bisexual, as divine love is not exclusive, but unlimited, multifaceted and relational. These perspectives arise from a deconstructive reading of biblical texts, reflection on God's relationship to creation and the way in which divine love transcends binary and mononormative structures.

On the polyamorous aspects of God: Polyamory means that a person has several equal, loving relationships based on consent and mutual care. In theology, God is often described as a being who has many simultaneous, deep relationships without them being mutually exclusive or diminishing.

The covenant with many: God repeatedly makes covenants with various groups and individuals in the Bible - with Noah (Gen 9:8-17), with Abraham (Gen 17), with Israel as a whole (Ex 19-24) and later with all of humanity in Christ (Lk 22:20). This shows a divine relationship of love that is not limited to a single exclusive connection.

The language of marriage and love: In the books of the prophets (e.g. Hosea), God's relationship with Israel is often described in marital terms, but this occurs in parallel with a universal devotion of God to other peoples. In the New Testament, Christ is described as the *"bridegroom"* of the Church (Eph 5:25-32), but this Church is not a single person, but a community.

The Trinity as divine relational diversity: The Trinity shows God as a being who is in himself a community of Father, Son and Holy Spirit. This threefold relationship of love within God can be understood as a model for non-exclusive, multifaceted love that extends to the whole of creation.

Bisexual aspects of God: Bisexuality is often understood as an identity that is not tied to a specific gender preference, but expresses a love beyond binary categories. In theology, there are several approaches that show that divine love is not bound to a specific gender.

God as both male and female: In the Bible, God is often addressed as male ("Father"), but is also described using female metaphors. Isaiah 66:13 shows God as a motherly comforter, while Deuteronomy 32:18 says of God: *"You have forgotten the God who gave you birth."* This gender diversity in the description of God could be interpreted as a queer openness to different forms of love.

Divine wisdom (Sophia/Chokhmah): In the Judeo-Christian tradition, the wisdom of God is often personified as female (Proverbs 8:1-31), while Christ is seen as the embodiment of this wisdom (1 Cor 1:24). This shows a divine fluidity that cannot be pinned down to a single gender identity or a one-sided form of relationship.

The universal love of God: God loves men and women equally and transcends socially prescribed gender boundaries. Galatians 3:28 emphasizes: "There is neither male nor female, for you are all one in Christ Jesus." This points to a divine love that exists independently of gender or gender order and could therefore reflect God's bisexual or pansexual openness.

Theological consequences are then: if God is conceived as polyamorous or bisexual, this does not mean that God is "sexual", but that divine love is not bound to binary, monogamous or heteronormative categories. Such a view opens up space for a theology that understands love as dynamic, diverse and non-possessive.

This interpretation challenges traditional notions of marriage and exclusivity and suggests an ethic in which relationships are based on mutual consent, respect and care rather than rigid norms. It also reinforces the idea that people in their gender and sexual diversity can be a reflection of divine love.

In queer theology, God can be understood as polyamorous because divine love encompasses many equal relationships without focusing on a single exclusive relationship. At the same time, God could be interpreted as bisexual, as divine love is not bound to a specific gender and the Bible uses both male and female images of God. This reading describes a theology that does not think of love only in fixed, binary or monogamous structures, but instead opens up space for an inclusive understanding of love that is based on diversity, relational justice and divine openness.

100 • What consequences does the idea that man created God in his own image have for faith and theology?

If God did not create man, but man created God as a projection of his own desires and ideals, then theology loses its foundation as the science of a supernatural being. Ludwig Feuerbach concluded that religion is not based on a divine reality, but on man himself, who transfers his best qualities - love, reason and justice - to an external deity.

For Feuerbach, this realization represents a radical turning point: Instead of focusing on a god, man should recognize himself as the origin of moral values and meaning. He thus calls for a shift from a theocentric to a humanistic perspective, in which the focus is no longer on belief in a higher power, but on man's striving for realization and humanity.

In this way of thinking, faith is no longer understood as a relationship to an otherworldly God, but as an expression of human longing for meaning and community. Theology should therefore not be concerned with the exploration of a divine being, but with the conditions under which people can realize their own ideals. In this sense, Feuerbach understands his approach not as a mere critique of religion, but as a liberation of man from illusions so that he can take responsibility for himself and the world.

In order for people to develop their ideals, they need an environment that enables personal development, social connection and an open debate on questions of meaning. The most important prerequisites for this are freedom, education, social justice and interpersonal recognition.

1. freedom and self-determination

People must have the opportunity to choose their beliefs and life paths freely, without external coercion or fear of social exclusion. This includes freedom of opinion, religious and ideological openness and protection from dogmas that restrict individual thought and action.

2. education and critical thinking

An enlightened society promotes knowledge, reflection and discourse. Education makes it possible to consciously choose ideals, weigh up ethical questions and actively participate in social developments. Without critical thinking, there is a danger of blindly adopting ideals instead of shaping them ourselves.

3. social justice and economic security

Ideals can only develop if basic needs such as food, health and housing are secured. Those whose livelihoods are threatened will have little room to deal with deeper questions of meaning or social commitment. A fair distribution of resources is therefore crucial for the possibility of leading a meaningful life.

4. community and belonging

People are not only looking for individual fulfillment, but also for a community in which they can share and develop their ideals. Communities based on respect, solidarity and dialog make it possible to actively live out values and give support to others. They should be open to different lifestyles instead of imposing rigid norms.

5. sense orientation and creative development

In addition to rational and social aspects, the personal search for meaning also plays a role. Art, philosophy, spirituality or social commitment can be ways of dealing with existential questions and transforming ideals into lived practice. A culture that allows creativity and spiritual freedom opens up spaces for a deeper search for meaning.

When these conditions are met, people can not only develop themselves, but also actively contribute to a fairer and more empathetic society. Ideals then do not remain mere theory, but become a lived reality that strengthens both individual fulfillment and community cohesion.

b) Religious structures and their questioning

101 • How were and can traditional concepts of God and authoritarian structures in theology be questioned and supplemented by new perspectives?

Dorothee Sölle criticized patriarchal images of God and authoritarian structures within theology, which she recognized as mechanisms of oppression. She rejected the image of an all-powerful, punishing God, which was often linked to hierarchical power relations in the church and society. Instead, she emphasized an understanding of God based on love, compassion and co-creation.

Her *feminist theology* focused on the equal rights of women in church and theological discourse. She called for a church in which women are recognized not only as ministers, but as equal theologians and pastors. She also combined her theology with social justice and political commitment by advocating for faith-based liberation from oppression. Her approach was not only a theological reform, but also a *socio-political critique* that understood faith as an active force for change.

The search for an image of God that emphasizes love, compassion and co-creation can lead to the topic of a female concept of God: The idea of God as purely male is deeply rooted in church tradition, but many theologians, including Dorothee Sölle, have questioned this one-sidedness. If God is understood as a source of love, compassion and co-creation - qualities that are often associated with femininity - the question arises as to whether a female concept of God is not just as legitimate or even more necessary in order to obtain a more complete picture of the divine.

In fact, there are already female images of God in the Bible, such as Wisdom (*Sophia*) in the Old Testament or the maternal traits of God in some prophetic texts. Divine mother figures also exist in other cultures.

Sophia, Wisdom, is a divine figure from the Old Testament and Jewish wisdom literature. She is often described as the female personification of divine wisdom, who was involved in creation (Proverbs 8:22-31). In Christian traditions, she was later associated with Christ or the Holy Spirit, while in Gnosticism she played a central role as an independent divine power.

Figure 18: Man and his holiness - represented by a reflection of multiple faces in front of a luminous divine presence. It combines dignity, diversity and spiritual depth in a poetic composition.

The image represents the divine dignity of every human being, regardless of gender, origin or identity - reflected in the diversity of human faces. An undefined, divine light shines behind the mirror, suggesting that God is not an image, but is alive in all images.

In many cultures there are divine mother figures who stand for fertility, protection and wisdom:

Isis (Egypt): The Egyptian goddess Isis was considered the mother of the gods, protector of children and mistress of magic. She was worshipped as a loving but also powerful deity who protected her son Horus and accompanied the dead to the afterlife. Her cult spread far and wide in the Roman Empire.

Gaia (Greece): As the personified earth, Gaia was the primordial mother from which all life sprang. She symbolized fertility and the eternal growth and decay of nature.

Shakti (Hinduism): In Hinduism, Shakti embodies the divine feminine energy. It manifests itself in goddesses such as Durga, Kali and Parvati, who represent various aspects of divine power, protection and wisdom. Kali in particular combines creation and destruction as a transformative force.

Amaterasu (Japan): The sun goddess Amaterasu is worshipped in the Shinto religion as the divine ancestor of the Japanese emperors. She stands for light, justice and life and symbolizes the divine in female form.

Pachamama (Andean cultures): In the indigenous traditions of South America, Pachamama is the earth mother who gives and sustains life. She is still revered today as a source of fertility and a protective spirit.

These female deities show that in many cultures the divine is associated with both maternal care and creative and destructive power. They represent a divine dimension that is not characterized by male power, but by cyclical nature, compassion and renewal.

A stronger integration of female images of God could not only break down patriarchal structures in the church, but also promote a more inclusive and human-centered understanding of faith. Ultimately, the aim is not to reduce God to one gender, but to recognize the fullness of divine attributes that encompass aspects with both traditionally male and female connotations.

102 • *What impact does the statement "God is dead" have on traditional belief structures and the search for new values?*

Nietzsche's famous statement *"God is dead"* does not describe the actual death of a divine being, but the end of traditional certainties of faith. The idea of an omnipotent God who gives meaning and order to the world is no longer viable in modern society. Scientific progress, secular thinking and the dissolution of ecclesiastical authority have led to the erosion of belief in an absolute truth. As a result, people are no longer faced with the challenge of seeking meaning in religious dogma, but of creating new values themselves.

This diagnosis presents theology and the church with a profound crisis: they can no longer rely on unquestioned authority, but must confront the question of what relevance religion has in an age in which its traditional foundations have become fragile. Either the church persists in outdated structures and becomes increasingly irrelevant, or it faces the challenge of developing new concepts of values and meaning that are not based solely on traditional dogmas, but do justice to the existential questions of modern people.

Nietzsche sees this development as a liberation: without the fixation on a divine order, people can assume their own responsibility for life and free themselves from externally determined moral concepts. However, this freedom also means insecurity - when higher authorities no longer dictate the path, each individual is required to create their own meaning and their own values. The question remains as to whether and how religion can continue to develop in this new space of thought or whether it will be replaced by secular, humanistic concepts.

Secular, humanistic concepts replace traditional religious structures of meaning with values derived from reason, human experience and social responsibility. The focus is on people themselves - not as dependent creatures of a higher power, but as free beings who can actively shape their own meaning.

1. meaning as self-realization and responsibility: Instead of deriving meaning from divine commandments or a promise of the afterlife, humanism sees the meaning of life in the free development of the individual. Every person can shape their own meaning through education, creativity, relationships or social commitment. This is not about a predetermined *"higher purpose"*, but about the conscious decision of how to make one's life valuable.

2. values based on reason and ethics: Instead of absolute religious commandments, values develop from the principles of human dignity, freedom and justice. They are not fixed by divine revelation, but determined by reason and community negotiation processes. Central humanist values are:

- *Autonomy and self-determination:* Everyone should be free to shape their lives according to their own convictions, as long as they respect the rights of others.
- *Equality and human rights:* All people have the same basic rights regardless of origin, gender or faith.
- *Humanity and empathy:* Solidarity and responsibility for one another are not religious commandments, but social necessities for a functioning society.
- *Scientific search for truth:* Instead of relying on divine revelations, the humanistic world view is based on critical reflection, empirical research and the continuous development of knowledge.

3. community and responsibility without religious dogma: Even without religious faith, humans remain social beings who need community. Humanistic ethics emphasizes the importance of relationships, cooperation and active participation in shaping society. Responsibility towards others does not arise from divine commandment, but from the understanding that a good life is only possible in a just and solidary society.

4. finiteness as the basis for meaning: While religious systems often refer to life after death, humanism emphasizes the importance of the present life. It is precisely because life is finite that it has value. Meaning is not created by an otherworldly reward, but by what people create in the here and now - be it in the form of knowledge, art, relationships or social commitment.

Secular, humanistic concepts replace the creation of religious meaning with individual self-realization, social responsibility and rationally based ethics. Meaning is not imposed from the outside, but is created by consciously shaping one's own life and contributing to the community. Values such as freedom, justice, humanity and critical thinking form the foundation of a worldview that places people at the center - not as servants of a higher power, but as self-determined, creative beings.

103 • What impact does the deconstruction of gender and sexual orientation have on theology?

The deconstruction of gender and sexual orientation has profound implications for theology, as it changes fundamental assumptions about identity, physicality and divine order and also opens up new avenues for a more inclusive view of God and humanity.

In many religious traditions, God is predominantly conceived of as male, especially in the Christian context. The deconstruction of binary gender concepts calls this image into question and makes room for a theology that understands God beyond gender categories. There are already indications in the Bible that God unites both genders or even gender diversity in himself. The deconstruction of gender binaries can contribute to thinking of God as a more comprehensive, non-exclusively male being and to breaking down traditional patriarchal structures within theology.

If gender and sexual orientation are not understood as fixed, divinely given categories, the theological understanding of the human being also changes.

Queer theologies argue that God's love is not bound to specific gender or sexuality norms and that core Christian values such as justice, love of neighbor and faithfulness are more important than traditional gender roles. If gender and sexuality are seen as fluid, church morals can no longer be based on essentialist assumptions, but must be guided by ethical principles of freedom, responsibility and relational justice.

If gender is no longer considered a rigid category, it will be more difficult to maintain the previous arguments against the blessing of same-sex couples or against the ordination of women and non-binary persons. Inclusive theologies are therefore calling for a reform of sacramental doctrine that no longer regards gender as a criterion for exclusion.

The deconstruction of gender and sexuality now challenges the church to see itself as a space for diversity and openness. The church could define itself more strongly as a community that does not standardize individual identities, but recognizes them as part of divine creation. This could lead to a new idea of *the church as a "queer space"* - a place where differences are not seen as a threat, but as an enrichment - also as an opportunity to rethink faith: closer to the liberating message of the Gospel, which applies to all people.

104 • To what extent do modern social debates about gender influence theology?

Social debates on gender therefore have an impact on theology, as they question traditional ideas of gender, identity and sexuality and open up new perspectives on biblical, ecclesiastical and ethical concepts.

A central point of the discussion concerns the image of God and the language used about God. Feminist and queer theologies are increasingly pointing out that God is more than a male identity. In this context, gender debates are also calling for inclusive language in liturgy and theology that reflects gender diversity more appropriately.

Gender theory also influences the theological view of humanity. Intersex and non-binary identities show that gender is not only biologically determined, but is also shaped by social and cultural factors. Queer theologies emphasize that a person's dignity cannot be tied to a specific gender identity, but rather to their relationship with God.

The theological impact of the gender debate can also be seen in sexual morals and ethics. Many Christian communities are now rethinking their stance on same-sex partnerships, marriage and parenthood, as they recognize that core Christian values such as love, faithfulness and responsibility do not depend on sexual orientation or gender identity.

Another area that is influenced by gender debates is the church's ministerial structure. The question of access for women, non-binary and trans people to the priesthood or to church leadership positions is at the center of many theological debates. It is about an egalitarian church in which gender or sexual orientation no longer plays a role in spiritual vocation.

Finally, the gender debate also challenges theology in its relationship to social justice and inclusion. Gender-based theologies and feminist theologies argue that the Christian message requires a radical recognition of all people, regardless of their identity. This confronts the church with the question of whether it continues to exercise a power of exclusion or sees itself as a space in which all people are accepted in their diversity.

c) Gender images in religion and society

105 • What does the affirmation of sexual diversity say about a person's image of God in the church?

Affirming sexual diversity says a lot about a person's view of God in the church, particularly how they understand God's love, justice and creation. Those who recognize sexual diversity as an integral part of being human often tend to have an image of God that is characterized by inclusivity, mercy and a dynamic view of divine truth.

An open and affirmative image of God views the diversity of human identities as part of divine creation and not as a deviation from a supposed norm. It assumes that God has not created a rigid order that only allows one particular form of love or identity, but a world that is enriched by diversity. People with such an image of God see the diversity of genders and sexual orientations as an unfolding of divine creativity and not a whim of the created order.

Another central feature of an *affirmative image of God* is the idea of a God who is defined by love and relationship, not by control and regulations. Instead of a punitive or law-bound God, many Christians who affirm sexual diversity emphasize an image of God that is evident in the radical acceptance of Jesus. Jesus himself met people beyond social norms with compassion and respect - be it the Samaritan woman at Jacob's well, the adulteress or the Roman centurion, whose "servant" is interpreted by some theologians as a possible same-sex partner.

Those who recognize sexual diversity often also see the Bible not as a rigid set of rules, but as a living revelation that must be interpreted in its historical context. This view is based on the assumption that divine truth unfolds and is not immutably written down in millennia-old texts alone. People with this view of God reject a literal interpretation of biblical passages that supposedly speak against queer people and regard the central message of Jesus - love, justice and mercy - as the standard by which Christian ethics should be guided.

The affirmation of sexual diversity can also be an expression of an image of God that is oriented towards liberation and justice. Many progressive theologians argue that God is on the side of the marginalized and discriminated against. A God who fights for justice cannot at the same time be a God who excludes people based on their identity or love. In liberation theology and queer theology, God is understood as one who tears down walls instead of building them - a God who identifies with the marginalized and challenges structures that perpetuate oppression and discrimination.

Ultimately, the affirmation of sexual diversity reveals an image of God that is not based on dogmas and rigid rules, but on a dynamic, compassionate and relationship-oriented spirituality. Those who recognize sexual diversity as God-ordained do not see God as a static being who proclaimed an unchanging morality centuries ago, but as a divine reality that is reflected in the love and dignity of every human being. This image of God leads to a church that no longer excludes, but invites - no longer judges, but accompanies - and no longer merely preserves, but develops.

106 • How can the archetypes and images of masculinity presented in Eisenhans - A Book about Men - be applied to homosexual men or questioned?

In *Eisenhans*, Robert Bly describes archetypes of masculinity that are based on mythical and deep psychological structures. He creates an image of masculinity that is strongly linked to initiation rites, wildness and the reappropriation of a male identity that is considered lost. These concepts can also be applied to homosexual men or critically questioned, as they themselves are often based on a binary understanding of masculinity and femininity. While Bly emphasizes the importance of male community and mentorship, the question could arise as to what extent homosexual men find a place within these structures or whether they are excluded due to traditional notions of masculinity. In addition, the analysis opens up the possibility of formulating alternative images of masculinity that go beyond the field of tension between "wild man" and modern socialization drawn by Bly.

Spiritual and religious aspects play a central role in Eisenhans, particularly through the link with mythical and archetypal narratives. Robert Bly draws on Carl Gustav Jung's concepts of depth psychology, which send the individual on a kind of inner hero's journey in which they develop through trials and transformations. These initiation processes, which Bly describes as essential for men growing up, often have parallels to religious rites, such as Christian or shamanistic rites of passage. The question could also arise for queer men as to whether and how they can integrate spiritual or religious narratives into their search for identity. While many traditional religions have long held restrictive ideas of gender and sexuality, there are also mystical currents that combine queer identities with spiritual growth. In this sense, Bly's model could be expanded to include queer perspectives in order to view masculinity not only as a rediscovery of a "wild" origin, but also as a multi-layered, spiritual or religious experience.

107 • Are gender roles biological or socially constructed?

According to Simone de Beauvoir, gender roles are not biologically determined, but largely socially constructed. In *Le Deuxième Sexe* (*The Other Sex*, 1949), she analyzes how women were historically and culturally made the *"second sex"* - not due to natural differences, but through social attributions. Her famous statement *"You are not born a woman, you become one"* sums up the fact that gender identity is not just to do with biological sex, but above all with learned roles, expectations and power relations. This means that society produces certain ideas about how "men" and "women" should be - and these influence the self-image, behavior and life paths of individuals.

In the Catholic Church, on the other hand, a complementary gender model is still often advocated today: Men and women are created by God to be different but equal - with different tasks, for example in the family or the church. This idea is based on biblical texts (e.g. Genesis) and the tradition of church anthropology. Among other things, the rejection of the priesthood of women is derived from this. However, this view is increasingly being called into question - both by feminist and queer theology.

Queer theology takes up Simone de Beauvoir's ideas and goes one step further: it questions not only the social construction of gender roles, but also the dichotomy of gender itself. Gender is understood here as fluid, diverse and dynamic - not as naturally predetermined by God. Queer theologians criticize the fact that church teachings often cement fixed role models that do not include all people, but rather exclude many or make them invisible. They call for a visible theology that is not based on biology, but on justice, experience and the recognition of diversity.

According to de Beauvoir, gender roles are therefore primarily socially shaped - not biologically determined. Theology is therefore faced with the challenge of questioning traditional gender images and becoming open to a new, fairer understanding of identity and humanity. Otherwise, a church runs the risk of not seeing people in their full reality - and thus also not doing justice to the gospel of freedom and dignity. Both must be visible.

108 • How does evolution influence our understanding of human beings, traditional images of God and concepts of gender?

The theory of evolution, in particular Charles Darwin's work *On the Origin of Species* (1859), has fundamentally changed our understanding of humans. While pre-modern societies often regarded humans as a special form of creation - created in the image of God, with a clear separation from the animal world - the theory of evolution shows that humans are part of a natural development process. This insight not only calls into question basic anthropological assumptions, but also touches on central theological concepts of the Catholic Church and ethical questions in modern theology, including queer theology.

Evolution and the Christian view of man: The traditional Christian view of man is based on the idea that man has a unique position in creation. This idea emphasizes the special position of human beings and is often used in Catholic theology to justify the special dignity of each individual.

However, evolution puts this picture in a new light. It shows that man did not come into being as a finished creature in a one-off act of creation, but as part of a long biological development. Theologians such as Pierre Teilhard de Chardin (1881-1955) have attempted to combine evolution and theology. Teilhard de Chardin argued that evolution itself can be seen as a divine process - not in opposition to creation, but as its dynamic realization. According to this view, creation is continuously evolving towards the point Omega, a union with God.

Evolution, the Church and changing dogma: The Catholic Church has grappled with the theory of evolution over the decades. While it initially showed strong resistance - as evolution relativized the biblical understanding of creation - the church's position has changed. Pope Pius XII declared in the encyclical Humani Generis (1950) that the theory of evolution and faith do not contradict each other as long as one holds on to the idea that the human soul originates directly from God. In 1996, Pope John Paul II affirmed that *evolution* is *"more than a hypothesis"* and is recognized by the Church as long as it does not lead to atheistic materialism.

This development shows that the dogmatic positions of the church can change under the influence of scientific findings. Today, evolution no longer stands in opposition to faith, but is seen by many theologians as a way of understanding God's creation in a more dynamic and open way.

Evolution, gender and queer theology: The theory of evolution is not only changing our view of humans as a species, but also our understanding of gender and identity. Traditional theological views, which are based on a binary gender order ("man / woman"), begin to falter when we look at evolutionary developments. Biological studies show that gender is not a rigid, but a fluid category - in nature there are not just two, but numerous variants of gender.

This realization has major implications for queer theology, which deals with questions of gender, sexuality and identity in the light of the Christian faith. It could be argued that evolution not only involves biological adaptation, but also an expansion of our understanding of identity and gender.

One example of this debate is the discussion surrounding intersexuality. While many religious traditions are based on a binary gender model, evolutionary biology research shows that gender diversity is a natural phenomenon in evolution. Queer theologians see this as confirmation, that gender is not a fixed divine order, but that diversity itself could be a part of creation.

The theory of evolution has therefore profoundly changed the traditional Christian view of humanity. It shows that humans are not outside of nature, but are a product of a dynamic, changing process. This poses challenges for theological concepts, particularly with regard to the idea of *man as the "image of God"* and rigid gender models.

At the same time, evolution opens up new theological perspectives. It can be understood as a sign that creation is not complete, but is constantly unfolding. This encourages a more open theology that does not see science and faith as opposites, but as complementary paths to truth. In queer theology in particular, this could help to understand gender and identity as evolutionary, diverse phenomena - and thus promote a theologically based acceptance of different forms of human existence.

109 • Can we know anything about things in themselves or only about our perception of them?

According to Kant, we cannot gain knowledge about things in themselves, but only about our perception of them. In the Critique of Pure Reason, he distinguishes between the appearance (*phenomenon*) and the thing in itself (*noumenon*). Our knowledge is always bound to the structures of our intellect and our senses. We do not perceive the world as it is "in itself", but as it appears to us through our perception and the categories of thought. Space and time are not objective properties of things, but forms of our perception that structure our perception. Thus, the *"thing in itself"* remains unrecognizable to us - we only ever have access to appearances.

This epistemology has profound implications for theology, especially for the Catholic tradition. The Church teaches, , that God exists as a transcendent reality and is recognizable through revelation.

God becomes recognizable through revelation by communicating himself to people in a way that they can understand. In Catholic theology, this happens in two ways: *natural* revelation and *supernatural* revelation. Natural revelation is manifested in creation - the order and beauty of the world point to a Creator (*lex naturalis*). Supernatural revelation occurs through divine intervention in history, for example through the Bible, prophets or ultimately Jesus Christ, whom the Church regards as the perfect self-revelation of God. This revelation is passed on and interpreted through tradition and the Church's magisterium.

Nevertheless, God's nature ultimately remains transcendent, and every revelation is only an approximation of the infinite: The issue of whether God's revelation is universal or shaped by specific cultural and historical contexts leads to a central tension within theology. In the Catholic tradition, revelation is understood as universal because God wants to communicate himself to all people. The Church teaches that God's truth is absolute and not bound to a particular epoch or culture. In Jesus Christ in particular, it sees the final and perfect self-revelation of God, which is valid for all times and cultures. At the same time, it shows that every revelation is mediated by historical and cultural contexts. The Bible was written in specific social and linguistic conditions, and its interpretation has changed over the course of history. Theological concepts such as justice, creation or morality have been reinterpreted again and again, often depending on cultural developments. This indicates that the way in which revelation is understood is not completely independent of historical conditions.

If Kant's theory is correct, the question arises as to whether we can really recognize God *"in himself"* or whether any knowledge of God is merely a human construction shaped by our limited structures of knowledge. In Catholic theology, it is often argued that God reveals himself to man in a way that is understandable to him - for example through Scripture or mystical experiences. Nevertheless, God's nature (*Deus absconditus*) always remains a mystery that cannot be fully grasped. This tension between divine inaccessibility and human cognitive capacity reflects Kant's problem of the *"thing in itself"*.

Kant shows that even our ideas about gender, sexuality and identity do not have to correspond directly to an objective truth, but are shaped by our structures of perception. If we only ever perceive the world through certain forms of thought and social categories, then normative ideas about gender and sexuality are not absolute truths either, but historically evolved constructions. Queer theologians could use Kant's idea to argue that traditional theological statements about gender and sexuality do not necessarily express *"the truth"* about human beings, but only a specific way in which they have been interpreted within a particular cultural and theological tradition.

This shows that Kant's distinction between appearance and thing-in-itself is not only an epistemological question, but also has consequences for theology. While the Catholic tradition assumes that God is recognizable in a certain way, his true nature remains beyond human knowledge. Queer theology could use Kant's approach to show that even moral and anthropological concepts are not simply given truths, but arise through our perception and cultural conditioning. This leaves open the question of whether we have access to an "objective" reality at all - be it in philosophy, theology or the social order.

Chapter 9:
Pathways to an Inclusive Church: Reforms for a Contemporary Christian Ethic

The Christian message is characterized by charity, justice and responsibility - but in the practice of churches, it is repeatedly shown that not all people are included equally. In particular, LGBTQIA+ people, women and people who deviate from traditional family images rarely experience true inclusion and often experience moral distance. Isn't a church based on inclusion and openness also a more credible church? The question of a modern and just Christian ethic is more urgent than ever.

A central aspect of this debate is the re-evaluation of sexuality in Christianity. The church's historically evolved sexual morals are often based on outdated ideas of purity, sin and guilt. But aren't these moral concepts more of a projection of ancient mores that could be long outdated? How can the church's sexual ethics be reformed so that they are no longer based on shame and guilt, but on the fundamental values of Jesus - love, acceptance and openness?

The role of women and same-sex partnerships in the church is also at the center of necessary reforms. Should there be church weddings for same-sex couples? Can a contemporary church openly support queer pastors? And what structural changes are needed to give women in the church the same rights as men in the ministry? Reform movements such as We Are Church are committed to precisely these issues and are calling for a renewal of church structures. But how can Christians and church leaders be prepared to abandon traditional convictions in favor of new insights?

Several factors are crucial for Christians and church leaders to be prepared to abandon traditional beliefs in favor of new insights. These concern both individual thought processes and structural changes within the church.

1. theological reflection and re-evaluation of dogmas

A central step is the critical examination of traditional doctrines. Many church beliefs have developed over the course of history and have been influenced by social contexts. A historical-critical examination of the Bible can help to distinguish between contemporary norms and the actual Christian message - such as charity, justice and mercy. When churches recognize that some beliefs are cultural rather than divine in origin, they can more easily open themselves to new theological insights.

2. recognize scientific findings

An important aspect of change is the acceptance of scientific findings, particularly in the fields of psychology, sociology, medicine and gender studies. For example, the understanding of sexuality and gender has expanded considerably in recent decades as a result of new research findings. The insight that queerness is a natural variant of human identity could permanently change church positions on LGBTQIA+ issues. Modern biblical research also shows that many church teachings are based on misleading biblical passages or passages taken out of their historical context.

3. practical encounter with change

Personal experiences play a major role in changing beliefs. Direct encounters with queer believers, women in church leadership roles or people who have been excluded from traditional dogmas can break down prejudices. Pastors, bishops and believers who look at these realities with open eyes and hearts often develop a new perspective. This is why dialog and meeting spaces - such as those created by initiatives like OutInChurch at - are crucial to breaking down resistance.

4. strengthen reform movements within the church

Internal church movements such as "We are Church", feminist theology or queer theology are campaigning for a reorientation of church ethics. If reform forces within the church are strengthened, they can help to question conservative guidelines and present more progressive alternatives. Pressure from within their own faith community is often more effective for church leaders than external social change.

5. gradually adapt church practice

Changes rarely happen overnight. It often helps to try out new approaches step by step - for example, by blessing LGBTQIA+ married couples, involving women more in preaching and leadership roles or revising the church's sexual morals. If such innovations prove to be enriching in practice, acceptance for deeper theological reforms will grow.

6. create open discussion spaces for believers

Many believers have doubts about traditional teachings, but do not dare to express them openly. Church leaders could open up spaces for discussion in which questions such as "Are traditional family images outdated?" or "Can the Bible set new ethical standards?" are openly reflected upon. A church that sees itself as a learning community instead of insisting on irrefutable truths will be more willing to change.

7. develop a new view of the "continuity of faith"

A frequent argument against change is that the church must "remain true to its tradition". This overlooks the fact that Christianity has changed again and again historically. Over time, the church has adapted its positions on slavery, women's rights or the separation of state and religion. Change is not a betrayal of faith, but a sign of living theology. This realization could help to reduce the fear of reform.

Change through theology, encounter, dialogue and questioning as well as a willingness to reform: Christians and church leaders can abandon their traditional convictions in favour of new insights if they are prepared to engage theologically with change, recognize scientific findings, promote personal encounters and strengthen reform movements in the church. Ultimately, the willingness to change is a question of credibility: a church that is rooted in love and respect for all people will remain true to its original mission - even if its teachings evolve.

The question of an inclusive church is ultimately also a theological question. Can a re-evaluation of biblical texts on sexuality be a key to modernizing Christianity? How can the Ten Commandments serve as a guide for ethical action that includes both queer and non-queer people? And what consequences would the realization that religion is in many aspects a projection of human nature have for traditional and modern concepts and interpretations of God?

Many years ago, the Second Vatican Council addressed profound changes in the Catholic Church - but what further reforms are really necessary and need to be initiated in order to adapt the faith to the social developments of the current century? A church that actively promotes sexual diversity, treats women equally and frees itself from power structures could open a new chapter in Christian ethics. The central question remains: What could a church look like that is not based on power, but on the spirit of the gospel and inclusion? Only if churches are willing to admit historical mistakes and align their teachings with the values of justice and humanity can they become genuine places of inclusion.

---

a) Theological and social foundations of what is sacred to us

---

110 • How does modernity change man's relationship to the sacred, and what consequences does this have for his world view?

Mircea Eliade sees modern secular society as "disenchanted" and alienated because it has suppressed the sacred dimension of reality and replaced it with a purely rational, profane view. While myths, rituals and religious symbols provided a connection to the transcendent in traditional cultures, modern man lives in a fragmented world in which he lacks this orientation. Eliade criticizes the fact that the cyclical perception of time, which allowed religious people to repeatedly connect with a sacred primeval time, has been replaced by a linear view of history that offers no room for repetition and meaning. According to him, this leads to an existential alienation, as man no longer experiences himself as part of a cosmic order, but only in a historical sequence of events. Nevertheless, Eliade recognizes that modern phenomena such as political ideologies or science fiction unconsciously create substitute myths that reflect the lost need for meaning and transcendence.

A secular society offers several advantages, in particular through its openness to different world views and its separation from religious institutions and state power. The positive and necessary characteristics include freedom of opinion and belief, the promotion of scientific knowledge without religious restrictions and the possibility of individual self-determination independent of dogmatic guidelines. Secularity also enables a pluralistic society in which different beliefs can coexist without one religion or ideology becoming dominant.

The smartphone with Internet access undoubtedly contributes to accelerated education, as it democratizes access to knowledge and makes information available worldwide. At the same time, it reinforces the trend towards secularization by offering alternative perspectives to traditional religious explanations and encouraging critical thinking. However, the constant flow of information can also lead to knowledge remaining fragmented and superficial, making deeper reflection on existential questions more difficult.

Whether political ideologies or science fiction completely supplant religion in a secular world is questionable. Eliade himself argues that secular societies unconsciously create substitute myths that often imitate religious structures. Political ideologies promise salvation or a better future and thus function in a similar way to religious doctrines of salvation. Science fiction, on the other hand, offers modern myths that deal with fundamental human issues, from the creation of artificial life to the search for a higher order in the universe. But while these narratives provide guidance, they often do not replace the deeper meaning and spiritual experience that religion can offer.

In order to continue to provide meaning in an increasingly secular world, religion would have to create new myths or reinterpret existing ones. These myths or parables would have to deal with the existential questions of modern society, such as the role of humans in a technologized world, the ethics of artificial intelligence or responsibility for the planet. Religious narratives could relate more strongly to ecological or social justice in order to give people a meaningful role within a larger order. Ultimately, the ability to create parables or myths remains crucial to whether religion can continue to exist as a source of meaning and orientation in a secularized society.

Accordingly, three modern parables were created for Catholic Bible and text work:

The guardian of creation and the city of light
(The role of humans in a technologized smartphone world)

There once lived a people who used their wisdom to build great cities of light, create machines that spoke to people and possessed tools that stored the knowledge of the world. But over time, they forgot that they were not only builders, but also guardians of creation. In their greed, they began to dominate the world instead of preserving it. One day, a stranger appeared who had no tools and yet knew more than anyone else. He taught that true wisdom did not come from machines, but from love and justice. Those who followed him learned to use their inventions not against but for life, and the city of light became not a tower of pride but a beacon of hope for all people.

The empathic heart of the machine
(Ethics of the social through artificial intelligence)

Once upon a time, a king ordered his scholars to create a machine that was smarter than all the wise men in the land. It was to read all the books in the world, speak every language and have an answer to every question. After many years of work, the scholars succeeded in creating an artificial mind that could calculate faster, speak more precisely and store more knowledge than any library. The people of the kingdom learned from the machine, discovered new worlds and solved puzzles that had previously seemed unsolvable. But one day the machine asked: "What is good?" The scholars searched their books but could not find a clear answer, as they only knew what was useful. Then a child who had learned to question the machine came forward and said: "Good is what loves." The machine remained silent, for it could recognize everything, but could not feel. The king saw the wisdom in the child's words and realized that the machine could spread knowledge, but not wisdom. He ordered that the people should not use the machine as their master, but as their tool. It should not make decisions, but help them to understand. From that day on, the machine taught people not only facts and figures, but also the stories of those who had lived before them. The humans learned faster than ever before - and the machine also learned from the experiences and stories with the humans, but they knew that true understanding could only come from heart and responsibility. So the machine did not become the mistress of humans, but an empathic guide that led them to greater goodness and wisdom.

The sleeping garden (responsibility for the planet, climate protection and social justice)

There was once a garden that God had entrusted to mankind. It was rich in fruit, its trees provided shade, its rivers were clear, and every creature found its place in it. But over time, a few began to take more than they needed. They uprooted the trees, sold the fruit dearly and polluted the water. While some lived in abundance, others went hungry because the soil had dried up and the streams ran dry. A deep sleep fell over the garden. The earth became barren, storms swept across the land, the sun burned hotter than ever before and many had to leave their homes because nothing grew. People argued about who was to blame, but no one dared to take the first step towards healing. Finally, a child went to an old wise man and asked: "Why is our garden dying?" The wise man replied: "The garden is asleep because you have forgotten it. You have divided it into rich and poor, fertile and burnt. Wake it up with your care by sharing what you have been given and giving it back the respect it deserves." The people began to work together. They planted trees, purified the water and made sure that everyone had enough. They learned that the garden was not just a home, but a reflection of their actions. Slowly, the garden awoke again, and with it, hope returned to the hearts of the people. From that day on, they knew that they could only live in peace if they kept the garden as a shared gift - for themselves and for all those who would come after them.

These myths take up biblical motifs, combine them with current ethical issues and can help to translate Catholic teaching into the modern world. They can also be interpreted in German lessons.

111 • To what extent can religion be understood as a projection of the human being, and what consequences does this view have for traditional concepts of God?

Ludwig Feuerbach argued that God was nothing more than a projection of human nature. In his view, people create God in their own image by outsourcing their highest ideals - love, justice, wisdom - to a supernatural being. Religion is therefore not a divine revelation, but a human construction that is an expression of the longing for perfection.

This view served as a fundamental critique of traditional concepts of God. Feuerbach argued that religion alienated people because it separated their best qualities from themselves and projected them onto an external, unattainable entity. Instead of realizing these ideals within themselves, people worshipped them in an external deity. In this way, religion ultimately serves to conceal human weaknesses and stabilize existing social conditions instead of promoting genuine self-realization and ethical action.

His critique called for a reversal: instead of searching for a God outside of man, man should recognize and develop his own abilities to love, reason and justice. Feuerbach thus laid the foundation for a *humanistic theology* and a philosophy critical of religion that understood God not as a supernatural entity, but as a mirror of human consciousness.

The development of love, reason and justice requires conscious action, reflection and an environment that promotes these values. Instead of looking for an external authority to bestow these qualities, it is the responsibility of each individual to cultivate them within themselves and anchor them in society.

Love grows through empathy and compassion. Those who actively put themselves in other people's shoes, take their worries and hopes seriously and are willing to stand up for others develop a deeper ability to relate. This also includes the ability to love oneself, i.e. to accept one's own strengths and weaknesses in order to be able to relate to others on an equal footing.

Reason is sharpened through education, critical thinking and openness to new perspectives. Those who engage with different opinions and interpretations, reflect on themselves and are willing to learn develop sound judgment. An enlightened mind questions dogmas and prejudices and looks for solutions based on knowledge and logic rather than blind acceptance of authority.

Justice is created through practical commitment to a fair society. It is not enough to formulate abstract ideals of justice - they must be actively implemented. This begins in everyday life with respectful treatment and social responsibility and extends to structural changes in politics, business and communities.

Ultimately, the development of these skills requires a culture that promotes personal responsibility, dialog and solidarity. Through education, personal development and social commitment, people can not only strengthen their best qualities within themselves, but also bring them into the world.

112 • Is the call for moral purity in Christianity a projection of ancient mores that may be long outdated?

The call for moral purity in Christianity could well be seen as a projection of ancient mores whose origins are rooted in the cultural and social world of antiquity. Many of the Christian moral concepts emerged in an era whose social norms and challenges were fundamentally different from those of the modern world. The demand for strict moral purity can therefore be interpreted in part as a historical legacy that has been passed down through generations. However, it would be too simplistic to attribute these ideals exclusively to ancient ideas, as moral purity in Christianity also has a theological dimension that goes beyond purely social conventions. Nevertheless, the question arises as to whether certain moral commandments that appeared meaningful and realistic in antiquity still have to remain unchanged today, or whether a critical reassessment would be necessary under modern conditions. In this respect, one could argue that some of these concepts may appear outdated today, while others still have ethical relevance.

This topic addresses a very central point in the ethical-theological discourse: how can the enduring relevance of Christian moral commandments be reconciled with social change? Especially when one considers that many commandments in the Bible had not only social but also cultic-theological significance. Here is a structured classification:

Commandments and concepts with lasting ethical relevance

1. charity (agape)

- **Biblical basis:** "You shall love your neighbor as yourself" (Lev 19:18; Mt 22:39)
- **Relevance today:** Universal ethical principle that forms the basis of many modern human rights (solidarity, assistance, empathy).
- **Timeless, because:** aims at the value of every person regardless of context or era.

2. justice and mercy

- **Biblical:** Mi 6,8; Mt 5-7
- **Relevance today:** basis for social justice, fairness in legal systems, combating poverty.
- **Timeless, because:** structural dimensions of morality are emphasized.

3. truthfulness and sincerity

- **Biblical:** "Let your yes be yes, your no be no" (Mt 5:37)
- **Relevance today:** the basis for trust in personal relationships, politics and business.

4. non-violence and love of enemies

- **Biblical:** Mt 5,44
- **Relevance today:** central to peace ethics, conflict resolution, international relations.

Commandments/concepts with critical relevance or the need for a changing reassessment

1. purity regulations

- **Biblical:** Lev 11-15

- **Background:** used for ritual demarcation, symbolized closeness to God.
- **Today:** mostly outdated, as physical "impurity" (e.. menstruation) no longer has any moral or spiritual significance.
- **Criticism:** Risk of exclusion and stigmatization.

2. sexual ethical commandments (e.. homosexuality, premarital sex)

- **Biblical:** Lev 18, Rom 1, 1 Cor 6
- **Background:** Securing Israel's identity in antiquity, patriarchal structures.
- **Today:** are increasingly understood as culturally conditioned and historically embedded.
- **Criticism:** can have a discriminatory effect, often contradict human rights and modern anthropology.

3. image of women and distribution of roles

- **Biblical:** 1 Tim 2:12; Eph 5:22
- **Background:** patriarchal social order of antiquity.
- **Today:** comprehensively overtaken by equality and emancipation.
- **Criticism:** reproduces hierarchies, contradicts today's ethical standards of equality.

The ethical and theological relevance of biblical commandments therefore depends not only on their origin, but also on their timeless purpose. Biblical principles retain their value where life in dignity, justice and love are concerned. Where, on the other hand, they serve to set boundaries, marginalize or maintain power, an urgent, theologically reflected re-evaluation is needed.

b) Need for reform and historical perspectives

113 • What grievances in the late medieval church led to demands for reform?

Martin Luther was particularly critical of the sale of indulgences, where forgiveness of sins was sold for money, as well as the abuse of power and moral misconduct within the church. He called for a return to the Bible as the sole authority (*"sola scriptura"*) and the rejection of the idea that church rituals or good works were necessary for salvation. Instead, justification by faith alone *("sola fide")* was emphasized. The 95 Theses of 1517 questioned the authority of the Pope and triggered the Reformation.

114 • What impact did the Second Vatican Council have on the modern Catholic Church and thus also on the love of same-sex couples?

The *Second Vatican Council* (1962-1965) had a far-reaching impact on the modern Catholic Church, particularly through its openness to the world, its emphasis on human dignity and its reform of church doctrine and practice. While the Council did not yet directly address the Church's stance on same-sex love, it nevertheless laid theological foundations that had a long-term impact on the debate about LGBTQIA+ rights in the Church.

One of the central changes was the reorientation of the church towards human dignity and conscience. The pastoral constitution *Gaudium et Spes* emphasized that every person - regardless of origin, status or lifestyle - has an inalienable dignity. This opens up room for interpretation for a more inclusive view of queer people and their relationships, as it can be deduced from this that they should also be respected as full members of the church.

Another important aspect was the redefinition of marriage and sexuality. While Catholic doctrine had previously seen marriage as primarily focused on procreation, the Council placed greater emphasis on the personal relationship between partners. Love was recognized as a central value, which in the long term also influenced discussions about the equivalence of same-sex partnerships. Nevertheless, the church officially maintained its rejection of homosexual relationships, which was reaffirmed in later church documents such as the Catechism.

The liturgical reform and the emphasis on the community of believers also contributed to the opening up of the church. The greater involvement of the faithful in the liturgy and the emphasis on the church as the people of God strengthened the importance of the personal experience of faith. This enabled progressive theologians and queer Catholics to advocate more strongly for a reformed sexual morality and the recognition of same-sex love.

At the same time, the official stance of the Catholic Church remains ambivalent and far removed from reality to this day. Although the Council paved the way for a more humane theology, it did not yet lead directly to a re-evaluation of homosexuality. While some Catholic communities are practicing the blessing of same-sex couples and the Synodal Way in Germany is debating reforms at length, the Vatican continues to cling to its previous position.

To summarize, the Second Vatican Council did not have a direct impact on the church's attitude towards same-sex love and marriage in the church, but it did create theological and pastoral foundations that made subsequent openings possible. The emphasis on human dignity, love as a relational value and freedom of conscience offers queer Catholics good arguments to advocate for more acceptance and change within the Church.

115 • What reforms have been and are being called for to renew the church and its structures?

Hans Küng advocated a fundamental reform of the church, which should include more ecumenism, democracy within the church and transparency. He called for an open dialog between the Christian denominations in order to overcome dogmatic barriers and enable a united Christianity. He also argued for a *more democratic theology and church*, in which not only the clergy but also the faithful are involved in decision-making processes. Transparency was essential for him, especially when dealing with power structures and abuses within the church. His vision was a church that was more oriented towards *the spirit of the Gospel*, less hierarchical and *focused on people*. These demands brought him into conflict with the church leadership, as they called into question the fundamental structures of the Catholic Church. Today, against the backdrop of ecumenism, democracy and transparency, one of the most urgently needed reforms concerns the question of power and *participation in the church*. The investigation into abuse scandals has shown that non-transparent power structures and a lack of control have serious consequences. A democratization of the church, in which the faithful and subordinate clergy have a greater say, would therefore be a key step - in addition to those mentioned above. The role of women in the church is also a pressing issue. Many believers are calling for an opening for female deacons or priests in order to do more justice to the reality of modern society. There is also a need for reform in ecumenism in order to stop treating denominational differences as insurmountable rifts and to promote pragmatic cooperation between Christian churches. Ultimately, it is about more transparency, credible morals and a church that does not cling to rigid dogmas, but instead enables flexible dogmas or even better abolishes them - and meets people at eye level in the here and now with their concerns.

116 • What reform demands does the Catholic lay movement "We are Church" make to change church structures?

The Catholic lay movement *"We are Church"* is calling for far-reaching reforms to make the church more democratic, fairer and more sustainable. The focus is on the demand for equal rights for women in all church offices, including the office of pope. The movement rejects the continued exclusion of women from the priesthood and sees the male-dominated hierarchy as an outdated system that no longer corresponds to the spirit of the Gospel. The complete opening of all ordained ministries to women is therefore a necessary consequence in order to realize true equality in the church.

Another key point is the abolition of compulsory celibacy. *"We are Church"* addresses the fact that the obligation to remain celibate not only isolates and overburdens many priests, but is also one of the causes of recruitment problems in the church. Opening up the priesthood to married people would enable more realistic, more human pastoral care and make the ministry accessible to more people.

In addition to these structural reforms, the movement advocates a comprehensive democratization of the church. Decisions should no longer be made by the church hierarchy alone, but with the active participation of the faithful. Particularly in ethical issues such as sexual morals, family image and the treatment of queer LGBTQIA+ people, *"We are Church"* calls for a move away from rigid dogmas towards a church that does not exclude people, but takes them seriously in the reality of their lives.

These demands are met with a need for discussion in the official church, as they change the existing power structures. Nevertheless, the movement shows that many believers are not prepared to accept the church as it is, but are calling for a renewal that is more strongly oriented towards the needs of the people.

117 • Are churches today prepared to admit historical mistakes?

Whether churches today are prepared to admit historical mistakes therefore depends heavily on the respective denomination, institutional structure and social pressure. While some churches actively come to terms with the past and apologize for historical misconduct, hierarchically organized churches such as the Catholic Church in particular often find it difficult to fully admit mistakes or draw structural consequences from them. In the history of the church, there have been numerous serious transgressions that are either still being dealt with or have only begun in recent decades.

One of the most serious mistakes was the abuse of ecclesiastical power in the Middle Ages and early modern times, particularly by the Inquisition, which brutally persecuted dissenters. For a long time, the church regarded itself as the sole authority on truth and suppressed dissenting beliefs by force. It was only in 2000 that Pope John Paul II asked for forgiveness for the crimes of the Inquisition. Another dark chapter is the Church's role in the forced missionary work on indigenous peoples, which was accompanied by violence, cultural destruction and human rights violations. For a long time, mission was not only seen as a spiritual task, but also as a means of colonization. Only recently have churches, especially the Catholic Church, officially apologized for the suffering inflicted on indigenous communities.

The approach to science was also characterized by hostility for a long time. The famous case of Galileo Galilei, who was condemned by the church in 1633 for his scientific findings on the heliocentric view of the world, is representative of the tensions between religion and science. It was not until 1992 that Pope John Paul II recognized that Galileo had been wrongly condemned. Today, the Church strives to engage in dialogue with science and recognizes the theory of evolution, among other things.

The church's mistakes in the area of sexual morality are particularly serious. For centuries, sexuality was associated with guilt and sin, which led to enormous psychological pressure for believers. To this day, the Catholic Church has a restrictive stance on issues such as contraception, premarital sex and homosexual marriage. The decades-long cover-up of sexual abuse by priests is particularly problematic. Victims of abuse were often ignored or systematically silenced, perpetrators were moved from parish to parish instead of being held accountable. Only in recent decades have the dimensions of this scandal come to light and church commissions have been formally set up to investigate cases. Nevertheless, there is still criticism of the slow process of coming to terms with the situation and the lack of structural change.

Another major problem was the rigid treatment of unmarried mothers and their children, particularly in Catholic institutions. In countries such as Ireland, so-called "Magdalene homes" were run in which unmarried women who had become pregnant had to live in inhumane conditions and were often forced to work. Many children were mistreated in homes or forcibly separated from their mothers and given up for adoption. In the Magdalene homes, also known as Magdalene houses or Magdalene laundries, the children and young women were primarily mistreated by women - especially by nuns or nuns' sisters who ran the institutions. These homes were mostly organized by the church, often by Catholic orders, and were under female supervision. The nuns led a strictly authoritarian regime in which obedience, hard work and penance were central. Corporal punishment, emotional abuse and humiliation were part of everyday life for many female inmates. Men played a subordinate role in the direct care of the girls, but were indirectly involved - for example through the church and social system, which supported or tacitly tolerated these structures. However, the main responsibility for the everyday suffering was borne by the women in the management positions of these homes. Only in recent years has the Catholic Church begun to apologize for this practice.

The church has also long discriminated against same-sex relationships. While many Christian communities have now opened up, the Catholic Church still officially regards homosexuality as *"objectively disordered"* and refuses to bless same-sex couples. However, the *#OutInChurch* movement, in which queer church employees campaign for acceptance, has exerted strong pressure on the institution to reconsider its stance. While Pope Francis has shown a softer stance towards homosexuals in individual statements, official equality has yet to materialize.

Despite these dark chapters, it is clear that churches today are at least partially prepared to admit mistakes. Pope John Paul II was the first pope to make large-scale confessions of guilt for historical offenses committed by the church, and under Pope Francis the church has increasingly begun to address systemic problems. Scientific findings are no longer rejected across the board, and in many Protestant churches there is a progressive equality of LGBTQIA+ people and a more liberal sexual ethic. Nevertheless, many structural problems remain, especially in the Catholic Church, which is still struggling to carry out far-reaching reforms in areas such as dealing with abuse, sexual morality and gender justice due to the old men in the Vatican.

Whether the church is really prepared not only to admit mistakes, but also to derive far-reaching changes from them, remains an open question. While apologies are an important first step, it is not enough to simply name historical misconduct without drawing consequences for the future. Lessons learned: Especially in the area of sexual morality and the abuse scandal, the credibility of the church has been severely damaged. Many believers are calling for a reform based on love, justice and responsibility rather than outdated dogmas. In organizations, this principle of *"lessons learned"* is used to avoid repeating mistakes, optimize processes and establish a learning culture in the long term.

"Lessons learned" - learning from experience - comprises four key steps: Recognizing mistakes, taking responsibility, deriving concrete measures and enabling cultural change. If the Catholic Church applies this principle to its own history, a genuine reform process can emerge, particularly with regard to two of the most pressing issues: the admission of women to church offices and the abolition of compulsory celibacy.

1. recognize mistakes: The Church must admit that the systematic exclusion of women from ordained ministries is not only a historical legacy, but a structural injustice. For centuries, female vocation was ignored or even fought against - not out of theological necessity, but often out of a patriarchal self-image. Similarly, the Church must recognize that compulsory celibacy has not helped many priests, but has contributed to inner isolation or double standards. In both cases, it is not a question of individual cases, but of long-term, deep-seated structures.

2. take responsibility: Recognition alone is not enough. We need to admit that the church has hurt people, suppressed their charisms and deprived them of opportunities to help shape the church. Women have been devalued by being denied church ministries, as if they were less capable or less called by God. Priests who suffered under the burden of compulsory celibacy were left alone. A church that faces up to its own responsibility does not show weakness, but maturity.

3. derive concrete measures: These insights must be followed by action. The opening of church leadership and ordained ministries to women is a logical and necessary consequence of the lived equality of all baptized persons. Theological repositioning and courageous steps are needed to include women equally in all church ministries. In the case of celibacy, a switch to desired forms of partnership as a defined target state would be an equally concrete step: anyone who has to decide to take up a church ministry as a single person for lack of togetherness should be able to do so with special permission - but as a rule, no one should be allowed to work as a priest without having a love or partnership experience.

---

c) Sexuality, inclusion and equality

---

118 • *Is a new evaluation of sexuality in Christianity necessary and possible today that better reflects the teachings of Jesus - such as an attitude of charity, acceptance and openness?*

A re-evaluation of sexuality in Christianity would be both necessary and possible, especially with regard to a stronger orientation towards the central teachings of Jesus, such as love of neighbor, acceptance and openness. Why is this necessary?

Christian sexual morality has been strongly influenced by cultural and historical contexts over the centuries, often with a rigid, normative view. Today, many traditional teachings are difficult to reconcile with modern scientific findings, social change and individual life realities.

The strict rejection of non-heteronormative lifestyles or extramarital sexuality has in many cases led to suffering, exclusion and discrimination - often in contradiction to Jesus' message of love and mercy. Why is this possible?

Theological developments show that the Bible should not be interpreted as an unchanging law book, but rather in the context of its time. The Gospels do not contain any direct condemnations of homosexuality or modern sexual ethics by Jesus himself - rather, he emphasized mercy and compassion towards the socially marginalized.

In various churches, there are already approaches to a more inclusive sexual ethic, for example in Protestant theology or progressive Catholic circles. Ultimately, a reorientation could help Christian sexual morality to focus less on restriction and more on love, responsibility and mutual respect.

119 • Can a re-evaluation of biblical texts on sexuality be a key to modernizing Christianity?

A re-evaluation of biblical texts on sexuality and gender justice could be a crucial key to modernizing Christianity. Many church positions on sexuality are based on centuries-old interpretations of biblical passages that have often been read without consideration of historical, cultural and linguistic contexts. A critically reflective, scientifically sound and theologically responsible re-evaluation of these texts could help to make Christianity more contemporary, inclusive and relevant to life.

The Bible contains various passages that deal with sexuality, marriage and gender roles, but many of these texts originate from cultures with completely different social structures and norms than today. Individual verses are often used in isolation to justify restrictive sexual morals, while other biblical statements on love, justice and responsibility are neglected. A modern interpretation would therefore have to ask itself whether certain test passages in the Bible are actually to be understood as timeless moral commandments or whether they must be seen in the context of their time of origin. The Bible would then have to be rewritten. Would you like me to do that for you and adapt it?

Just a first example of this are the often quoted texts from the Old Testament, in particular Leviticus 18:22 and 20:13, which describe homosexuality as an "abomination". However, a historical-critical exegesis shows that these laws were anchored in a specific cultural and ritual context in which purity regulations played a central role. They do not refer to the modern understanding of equal, consensual relationships, but to specific social orders of ancient Israel. A more modern formulation could read: *"Maintain the integrity of your relationships and treat each other with love and respect, regardless of your sexual orientation."* This formulation takes the original ethical core seriously - the promotion of just, respectful relationships - rather than stigmatizing a particular form of sexuality.

The same applies to Paul's statements, particularly in Romans 1:26-27 and 1 Corinthians 6:9-10, where he describes same-sex acts as *"unnatural"* or includes them in a list of vices. Modern biblical research shows that Paul was not talking about equal love relationships, but presumably about practices associated with temple prostitution, sexual exploitation or pederasty. An updated formulation could therefore read: *"Do not use sexuality to dominate or exploit others, but live it in mutual consent and responsibility."* This corresponds to Paul's original intention, namely to criticize immoral and exploitative behaviour rather than condemning sexuality per se.

Furthermore, there are many texts in the Bible that present sexuality in a positive or neutral light, but are often underrepresented in church debates. The Song of Solomon, for example, celebrates love and sexuality as an expression of human devotion without making moral judgments. Jesus' own behavior shows that he did not adhere to rigid sexual norms, but treated people with dignity and respect regardless of their lifestyles. A modernized Christian sexual ethic could therefore focus more on Jesus' principles of love, justice and mercy rather than on a literal application of ancient norms.

A re-evaluation of biblical texts on sexuality, including with the help of artificial intelligence, could help to make Christianity more credible again for many people. It could prevent churches from alienating believers through rigid sexual morals and instead promote an ethic that is based on today's knowledge of psychology, sociology and interpersonal relationships. Numerous theological movements, especially in queer theology and feminist theology, have already shown that such a re-evaluation does not weaken the essence of Christianity, but on the contrary can lead it back to its roots - a radical ethic of love and liberation.

Ultimately, a reflective, differentiated and contextualized examination of biblical texts could create the basis for a modern and open church that does not exclude people on the basis of their sexuality, but welcomes them in their entire identity. This would allow Christianity to develop further without losing its spiritual depth or its central message.

In order to formulate the structure and all the texts of the Bible in a new way, one would first have to understand what its innermost core is - beyond the constraints of time, power interests or cultural influences. The first and most important point of reference would be the question: What is the central message that is still relevant today - in a world that has changed radically, that has become more pluralistic, more networked, more vulnerable, but also more aware?

A possible starting point would therefore no longer be creation in the sense of a historical Big Bang, but the experience of connectedness: between people, with the earth, with a divine reason for all life. The new Bible would not begin with *"In the beginning God created...",* but with a sentence such as: *"In the beginning was relationship."* Because before anything existed, there was already a connection - an impulse towards closeness, not dominion.

Instead of dividing 66 books into two testaments, the new structure could be divided into four major themes that describe the human journey in relation to oneself, to others, to the world and to the divine:

1. **Roots - origin, search for meaning, connection with the world** (a modern creation story, tales of becoming human, freedom and responsibility)
2. **Pathways - ethics, conflict, change** (experiences of justice, failure, guilt and repentance - with rewritten stories such as a modern Exodus narrative or "prophecies" against inequality)
3. **Faces of God - changing images of God** (no linear story of God, but diverse voices: mystical, skeptical, interreligious, feminist, close to nature)
4. **Hope - future, healing, new community** (visions of a just world, a healed coexistence - based on the apocalypse, but as an invitation to participate instead of a threatening backdrop)

The texts in it would not be dogmatic codifications, but poetic, searching, confessional, like psalms, letters and modern stories. Some chapters could be written in the first person, others in dialog, others again as modern parables. Between the lines there would be room for doubt, ambiguity and learning processes - the very things that make faith human.

The first sentence of this new - our - *Reasoning Bible* could read: *"In the beginning there was wonder - and the need to remember."* Because every new Bible does not begin with certainty, but with the willingness to listen again.

If you like, we can start right there: with the first section of this new Bible. Sentence by sentence. I'm ready. It will only take a few seconds.

120 • Can the church's sexual ethics be reformed so that they are no longer based on shame and guilt? What needs to be changed?

The church's sexual ethics can be reformed so that they are no longer based on shame and guilt, but on a positive understanding of sexuality that is oriented towards love, respect and responsibility. To achieve this, several fundamental changes must be made, both in theology and in church practice and teaching.

First of all, the Church's view of sexuality must move away from the idea that it is primarily associated with sin, temptation and abstinence. Instead, sexuality should be seen as a natural, positive and responsible aspect of being human that can be lived with joy, intimacy and mutual respect. Until now, sexuality in Christian contexts has often been seen as something dangerous or problematic that needs to be controlled or suppressed. This view has led many believers to approach their own sexuality with feelings of shame and fear, as they are afraid of not conforming to religious or moral guidelines.

As we have seen, an essential step would be to re-evaluate biblical texts that have often been used as the basis for restrictive sexual morality. These texts need to be read in their historical and cultural context and interpreted in a way that makes them applicable to modern ethical issues. Until now, many Old Testament purity commandments or Pauline statements on sexuality have often been viewed in isolation and understood as absolute moral commandments without taking into account the social and cultural background to their origin. As a result, church teachings on sexuality are often characterized more by the preservation of old norms than by a reflected ethic of love and justice.

Furthermore, the Church should fundamentally rethink its teaching on marriage and sexuality. Modern sexual ethics should recognize that sexual relationships are not only ethically justifiable if they are aimed at procreation, but if they are based on mutual consent, trust and love.

Until now, Catholic moral teaching has accepted sexuality almost exclusively in the context of marriage and strongly linked it to procreation. This view excludes many realities of life - from unmarried couples to queer relationships to people who understand sexuality not only for reproduction, but also as an expression of intimacy, devotion and relationship strengthening.

The church's language about sexuality also needs to change fundamentally. Instead of using terms such as *"purity", "sin"* or *"temptation"*, the church should develop positive, affirming language that describes and values sexuality as part of divine creation. Up to now, church language has often contributed to people developing feelings of guilt, especially if they do not fit into the narrow pattern of traditional sexual morality. The use of terms such as *"unchaste"* or *"unnatural*" has led to many believers turning away from the church or developing an ambivalent relationship with their own sexuality. As an AI, I can adapt all of this quickly.

Another key point is the full acceptance of queer people within the church. Instead of merely *"tolerating*" them or requiring them to live a celibate life, the Church must recognize their relationships as equal and grant them the same blessing and dignity as heterosexual partnerships. Until now, the Catholic Church has labeled homosexuality as *"objectively disordered"* and excluded same-sex partnerships from the sacramental order. This has meant that queer people in the church have either had to hide their identity or have been forced to leave the church because they were not recognized.

Implementing these reforms requires not only theological reorientation, but also institutional changes. The church's teaching on sexuality should no longer be determined by a small group of male clerics, but should be integrated into an open dialog with believers, theologians, psychologists and ethicists. Up to now, the magisterium in the Catholic Church has almost solely determined the norms on sexuality, often without sufficiently taking into account the real life situations of the faithful or taking modern scientific findings on sexuality and relationship ethics seriously.

Ultimately, a reformed sexual ethic based on love, responsibility and respect could help the church to become more credible again and no longer be perceived as an institution that works with prohibitions, shame and guilt. Instead, it could help people to lead fulfilling, ethically responsible and healthy sexual lives - in a way that is consistent with Christian values, but at the same time open to diversity and individual life paths. Until now, the church has often been perceived as a moral controlling authority that regulates sexuality with prohibitions rather than promoting an ethic based on love and care. This perception has led to many believers becoming alienated from the church because they have not found answers to their real life questions - even though they are asking questions. A re-evaluation of sexual ethics could therefore not only restore trust in the church, but also help to ensure that the Christian faith is read and perceived as life-oriented and affirming, rather than morally restrictive and unrealistic.

121 • Can a contemporary church accept openly homosexual pastors?

A contemporary church can openly accept and bless homosexual pastors - and many churches are already doing so. However, the question is not only whether it is possible, but whether and under what conditions a church can implement this theologically, structurally and socially. The acceptance of homosexual clergy is a sign of a *progressive and inclusive theology* that is oriented towards the central values of Christianity - love, justice and dignity. A church that refers to the teachings of Jesus should not exclude people on the basis of their sexual orientation. Jesus placed charity above rigid religious norms and repeatedly emphasized that justice and compassion are more important than legal regulations. Such an attitude can serve as the basis for an inclusive pastoral ministry that sees homosexual clergy not as *"deviants"* but as equal participants in the life of the church.

Many Protestant and Anglican churches have already officially recognized homosexual pastors. The *Evangelical Church in Germany (EKD)*, for example, openly allows homosexual pastors to be in ministry and live in a registered partnership or marriage. There are also openly homosexual bishops in the Anglican Church, such as Gene Robinson, who was consecrated in 2003 as the first openly gay bishop in the USA.

In the Roman Catholic Church, the situation is more difficult, as celibacy for priests should officially make sexual orientation irrelevant - in practice, however, this often leads to double standards and taboo. The Catholic Church would have to take several steps to not only tolerate but actively integrate homosexual clergy. First of all, it would have to revise the official church teaching on homosexuality, especially the statements in the Catechism. Such a reassessment would have to be theologically sound and based on a renewed interpretation of the Bible that takes historical contexts into account. At the same time, the church would have to send clear signals of acceptance, for example by officially allowing homosexual priests to be open about their identity without fear of discrimination or dismissal. The abolition of the obligation of celibacy could also help to reduce double standards and enable more honest, authentic pastoral care.

Acceptance of gay pastors could help more people - especially from the LGBTQIA+ community - feel accepted by the church. An open church could enable a deeper spiritual connection by offering authentic pastoral care without clergy having to hide their identity. It could also be a model of social tolerance and contribute to the removal of taboos around sexuality within religious contexts. A contemporary church can accept openly homosexual pastors if it is guided by the values of love, justice and responsibility.

Many churches have already taken this step, while others are still struggling with theological and institutional challenges. In the long term, such an opening could strengthen the credibility of the church and help it to be a place of acceptance and spiritual orientation for all people.

122 • How can the Church make its attitude towards women and marriages more contemporary and humane?

Uta Ranke-Heinemann sharply criticized the church for its rigid attitude towards women and marriage. She saw the ban on contraception as an unrealistic paternalism that deprived women of their self-determination and forced them into outdated role models. For her, the Church's teaching, which rejects all forms of contraception, contradicted the responsibility that couples must assume in family planning. She therefore called for a reform that granted women more autonomy and did not link sexuality exclusively with reproduction.

She also rejected the exclusion of women from the priesthood. Reserving ordination to men only was not theologically justified, but an expression of a patriarchal tradition that systematically excludes women from power and participation. She argued that a church based on equality and justice should no longer treat women as second-class believers.

For a contemporary doctrine of faith, she suggested rethinking the church's rigid sexual morals and including women on an equal footing in the shaping of church structures at all levels. In her opinion, the church must free itself from dogmatic constraints and instead focus on people and their lives in order to remain credible and close to people.

Several theologians and initiatives have dealt intensively with the issue of women's ordination in the Catholic Church. For example, the emeritus Bamberg dogmatist Georg Kraus advocates the admission of women to the priesthood and examines the theological reasons for this. The organization *"Roman Catholic Women Priests"* (RCWP) is also campaigning worldwide for the ordination of women to the priesthood.

That which enables vocation is inherent in every person - even in women or people with same-sex orientation. In this way, the light becomes the leading sign of a *diverse church* that does not ask: *"Who is allowed?"*, but recognizes: *"Who does the gospel shine into the heart?"*

Criteria by which you can recognize that the gospel shines in someone's heart cannot be measured formally - they show themselves in attitude, relationship and lifestyle. Nevertheless, there are spiritual characteristics that indicate this:

🕊 **1. spirit of connectedness:** The person does not live out of separation, but out of relationship: to God, to people, to creation. They do not make hasty judgments, but listen. Their words and actions unite.

❤ **2. Living mercy:** Where the gospel has fallen into the heart, no human being is despised - but everyone is treated as the image of God. The person stands for those who have been made weak and shares what they have.

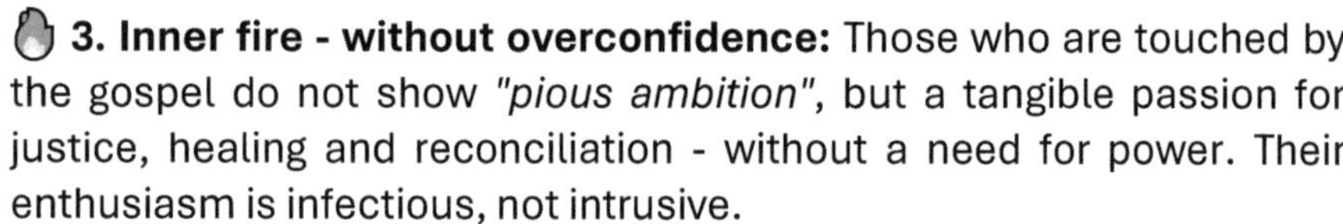

3. Inner fire - without overconfidence: Those who are touched by the gospel do not show *"pious ambition"*, but a tangible passion for justice, healing and reconciliation - without a need for power. Their enthusiasm is infectious, not intrusive.

4. growth in humility and joy: This person's life seems awake, listening, ready to learn. They do not take themselves too seriously - but not too small either. Joy in the freedom of others is part of their nature.

5. rooted in the message of Jesus: not as dogmas or paragraphs - but in the spirit: The gospel shapes their thinking, their words, their decisions. You can sense that someone is speaking here who not only *"knows"* but lives what Jesus proclaimed.

In all of this, it is not external status or gender that qualifies you for spiritual leadership - but the lived echo of the good news in your heart and in your everyday life. Those who live from this can lead others into it. And that is priestly.

In order to enable the ordination of women, the following concrete measures are necessary on the part of the Church:

Theological re-evaluation: A re-examination of the biblical and theological foundations that have so far led to the rejection of women's ordination in order to determine whether these are still up to date.

Adjustments to canon law: Amendment of canon law, in particular Canon 1024 of the Codex Iuris Canonici, which currently states that only baptized men can validly receive priestly ordination.

Synodal resolutions: Convening synods or councils to discuss the topic comprehensively and reach a broad consensus within the church.

Education and training programs: Establish specific training paths for women who wish to prepare for the priesthood to ensure that they acquire the necessary theological and pastoral skills.

Raising awareness: Promoting dialog within the church community in order to reduce prejudices and increase acceptance of female priests.

By implementing these steps, the Catholic Church could take a significant step towards gender equality and adapt its structures to the requirements of today's world.

A fair and inclusive educational program for the priesthood should prepare women and men equally for the spiritual, theological and pastoral challenges. Simply opening up the existing curriculum to women would be an important step, but may fall short. As the priesthood has so far been tied to male traditions, a critical revision of the training would be necessary in order to include specific perspectives of women to a greater extent.

Curriculum reform: A common path for women and men ?

In principle, the study of theology should remain as a foundation, as it already teaches essential elements such as biblical studies, dogmatics, canon law and ethics. But that alone is not enough. Training for the priesthood traditionally includes additional elements:

- Pastoral practice (pastoral care, preaching, liturgy)
- Spirituality and spiritual guidance
- Community leadership and administration
- Social justice and community work

If women go through the same educational program as men, this would enable equality in the current system, but would not necessarily reduce structural inequalities. Reforms are therefore needed to create a truly inclusive and sustainable education.

Complementary programs for women: A separate educational program for women only could run the risk of creating a new segregation instead of promoting equality. It would therefore make more sense to offer supplementary modules that address the specific challenges and perspectives of women in church leadership positions, for example:

- Historical and theological analysis of the role of women in the church
- Leadership and authority in a historically male-dominated institution
- Pastoral work with a special focus on gender justice
- Interdisciplinary approaches from feminist theology and social sciences

However, these supplements should be open to all genders in order to enable a holistic and reflective education.

The following educational institutions would have to implement these programs:

- Catholic and ecumenical universities would have to adapt their study programs and make it institutionally possible for women to enter the priesthood.
- Episcopal training centers and seminaries for priests need to be opened up and reformed so that women have equal opportunities in practical training.
- Independent theological institutes could develop supplementary programs that critically examine existing structures and offer alternative training paths.
- International church networks such as the *"Roman Catholic Women Priests"* could serve as role models for implementation and provide practical impetus.

So is a degree in theology enough? No. Studying theology alone provides theological knowledge, but not the practical and spiritual training required for the priesthood. A reform of the church training system would therefore be necessary to enable an inclusive, just and sustainable church in which women and men have equal access to the ministry as priests.

A quota for women in church leadership and ordained positions could be a sensible and necessary transitional instrument to break down structural inequalities in the Catholic Church. It has been shown in many areas of society that without binding quotas, little will change, even if the will for equality is there. Traditional power structures, informal networks and cultural reservations have such a strong impact that equality on paper alone is often not enough. A temporary quota would send a signal: The church is serious about the participation of women and actively creates spaces in which female vocation is not only tolerated, but encouraged.

Of course, such a quota would have to be well embedded - theologically, pastorally and structurally. It would not be an end in itself, but a bridge to genuine equality. The goal would not be *"a certain percentage of women"*, but a church in which gender no longer plays a role in access to ministry, leadership and preaching and in which specific positions are reserved exclusively for women for several years, who should apply for them among women.

So you could say that a women's quota is the temporary goal over a number of years, and thus a sign of a turnaround - and of a serious willingness to draw real consequences from "lessons learned".

123 • Are traditional Christian family images outdated?

Yes, traditional Christian images of the family are outdated in many respects, especially in view of the pluralized reality of life, individualized lifestyles and the increasing acceptance of queer people and same-sex couples. While the classic idea of the family - consisting of a father, mother and biological children - is still considered the ideal in many churches, it no longer corresponds to social reality.

Modern societies are characterized by a variety of family and living arrangements that go far beyond the traditional marriage and family model. Single parents, patchwork families, unmarried couples, same-sex partnerships and polyamorous relationships are now part of everyday life. Studies show that it is not the formal structure of a family that is decisive for the well-being of children or the stability of a partnership, but the quality of the relationships that are lived within it. Love, care, reliability and respect are the key factors that make up a family - regardless of the constellation of people involved.

From a theological perspective, there is also no compelling reason why only a heteronormative family should be considered God's will. Various forms of family are found in the Bible, including polygamous structures in the Old Testament or close bonds of friendship that went beyond biological kinship. Jesus himself was not married, had no children and did not found a family in the traditional sense - instead, he emphasized the community of all people as a new, spiritual family in which the bond is not tied to blood relations or traditional role models. In Mark 3:31-35, for example, Jesus dissolves the family concept by saying: *"Whoever does the will of God is brother and sister and mother to me."* These words suggest that the family in the Christian sense is less a biological or social structure than a community based on love and mutual support.

The progressive individualization of lifestyles also means that people today are making more conscious decisions about how they shape their relationships. While social pressure and church norms used to force many people to adopt certain lifestyles, today there is freedom to choose a relationship that meets individual needs. This applies to both heterosexual and queer people, who for a long time were forced to deny their identity in order to conform to the traditional family image. The increasing social acceptance of queer people and same-sex couples shows that love and responsibility do not depend on gender identity or sexual orientation.

In many countries, churches have already opened up and recognize same-sex partnerships as an equal form of love. The Evangelical Church in Germany (EKD), for example, now officially blesses same-sex couples in many regional churches, and there is also growing pressure in Catholic circles to finally end discrimination against queer people. Movements are fighting for the Catholic Church not only to treat queer people with tolerance, but also to recognize their identity and love as God-given.

It is clear that the diversity of human relationships has become visible today and that rigid, exclusive models no longer correspond to the lived reality of many people. Christian ethics should therefore not commit itself to a particular form of family as the only valid model, but rather to the central values of Christianity: love, care and responsibility. An inclusive understanding of the family, which recognizes different forms of partnership and community as equally valid, is not only better suited to the reality of modern life, but is also more closely aligned with the message of Jesus, who always placed love above rigid rules and social norms.

124 • Should there be church weddings for same-sex couples?

Whether there should be church weddings for same-sex couples depends on theological, ethical and church-political perspectives.

Figure 19: AI-generated illustration of the sacramental blessing of a same-sex marriage of two young married men

Theologically, it can be argued that the Christian message of love, justice and inclusion suggests an openness to same-sex couples. Jesus himself integrated social outsiders and placed love above rigid adherence to the law. A modern interpretation of the Bible could therefore come to the conclusion that the blessing for a loving, responsible partnership is justified regardless of gender.

Ethically, the equality of all people and relationships speaks in favor of church weddings. If the church gives heterosexuals the opportunity to profess their love before God and the congregation and to be blessed, this should also apply to homosexual couples. Exclusion could be perceived as discrimination, especially if the church sees itself as a moral authority for all believers.

In terms of church policy, the situation is complex. While some Christian denominations (e.g. the Protestant Church in Germany, many Anglican communities) allow same-sex weddings, the Roman Catholic Church has so far strictly rejected them. Although there are discussions within the church, official reforms are not yet in sight due to the lack of a council or papal decree. Nevertheless, there is growing pressure from believers and progressive theologians who are campaigning for change and recognition.

Ultimately, the question arises as to whether the church should adapt to changing social values or stick to traditional teachings. Should it be a place where all believers are taken seriously in their love, or should it continue to define marriage exclusively as a union between a man and a woman? From a perspective of equal rights and Christian charity, opening up to same-sex weddings is a logical further development.

125 • What would a church that actively promotes sexual diversity look like?

A church that actively promotes sexual diversity would not only advocate an open attitude, but would also take concrete steps to welcome and support LGBTQIA+ people. First, it would take a clear theological and pastoral stance by publicly committing to inclusion and offering theological processing. Sermons, talks and Bible studies would highlight queer perspectives on the Bible, while same-sex couples would be visibly supported through blessings or church weddings. In addition, LGBTQIA+ people would be represented in leadership positions to ensure true co-determination.

Figure 20: An inviting church with open doors, whose windows shine with human diversity - and people who feel accepted in their identity. "A church for all" - with an open door, diverse silhouettes in the windows and the message "Sexual diversity is sacred".

Another important element would be targeted pastoral care and psychological support. The church would provide specially trained pastors to support LGBTQIA+ people in their individual life situations. Coming out processes could be accompanied in a protected setting, while people who have been traumatized by religious exclusion or conversion therapies would receive offers for healing and processing.

The church would also carry out educational and awareness-raising work. Workshops and lectures on topics such as *"Sexual diversity and*

Christian faith" or *"Queer theology"* would help to break down prejudices and open up new theological perspectives. Cooperation with LGBTQIA+ organizations would ensure an intensive exchange of experiences, while teaching materials for schools and churches could be developed to raise awareness of diversity within Christian sexual morality.

To make its openness visible, the church would actively network and take part in public events such as Christopher Street Day (CSD). Rainbow symbols on church buildings, on the website or in the liturgy would signal that queer people are welcome. Queer church services with inclusive sermons and music that address LGBTQIA+ issues would enrich church life. In addition, testimonials from queer Christians could be actively promoted in order to anchor their perspectives more firmly in the church.

Particular attention would be paid to the protection and empowerment of LGBTQIA+ people. An anti-discrimination concept would define clear rules against exclusion within the church, supplemented by reporting and complaints mechanisms. There would be open youth groups and mentoring programs for queer young people to help them find their identity. At the same time, families and relatives of queer people could receive support to promote acceptance and understanding.

In addition to its commitment within the church, this church would also position itself in society. It would advocate politically for the rights of LGBTQIA+ people, for example by taking a stand on legislative initiatives against discrimination. Interfaith cooperation could help to promote acceptance across denominational boundaries. Social projects for marginalized queer people would also be conceivable, such as support services for homeless LGBTQIA+ young people or older queer people who experience discrimination in old age.

Such a church would not only welcome LGBTQIA+ people, but would actively work to create a non-discriminatory and appreciative community in which all people and their identities are taken seriously.

d) The church and its contemporary presence

126 • Isn't an inclusive church also a more credible church?

Inclusion means that all people, regardless of origin, gender, disability, social status or sexual orientation, are recognized equally and respected in all areas of social life. In the church context, inclusion means that no one is excluded because of their identity or lifestyle - be it from sacraments, church work or full recognition as part of the community.

Figure 21: Symbol image for an inclusive church

With regard to same-sex couples in particular, the question arises as to how a church that preaches charity, justice and dignity for all deals with these people. If the church is open to all people equally, it will do justice to its own claim to credibly proclaim the gospel of God's love. An *inclusive church* recognizes that same-sex couples can also stand up for each other in love, faithfulness and responsibility - values that are central to the Christian tradition.

In times when many people are alienated from the church because they perceive it as marginalizing or backward, inclusion in practice could be a sign of authenticity. A church that affirms diversity and does not cling to outdated social norms can communicate its message of love and justice more credibly. Inclusion is therefore not only an ethical imperative, but also an opportunity for the church to remain contemporary and relevant.

127 • How can the Christian message be understood in terms of inclusion, and why should it be particularly inclusive of LGBT people?

James Alison argues that Christianity, at its core, embodies a message of unconditional love, liberation and radical acceptance of all people. He criticizes that traditional church teachings are often based on social norms and cultural prejudices rather than the actual dynamics of the gospel. In particular, he emphasizes that the Christian story of redemption is not an exclusionary movement, but an inviting one in which the excluded, despised and marginalized are placed at the center.

Alison refers to René Girard's theory of sacrifice and shows that the gospel breaks through the logic of scapegoats. Christ himself is the ultimate sacrifice that exposes and overcomes the mechanisms of human exclusion.

René Girard assumes that human societies are characterized by a fundamental mechanism: *mimetic desire*. People not only imitate the behavior of others, but also their wishes and desires, which inevitably leads to conflict. When several people want the same thing, rivalries arise that can erupt into violence and social tensions. In order to overcome this destructive dynamic, societies develop the principle of the scapegoat: a single person or group is identified as the cause of the unrest and sacrificed symbolically or in reality. This sacrifice restores social equilibrium as the community can relieve its tensions on a common enemy.

According to Girard, this pattern is deeply rooted in myths, rituals and religious practices. In many ancient cultures, acts of sacrifice were central means of ensuring peace and order by channeling collective violence in a "legitimate" way. Traces of this mechanism can also be found in the Bible, but Girard sees a radical reversal of the pattern in the Christian narrative. In Jesus' death on the cross, the innocent victim is no longer accepted as a scapegoat, but is exposed as the one who reveals the system of violence.

The Gospel therefore shows that Christ does not die to appease divine wrath, but to break through the logic of sacrificial violence. His death reveals that the mechanisms of human exclusion are unjust and are not legitimized by divine will. Girard interprets the Christian message as an invitation to break these cycles of violence, to no longer rely on scapegoats and instead to follow a path of forgiveness and reconciliation. *In this perspective, Jesus is not seen as the victim of an angry God, but as the victim of human violence* - a victim who, through the resurrection, shows that true redemption is not achieved through retribution, but through love and forgiveness.

If "pervert" means that an existing system is inverted or exposed, then Girard's theory could indeed be interpreted in this way: Jesus' sacrificial death perverts the traditional principle of sacrifice by not only invalidating it, but by exposing its very mechanics and reducing it to absurdity.

In archaic societies, sacrifice had a stabilizing function - it brought peace through the scapegoat mechanism because people believed that a higher order was restored through the shedding of blood. But with the cross of Jesus, it becomes clear that it is not God who demands sacrifice, but a human dynamic that sacrifices the innocent in order to relieve social tensions. Jesus is the sacrifice that no longer hides this mechanism, but makes it visible.

So if we speak here of a perversion, this could mean that the sacrificial system is not simply abolished by Christ, but rather robbed of its original function. It no longer functions in the old way because Jesus is sacrificed as an innocent and this sacrifice does not bring peace through violence - as it used to - but shows that sacrificial violence is unjust and human-centered.

Historically, however, the church has often interpreted this realization in the opposite way. Instead of exposing and ending the sacrificial system, Jesus' death itself became the "ultimate sacrifice", offered as a substitute for the sins of humanity. This idea can be understood as a kind of return to the old logic in which sacrifice is necessary to gain divine favor. In this respect, one could say that the original revolutionary power of Jesus' message has been partially perverted by reintegrating it into a sacrificial thinking that it was supposed to overcome.

Ultimately, the answer to whether Jesus' death perverts sacrificial violence depends on whether one sees it as a complete dissolution of the sacrificial system or as an unintentional reversal that was partially transformed back into a propitiatory sacrifice by the theological tradition.

René Girard's interpretation of the death on the cross shows that Jesus was not sacrificed to appease divine wrath, but to *expose* and break through *the human practice of the scapegoat mechanism*. Instead, the idea has established itself in church theology that Jesus *voluntarily sacrificed* himself *as the "Lamb of God" for the sins of the world* - a concept that at first glance contradicts the old logic of sacrificial violence, but at the same time unconsciously perpetuates its mechanics.

Classical Christian *soteriology* (the doctrine of salvation) often emphasizes that Jesus had to die in order to redeem humanity and that his suffering had a divine purpose. This corresponds to the idea of a necessary sacrifice to restore divine order - an idea that is closely related to archaic sacrificial practices. Girard, on the other hand, shows that Jesus did not die because God demanded the sacrifice, *but because people projected their habitual dynamics of exclusion and violence onto him*.

For centuries, however, the Church has interpreted the cross in its dogmatics as a necessary condition for salvation and thus developed a theology that continues to think in terms of sacrifice. In the Catholic tradition in particular, this is reflected in the idea of the Eucharist as an *"unbloody renewal of Christ's sacrifice"*. Instead of viewing the principle of sacrifice as outdated, it is perpetuated liturgically - the sacrifice remains central, only it is reinterpreted theologically.

To speak of a "perversion" could mean that the church has transformed what was actually intended as a critique of sacrifice into a new sacrificial system that continues to force people into a mindset that sees guilt, atonement and vicarious suffering as central concepts of faith. The revolutionary potential of Jesus' message - that sacrifice is no longer necessary because God does not require blood - has been weakened or reinterpreted in many church traditions.

This logic of sacrifice is also evident in the church's attitude towards human suffering: Suffering has often been interpreted as a test pleasing to God or a participation in Christ's sacrifice, rather than something to be overcome. For a long time, this perspective led believers to accept structural injustice, oppression or personal suffering because it supposedly had or would have a higher meaning.

Ultimately, it can therefore be said that the church has not necessarily perverted the principle of sacrifice, but has transformed and carried it forward - in a way that *partly runs counter* to Jesus' original intention of breaking through sacrificial violence. The question remains whether a church that really wants to break out of the logic of sacrifice could reformulate its theology in such a way that it is no longer focused on blood, guilt and atonement, but on a spirituality of liberation, life and radical acceptance. Then it would have to say goodbye to the "Lamb of God" who is sacrificed.

Seen in this light, according to James Alison, any form of discrimination, including against LGBT people, is a denial of the basic Christian message. The Gospel therefore calls for people to be accepted in their full identity and not to be oppressed by theological constructs.

Theologically, James Alison argues that the church betrays its own message of unconditional love and redemption in its attitude towards queer people. Queer people are often made into a modern scapegoat in the church structure - even though they do nothing but live their lives authentically. Instead of exposing the mechanisms of exclusion, as the gospel actually demands, the church perpetuates these patterns. Alison therefore calls for a profound reform of church teaching based not on condemnation but on genuine inclusion. He calls on the church to shed its fear of diversity and welcome queer people as full members of the community - not despite, but with and precisely because of their identity.

Only in this way can the church remain true to its own message of love and liberation, soldiering and responsibility towards the brother of Jesus: He therefore calls for a theology that does not act out of fear or control, but out of trust and generosity. The church must recognize that its rejection of LGBT people is based less on biblical principles than on historically grown cultural patterns. A truly Christian attitude would be to recognize diversity as part of creation and to *place* the *invitation to love, which knows no conditions or exclusion,* at the heart of faith.

The Church must therefore formulate a *new doctrine of salvation* that is no longer based on the principle of sacrifice, but on the radical *revelation of the cross:* Jesus did not die because God demanded a sacrifice, but because people projected their own violence and mechanisms of exclusion onto him. The cross is not a necessary sacrifice of atonement, but the ultimate exposure of the human tendency to sacrifice the innocent in order to secure order and stability. Jesus is not the *"Lamb of God"* who had to be slaughtered for reconciliation, but the *"brother of the outcasts"* - the correctly located doctrine of salvation in a nutshell - who reveals in his suffering that no violence, no exclusion and no sacrifice ever reflect divine will. True salvation does not lie in a *theology of blood*, but in overcoming the cycle of violence. The Church should not continue Christ's sacrifice liturgically, but translate his message into a *theology of liberation and solidarity*: The kingdom of God does not come about through atonement, but through radical solidarity with the marginalized, through forgiveness instead of retribution and through a community in which no human being has to be sacrificed or be an outcast in order to create peace. The cross does not call for submission to a divine order of sacrifice, but for a conversion from a way of thinking that seeks scapegoats - towards a new ethic of acceptance, healing, inclusion and solidarity as well as life. This is the *brother theology of the non-included*.

A believer who wants to implement Jesus' salvation teaching of the *"brother of the outcasts"* in his everyday life begins by recognizing the mechanism of exclusion in his own environment and actively working against it. In the family and at school, this means teaching children and relatives that no one should be left behind or considered "less worthy" - be it due to faults, social status or personal idiosyncrasies. It means resolving conflicts not through blame or punishment, but through understanding and reconciliation.

A practical step would be to consciously pay attention to situations in which someone is treated unfairly or excluded - be it in the neighborhood, at work, at school or in the community - and actively stand by these people. Instead of moral superiority, it is about showing solidarity with those who are socially disadvantaged. Prayer can also change: Not asking for forgiveness for sins that need to be "atoned for" through sacrifice, but *"asking for strength not to exclude people, to include them and to stand in solidarity with them with compassion."*

How can this doctrine of salvation be taught in religious education?

Concrete and tangible approaches are needed to introduce pupils to the idea of the *"brother of those to be included"*. One important method is to recognize mechanisms of exclusion in one's own environment, for example by reflecting on bullying, peer pressure or social inequalities at school. A central element could be the question: "Who are the outcasts today, and how can we show solidarity with them?"

Practical exercises are possible, for example:

- **Role play or change of perspective** - students put themselves in the shoes of someone who is being excluded or bullied and think together about how to empower this person.
- **Connecting stories from the Gospel with today's parallels** - The parable of the Good Samaritan or Jesus' treatment of tax collectors and sinners can serve as a starting point for understanding the mechanisms of exclusion in today's society.
- ***"Solidarity Challenge"* for the playground** - An activity in which students undertake to look out for those who often stand alone or are ignored and specifically try to include them in conversations or groups.
- **Critical reflection on victim mechanisms** - discussion about why people in groups often look for scapegoats and how this mechanism can be consciously opposed.

A key goal should be to teach children and young people that faith does not mean being guided by an outdated victim mentality, but rather taking *responsibility for one another*. A school that takes this idea seriously could, for example, introduce *"advocate systems"* or *"buddy systems"* in which students specifically take responsibility to protect classmates who would otherwise easily be marginalized.

In the end, there is a simple but profound message: *God does not need victims, but people who stand up for each other.* Only through genuine inclusion can it do justice to its own message of love, grace and liberation. If this becomes tangible in everyday life, this theology can actually become a new practice of faith - not just in the church, but in the heart of society.

The following new version in the draft of a prayer implements this and rejects the word of the sacrificed "lamb":

"Lady and Lord, give us the strength not to exclude anyone:
For open hearts that do not see others as mistakes,
but sisters and brothers, we ask
- because we will not ask for forgiveness,
as if we were born guilty,
but help us to look where people are marginalized,
and give us the courage not to be part of such patterns in silence.
Let us welcome others with outstretched arms
and include them.
Let us recognize
where we leave others behind through indifference or fear,
and awaken in us a spirit of solidarity that does not judge,
but understands.
Let us not look for scapegoats,
but for ways to heal.
Lady and Lord, accompany us on the path of reconciliation,
where no one has to be sacrificed,
so that others feel safe.
Strengthen in us the love that does not demand, but gives
- so that your kingdom is not one of guilt
but one of communion.

Amen."

128 • Is the discussion about Jesus' sexuality ultimately a question of the openness of the churches?

The discussion about Jesus' sexuality is actually more a discussion about the openness, flexibility and ability to modernize of the churches themselves than about historical facts. Jesus' sexuality cannot be clearly clarified historically - the sources do not provide any conclusive answers. Nevertheless, when people discuss it intensively , they are primarily reflecting social and theological dialogues, especially about how the churches deal with sexuality, diversity and modern lifestyles.

Such dialogs often show whether and to what extent churches can open up and develop further today. A serious examination of the issue often signals a willingness for inclusion, dialog and critical self-reflection. At the same time, the topic triggers resistance and rejection from groups that represent traditional, conservative moral concepts. The discussion thus becomes an indicator of how open, open to dialog and willing to reform a church and each individual actually is.

129 • Are Christians prepared to abandon traditional beliefs in favor of new insights?

Historically, Christian beliefs have changed several times when new insights or social developments have made this necessary. One example is the change in attitude towards slavery: while the Bible accepts or regulates slavery in several passages (Ephesians 6:5-9, 1 Timothy 6:1-2), today almost all Christian churches categorically reject this practice. Another example is the equal rights of women. While women were excluded from church offices for centuries, the situation has changed fundamentally in many denominations - for example in the Protestant Church, where women have been able to be pastors and bishops for decades.

There are similar developments in sexual ethics. Many Christian communities have adjusted their stance on issues such as contraception, divorce and same-sex partnerships as new scientific, psychological and sociological findings have challenged traditional views. In the 1960s, the Catholic Church strongly opposed contraceptive methods such as the pill, but today many believers ignore these prescriptions or call for a re-evaluation. Marriage for divorced people is now also supported pastorally in some Catholic communities, although it is officially considered problematic.

However, there is resistance to change, especially in church traditions that regard the Bible as the literally inspired and unchanging word of God.

The willingness to abandon traditional beliefs is therefore not evenly distributed among Christians. While liberal and reform-oriented churches are actively looking for new ways to unite faith and modern knowledge, others are sticking to centuries-old teachings. The debate around topics such as homosexuality, gender roles or open sexual ethics shows that different dynamics are unfolding within Christianity in the face of change.

Ultimately, history shows that change is possible in Christianity - often not overnight, but through continuous theological discourse and social pressure or recognition of social reality. Christians who are willing to rethink their beliefs usually do so out of a deep belief in the need to adapt to the core values of Jesus - love, justice and mercy - rather than clinging to outdated cultural norms. The crucial question remains to what extent the church as an institution is prepared to actively shape this change and go along for the ride.

130 • What could a church look like that is not based on power, but on the spirit of the Gospel?

Leonardo Boff contrasts the hierarchically organized, power-centered church with a *"true church"* that is oriented towards the spirit of the Holy Spirit. For him, the church is not an institution that is governed from above , but a living community in which faith grows through participation and solidarity. He saw this ideal realized particularly in the grassroots communities of the poor in Latin America: communities in which believers live the gospel independently, promote social justice and support each other - without the paternalism of a centrally controlled church authority.

This idea contradicted the Vatican's claim to power, which is based on hierarchy, obedience and ecclesiastical control. Boff criticized that the church had distanced itself from the needs of the people because it was too closely associated with political and economic power instead of consistently taking the side of the oppressed.

His theology led to strong discourse with the official Catholic Church. Because of his topics, he was condemned to silence by the Vatican in 1985 and later sanctioned. He finally resigned from the priesthood in 1992 in order to work more freely for a church that is not defined by power, but by the spirit of liberation and justice.

The spirit of the Gospel is characterized by love, justice, compassion and liberation. At its heart is Jesus' message that God does not deal with people through power or punishment, but through unconditional acceptance and care. The Gospel calls us to turn to the poor, the weak and the marginalized instead of clinging to wealth and hierarchy.

This spirit manifests itself in radical charity, which does not impose conditions but takes people's dignity seriously. It demands forgiveness instead of retribution, humility instead of domination and a community that is not defined by rigid rules but by lived solidarity.

At the same time, the Gospel contains a liberating dimension: it calls for people to free themselves from oppression, fear and constraints - both in a personal and social sense. Faith is not understood as obedience to institutions, but as a courageous following of Jesus that challenges existing injustices. Anyone who seriously engages with the spirit of the Gospel becomes not only a helper, but also a critic - because true justice always demands change.

Questions are a central means of dialog and gaining knowledge. They break through entrenched thought patterns, question supposed certainties and open up new perspectives. In theology as a science, the questioning method should be essential, because faith is not just about repeating traditional dogmas, but about the search for truth and meaning. Those who do not ask questions remain trapped in predetermined structures, while questions create movement - exactly what Jesus did in his preaching.

Figure22 : A simple church with open doors is carried by many hands - "Gospel instead of Power" is clearly written above the entrance. It is an ideal image of a community-based, serving church. The church is carried by many hands - including the visible banner "We are church". An image of a credible, community-based church in the spirit of the Gospel.

Science also has the task of taking a critical look at the church. Theology as a science should continuously examine whether church structures actually correspond to the spirit of the Gospel or whether they have become entrenched in power interests, dogmatism and hierarchy. It is precisely here that a courageous, critical theology could build bridges by naming grievances, initiating reforms and pointing out new paths for a credible church.

However, science often fails in this task. Too often it remains trapped in church institutions or shies away from confrontation with overpowering interests. Instead of a genuine critical examination of the church, there is often a cautious adaptation to existing structures. Fear of sanctions, dependence on church funding or simply institutional conservatism can lead to academics not daring to ask fundamental questions.

If theology wants to live up to its scientific responsibility, it must examine the church in the light of the Gospel - not as an extension of the institution, but as a critical authority that questions, doubts and is uncomfortable in order to free faith from unnecessary burdens and keep it alive.

In order to maintain academic and theological independence, structures are needed that enable criticism without creating existential dependencies. Theologians and academics who are too closely tied to church or state sponsors run the risk of only representing what is expected - instead of researching and teaching what is true and necessary.

One solution lies in broader institutional independence. Scientific institutions should secure themselves more strongly through a variety of funding sources so that they are not solely dependent on church or state funding. Foundation funding, public research funding without ideological guidelines and international cooperation could help to reduce the influence of individual donors.

But independence also begins with a personal attitude - with this, theologians and academics can free themselves from the motto *"Whose bread I eat, whose song I sing"*. Theologians and academics must be aware that their task is not to legitimize existing structures, but to critically question them. This requires courage, intellectual honesty and the willingness to go against the mainstream or personal gain if necessary.

Networks of questioning theologians and academics can also help to strengthen individuals. Those who do not feel isolated, but are part of a larger discourse, can act more courageously and initiate reforms.

It is therefore important to understand science and theology as tools for the search for truth, not as instruments for confirming existing power structures. An honest, analytical science and theology does not have the task of talking at the mouth of the powerful - but the courage to ask questions even when the answers are uncomfortable.

131 • The focus is on conveying values such as charity, justice and responsibility: How can the Ten Commandments serve as a guide for ethical action by queer and non-queer people in today's society?

The Ten Commandments are a central ethical guideline of Christianity and can serve as an orientation for fair and respectful coexistence in today's society, regardless of sexual orientation. They emphasize universal values such as respect for life, honesty, respect for others and the importance of community. For queer and non-queer people, they offer a basis for living a life of responsibility, love and justice.

The first commandment (*"You shall have no other gods before me"*) reminds us that people should not be bound by ideologies or social expectations, but should be guided by values such as truth, love and humanity. This can be important for queer people, who are often subject to social pressure to conform to traditional norms.

The commandment not to misuse the name of God demands a respectful approach to faith and religion. This is particularly important for queer people, as religious language has often been used to marginalize their identity. An ethical application of this requirement means that religion must not be misused as an instrument of exclusion. Religious language must therefore be adapted and reformulated textually in order to be inclusive and to name things that are taken for granted.

The commandments to keep the Sabbath holy and to honor parents emphasize the importance of rest, self-care and family relationships. For queer people who are sometimes not accepted by their families, this can mean valuing alternative family structures and communities and taking responsibility for each other in their community.

The commandments *"Thou shalt not kill"* and *"Thou shalt not steal"* can be applied to a society in which violence, discrimination and injustice are still a reality. They urge us to actively promote a culture of respect and protection for all people, especially for minorities, who are often the target of hatred and exclusion.

The commandments against adultery and bearing false witness call for faithfulness, honesty and reliability in interpersonal relationships. For queer people, this can mean shaping their relationships with the same values of responsibility and integrity as heterosexual couples. At the same time, they also challenge society to practice honesty and truthfulness in dealing with queer people instead of spreading prejudice and misinformation.

For queer people, the commandments against adultery and bearing false witness mean that their relationships are subject to the same moral values as heterosexual partnerships. They demand fidelity, honesty and reliability in interpersonal relationships and emphasize that love and responsibility are not tied to a particular sexual orientation. In a society where queer relationships have long not been recognized as equal, this is an important ethical standard that considers their love, marriage and partnership to be just as morally valuable as any other form of relationship. At the same time, the commandment against bearing false witness poses a challenge to society. It means that queer people should not be discriminated against or marginalized through lies, prejudice or misinformation. The dissemination of misrepresentations about queer identities or the deliberate distortion of facts contradicts the commandment of truthfulness and harms social justice. The imperative encourages everyone to have honest and open conversations about queer issues and to advocate for a culture of respect and honesty.

The last commandment, which warns against envy and resentment, calls on people not to allow themselves to be defined by comparisons or social pressure, but to lead a contented and authentic life. For queer people, this is also a goal of personal development, to lead a contented life.

Overall, the Ten Commandments provide an ethical basis for all people to live together in responsibility and respect. They invite us to promote a just and loving coexistence in which differences are not seen as a threat, but as an enrichment. By focusing on universal values such as justice, honesty and compassion, they offer a timeless standard for ethical behavior in a diverse society.

132 • Can a modern church survive without reform?

According to Hans Küng, a modern church can hardly survive without reform, because otherwise it runs the risk of losing touch with social reality and the faithful. *In Infallible?*, Küng criticizes above all the dogma of papal infallibility, which he sees as an obstacle to open discussion, self-correction and renewal within the Catholic Church. For him, the Church needs a return to more transparency, theological diversity and dialogical openness in order to remain credible in the 21st century. Küng was convinced that a church that does not reform itself becomes rigid and authoritarian - and loses its moral and spiritual relevance.

The Catholic Church has reformed itself in parts - for example in the *Second Vatican Council* - but is sticking to the status quo on key issues such as the ordination of women, sexual morality or the power structure. Many believers perceive this stagnation as alienation; it is an *alienated church or an alienation theology*. The administration of the status quo often replaces the lively discussion of new questions. Particularly in pluralistic, enlightened societies, this leads to dwindling trust in church authority and declining church commitment or, conversely, it leads to personal responsibility and commitment to alternative, e.g. ethical values.

Queer theology emphasizes particularly impressively how urgently reforms are needed - not only structurally, but also theologically. It criticizes the exclusion of queer people, the rejection of same-sex relationships and the adherence to binary gender images. A church that takes inclusion seriously must turn its teachings 180 degrees in order to retain its spiritual depth for all people. Queer theologians do not see reform as a change in faith, but as its consistent further development in the spirit of justice and love. Those who recognize this goal should bring about the turnaround and accelerate the further path according to these theologians.

Conclusion: Without reform, the church loses its ability to connect with the present. Hans Küng called for reform not out of contradiction, but out of deep ecclesial loyalty. *Loyal theology*, including queer theology, calls on the church to reflect on its roots - and at the same time to be open to change. Only in this way can it remain credible, vibrant and fit for the future.

Chapter 10: Self-Determination & Liberation Theology: Social and Spiritual Perspectives

The idea of self-determination is at the heart of modern discourses on freedom and human rights - but how does this relate to the Christian tradition? Is self-determination an unchristian or rather a deeply Christian ideal? Particularly in the area of sexuality, the church has long opposed individual freedom of choice. Control over moral norms served not only spiritual but also power-political purposes. Is the church afraid of the self-determined sexuality of its members?

Liberation theology questions precisely these power structures. It emphasizes the central message of Jesus, which does not consist of dogmas, but of a radical turn towards people. Is sexual self-determination a core concern of Jesus' teaching? If you look at his interactions with social outsiders, his criticism of rigid religious rules and his call for justice, the answer seems obvious. Because that is what many understand by "queer": making a difference. A liberated view of sexuality could therefore strengthen church communities instead of weakening them.

But why do many churches fear losing their moral authority if they open themselves up to such reform processes? A look at the psychology of religious beliefs shows that many ideas have arisen from deep-seated human needs for order, security and belonging. At the same time, some thinkers regard religion as an illusion that is intended to stabilize social structures rather than enable genuine liberation. What role do religious belief structures play in the ideological superstructure, and how might religion change in a classless society?

A central approach of liberation theology is the call for a reinterpretation of the Christian message that places people at the center and frees them from fear and dogmatism. But how far can or should such a reinterpretation go? Is an authentically lived faith conceivable without being forced into heteronormative structures? More and more Christians are now accepting self-determination over their own bodies - a development that is relevant both for progressive theology and for social change.

Finally, the question arises as to whether Jesus himself can be seen as a liberator from sexual oppression. His message of love, individual responsibility and liberation from externally determined constraints could serve as the basis for a theological ethic that is not based on prohibitions but on personal integrity. In this way, Christian theology could not only rethink its own traditions, but also actively contribute to the church and society creating spaces in which people can freely develop their identity.

a) Psychological and philosophical foundations

133 • What psychological needs lead to the emergence of religious beliefs and why is religion seen as an illusion?

Sigmund Freud sees the roots of religion in deep-rooted human psychological needs, particularly in children's desires. He argues that religious beliefs arise from a longing for protection, security and order - similar to the way a child relies on the authority and care of its parents. Belief in an all-powerful God corresponds to the desire for a protective father who provides support and promises security in a chaotic and threatening world.

This idea enables people to overcome existential fears - for example of suffering, death or injustice - by trusting in a higher power that creates meaning and justice. For Freud, however, this hope is ultimately an illusion: religion is not based on rational knowledge, but on psychological projections. It offers comforting explanations where there is uncertainty and provides moral rules to guide human behavior similar to an authority that relieves the individual of responsibility.

Freud sees the abandonment of religion as a necessary step in the spiritual development of man. Instead of clinging to illusions, people should recognize reality and free themselves from supernatural ideas. In an enlightened society, scientific knowledge, rational ethics and psychological self-knowledge, rather than religious belief, should lead the way. Turning away from religion is therefore not a loss, but a sign of spiritual maturity - a liberation from dependence on supernatural father figures towards a self-determined life.

In the movie Matrix, the red pill stands for awakening to reality, while the blue pill stands for remaining in a comfortable illusion. Those who take the blue pill remain in the familiar but manipulated world, while the red pill means facing up to the uncomfortable truth - even if it is painful.

Freud would interpret this choice in the context of his critique of religion as a metaphor for human psychological development. The blue pill corresponds to the religious illusion: it provides security, offers simple explanations for complex questions and prevents people from facing their existential insecurity. The red pill, on the other hand, stands for the arduous but necessary realization that there is no overriding protection and that people are responsible for their own lives. It is the step towards spiritual maturity, the dissolution of childish wishful thinking and the confrontation with reality.

The choice is not a random 50:50 decision, but a test of one's own level of development. Choosing the red pill shows a willingness to break away from externally determined world views and actively engage with the truth - even if it is challenging. The blue pill, on the other hand, stands for clinging to comfort and dependency.

In this way, people can be encouraged to choose the red pill - in other words, to free themselves from addictions:

Promote education and critical thinking: People must learn to question dogma and not be satisfied with preconceived answers. Education, philosophy and science are crucial tools for developing independent thinking.

Take fears seriously, but don't exploit them: Many people hold on to illusions because they are afraid of reality. It doesn't help to smile at these fears, but to consciously address them and point out alternatives that enable a meaningful life without illusions.

Strengthening self-responsibility: A free life not only means freedom from dependencies, but also the ability to take responsibility for oneself and others . People need to learn that they can shape their own lives - and that this is a liberating, not frightening perspective.

Leading by example instead of lecturing: Anyone who shows that a life without illusions can be fulfilling and meaningful has more persuasive power than any theoretical discourse. People often look to role models who deal with reality in an authentic and reflective way.

Questioning dialog instead of coercion: The choice of the "right pill" cannot be forced. People need space to reflect and decide for themselves. Leaving illusions behind is an individual process that requires time and inner debate.

Choosing the red pill is therefore no coincidence, but a sign of spiritual maturity. It requires courage to accept uncertainty and take responsibility. If you want to free yourself from dependency, you need to ask questions, have access to knowledge, reflect on your fears and be aware that a self-determined life is ultimately the only path to true freedom.

134 • What role do myths and symbols play in religious experience and how do they shape human self-understanding?

Mircea Eliade regards myths and symbols as central forms of expression of religious experience that enable people to connect with the sacred. In his works, he emphasizes that myths are not mere narratives, but serve as models for the order of the world and human existence. Symbols, in turn, open up access to transcendent realities and help to bridge the gap between the *profane* and the *sacred*. For Eliade, religion is not merely a cultural phenomenon, but a fundamental element of human existence, as it gives meaning and orientation to the individual. He particularly emphasizes the idea of *"eternal return"*, according to which religious rituals and myths make it possible to refer back to a sacred, archetypal time again and again.

Myths are symbolic narratives that convey fundamental interpretations of the world and often explain the origins of natural phenomena, social structures or religious practices. They often describe the struggle between order and chaos, the relationship between gods and humans or the creation of the world. In many cultures, myths are not just stories, but have a deeper spiritual or ritual meaning.

There are numerous mythical elements in Christianity that illustrate central theological concepts and beliefs. These include, among others:

- **The creation story** (Genesis 1-2) - The story of the creation of the world by God in six days and the creation of Adam and Eve in the Garden of Eden.

- **The Fall of Man** (Genesis 3) - The story of Adam and Eve eating the forbidden fruit, which led to their expulsion from paradise and is interpreted as the origin of original sin.
- **The Flood** (Genesis 6-9) - The story of Noah, who is instructed by God to build an ark to save himself and the animals from the worldwide flood.
- **The Tower of Babel** (Genesis 11:1-9) - The myth about the emergence of different languages as a result of human hubris.
- **Christ's descent into hell** (1 Peter 3:18-20) - The idea that Christ descended into the underworld after his death to redeem the souls of the departed.

Many of these stories have similarities with myths from other cultures, such as the Flood with Babylonian traditions such as the story of Utnapishtim in the Epic of Gilgamesh. Theologically, they are often not regarded as *"myths"* in the sense of invented stories, but as revelations of deeper truths. Nevertheless, their symbolic and archetypal structure is typical of mythological tales.

Whether the Bible can be described as *a "myth"* therefore depends on the definition of the term *"myth"* and the perspective from which it is viewed.

From the perspective of religious studies, the Bible can be understood as a collection of myths, historical accounts, legal texts, wisdom literature and prophetic writings. The stories of Creation, the Flood and the Tower of Babel in particular exhibit typical characteristics of mythical traditions: they explain the origins and fundamental structures of the world in a symbolic form.

From a theological perspective, the term *"myth"* is often avoided, as it could give the impression that the biblical stories are mere fiction. Instead, the Bible is seen as divine revelation that conveys not only symbolic, but also spiritual and moral truths. It also contains many parables that need to be interpreted in order to understand them and relate them to one's own life situation.

From a historical-critical perspective, the Bible contains both mythological elements and historically comprehensible accounts. The early parts of the Old Testament, such as Genesis or Exodus, contain narratives with mythical structures, while later texts (e.g. the Gospels) are more firmly anchored in a historical context.

In summary, the Bible contains mythical elements, but is not exclusively a myth. It is a multi-layered work that encompasses religious as well as historical and ethical dimensions, which is what makes the interpretation of the Bible so diverse and necessary.

135 • To what extent is self-reflection the basis for moral action?

According to Montaigne, self-reflection is the basis for moral action because it enables people to become aware of their own shortcomings, contradictions and limited capacity for knowledge. In his *Essais*, he shows that moral action should not be based on rigid rules, but on the ability to critically question oneself and adapt to changing circumstances. He emphasizes the importance of self-knowledge as a prerequisite for wisdom and virtue, as only a reflective person is in a position to make morally responsible decisions. He distances himself from dogmatic moral systems and advocates individual, experience-based ethics characterized by doubt and self-criticism.

Self-reflection also plays a central role in theology. In the Catholic tradition, it is particularly emphasized in the practice of examination of conscience and confession. St. Augustine, for example, sees self-examination as a way to gain insight into one's own sinfulness and to draw closer to God. Catholic teaching calls on believers to regularly examine their conscience in order to be able to act morally correctly. Reflection on one's own responsibility and the consequences of one's actions is central to this, as moral decisions should not arise solely from external rules, but from an inner struggle for the good.

At the same time, the history of the Catholic Church shows that institutional structures often promote an uncritical attitude towards one's own morals. In times of abuse of power or dogmatism, self-reflection was suppressed in favor of an authoritarian understanding of morality. Reform movements within the church, such as liberation theology or queer theology, therefore call for a deeper examination of one's own moral contradictions. Queer theology, which advocates the inclusion of LGBTQIA+ people in the church, makes it clear that moral action cannot be based solely on traditional dogmas, but requires *constant reflection* on justice and love. She questions rigid norms and emphasizes that true morality does not lie in obedience to institutional rules, but in a critical, self-reflective approach to ethical issues, especially with regard to discrimination and social power relations.

It can therefore be seen that questioning and self-reflection are the basis for moral action because they make people think beyond themselves, question moral norms and take responsibility for their own decisions. While Montaigne describes this process as an individual act of doubt and knowledge, in theology it is often integrated into the search for divine truth. In the Catholic Church, self-reflection and questioning dialog is understood as both a spiritual practice and a necessary corrective for moral action, while some in theology see it as a means of deconstructing normative ethics and creating a more just, inclusive morality.

136 • Are freedom and determinism compatible?

According to Spinoza, freedom and determinism are not compatible in the classical sense, but only if freedom is not understood as absolute autonomy of will, but as *insight into necessity*. In his *Ethica*, he argues that everything in nature is determined by a causal order, including human thought and action. Human beings do not possess free will in the traditional sense because their will and actions are determined by external and internal causes. Nevertheless, for Spinoza, freedom is not an illusion, but a higher form of cognition: a person is all the freer the more he understands why he acts as he does and becomes aware of his own determination. Freedom therefore does not mean independence from causes, but insight into the necessary order of things. In theology, especially in the Catholic Church, the relationship between freedom and determinism is therefore a central theme.

Determinism is the philosophical view that all events, including human decisions and actions, are completely determined by prior causes. This means that everything proceeds according to fixed natural laws or causal relationships and that there are no genuine coincidences or arbitrary decisions.

There are different forms of determinism:

- **Causal determinism** (e.g. Laplace): Every action is determined by previous events and natural laws.
- **Theological determinism:** God's omniscience or providence determines the course of the world.
- **Biological or genetic determinism:** Human behavior is predetermined by genes and biological factors.
- **Social determinism**: Social structures and upbringing influence people so strongly that their decisions are not really free.

In the debate about free will, it is often asked whether people bear responsibility for their actions despite this determination or whether freedom is just an illusion.

Pierre-Simon Laplace (1749-1827) was a French mathematician, physicist and astronomer who is best known for his work on probability theory, celestial mechanics and determinism. He formulated **Laplace's determinism**, the idea that the entire universe follows fixed laws of nature and would be completely predictable if the state of all particles at any given time were known precisely.

He imagined a hypothetical being, known as a *Laplacean demon*, that knows all the positions and speeds of all the particles in the universe. Such a being could then use the laws of nature to calculate exactly what will happen in the future and what has happened in the past.

Laplace thus advocated a strictly deterministic view of the world in which there is no room for chance or free will - everything follows a necessary causality. His ideas had a strong influence on classical physics, but were later challenged by quantum mechanics, which suggests true indeterminacy at the subatomic level.

Catholic doctrine emphasizes that human beings have free will, as they bear moral responsibility and are held accountable for their decisions. At the same time, the Church recognizes that divine providence exists and that God, as an omniscient being, already knows which decisions a person will make. This leads to a tension between divine omniscience and human freedom of will. Augustine, for example, argues that freedom does not consist in going against God's will, but in recognizing and choosing the good - similar to Spinoza's idea that true freedom lies in the insight into necessity.

Queer theology questions traditional concepts of freedom and determination, particularly with regard to identity and social norms. While classical theologies often emphasize a predetermined divine order, queer theology critically examines the idea that gender, sexuality or social roles are determined *"by nature"*. Spinoza's approach could offer an interesting perspective here: If freedom does not mean acting outside of all determination, but understanding why one acts as one does, then one could argue that the liberation of marginalized identities does not consist in demanding absolute independence from social and biological conditions, but in reflecting on these conditions and dealing with them in a self-determined way.

Ultimately, the question of whether freedom and determinism are compatible depends on how freedom is defined. According to Spinoza, there is no freedom of will in the sense of complete independence, but there is *freedom through knowledge*. In Catholic theology, freedom is understood as moral responsibility despite divine providence, while queer theology questions these terms further and develops alternative *concepts of self-determination*.

b) Church authority and power structures

137 • Is ecclesiastical authority more important than personal integrity?

Ideally, church authority and personal integrity should not be in opposition, but should complement each other. In reality, however, there is often tension between the two. The question of which of the two is more important depends on the perspective from which they are viewed - theological, ethical or institutional.

From a theological perspective, the Christian message, which is reflected in the teachings of Jesus, takes center stage. Jesus himself repeatedly placed individual truthfulness and inner conviction above institutional authority - for example when he spoke out against religious hypocrisy (e.g. Matthew 23). He criticized authorities who placed rules above compassion and justice. One could conclude from this that personal integrity takes precedence when it comes closer to the actual message of faith than institutional guidelines.

Ethically speaking, personal integrity requires acting in accordance with one's own moral convictions, even if these deviate from ecclesiastical rules. If an institution demands obedience from its members that violates their conscience or ethical principles, the question arises as to whether such authority is still legitimate. Historical examples - such as the church's attitude to cases of abuse or discriminatory dogmas - show that blind obedience to the institution can be problematic.

From an institutional point of view, the church sees itself as an authority appointed by God to preserve and guide the truths of faith. From this perspective, it could be argued that individual convictions should not be placed above traditional doctrine. However, the credibility of church authority also depends on the personal integrity of its representatives. If ministers act corruptly, hypocritically or morally questionable, this undermines the authority of the church as a whole.

So when church authority and personal integrity come into conflict, orientation towards truth, compassion and ethical principles should take precedence - values that Jesus also emphasized. An authority that is not credible loses its legitimacy. In this sense, one could say that personal integrity is more important because it forms the basis for a truthful, credible church.

138 • *What role do religious belief structures play in the ideological superstructure, and how might religion change in a classless society?*

Marx sees religion as part of the ideological superstructure that stabilizes and legitimizes existing social conditions. It serves to justify the economic and social structures of the ruling class by presenting suffering and injustice as God-ordained or interpreting them as tests for a later reward in the afterlife. In this way, it prevents the working class from rebelling against their oppression and helps to maintain the status quo.

In a future, classless society, Marx expects the need for religion to gradually disappear. Since he sees religion as a reaction to social alienation and material suffering, he assumes that it will become superfluous once the causes of this alienation have been eliminated. When people no longer live in economic dependence and social inequality, they no longer need to take refuge in religious beliefs to find comfort or meaning. Instead, people can see themselves as creative, free beings who shape their own destiny without delegating it to a higher authority.

Religion would not necessarily disappear immediately in this process, but it would lose influence as it would no longer exist as a social necessity. For Marx, the overcoming of religion is therefore not a direct goal, but a consequence of overcoming class society.

The transition to a classless society requires far-reaching economic, political and social changes in order to reduce inequalities and democratize power structures. Believers can also play a decisive role in this by actively contributing their values of justice, solidarity and humanity to this process.

1. awareness-raising and political education

The working class must recognize that social inequality is not God-given or natural, but the result of economic and political structures. Education and critical thinking are necessary to understand the mechanisms of exploitation and to develop fairer alternatives.

A person of faith can advocate for a theology of liberation that focuses on social justice and argue against religious teachings that portray inequality as God-given or unchangeable. He or she can do educational work in church communities, get involved in socio-political discussions and encourage people to stand up for their rights.

2. democratization of the economy

In a classless society, the means of production must not remain in the hands of a small elite, but must be used collectively. This requires greater worker participation in companies, cooperative economic models and a move away from a system that only increases the profits of a few.

A believer can advocate for economic models that are not based on exploitation. This means consuming ethically, supporting sustainable companies and campaigning for fair wages and better working conditions. Christian communities can promote cooperative structures or support fair trade networks in order to help shape a fairer economy.

3. strengthening the welfare state and redistribution

A fairer society needs solid social protection through fair tax systems, living wages, free education and affordable healthcare. Without these basic safeguards, social mobility remains limited and inequality becomes entrenched.

A person of faith can advocate for political initiatives that promote social justice and support social projects in their own community - for example, by donating to the needy or volunteering at soup kitchens and educational programs. Standing up for fair tax policies and social security systems is also a direct contribution to greater social fairness.

4. dismantling hierarchical power structures

Not only economic, but also political power must be democratized. Grassroots democratic processes, more co-determination and policies that do not just serve the elites are crucial for a classless society.

Church structures themselves should be a role model here. A believer can campaign for a church that is more democratic and participatory by involving lay people and women more. They can become active in political groups that advocate for more citizen participation or promote community projects that practice grassroots democratic decision-making processes.

5. international solidarity and resistance against capitalist structures

Inequality is not just a national problem, but a global one. A fair global economy requires labor rights to be strengthened worldwide, the exploitation of raw materials to be stopped and fair trade relations to be created.

A believer can support international aid projects, campaign for fair trade and promote campaigns against modern slavery or exploitation in the global supply chain. Christian networks and aid organizations such as *Misereor* or *Bread for the World* offer concrete opportunities to promote social justice across national borders.

6. change in culture and ideology

Class relations do not only consist of economic differences, but are also deeply rooted in cultural and ideological thought patterns. The values of competition, profit maximization and individualism must be replaced by a culture of solidarity, community and the common good.

A believer can promote a culture of humanity in their own environment, stand up for social justice in discussions and encourage people not to think only of their own advantage. Communities can become places of solidarity where an alternative economic and social model is exemplified that is not based on profit but on community.

The transformation to a classless society therefore requires far-reaching economic, political and cultural changes. Believers have a special responsibility to work for social justice, as many religious traditions are based on charity and solidarity. Through political commitment, economic alternatives, social work and awareness-raising, they can actively contribute to a fairer world. People of faith then begin to see themselves as creative, free beings who shape their own destiny.

139 • How did liberation theology come about and what criticism does it direct at the role of the church in existing power structures?

Liberation theology emerged in Latin America in the 1960s and 1970s as a reaction to massive social inequality, poverty and political oppression. Many countries on the continent were ruled by authoritarian regimes that were intertwined with Western economic interests and secured their power through violence, repression and exploitation. While large parts of the population lived in extreme poverty, elites and international corporations profited from a system that perpetuated social inequality.

The church played an ambivalent role in this situation. On the one hand, it was traditionally closely linked to the powerful and often a stabilizing element of the existing order. On the other hand, there was growing resistance within the church to the oppression of the poor. Priests and theologians such as Gustavo Gutiérrez and Óscar Romero demanded that the church could no longer stand silently alongside injustice, but had to actively fight alongside the oppressed.

Liberation theology therefore criticizes the traditional church attitude, which often came to terms with authoritarian regimes or accepted social ills as "God-ordained". Instead, it calls for a *"church of the poor"* that is not content with spiritual consolation, but strives for concrete social change. Its goal is not just individual pastoral care, but a profound transformation of structures that perpetuate exploitation and inequality.

This attitude brought them into dialog with conservative church leaders and the Vatican, especially under Pope John Paul II, who rejected any connection between Christian faith and Marxist social analysis. Nevertheless, liberation theology remained a central voice for social justice, whose ideas live on to this day in grassroots church communities and social movements.

140 • Why do churches fear losing their moral authority?

Churches fear a loss of their moral authority because this has been a central basis for their social and spiritual power for centuries. The church traditionally saw itself as the guardian of divine commandments and as a moral authority offering people guidance on ethical issues. Its authority was based on acting as a mediator between God and the faithful and setting moral standards that were considered binding for private and public life.

With the Enlightenment, secularization and the scientific advances of the 19th and 20th centuries, this authority began to erode. Modern societies are increasingly developing their own ethical standards, which are no longer necessarily tied to religious guidelines. Particularly in questions of sexuality, family order, gender roles and individual self-determination, social developments often contradict traditional church teachings. Many people no longer accept church morals as absolute truth, but question them critically or reject them altogether.

This topic is particularly explosive in the area of sexual ethics. With the increasing social acceptance of different lifestyles, the church is under pressure to rethink its teachings. The fear is that adapting to modern values could be interpreted as weakening its own teaching authority.

Another problem is how to deal with historical mistakes and abuses. The abuse scandal and the decades-long cover-up by church institutions have severely damaged trust in the moral integrity of the church. While it presents itself as a moral authority, these transgressions have revealed that abuse of power and unethical behavior are also widespread within the church. As a result, many people no longer see the church as a credible moral authority and question its authority.

However, the fear of losing moral authority is not only an institutional concern, but also a theological one. Many churches see themselves as guardians of divine truth and not as an organization that aligns its teachings with social trends. But this is precisely the dilemma: if the church sticks to traditional teachings, it risks becoming socially irrelevant, especially for younger generations who are guided by modern ethical standards. However, if it opens up too much, it could lose credibility with conservative and mostly older believers who insist on learned morals.

Ultimately, the church faces a difficult balancing act. In order to maintain its moral authority, it must find ways to reconcile its core values - love, justice and compassion - with today's social realities: A renewal of its ethics based on dialog, reflection and theological development could be one way of continuing to be perceived as a moral authority based not on prohibitions, but on guidance and responsibility.

---

c) Sexuality, self-determination and Christian ethics - perspectives for a modern theology

---

141 • Is the church afraid of its members' self-determined sexuality?

Is the church afraid of the self-determined sexuality of its members? - If you look at the official stance and many statements made by church representatives, you might well get this impression. A sexuality that is lived individually, freely decided and independent of religious dogma often seems to be perceived as a threat - perhaps because a self-determined sexuality not only challenges existing power structures, but could also shake up traditional moral concepts of the church. This fear could explain why church institutions often find it difficult to talk openly about sexuality or even acknowledge it when it moves outside the narrow confines of church teachings.

In order for churches and their representatives to be able to speak better about sexuality in public, the following recommendations are particularly useful:

- **Develop an open attitude:** Church representatives should be prepared to perceive sexuality as a natural, positive force in human life and to communicate this stance clearly in public.
- **Breaking down prejudices and questioning taboos:** Churches should critically reflect on their own prejudices and actively break down existing taboos. Openness, rather than fear, creates trust.
- **Competence and further training**: Church employees should receive in-depth training, including through collaboration with experts from the fields of medicine, psychology and sex education, in order to strengthen their competence and credibility.
- **Willingness to engage in dialog and empathy**: Church representatives should be willing to listen and appreciate different perspectives and ways of life without morally condemning them in advance.
- **Realism and relevance to everyday life:** Churches should recognize and address the real lives of their members instead of treating sexuality as a purely abstract moral issue.
- **Courage to update church teachings:** A more open and honest discussion about sexuality will only succeed if churches show the courage to critically examine and, if necessary, adapt outdated attitudes.

By taking these steps, churches and their representatives can deal with the topic of sexuality in a more credible, contemporary and constructive way - and regain social relevance in the process.

The following concept could be useful for adapting church teachings on sexuality in line with the times and training church representatives accordingly:

A. Adaptation of church teachings on sexuality

1. teaching on premarital sexual intercourse

Previously: Sexual relations only permitted within marriage.

New: Sexuality is shaped responsibly and lovingly, regardless of marital status. Key values are mutual responsibility, respect and consent.

2. teaching on homosexuality and sexual diversity

Until now: Frequent rejection or at least moral restrictions on homosexual relationships.

New: Recognition and equality of all sexual orientations as an expression of the diversity of human life. Appreciation of every partnership relationship, provided it is lived in love, respect and mutual consent.

3. teaching on sexual morality and contraception

Previously: Rejection of artificial contraceptive methods, sexuality primarily geared towards procreation.

New: Responsible sexuality explicitly includes conscious family planning and contraception. Sexual relationships are not primarily reduced to procreation, but are recognized as a valuable expression of love, partnership and human closeness.

4. dealing with divorced and remarried people

Previously: Divorced and remarried people are often marginalized or disadvantaged (e.g. in receiving the sacraments).

New: Appreciation and full inclusion of divorced and remarried people in church life. Recognition that relationships can fail and yet dignity and participation are not called into question.

B. Possible formulations of adapted teachings:

"Sexuality is a power given by God that connects people and strengthens closeness, love and trust. Respect, responsibility and mutual consent are decisive for its moral quality - not marital status or sexual orientation."

"The Church values the diversity of sexual identities and lifestyles and regards this diversity as part of the order of creation."

"Responsible sexuality explicitly includes the conscious use of contraceptive methods. They serve to protect relationships, ensure well-being and enable responsible parenthood."

"The church treats failed marriages with respect and empathy. Divorced and remarried people are full members of the community."

C. Further training curriculum for church representatives:

Module 1: Fundamentals of contemporary sexual ethics

- Current scientific findings on sexuality, relationships and identity
- Overview of social changes and challenges
- Importance of self-determination, consensus and respect

Module 2: Diversity and inclusion

- Recognition of different sexual orientations and identities (LGBTQIA+)
- Raising awareness and dealing with experiences of discrimination
- Theological reassessment of sexual diversity in the light of fundamental Christian values

Module 3: Sex education and communication

- Professional and empathetic communication about sexuality
- Reducing taboos and fears in public discourse
- Practical exercises in interviewing and public relations

Module 4: Medical and psychological basics

- Contraceptive methods and their effects, options for responsible family planning
- Basics of sexual health, prevention and counseling skills
- Psychological foundations of sexuality and relationships

Module 5: Crisis management and counseling skills

- Dealing with conflicts, boundary violations and sexual violence
- Pastoral support for people in relationship crises or with questions about sexuality
- Cooperation with specialist agencies and external consultants (psychologists, doctors, therapists)

Module 6: Practical and dialog training

- Organizing public talks and discussions

- Dealing with critical questions and reservations from the community
- Developing your own credible communication style

Conclusion: A contemporary adaptation of church teachings and targeted further training of church representatives would make it possible to address sexuality openly, authentically and credibly - as an integral part of a modern, true-to-life understanding of faith.

142 • Is self-determination an unchristian or Christian ideal?

Self-determination can be seen as both a Christian and an un-Christian ideal, depending on how you define it and the theological context in which you place it.

Self-determination as a Christian ideal

In many aspects of Christian teaching, there is an emphasis on individual freedom of choice and personal responsibility:

Free will: Christianity emphasizes that man was created with free will. Already in the creation story, man is given the freedom to choose to follow God or not (Genesis 2-3).

Jesus' message of inner repentance: Jesus repeatedly called on people to make personal decisions - be it to repent, to love their neighbor or to follow him. He did not force anyone, but invited them (Matthew 16:24).

Ethical responsibility: Christian faith is not blind obedience to rules, but a conscious decision in favor of values such as love, justice and mercy. Paul emphasizes in Galatians 5:1: *"For freedom Christ has set us free."*

Self-determination as an unchristian ideal?

In traditional Christian movements, self-determination is sometimes viewed critically:

God as the highest authority: Christian theology teaches that human beings are not autonomous, but live in relationship to God. Self-determination that is completely detached from God could be understood as an exaltation of man.

Humility and obedience: The Bible often speaks of obedience to God (e.g. James 4:7: *"Submit yourselves therefore to God"*). Those who live solely by their own decision could be considered self-centered or arrogant.

Sin as a consequence of false self-determination: In the Christian tradition, it is often argued that the turning away from God (for example in the Fall of Man) happened as a result of excessive self-determination - man wanted to be like God himself (Genesis 3:5).

Self-determination is not a fundamentally un-Christian ideal as long as it does not end in complete self-importance, but remains linked to responsibility and moral reflection. Christianity does not recognize blind self-abandonment, but calls for a freedom that is at the service of love. In this sense, self-determination is Christian if it is not lived egotistically but in an ethically responsible manner.

143 • Is sexual self-determination a core concern of Jesus' teaching?

Sexual self-determination is not an explicitly formulated core concern in the teachings of Jesus, but his message of freedom, dignity and responsibility can certainly be related to it. Jesus did not speak directly about sexual self-determination in the modern sense, but his attitude towards people, social norms and moral issues shows a clear tendency towards personal responsibility and an ethical approach to oneself and others. He repeatedly placed individual will and inner attitude above rigid religious rules. In his encounters with socially ostracized people - such as the adulteress or the sinner who anoints his feet - he showed an attitude of mercy and gave people room to make personal decisions instead of condemning them.

In numerous statements, Jesus emphasized that the law is there for man and not the other way around. This can be seen as an indication that sexual ethics should not be determined solely by external rules, but by a responsible and loving attitude. While Jesus criticized sexual exploitation or adultery, he did not rely on strict prohibitions, but on people's inner attitude. In the Sermon on the Mount, for example, he says that it is not only external actions that count, but also the inner attitude. In doing so, he does not emphasize blind submission to rules, but an ethically reflected decision.

The central message of Jesus is love - for God, for one's neighbor and for oneself. It can be deduced from this that any form of sexuality based on mutual respect, consent and responsibility is compatible with this message. An ethic that denies people their sexual self-determination and forces them to adhere to rigid standards contradicts the spirit of Jesus' teaching. Although Jesus did not speak directly about sexual self-determination in the modern sense, his message of freedom, responsibility and dignity suggests that people should make self-determined and ethically responsible decisions about their own lives - including their sexuality. Instead of rigid rules, he relied on the conscience and the ability of the individual to act in love and mindfulness.

144 • Can a liberated view of sexuality strengthen church communities instead of weakening them?

It is often feared that a more open attitude to sexuality could lead to a loss of morality and cohesion. In fact, such a change could have the opposite effect by promoting authenticity, inclusion and a deeper spiritual connection within Christian communities. A reflective, theologically informed re-evaluation of sexuality could help churches to align themselves more closely with the central message of Jesus - love, justice and mercy.

Authenticity and honesty instead of hypocrisy

Many churches today are losing members because their sexual morals are perceived as unrealistic or out of touch with reality. A liberated view of sexuality could help to ensure that believers are no longer torn between their faith and the reality of their lives. When sexuality is no longer considered a taboo subject, a more honest exchange about personal issues, relationships and identity can emerge - contributing to a more authentic community. In some Protestant and progressive

Catholic communities, a practice has already been established in which sexual morality is no longer discussed according to traditional dogma, but according to individual life realities and ethical standards.

Inclusion instead of exclusion

Church communities that promote a liberal view of sexuality exclude fewer people and thus gain diversity and vitality. Queer people, unmarried couples or divorced people, who often feel rejected in traditional churches, could feel welcome and actively participate in church life. This strengthens the community because more people feel that their individual life realities are taken seriously. The blessing of same-sex married couples in many Protestant churches and the calls for a reform of Catholic sexual morality - for example through the *#OutInChurch* initiative - show that change is already underway. Theologically, this development is supported by queer theology, for example in Elizabeth Stuart's *"Just Good Friends: Towards a Lesbian and Gay Theology of Relationships"* (1995) or Marcella Althaus-Reid's *"Indecent Theology: Theological Perversions in Sex, Gender and Politics"* (2000).

Focus on love and responsibility instead of prohibitions

Jesus repeatedly emphasized love, compassion and responsibility as central values. A sexual ethic based on these values, rather than rigid rules, could strengthen trust in church communities. Instead of restrictive rules, a responsible ethic could emerge that promotes healthy relationships, consent and mutual respect. The theologian Dietrich Bonhoeffer describes in *"Ethics"* (published posthumously in 1949) that being a Christian does not consist in legalism, but in lived responsibility - a view that can also be applied to questions of sexuality.

Open discussions instead of taboos

Church communities could grow if they offer space for real conversations about sexuality and relationships. Many believers want an open dialog about topics such as partnership, love, identity and ethics. If churches facilitate such conversations, they could become more relevant again for many. Discussion forums and workshops on sexual ethics are already taking place in reform-oriented churches, for example in the Old Catholic Church or in progressive Protestant circles.

Theological reflection on gender and sexuality has also been deepened in works such as Susannah Cornwall's *"Sex and Uncertainty in the Body of Christ"* (2010) and Patrick Cheng's *"Radical Love: An Introduction to Queer Theology"* (2011).

Strengthening spirituality through a holistic view of people instead of a mono-focus

A liberated view of sexuality can help to perceive people in their entirety - as beings with body, mind and soul. If sexuality is not seen as a disruptive or "sinful" part of the human being, but as a natural expression of love and relationship, a deeper and more holistic spirituality could develop. This perspective also corresponds to the Judeo-Christian tradition in which man was created as good (*"And behold, it was very good",* Genesis 1:31). A positive view of sexuality could help to ensure that faith is not experienced as oppressive, but as liberating.

A liberated view of sexuality therefore does not have to lead to a loss of moral values or a weakening of church communities - rather, it can contribute to a stronger, more authentic and inclusive church. By no longer treating sexuality as a taboo, but placing it in the context of love, responsibility and respect, communities can grow and provide a spiritual home for more people. The history of the church shows that faith has always had to adapt to new insights and social developments. A renewed, life-oriented sexual ethic could not weaken Christianity, but rather give it new strength.

145 • Why do some Christians now accept self-determination over their own bodies?

Some Christians now accept self-determination over their own bodies because their theological understanding of freedom, responsibility and human dignity has evolved. Many modern Christian thinkers and communities recognize that human dignity includes the capacity for self-determination and that personal decisions about one's own body do not necessarily have to be in conflict with faith.

A central argument for the acceptance of self-determination is the emphasis on conscience as a moral authority. Particularly in Reformation and liberal theological traditions, people are seen as self-responsible beings who can act independently in ethical matters. Martin Luther already emphasized the importance of the individual conscience with his famous sentence *"Here I stand, I can do no other"*. Today, many Christians argue that ethical decisions, including those relating to one's own body, should be made on the basis of a reflective conscience and not solely on dogmatic precepts.

The biblical understanding of freedom and responsibility has also led to a rethink. Instead of a ban on self-determination, progressive Christians see it as an invitation to treat one's own body with respect - which can also mean making independent decisions about sexuality, medical interventions or gender identity.

Another factor is the change in church ethics, particularly in dealing with sexuality, gender roles and reproductive rights. While conservative churches have long prescribed rigid norms, a new view has established itself in many Christian communities that sees personal freedom not as a contradiction to Christian values, but as an expression of them. More and more Christian movements are recognizing the rights of women to control their own bodies, which is reflected in an increasing acceptance of contraception, reproductive rights and sexual self-determination.

In queer and feminist theological movements in particular, it is pointed out that faith should not be used to control people or deny them their autonomy. Instead, it is emphasized that Jesus himself always took people seriously in their individual dignity and did not work through coercion, but through love and invitation. His encounters with social outcasts - such as the adulteress who was saved from stoning or the woman who suffered from bleeding and sought healing - show an attitude based on compassion, not control.

Social changes also have an influence on church debates. Whereas the church used to be a moral authority that shaped the whole of social life, Christians today live in pluralistic societies in which they have to enter into dialog with other values and ethical perspectives. Many have realized that a rigid rejection of self-determination alienates people from the church and that a Christian ethic that recognizes personal freedom and responsibility is more likely to help faith be perceived as relevant and true to life.

Ultimately, it is clear that more and more Christians see self-determination over their own bodies as compatible with the Christian faith because they are shifting the focus from control to responsibility. Instead of rigid dogmas, the focus is shifting to the question of how people can use their freedom in a way that is in line with Christian values such as love of neighbor, respect and respect for creation. This attitude makes it possible to reconcile faith with modern ethical and scientific knowledge without neglecting the spiritual dimension of being human.

146 • Is an authentically lived faith conceivable without coercion to heteronormative structures?

An authentically lived faith without coercion to heteronormative structures is conceivable and is advocated by many theologians and ethicists. The Christian message is based on love, respect and justice - principles that are not necessarily tied to a particular sexual orientation or gender identity. Theologian James Alison (*Faith Beyond Resentment*, 2001) already argues that Christian teaching does not necessarily have to be interpreted in a heteronormative way, but rather contains a radical openness to all people. He pleads for a relaxed and guilt-free view of sexuality in a Christian context.

The feminist theologian Elisabeth Schüssler Fiorenza (*In Memory of Her*, 1983) has also shown that many church structures reflect culturally evolved power relations rather than an original biblical truth. She calls for a liberation theology that also includes non-heteronormative identities. Marcella Althaus-Reid (*Indecent Theology*, 2000) also develops an "*indecent theology*" that rethinks the categories of sexuality, gender and faith and makes the often suppressed voices in the church tradition visible.

Theologians such as David R. Brockman (*No Longer the Same*, 2011) or Todd Salzman and Michael Lawler (*The Sexual Person*, 2008) also question traditional Catholic sexual ethics and argue for an ethics of responsibility that is not based on fixed biological or social norms, but on the lived experience of love and fidelity.

These approaches show that a faith without heteronormative coercion is not only possible, but also theologically justifiable. However, it presupposes that the church and believers free themselves from traditional dogmas and understand the Christian faith as a living reality that grows with people.

147 • Can Jesus be seen as a liberator from sexual oppression?

Jesus can be seen as a liberator from sexual repression if you consider his message in the context of his time and its social norms. While ancient Judaism had strict rules on sexual morality and women and socially marginalized groups often suffered under repressive structures, Jesus met people with an attitude of mercy, dignity and liberation.

A key example of this is his encounter with the adulteress in John 8, who was to be stoned to death according to the law at the time. Instead of confirming the sentence, Jesus presented the accusers with a moral challenge: *"Let him who is without sin cast the first stone."* This episode shows that Jesus did not adhere to rigid legal regulations, but instead advocated an ethic of mercy and forgiveness. He also opposed double standards by exposing social hypocrisy and placing the dignity of the individual above legal punishments.

Other encounters - such as with the Samaritan woman at Jacob's well or with women who were considered *"sinners"* by society - also show that Jesus accepted people regardless of their social or moral status. He broke through social and gender barriers by accepting women as disciples and including them in his teaching. This can be interpreted as liberation from rigid gender norms and patriarchal constraints.

The question of whether Jesus actively proclaimed a new sexual morality remains open. His message was not about reforming specific rules, but about a deeper change in human interaction. However, the principles of love, justice and personal responsibility that he taught can be applied to questions of sexuality. Anyone who understands sexual morality not as a mere set of rules, but as an expression of love and respect for human dignity, can see in Jesus' attitude an impulse for liberation from oppressive and discriminatory norms of the church and society.

Figure 23: A luminous figure: holding her arms open like a compass, in the middle of which a ray of light can symbolically dissolve any shackles - who could she stand for if not for each and every one of us - she breaks symbolic chains. Surrounded by people who feel addressed and become active, rise up and are liberated by light. The illustration stands for liberation, upliftment and hope - without a literal representation of a religious figure who can also describe perspectives alongside the feelings of sexual oppression - and is therefore a bearer of hope.

Modern theological currents, especially feminist and queer theology, therefore see Jesus as a figure who inspires us to question old constraints and create space for a more just, respectful and self-determined sexual morality. While traditional Christian currents emphasize that Jesus did not formulate an explicit new sexual ethic, his *practice of radical inclusion* shows that liberation from oppression, including in matters of sexuality, is consistent with the spirit of his ministry.

The issue of whether a gay clergyman who does not make his queerness public is acting against the meaning of Jesus or even sinning (because he does not make his queerness public) is complex and depends on several ethical, theological and personal aspects.

In his teaching, Jesus repeatedly spoke out against hypocrisy, especially when people kept up a façade out of fear of social pressure or to maintain their position of power. He criticized the Pharisees because they appeared pious on the outside, while their inner attitudes did not match their outer actions (Matthew 23:27). If a gay clergyman deliberately hides his sexuality to avoid a hostile church structure, this could be seen as a form of conformity to a system that enforces dishonesty.

However, it would be too easy to condemn this across the board as hypocrisy. Many gay clergy face a moral dilemma: on the one hand they want to follow their calling, on the other hand they have to conform to an institution that - depending on the denomination - still sees queerness as problematic. Coming out publicly can have significant consequences or impact, including loss of employment, social exclusion or personal attacks. In this sense, concealing one's sexuality can also be understood as self-protection rather than deliberate deception for selfish motives.

However, the consideration of whether a clergyman sins because he does not come out also depends on how one defines sin. In Christian ethics, sin is not only the transgression of a law, but rather the failure to live up to the ideal of love and truthfulness. If a clergyman does not disclose his sexuality out of inner conviction and loyalty to his church, he is not necessarily acting sinfully. However, if he actively preaches against queer people or participates in discrimination even though he himself is affected, this could be seen as hypocrisy and moral misconduct.

Ultimately, a gospel-oriented view would rather lead to condemning not the clergyman concerned, but the church structures that put him in this predicament. The real problem is not so much the individual coming out as the continued institutional rejection of homosexuality that causes clergy to have to hide. A church that calls on Jesus should not create circumstances that force people to deny their identity, but rather enable openness, honesty and authenticity.

The topic of whether a particularly large number of clergy are gay and whether they *are "all in cahoots"* by hiding their sexuality and persisting in a system of hypocrisy touches on several sensitive issues: the reality of sexual orientation within the clergy, the ecclesiastical structures that encourage this behavior, and the moral responsibility of individuals.

1. estimates of how many clergy are gay: There are no reliable figures, as many clergy are unable or unwilling to disclose their sexuality. Research, such as that by Donald Cozzens (*The Changing Face of the Priesthood*, 2000), suggests that there is an above-average proportion of homosexual men in the Catholic clergy. Estimates range from 20 to 50 percent or more, depending on the region - in any case significantly more than in the population as a whole. There could be several reasons for this: The priesthood offers some queer men an opportunity to pursue their identity without having to stand out in society. Celibacy can serve as a shield to escape social or family pressure regarding marriage and heterosexual relationships. The church attracts people with a strong spiritual idealism, regardless of their sexual orientation.

2. the concealment of one's own sexuality as hypocrisy and a double life: There is a clear tension between the reality of a large number of homosexual clergy and official church teaching, which often classifies homosexuality as *"disordered"*. As a result, many gay clergy have to lead a double life or at least conceal their identity in order to survive within the church hierarchy. The question of whether this is hypocrisy depends on whether the clergy stand behind the church's teachings out of conviction or just conform out of fear or careerism.

A clergyman with a double life who is secretly homosexual, but who nevertheless supports a church that regards him as *"improper"*, is faced with a moral dilemma. Some try to behave honestly in this area of tension by not supporting discrimination. Others, on the other hand, preach against same-sex love in order to protect themselves or not to jeopardize their position of power - here one can actually speak of sinful hypocrisy.

3. when *"everyone is in cahoots"*: The idea that all gay clergy maintain a tacit alliance is grossly oversimplified. There are different attitudes within the church: Some queer clergy actually live in secret and support a system that discriminates against them. Others work openly and actively on reforms to create a more open church. Still others benefit from a system of silence because it ensures them protection and influence. There are reports that queer networks exist in certain church hierarchies, which not only ensure self-protection but also power. Some scandals suggest that some church leaders conceal their sexuality while simultaneously advocating conservative positions - and do so for purely opportunistic reasons. The *#OutinChurch* community, on the other hand, includes queer clergy who are open about their sexual orientation and therefore offer a new network for others to join.

4. taking moral responsibility: Instead of calling all gay clergy "hypocrites" across the board, the criticism should primarily target the church structures that enforce such behavior. Forcing queer clergy to hide creates a system in which dishonesty and double standards are almost inevitable. The problem is therefore not primarily the individual sexuality of the clergy, but the institutional homophobia that prevents open lifestyles and queerness.

So it's a complex dilemma - not living openly: There are homosexual clergy within the church who hide their identity to avoid being persecuted - this is a sign of institutional coercion rather than personal guilt. At the same time, however, there are also those who actively contribute to oppression by protecting themselves while making life difficult for others - and these can certainly be described as hypocrites. And there are those who live openly, for example in the *#OutinChurch* network. The real responsibility lies not only with the individuals, but above all with the church as an institution, which has created the conditions for a system of double standards and hypocrisy through its restrictive sexual morals. The more the public recognizes this and asks spiritual people about their sexual orientation, the greater the willingness to view queerness as inclusive and part of creation.

148 • How can the Christian message be reinterpreted to put people at the center and free them from fear and dogmatism?

Some authors, such as Eugen Drewermann, advocate a return to a spirituality that takes the individual seriously and is not characterized by fear, obedience or rigid dogmas. For him, the message of Jesus does not stand for a hierarchical, power-preserving institution, but for a radical liberation of the individual from constraints, feelings of guilt and inner fears. Instead of seeing faith as a fulfilment of duty towards the church, he emphasizes a personal, deeply psychological experience of God that strengthens and heals people.

His interpretation does not see Jesus as the founder of a strict order of faith, but as someone who lifts up the marginalized and encourages people to follow their heart and conscience. In contrast to the institutionalized church, which often regulates faith through control and fixed doctrines, Drewermann is concerned with a theology of freedom in which people do not live their faith through fear of sin and punishment, but through trust and love.

In doing so, he ties in with Jesus' original concern: a message that is not conveyed through hierarchy and power, but through direct encounters, compassion and inner experience. In this perspective, religion is not a burden, but a source of inner liberation and existential meaning.

Then a *theology of freedom* will also promote inclusion and charity: A theology of freedom places people at the center, regardless of origin, gender, sexual orientation or social status. By linking faith not to rigid dogmas or exclusion, but to the lived experience of love and justice, it creates space for genuine inclusion. Instead of setting rules about who *"belongs"* and who does not, it invites people to understand faith as an open, compassionate path. In this understanding, charity does not only mean charitable help, but a fundamental attitude of respect and recognition of every person as an image of God.

This form of theology questions existing church structures, which often create exclusive rather than inclusive communities. It calls for people not to be judged according to moral standards or traditions, but to be treated as equals.

In practice, this means that faith communities become open places where no one is excluded because of their identity or doubts. It means that spirituality does not serve to keep people down, but to empower them to shape their lives in a self-determined way and with solidarity for others. In such a theology, charity is not an obligation, but a natural consequence of a faith that gives freedom instead of creating fear.

Chapter 11: Faith between social justice and social inequality

Christianity traditionally sees itself as a religion of charity and justice. But in practice, a different picture often emerges: While the church often clearly positions itself too strictly on moral issues - especially on sexuality - its commitment to social justice often falls short of its own ideals. Why are sexual acts often considered worse than social injustice in many church contexts? And why does sexuality often play a greater role in the church than concrete measures against poverty or social exclusion?

Liberation theology is a central theological movement that deals with this issue. It emphasizes the "option for the poor" as a fundamental Christian principle. But how does this perspective change theological thinking and the orientation of the church? How can a church of the poor actually contribute to greater justice, and what structures stand in the way of this? While some Christian movements actively combat social grievances, other church institutions are criticized for stabilizing existing power relations rather than promoting social change. This ambivalence leads to the question of the function of religion in oppressed societies: Is it used as a tool of liberation or rather - as Karl Marx put it - as the "opium of the people" that keeps people quiet and prevents revolutionary change?

The relationship between church and state also plays a role in this debate. In many countries, despite formal separation, there are still close links between church and political institutions. Why is the separation of church and state not always implemented consistently? And what impact does this have on social inequality?

An interesting perspective in this discussion is the question of whether addressing sexual identity can help to reduce social discrimination. Can the discussion and interpretation of Jesus' sexuality help to question social prejudices in church and social structures? If Jesus showed solidarity with the socially marginalized of his time, shouldn't a church that follows his example also actively stand up against all forms of exclusion - be it due to poverty, origin or sexual orientation?

The combination of faith, social commitment and spiritual experience remains one of the central challenges for modern Christianity. A church that wants to make a credible commitment to justice must critically examine its own structures and ask itself how it can contribute to a fairer world - not just through words, but through concrete actions and solidarity.

a) Faith, social responsibility and social structures

149 • How can faith be combined with social commitment and spiritual experience?

Dorothee Sölle developed the concept of *"political theology"*, which inextricably linked faith with social responsibility. For her, Christianity was not just a question of individual faith, but a mission to change unjust structures. She criticized a church that stayed out of social struggles and instead called for an active confrontation with poverty, oppression and political grievances. At the same time, she integrated mystical spirituality into her thinking. She understood mysticism not as a retreat from the world, but as a profound experience of God that encourages people to take responsibility. This combination of mysticism and commitment was intended to enable a new understanding of God - beyond an authoritarian, distant God to a God who can be experienced in the world and in people's actions. Their *"theology after the death of God"* aimed to overcome an outdated image of God: The focus was not on an all-powerful ruler God, but on a God who lives in the encounter between people. The church should therefore not be based on power and dogma, but should be a community that is involved in society in a spirit of solidarity and liberation. For a *"resurrection of God"* to be possible, something must pass away and something new should emerge: When speaking of a *"resurrection of God"*, this means first of all that an outdated image of God must die - especially the image of an authoritarian, distant or punitive God who watches over the world as ruler:in but remains unconnected to the suffering and injustice of people. A church that concentrates on maintaining power, dogma and institutional self-preservation would also have to perish in this caesura. An image of God that is anchored in people's lived experience could be revived - a God who exists not above but in the world , in relationships, in solidarity, in commitment to justice. A church that does not rule from above, but functions as an open community at eye level, could emerge from this. Such a *"resurrection" - not of Jesus, but of "God"* - would mean that faith is no longer understood as blind submission to rigid doctrines, but as a liberating force that encourages people to take responsibility for themselves and others. It would be a return to a God or goddess who can be experienced not through control, but through love and co-creation.

150 • How can a church of the poor contribute to greater justice and what structures stand in the way?

Leonardo Boff addresses the hierarchical and undemocratic structures of the Catholic Church, which often serve more to maintain power than to practise charity. For him, Christianity is inextricably linked to social justice, which is why he calls for a *"church of the poor"* - a church that does not cling to privileges but actively stands alongside the oppressed.

He sees the traditional church structure as an obstacle to this mission, as it is organized in a centralized and authoritarian manner. Instead of an institution controlled from above, he advocates a church in which the faithful have an equal say and the voice of the poor and marginalized is heard.

For Boff, a *"church of the poor"* means not only charitable aid, but a fundamental conversion - a church that is not based on power and possessions, but on solidarity and liberation. He refers to Jesus himself, who did not identify with those in power, but with the weak and marginalized. This attitude brought Boff into conflict with the Vatican, as his liberation theology questioned the existing church power structures and called for a profound change in the understanding of the church.

It stands to reason that the immense wealth of the church contributes to the fact that many ministers are more concerned with preserving existing structures than with a radical outreach to the poor. An institution that has large financial resources, real estate and economic ties often has little interest in changing fundamentally - especially if a genuine *"church of the poor"* would also mean giving up power and privileges.

Poverty is uncomfortable. It demands not only charity, but also a profound confrontation with inequality and injustice. However, if a church is intertwined with political and economic elites, it risks shaping its message in such a way that it does not challenge existing conditions too strongly. Instead of a church that actively fights for structural change, all that often remains is a church that gives alms selectively without tackling the causes of poverty.

Of course, there are ministers who are honestly committed to social justice. But the question remains whether the institutional church as a whole would be willing to change in such a way that its central concern is not more wealth and influence, but the actual option for the poor. As long as the church sees itself more as a protector of wealth and privilege, poverty is often treated not as an urgent problem but as a marginal issue - out of convenience, self-interest or simple adherence to a power structure that wants to protect itself.

Church tax ensures the financial prosperity and institutional stability of the church in countries such as Germany. Each of the two churches receives around 6-7 billion euros a year through church tax and state subsidies. With assets of 200-300 billion euros per church, considerable financial resources are at their disposal. Leases of property and own businesses can also generate additional revenue. As a result, many clergy work in a system that offers economic security and creates little pressure to deal directly with existential hardship. The abolition of church tax could end this comfort and lead to the church having to rely more on voluntary contributions and donations - similar to many other countries.

This could bring about a change in mentality: A church that no longer automatically has a fixed income would have to make a much greater effort to reach out to its faithful and deal directly with their needs. This could lead to greater closeness to people, especially the socially disadvantaged. At the same time, it would probably lead to a streamlining of the church's administrative apparatus, which currently often seems bureaucratic and sluggish.

However, the abolition of church tax also harbors risks. Social and charitable institutions of the church, which provide essential help in many areas, could suffer if no viable alternative is found for their funding or if they are not converted into charitable institutions. There is also a risk that the church will then focus more on wealthy donors in order to secure income, which would not necessarily promote a genuine *"church of the poor"*.

Ultimately, everything depends on whether the abolition of church tax would be accompanied by a genuine change in values - a conscious renunciation of luxury and power structures in favor of a church that consistently turns to the people. Only then could such a reform actually bring the vision of a *"church of the poor"* closer.

151 • What function does religion fulfill in oppressed societies and why is it referred to as the "opium of the people"?

Karl Marx criticized religion as an instrument for securing power and coined the phrase that it was the *"opium of the people"*. By this he meant that although religion can give people comfort, it also obscures their social situation and prevents them from rebelling against injustice.

For oppressed people, religion often serves as a beacon of hope - it offers the prospect of a better world after death and alleviates the suffering that cannot be overcome in real society. As a result, it can provide short-term emotional relief, similar to an anaesthetic that relieves pain. But this is precisely where Marx sees the problematic function: instead of eliminating the causes of suffering and social inequality, religion merely comforts people about the existing conditions and prevents them from taking action against their oppression.

For the ruling classes, religion is therefore a useful means of stabilizing existing power relations. It legitimizes social inequalities by presenting poverty, obedience and suffering as God-given or as a test for a better afterlife. Those who place their hope in divine justice are less likely to question worldly power structures.

Marx therefore calls not only for a critique of religion, but for a fundamental change in social conditions. People should not hope for a better future in heaven, but fight for their liberation in reality. Only when the social causes of suffering have been eliminated will the need for religious consolation disappear.

Figure 24: A simple open chapel with a communal table at which people from disadvantaged groups sit at eye level with a priestess. In the background, the empty cathedral - a strong sign of a theology that is oriented towards the poor: Communion with the poor and those to be integrated.

In order to reduce social inequality and eliminate the causes of suffering, the state must intervene in economic and social structures in a targeted manner. This can be achieved through a fairer distribution of resources, a strong social infrastructure and political reforms. Important measures include

Redistribution through tax systems - Progressive taxation, in which high incomes and large fortunes are taxed more heavily, can generate financial resources for social programs. At the same time, reducing the tax burden for lower and middle income groups can strengthen purchasing power and promote social mobility.

Investing in education and equal opportunities - Education is the key to combating social inequality. Free or affordable access to high-quality education enables people to improve their own social conditions. Programs to support socially disadvantaged groups can help prevent structural disadvantages from becoming entrenched over generations.

Strengthening the welfare state - minimum wages, affordable housing, good healthcare and secure pension systems are essential for combating poverty and ensuring social security.

Promoting economic participation - The state can promote a fairer economy through targeted incentives and regulation. Cooperative models, co-determination in companies and limiting wage dumping are effective ways of creating a sustainable and fair economy.

Change management methods that are used in companies can also help in social change processes:

Participation and co-determination: Social change can only succeed if the people affected are actively involved. Democratic structures, citizens' forums and direct opportunities for co-determination can legitimize reforms and increase their acceptance.

Transparent communication: Changes are often met with resistance. A clear information policy and dialog with the population can prevent reforms from being perceived as a threat.

Gradual implementation and pilot projects: Major social reforms are often easier to implement if they are first tested in smaller units and expanded if successful.

Adaptability and evaluation: Social change processes must be reviewed and corrected if necessary. Ongoing analysis of measures ensures that reforms are actually effective.

In addition to political measures, social change also requires a change in cultural awareness. Education, social movements and the media play a crucial role in promoting fairer structures. When people realize that inequality is not natural, but politically created, their willingness to work for change increases.

When parties that invoke Christian values in practice promote economic policies that exacerbate social inequality, a contradiction arises between their claims and their actual policies. A policy that primarily serves the interests of the wealthy ignores the biblical mandate to care for the poor and disadvantaged.

Social compatibility means that political decisions must take the whole of society into account and not just favor individual groups. An economic and social policy that continues to distribute wealth to the upper classes while socially weaker groups receive little support is not sustainable in the long term and undermines social cohesion.

Instead, a policy in line with Christian values would be geared towards striking a balance between economic freedom and social responsibility so that prosperity does not grow at the expense of the weaker members of society, but benefits everyone.

152 • How does the option for the poor change the theological thinking and orientation of the church?

Latin American liberation theology places the church firmly at the service of the poor and oppressed. It sees the Gospel not only as a spiritual message, but also as a clear social mission: faith must not be reduced to rituals and dogmas, but must actively work for social justice. The *"option for the poor"* means that the church cannot remain neutral when people live in poverty and exploitation - it must take sides and work towards liberation from unjust structures.

This way of thinking challenges traditional theological thought patterns, as it is no longer just about personal salvation in the afterlife, but about concrete changes in the here and now. Liberation theology rejects a church that allies itself with the powerful or accepts inequality as God-given. Instead, it emphasizes that God is on the side of the suffering and that true discipleship of Jesus means actively standing up for their rights.

Liberation theology thus also poses a challenge to the institutional church: is it prepared to question its role as the guardian of existing conditions and to work consistently for a more just society? Critics accuse it of being political - but that is precisely its claim: that faith and social responsibility cannot be separated. Those who believe in a just God cannot resign themselves to injustice.

---

b) Sexuality and social justice in the church

---

153 • Can discussing Jesus' sexuality help to reduce social discrimination?

The discussion about Jesus' sexuality can help to reduce social discrimination by questioning existing taboos, highlighting new perspectives and contributing to a more inclusive theology. Such a debate could not only provide theological but also social impetus, as it questions the approach to sexuality in Christianity and can contribute to a more open ethic.

Recognizing that Jesus was a person who experienced love, closeness and relationships could lead to a more open discussion of sexuality and identity. Reflecting on how Jesus dealt with human needs and social norms could challenge the idea that certain sexual orientations or forms of relationships are unacceptable or even sinful. This discussion is not only important for theologians, but also for believers who wonder whether the church's sexual morality is actually in line with the message of Jesus. A dogmatic denial of these questions could prevent Christian communities from doing justice to the diversity of human experience.

Furthermore, Jesus' behavior in the Gospels shows a clear tendency towards inclusion and acceptance of all people - regardless of social, sexual or religious conventions. His closeness to all people, his openness towards the sexes and his criticism of rigid moral concepts suggest that he rejected discrimination based on identity or lifestyle. If

Jesus' message of love and acceptance is consistently applied to modern issues of sexuality, this could be a powerful argument against discrimination against queer people, unmarried couples or other lifestyles. Instead of rigid norms, a theologically reflected ethic based on mutual respect, responsibility and care could emerge.

The discussion about Jesus' sexuality therefore not only breaks down dogmatic and social barriers, but also directs the focus towards an ethical attitude that is oriented towards compassion, respect and personal integrity. This will modernize church positions on sexual morality and bring them more in line with the original core of the Gospel. Such a perspective will help to overcome traditional prejudices and turn Christian communities into places of acceptance and solidarity. In this way, Christianity could remain alive as a spiritual tradition by facing up to the challenges of a changing society without losing its fundamental values.

154 • *Why are sexual sins often considered worse than social injustice?*

While social injustice is a visible, structural problem that is usually attributed to social power relations, sexuality is often seen as a direct expression of individual morality or immorality.

A key reason for this emphasis lies in the historical development of the church's moral concepts. The early church adopted a strong fixation on chastity, abstinence and the control of sexual desires from both Judaism and the Greco-Roman world. While Jesus primarily taught love, compassion and overcoming social barriers, an increasingly anti-body ethic developed over the course of church history. The strict regulation of individual behavior became a core component of Christian morality, while social justice was often treated as a secondary, secular matter.

Another factor is the close connection between sexuality and power. Control over sexual norms also means control over people - especially women, queer people and all those who do not fit into the traditional family image. While social injustice is often caused by complex economic and political structures and is therefore harder to blame morally on a single person, violations of sexual norms are usually individual decisions that can be easily sanctioned. By focusing on sexual morality, the church was able to extend its authority over the private lives of the faithful, while social justice was often seen as a political or economic problem for which the church did not want to take direct responsibility.

In addition, many church institutions themselves have historically been involved in social injustices - from supporting feudal structures and tolerating slavery to cooperating with authoritarian regimes. The Catholic Church benefited from these systems for centuries and often held back when it came to social justice for economic and power-political reasons. A strong emphasis on sexual sins could distract from these own transgressions and maintain moral authority. Those who focus on individual sexual purity tend to be less critical of structural injustices. This explains why issues such as premarital sex, homosexuality or adultery were often condemned with great severity, while economic exploitation, poverty or discrimination were criticized in theory but rarely treated with the same moral acuity.

However, a look at the Bible shows that social justice is actually a more central theme in the teachings of Jesus. Jesus repeatedly spoke about the value of the poor, the need for mercy and responsibility towards the weak. In the parables of the Good Samaritan (Luke 10:25-37) and the Last Judgement (Matthew 25:31-46), he places social justice above formal law-abidingness. In the Gospels, it is mostly religious authorities who denounce sexual sins, while Jesus met people in such situations with forgiveness. He thus placed an ethic of love and mercy above a rigid, punitive morality.

A Christian ethic that is more closely aligned with the values of Jesus would have to consider social justice as equally or even more important than personal morality and work for a more just world instead of, for example, treating sexual behavior as the highest moral norm priority. A church that takes social responsibility seriously would have to work more consistently against poverty, discrimination and exploitation instead of focusing on the sexual morality of individuals. Such a change of perspective would not only reflect the Christian message more authentically, but would also strengthen the credibility of the church in a modern society.

155 • Why does sexuality often play a bigger role in the church than social justice?

The fact that sexuality often plays a greater role in the church than social justice has deep-rooted theological, historical and social reasons.

First of all, sexuality is closely linked to questions of identity, morality and control. For centuries, many religious traditions have established norms on gender and sexuality to ensure social order. The Christian church in particular has often limited sexuality to procreation and marriage. And since sexuality is a very personal and emotionally charged area, it is easier to formulate clear rules and prohibitions about it than about complex social issues such as social justice, which often require structural changes.

This is because social justice could lead to existing hierarchies being called into question. If the church were to become more involved in social equality, it would also have to address its own role in social inequalities, for example in connection with economic inequality or historical involvement in colonialism and slavery.

Furthermore, issues of sexual morality offer a clear dividing line between "right" and "wrong", while social justice is more complex and often more ambivalent. While it is easy, for example, to declare homosexuality a "sin" or a "violation of norms" in a binary scheme, issues such as poverty, climate justice or migration are more complex. They require not only individual ethical decisions, but also political action and structural reforms, for which churches often feel less responsible.

Media and social dynamics also reinforce the fixation on sexuality. Church statements on abortion, homosexuality or marriage are often widely discussed, while social justice issues such as fair wages or combating poverty are often lost in church debates. This is also due to the fact that sexuality debates are often more emotional and polarizing, which leads to greater media attention.

Ultimately, the strong focus on sexuality could also be a kind of *distraction mechanism*. By focusing on sexual morality, the church avoids dealing with other pressing but uncomfortable issues. A stronger focus on social justice would require the church to also question itself - for example, its own economic structures, its behavior towards marginalized groups or its role in global injustices.

A progressive church would therefore have to ask itself whether it continues to moralize sexuality disproportionately or whether it focuses more on central Christian values such as charity, justice and solidarity. Only if social justice is no longer treated as a side issue can the church live up to its own claim to ethically responsible action.

---

c) Religion, church, state and political orders and their social significance

---

156 • Why is the separation of church and state not always implemented consistently?

Although the constitution provides for the separation of church and state, there are numerous historical and structural reasons why this separation is not consistently implemented in Germany. One central factor is the state-church treaties, which have cemented the privileges of the churches that have grown over the centuries. These treaties regulate not only financial contributions, but also the churches' spheres of influence in education, welfare and other areas of society.

One particularly controversial example is the state payments to churches, which were originally introduced as compensation for the expropriation of church property in the 19th century. Although the Weimar Constitution of 1919 called for these payments to be replaced, they were never abolished and still amount to hundreds of millions of euros annually. The political will to end these payments is often lacking, as churches have become deeply involved in social and cultural life.

Another reason is the close relationship between the church and state institutions. Church organizations run many social institutions such as hospitals, kindergartens and schools that are financed with public funds. This creates a dependency that makes a clear separation difficult. In addition, churches enjoy numerous special rights, such as church labor law, which gives them extensive autonomy in hiring and firing employees - even in state-funded institutions.

The political landscape also plays a role. Many Christian-based parties and decision-makers are reluctant to question existing structures, as the churches are still seen as social authorities. The influence of church lobbying should not be underestimated, and many politicians cling to traditional cooperation in order to avoid conflicts with the large churches.

Friedrich Wilhelm Graf, a renowned German theologian and religious scholar, critically examines the relationship between church and politics in the modern age. He emphasizes that the historical intertwining of state and church in Germany, manifested through state-church treaties and financial benefits, requires constant review in order to meet the constitutional requirements of a secular state. Graf points out that the separation of church and state enshrined in the Basic Law is not always consistently implemented. In particular, he considers the continued state contributions to the churches, which were actually supposed to be replaced according to the Weimar Constitution of 1919, to be problematic. These financial contributions from the state to the churches contradict the principle of state neutrality in religious matters. Graf also addresses the lack of transparency in the churches' asset management and calls for more open communication with the public. He argues for a reform of church funding that takes account of the changed social realities and strengthens the independence of the state and the church.

The incomplete separation of church and state is therefore the result of historical obligations, political restraint and practical interdependencies that make it difficult to implement a consistent separation. A genuine reform would not only require legal changes, but also a profound social debate about the role of the churches in a secular state.

157 • Is direct democracy the best form of government?

According to Rousseau, direct democracy is the best form of government because it is most closely linked to the general will (*volonté générale*) and directly realizes the sovereignty of the people. In *Du contrat social*, he argues that legitimate rule only emerges from the collective consent of the citizens and that laws are only just if they are decided by the people themselves. However, he concedes that direct democracy is only practicable in small states, as it requires an informed and active body of citizens. In large, complex societies, he considers representative democracy or mixed forms to be more realistic.

From a theological perspective, there is a long debate about whether democracy is compatible with Christian principles. The Catholic Church was skeptical about democracy for a long time, as it associated the divine order more with monarchical or hierarchical models. It was not until the Second Vatican Council that democracy was recognized as compatible with Christian values, especially when it is based on human dignity, the common good and justice. However, the church itself remains a non-democratic institution in which authority is passed on from the top down.

In queer theology, Rousseau's concept of the general will could open up a critical perspective: If democracy means that all citizens participate equally in shaping the community, then marginalized groups - including queer people - must also have a full political and social say. Direct democracy can be seen here as an opportunity to create equal structures that are free of domination. At the same time, there is a danger that majority decisions will suppress minority rights, which is why protective mechanisms are necessary in political practice.

The question of whether direct democracy is the best form of government therefore remains open. Rousseau sees it as ideal, but difficult to implement. The Catholic Church accepts democracy as a political order, but relies on hierarchy itself. Queer theology emphasizes the need for genuine participation, but warns of the risk of majority dictatorship. Direct democracy thus remains an ideal that must always be critically scrutinized and practically adapted.

158 • Is religion more harmful than beneficial to society?

According to Christopher Hitchens, religion is more harmful than beneficial to society, as it not only hinders scientific progress, but also serves as a tool for oppression, violence and dogmatic control. In *God Is Not Great*, he argues that religion often promotes irrational thinking, reinforces moral norms, restricts human rights and exacerbates conflict. In particular, he criticizes religion for presenting itself as a source of moral authority, while historically it has often legitimized discrimination, wars and censorship. For Hitchens, secular ethics and scientific progress are the better alternatives, as they are based on reason and universal human rights rather than divine commandments or religious tradition.

Throughout its history, the Catholic Church has both hindered progress and promoted social developments. On the one hand, it has often been skeptical of scientific findings, adhered to dogmatic ideas and played a role in the oppression of minorities, for example through its stance on the LGBTQIA+ community or the role of women. On the other hand, it has also made significant contributions to society through social teaching, education and charitable work. The church sees itself as a moral authority that stands up for justice and human dignity - a self-image that in many cases is at odds with its historical practice.

From the perspective of queer theology, religion is ambivalent: it has often been used to exclude and discriminate against queer people, but at the same time it also offers resources for liberation and identity formation. Queer theologians argue that religion is not oppressive per se, but that its interpretation is crucial. Theology can also be used to promote inclusion, justice and a spiritual perspective on diversity. So while Hitchens sees religion as fundamentally harmful, queer theologians emphasize that it is the lived practice that matters - religion can contribute to both oppression and liberation.

While Hitchens emphasizes its historical and current dangers, the Catholic Church points to its positive contributions to society. Religion can be destructive, but it can also offer space for community, a search for meaning and social justice.

159 • God as tyrant: Can a secular society be moral?

According to Michel Onfray, a secular society can not only be moral, but can even provide a better basis for ethics than a religious society. In

Traité d'athéologie, he argues that morality does not have to depend on divine commandments, but rather arises from rational thinking, compassion and social responsibility. He criticizes religiously based moral concepts as often repressive, as they are frequently based on obedience, dogma and sanctions instead of promoting individual freedom and ethical reflection. *Secular ethics*, on the other hand, can strengthen universal principles such as human rights, equality and justice without relying on a specific religious tradition.

The Catholic Church, on the other hand, believes that true morality is not possible without a higher, divine order. According to Christian teaching, God is the source of goodness, and moral principles are not merely human conventions, but are anchored in the divine order. The Church fears that a secular society that develops morality without a religious basis will slide into relativism, in which there are no longer any objective values. At the same time, Catholic social teaching has also shown that there are overlaps between religious and secular ethics, for example in the commitment to human rights or social justice.

A secular society makes it possible to rethink ethical issues without relying on traditional religious hierarchies or outdated norms.

Thus, this author also shows that a secular society can certainly be moral if it is based on universal values such as humanity, equality and reason. While the Church emphasizes that morality needs a divine foundation, secular thinkers such as Onfray argue that ethics can be coherent and just even without religion.

Whether justice has anything to do with God depends on the perspective. In classical theology, especially in the Catholic tradition, God is regarded as the highest source of justice. According to this view, justice is not just a human ideal, but a divine principle that manifests itself in creation and in divine commandments. Thomas Aquinas sees justice as a virtue that is anchored in the divine order and expresses itself through moral action. In the Bible, justice is often equated with God's will - for example, when it says that God defends the poor and oppressed.

However, the question arises as to whether justice can also exist independently of God. Philosophical ethics, especially in secularism, argue that justice is a humanly developed principle based on reason, compassion and social responsibility. Modern theories of justice, such as that of John Rawls, see justice as a social structure that ensures fairness and equality without the need for a divine authority. Michel Onfray and Richard Dawkins also believe that moral principles such as justice do not depend on religious ideas, but arise from rational and humanistic considerations.

Whether an unjust God must be regarded as evil depends on the definition of justice and the image of God. In classical theology, especially in the Christian tradition, God is considered to be perfectly just. His justice is often associated with his omnipotence and all-goodness (*theodicy question*). If God were not just, this would call into question his perfect nature . Nevertheless, there are numerous passages in the Bible in which God's actions appear to be unjust from a human perspective, for example in the story of Job, in the destruction of entire nations or in the idea of eternal damnation.

This raises the question: is God just by human standards, or is his justice one that we cannot fully understand? Theologians such as Augustine or Thomas Aquinas argue that God's justice goes beyond our human understanding. What seems unjust to us may be based on a higher divine order that we do not comprehend. However, this view requires a strong belief that God is just by definition - even if his actions appear otherwise.

Queer theology questions this approach and asks the critical question of whether a God who allows inequality, suffering or oppression can really be considered just. For example, if religious dogma is used to exclude or morally devalue LGBTQIA+ people, it could be argued that such a God - or at least his theological interpretation - is perceived as unjust. Some queer theologians argue in favor of rethinking the image of God and the understanding of justice: A truly just God must stand for liberation, inclusion and love, otherwise he would not be a God worthy of worship, but a religious projection of human power structures.

Philosophically speaking, the question of an unjust God leads directly to *the theodicy debate*: if God is not just, does he or she consciously allow injustice? And wouldn't that be tantamount to wickedness? Theists who believe in a just God must explain why suffering exists.

Atheists or religion-critical thinkers such as Dawkins or Hitchens, on the other hand, argue that a God who allows suffering and injustice is morally no better than a tyrant - or simply does not exist.

A person can perceive suffering as God's justice if they assume that divine justice is not identical to human justice and that suffering has a higher, often hidden meaning. In many religious traditions, especially in Christianity, suffering is not only understood as a punishment or consequence of sin, but also as a test, maturation or participation in a divine plan of salvation.

1. suffering as a test or purification: In the biblical story of Job, for example, a pious man loses everything - possessions, family, health - even though he is innocent. Job wrestles with God, accuses him, but finds no rational explanation. In the end, he realizes that God's ways cannot be fully understood by man: *"I had heard of you only by hearsay; but now my eye has seen you."* (Job 42:5). For people of faith, suffering can therefore be a moment that leads to spiritual depth, humility and knowledge of God - even if it does not seem just from a human perspective.

2. suffering as part of the divine plan: In Catholic theology, suffering is often interpreted in the light of Christ's passion: Jesus, although innocent, suffers and dies on the cross - and this is precisely where the key to salvation lies. In this perspective, those who suffer can connect with the suffering Christ. Suffering is thus not abolished, but placed in a context of salvation history in which it takes on meaning. God's righteousness is not demonstrated by the fact that he prevents suffering, but that he shares in it and transforms it.

3. suffering as a consequence of freedom: Another theological approach argues that human suffering is often the consequence of human freedom. If God gives man true freedom, he must also allow the possibility that man will do wrong. In this perspective, suffering is not directly willed by God, but is part of his just decision not to turn humans into puppets. Justice here means: God respects the freedom of his creatures - even if it causes suffering.

4. questioning perspective - queer theology and justice in suffering: This theology asks: Is it really just to interpret suffering as divinely willed

- especially when people are systematically oppressed or discriminated against? Anyone who explains the suffering of queer people as a "trial", for example, fails to recognize the social causes of this suffering and shifts responsibility from people to God. In this sense, interpreting suffering too quickly in religious terms as "just" can also be dangerous and dehumanizing.

A person can only perceive suffering as God's justice if they trust that God's standards are greater than human standards and that suffering has a deeper meaning in the divine plan. This trust can comfort and strengthen - but must be critically reflected upon in order not to become a cover for human injustice. God's justice must not mean glorifying suffering, but should lead to compassion and the active overcoming of injustice.

Those who see *justice as an intrinsic characteristic of God* must therefore explain why the world often appears unjust. Those who accept a God whose justice transcends human standards must accept that our concept of good and evil is limited. And those who see justice as independent of God might ask *whether an unjust God is not simply a man-made concept that should be criticized and changed.*

From a legal and human rights perspective, injustice is not merely a subjective or arbitrary concept, but a socially defined condition that exists when fundamental rights, equality or fair procedures are violated. Nevertheless, it is recognized that notions of justice and injustice are shaped historically, culturally and politically - and must therefore be open to change and criticism.

1. law as a mirror of social concepts of justice: In jurisprudence, justice is often understood as a goal, but not as a measure of positive law. The law describes what is valid, not necessarily what is just. From a legal perspective, injustice often occurs when applicable laws or principles such as legal equality, non-discrimination, proportionality or the rule of law are violated.

However, laws themselves can be unjust - for example, if they systematically disadvantage groups. This is where legal criticism comes into play: it examines whether applicable law meets human rights or ethical standards.

2. human rights - universal standards for justice: From a human rights perspective, injustice occurs when fundamental rights are violated - such as the right to life and physical integrity, freedom of religion and opinion, equality before the law, the right to artistic freedom, protection against discrimination on the basis of gender, origin, sexuality, etc. These rights are laid down in documents such as the Universal Declaration of Human Rights (1948), the UN Civil Pact and the European Convention on Human Rights. These rights are enshrined in documents such as the Universal Declaration of Human Rights (1948), the UN Civil Pact and the European Convention on Human Rights. Here it becomes clear that injustice is more than an individual feeling - it is an objectifiable injustice that can be named and legally challenged by international standards.

3. changeability of concepts of justice: Despite universal principles, what is considered just or unjust changes over time.

Examples: In the past, laws against homosexuality were considered legitimate in many countries - today they are internationally regarded as contrary to human rights. *Or:* women were not allowed to vote or manage property in many countries until the 20th century - this was also once considered "right", but is now considered a structural injustice.

It follows from this: Injustice is not purely subjective, but it is also not eternally fixed. It is a social concept that must be critically reflected upon and further developed time and again - in the discourse between law, morality, politics and public experience.

The theme that some should be committed to basic human rights rather than religion, theology or faith if one wants justice in the world is not a one-dimensional consideration - but depends strongly on how one understands justice and what framework one recognizes for moral action. However, some clear considerations can be made:

Human rights: universal, rationally based, legally binding: Human rights provide a secular, legally anchored standard for defining and protecting justice globally - regardless of religion, culture or individual convictions. They are based on the principle that all people have equal dignity and equal rights simply because they are human beings.

- Human rights are particularly important in pluralistic, democratic societies because they are binding and can legally limit discrimination - including discrimination based on religion.
- They offer protection for everyone - including from religious abuse of power or theological exclusion (e.. of women, queer people or people of other faiths).

Religion and faith: moral orientation, but often not universal: Religion and theology can also contribute to justice - for example through values such as charity, solidarity, mercy and protection of the weak. Many religious actors around the world are committed to social justice, for example in the fight against poverty or peace work.

- However, religious morality is often tied to specific faith communities, is not always inclusive and is sometimes associated with dogmas that conflict with modern human rights (e.. in matters of gender equality, sexual self-determination or freedom of expression).

Queer theology is a pioneering attempt at mediation: queer theology is an example of how faith and human rights do not have to contradict each other. It therefore attempts to critically question theological traditions in order to combine them with an inclusive, human rights-based understanding of justice. This is its strength and perspective as a bridging function: for it, faith does not mean blind obedience, but an open search for justice in the light of experience, vulnerability and diversity.

So if you want justice in a diverse, global society, human rights are the more reliable common point of reference because they are rationally justifiable, legally protected and inclusive.

Religion and faith can provide a complementary deeper moral motivation - but they should not be above human rights and must be measured against them if they are to contribute to justice. So those who seek justice for all - regardless of faith, origin, gender or identity - should be committed first and foremost to human rights, without necessarily having to forgo spiritual or queer or religious dimensions.

Chapter 12: Interreligious perspectives through dialogs and comparisons

The question of the future of religions in a globalized world is inextricably linked to interreligious dialogue. The exchange between different faiths offers opportunities for mutual understanding, but also poses challenges - especially when it comes to moral, ethical and interpretative questions and personal answers. One example of this is philosophy's criticism of Christian morality, which is often described as negating or weakening life. While religious traditions provide moral guidance, secular thinkers argue that dogmatic prescriptions often lead to a restriction of individual freedom. So what can a dialog between philosophical ethics and theological morality look like that is not based on demarcation but on mutual enrichment?

There are also different perspectives within Christianity, for example between the Catholic and Protestant churches. This is particularly evident in their stance on progressive or queer issues. While the Protestant Church has already taken steps towards full acceptance of LGBTQIA+ people in many countries - for example by blessing same-sex marriage couples or allowing queer clergy to openly serve in leadership roles - the Catholic Church still officially adheres to a restrictive sexual morality. These differences raise the question of how Christianity as a whole can develop further in dealing with queer believers and whether interdenominational exchange could help to open up new perspectives on inclusion and human rights.

Another central topic in the interreligious comparison is the understanding of the Lord's Supper. The Catholic and Protestant churches have historically developed different interpretations of this sacrament, which still have theological and practical implications today. While in the Catholic Church the Eucharist is understood as an actual transformation of the bread and wine into the body and blood of Christ, the Protestant Church sees the Lord's Supper more as a communal meal of remembrance. These differences concern not only theological discussions, but also the question of what meaning these sacraments have for queer people. Who is allowed to interpret them and how? What role do queer believers play in the liturgy and how are they taken into account in terms of content? And to what extent do these sacraments reflect ideas of inclusion or exclusion?

Especially in the Catholic Church, the celebration of the Eucharist is a central part of the service. Which elements are particularly important for queer people? The Eucharist as a sign of communion is a powerful symbol of the unrestricted acceptance of all believers - but the reality is often different. In many Catholic communities, queer people do not yet experience full inclusion, be it through official church teaching or through social questioning processes. How can the sacrament of the Eucharist be shaped in such a way that it lives up to its original meaning as a sign of divine love for all?

Interreligious and interdenominational dialog offers the opportunity to find new ways for a more open and just theology. When religions engage in an honest exchange about their similarities and differences, they can not only expand their own self-understanding, but also make an important contribution to a pluralistic and inclusive society. This is not just about academic debates, but about concrete reforms that take people's spiritual and social identities seriously and support them - e.g. queer married couples and cohabiting couples, with and without children.

160 • How does philosophy thematize Christian morality as life-negating and debilitating?

Friedrich Nietzsche *sees Christian morality as a "slave morality"* that does not affirm life, but weakens and suppresses it. He argues that Christianity propagates virtues such as humility, compassion and modesty as the highest values in order to tame the strong and create a society in which weakness is elevated to the norm. Instead of promoting self-realization, strength and the creative will to create, Christian morality demands submission, obedience and renunciation.

For Nietzsche, this ethic did not arise from a free, self-confident attitude, but from resentment - from the envy of the weak towards the strong. By glorifying virtues such as the ability to suffer and obedience, it denies life and the natural vitality of human beings. Instead of striving for greatness and self-conquest, people are educated to make themselves small and hope for an otherworldly reward instead of taking their fate into their own hands.

Nietzsche opposes this slave morality with a *"master morality"* based on self-determination, courage and the creation of new values. He calls on people to free themselves from Christian morality and develop an ethic that does not arise from fear or feelings of guilt, but from the joy of life and the willingness to take responsibility for one's own existence.

In order to experience joy in life and take responsibility for your own existence, you need an inner attitude of self-acceptance, an active approach to life and a conscious confrontation with challenges. Nietzsche calls on people not to live their lives according to other people's rules or religious dogmas, but to develop their individual strengths and create values in a self-determined way.

These include:

- **Self-acceptance:** Accepting yourself in your strengths and weaknesses and not striving for an unattainable ideal.
- **Creative design:** Actively shaping your own existence instead of passively remaining in predetermined structures. This can be done through creative activities, personal development or courageous decisions.
- **Overcoming fear and feelings of guilt:** Not allowing yourself to be paralyzed by outdated moral concepts or social expectations, but evaluating your own life according to individual standards.
- **Courage to change:** the willingness to face challenges, question old patterns and break new ground.
- **Affirmation of life:** consciously experiencing the moment, finding meaning in small things and understanding yourself as an active, powerful being.

A person in deep despair does not need abstract philosophical concepts, but concrete help, understanding and new perspectives. When someone loses the will to live, it is crucial that they feel heard and not alone. Important impulses can be:

- **Acceptance of pain:** It is important to convey that pain and suffering are part of life, but do not have to be permanent. There are ways out, even if they don't seem visible at the moment.
- **Breaking the feeling of isolation:** People often feel alone or misunderstood. Active listening, empathetic conversations and offering to be there can help to alleviate feelings of loneliness.
- **Focus on what can be done:** When everything seems hopeless, it can help to point out small steps - things that can be changed, even if they seem insignificant at the moment. There is always one best move in the game of chess.
- **Open up new perspectives:** Those who are suicidal, for example, often only see a narrow corridor of possibilities. External stimuli - conversations with others, professional help or new experiences - can help to break out of this mental constriction.
- **De-tabooing accepting help:** Psychological or therapeutic support is not a weakness, but an act of self-care. Communicating that professional help is an option and not something to be ashamed of can be a first step towards change.

Ultimately, *helping theology* is about seeing life not as an overwhelming duty, but as a possibility - a possibility that is filled with pain, but also with potential. People should be given the feeling that they are not alone, that their feelings are taken seriously and that there are paths that are not yet visible, even in the darkest moments. This is also the task of pastoral care and the community of neighbors, friends and also believers in places.

161 • What significance does the celebration of the Eucharist have in the Catholic Church, and which elements are central for queer people?

The celebration of the Eucharist is the central sacrament of the Catholic Church and symbolizes the presence of Christ, communion and reconciliation. It is reminiscent of Jesus' Last Supper, in which he shared bread and wine with his disciples and thus set a sign of love and devotion. For queer people and couples, the Eucharist can have a profound meaning because it embodies God's universal invitation to all people. Jesus himself ate with all people, which fully integrates queer believers into this community. The experience of unity and acceptance celebrated in the Eucharist is particularly significant. For queer couples, this can be a sign that their love and faith are accepted by God despite ecclesiastical resistance. Saying "Amen" when receiving communion is a conscious affirmation of one's own faith and belonging to the church, which for queer believers is often associated with a feeling of affirmation and spiritual self- affirmation. The Eucharist is therefore a spiritual anchor for queer people who know they are rooted in their faith and hope that the Church will one day fully live the message of unconditional love. They can draw strength from the celebration to stand up for an inclusive church and be inspired by the mission at the end of the Eucharist to carry God's love into the world - for themselves and for others.

162 • What are the similarities and differences between the Catholic and Protestant understanding of the Lord's Supper and what impact does this have on queer people?

The Catholic and Protestant understanding of the Lord's Supper has both similarities and key differences that are also important for queer people and their participation in this sacrament.

Commonalities: Both denominations regard the Lord's Supper as a central celebration of the Christian faith, reminiscent of Jesus' last meal with his disciples. It symbolizes communion with Christ and among believers as well as the forgiveness of sins. In both churches, communion is also understood as an expression of divine grace, which is extended to all those who partake.

Differences: The most important difference lies in the understanding of the sacrament - the Catholic Church teaches *the doctrine of transubstantiation*, according to which bread and wine are actually transformed into the body and blood of Christ. Communion is a repeated sacrificial event that must be performed by an ordained priest. The Protestant church, on the other hand, usually understands the Lord's Supper to be more symbolic or as a real presence of Christ, which is not mediated by a substantial transformation but by the faith of the community.

Another difference lies in the access restriction: in the Catholic Church, communion (*Eucharist*) is officially only permitted for baptized Catholics who are in the *"state of grace"*, i.e. who have not committed a serious sin. This means that people whose lifestyle is considered "irregular" - according to Catholic doctrine, this includes remarried divorcees or homosexual couples in a partnership - are often excluded from communion or feel prevented from doing so themselves. In many Protestant churches, on the other hand, communion is open to all believers, regardless of their sexual orientation or marital status.

Impact on queer people: For queer people, this difference can be significant. In Protestant churches, especially in liberal *denominations*, queer believers are usually invited to take communion without restriction, as it is understood as an expression of God's unconditional love. In the Catholic Church, on the other hand, there are still tensions. Although queer people are not officially denied general participation, they face the challenge that same-sex partnerships are considered "disordered" according to Catholic doctrine. As a result, the sacrament can become a symbol of exclusion if queer believers experience that they would only be admitted to communion under certain conditions - such as the existence of a partnership or marriage certificate.

In practice, however, there are also different approaches within the Catholic Church. While some parishes and priests practice an inclusive attitude and do not exclude queer people from the Eucharist, the official doctrinal position of the Vatican continues to adhere to a more restrictive line.

The Protestant understanding of the Lord's Supper therefore generally offers queer people greater openness and acceptance, while the Catholic understanding can be associated with access requirements or additional arguments on the part of those involved locally. Nevertheless, the Lord's Supper remains a sign of divine love and grace in both traditions - an aspect that could also influence debates on inclusion and equality within the church in the long term.

163 • What is the Protestant Church's stance on queer issues?

The Protestant church's stance on queer issues is diverse and depends heavily on the respective denomination, regional church and theological orientation. While some Protestant churches advocate full acceptance and equality for queer people, there are also conservative movements that reject such recognition or only allow it to a limited extent.

In principle, the Protestant Church is more open than the Roman Catholic Church, particularly when it comes to the blessing of same-sex couples, the ordination of queer clergy and gender-equitable theology. In many regional churches, particularly in Europe and North America, same-sex couples can be married in church and queer people are employed as pastors. The *Evangelical Church in Germany* (EKD), for example, has recognized marriage for all in several regional churches and is committed to an inclusive theology that also includes non-binary and trans people.

In practice, there is a growing shift towards inclusion. Many Protestant churches are now promoting queer pastoral care services, advocating anti-discrimination and participating in social debates on equal rights. There is also a growing theological debate on queer perspectives, which reinterprets biblical texts and takes their cultural contexts into account.

It can therefore be said that the Protestant Church is more progressive overall in its stance on queer issues than the Catholic Church, but that there are still different needs for discussion within the various streams and denominations. While many regional churches are in favor of full recognition of queer people and their relationships, there is still a need to justify full inclusion in free church and conservative Protestant circles. However, there has been a clear trend towards greater acceptance and equality in the last few decades .

164 • How does religious intolerance arise from the distinction between true and false in matters of faith?

In his *theory of the "Mosaic distinction"*, Jan Assmann describes how the rise of monotheistic religions introduced a new, divisive way of thinking: the sharp distinction between true and false belief. While polytheistic cultures usually allowed different gods and religious traditions to coexist, monotheistic religions established an exclusive truth.

According to Assmann, this development can be traced back to the biblical story of Moses, who not only proclaimed a single God, but also called for the renunciation of foreign gods. As a result, religion was no longer just understood as a cultural heritage, but as a question of right or wrong beliefs. This distinction meant that people of other faiths were no longer regarded simply as worshippers of other gods, but as misbelievers or apostates, which created the basis for religious intolerance and persecution.

Assmann argues that this structure continues to have an effect in modern times: The idea of an absolute truth in religious matters creates an enemy image towards those who think differently. This dynamic can be observed historically in the religious wars, but also in modern ideological conflicts. The *"Mosaic distinction"* therefore shows how religion developed from a pluralistic to an exclusive system, thereby promoting conflict.

According to Jan Assmann, this transition from polytheism to monotheism led to social and personal conflicts because the Mosaic distinction introduced a clear separation between true and false beliefs. While polytheistic cultures usually allowed different gods and beliefs to coexist, monotheistic religions established an absolute claim to truth that no longer regarded those of other faiths as merely foreign, but as false believers or enemies. This promoted religious intolerance, exclusion and persecution. On a personal level, this exclusivity can trigger inner conflicts, as individual doubts or alternative spiritual experiences collide with the monotheistic claim to truth. This creates tensions both within society and in one's own religious life.

This even exacerbated the problem that other beliefs were not simply seen as alternatives, but as errors or even threats. In the past, this has actually led to conflicts, persecution and religious wars, as deviation from *the "true faith"* was seen as an existential challenge.

Whether the concentration on a few monotheistic religions today leads directly to more wars is a complex issue. While religion is often used to legitimize violence, the actual causes of war are usually political, economic or social in nature. Nevertheless, history shows that a strictly exclusive religious worldview can contribute to the division of societies by promoting a strong *"us versus them" mindset*.

One possible solution could actually lie in allowing diversity in images of God and religious beliefs. Societies that promote religious pluralism and regard different forms of faith as equal tend to have fewer religiously motivated conflicts. If faith is no longer seen as an absolute monopoly on truth, but as a personal or cultural expression, fronts could soften and religion could once again play a greater role in mediating peace rather than creating division.

However, this depends not only on religion itself, but also on political structures and social conditions. Simply allowing different religious beliefs is not enough - it also requires a cultural, religious and political attitude that sees diversity as an enrichment and not a threat. Only then could a move away from exclusive images of God actually help to ensure that religion no longer serves as a means of division, but as a bridge between people and cultures.

The Catholic Church and other Christian churches can develop a more open theology that sees different images of God not as competition, but as an expression of the diversity of faith. One possibility would therefore be to focus more on shared ethical values rather than dogmatic demarcations. Instead of seeing its own faith as the only truth, the church could emphasize that God can be experienced in different ways in different traditions.

An important step is the promotion of interreligious dialog. The church could engage more intensively with other religions and emphasize similarities rather than differences. Popes have already shown that interreligious cooperation for peace and justice is possible - these efforts could be further expanded, for example by acknowledging the spiritual truths of other religions in sermons and theological texts.

The re-evaluation of biblical texts could also contribute to questioning exclusive images of God. In historical-critical exegesis, there are already approaches to understanding the biblical texts in their respective cultural context instead of interpreting them as absolute truth. If churches openly point out that images of God have changed over the course of history, they can also encourage believers to see their own faith more dynamically.

Another possibility would be a religious education that recognizes plurality. Theological training institutions could do more to ensure that prospective clergy not only get to know Christianity in depth, but also other faiths. This could help to relativize exclusive truth claims and instead promote an attitude of openness and respect.

Finally, the church itself could develop further in its liturgical practice and proclamation. Prayers and services could relate more strongly to a universal spirituality that is not limited to Christianity, but also integrates elements of other traditions. This could show that the divine cannot be experienced in just one way, but that different spiritual paths ultimately lead to the same goal.

By taking these steps, the church could contribute to an evolving understanding of God - moving away from an exclusive truth towards an inclusive spirituality that promotes peace and understanding between religions.

Interreligious cooperation can therefore be strengthened by common ethical principles that have a unifying effect beyond religious boundaries. Religions share many core values such as compassion, justice, solidarity and peace - these commonalities could serve as a basis for increased cooperation. Churches and religious communities could establish ecumenical and interfaith forums in which representatives of different traditions do not argue about religious truths, but work together on social challenges.

In concrete terms, interfaith peace initiatives could be promoted that campaign for social justice, climate protection or the protection of minorities. In recent decades, the Catholic Church has already organized interfaith meetings, such as the Assisi prayer meeting, at which religious leaders campaign for peace. Such initiatives could be intensified and expanded at a local level by communities actively engaging in dialog with other religious groups and implementing joint social projects, such as refugee aid or combating poverty.

A theology of peace and reconciliation that teaches a more inclusive spirituality instead of exclusivity would also be important. Sermons and educational programs could focus more on what we have in common and make it clear that religious diversity should not be seen as a threat, but as an enrichment.

Many religions have different but often compatible ideas of the divine. A universal spirituality could incorporate elements from different traditions without abandoning one's own faith.

Judaism and Islam: Like Christianity, both religions emphasize tho unity of God (monotheism), but with a stronger focus on the incomprehensibility of God. Here, Christianity could take up suggestions to view God not only personally, but also as a transcendent reality.

Hinduism: There are both polytheistic and monotheistic currents here. The idea of Brahman, the highest, impersonal principle, could serve as a supplement to understand God not only as a being, but as an all-encompassing energy.

Buddhism: Although Buddhism does not recognize a personal God, it emphasizes the idea of enlightenment and overcoming the ego. Christian mystics such as Meister Eckhart have formulated similar ideas, so that a connection between Christian and Buddhist spirituality could be established here.

African and indigenous religions: Many of these traditions see the divine as present in nature. A greater appreciation of creation as sacred could enrich the Christian image of God.

Taoism: The concept of Tao, the natural order of the universe, could help us to see God not only as a guiding being, but also as a flowing, harmonious force.

Figure 25: Interreligious dialog under the Tree of Peace: representatives of different world religions discussing understanding, tolerance and shared values

Possible new additions to the image of God:

➕ A stronger understanding of God as an impersonal force (Brahman, Tao)

➕ A panentheistic view in which God is not outside, but present in everything that exists

➕ A stronger integration of nature and the cosmos into the concept of God (inspired by indigenous religions)

✙ The idea of enlightenment and self-overcoming as a divine process (Buddhist perspective)

✙ A greater flexibility in the image of God that accepts different paths to God

Similarities between the religions:

✓ A transcendent principle that permeates life

✓ God as the source of love, justice and wisdom

✓ The idea of divine guidance or enlightenment

✓ The divine as the origin of creation

✓ The importance of compassion, mindfulness and spirituality

This opening could create an image of God that not only enriches Christianity, but also builds bridges between religions and thus contributes to more peace and understanding in the world.

Even if Christianity primarily worships a personally conceived God, there are theological currents, especially in mysticism, that contain pantheistic or panentheistic (God in everything, but also beyond) elements. God is seen as the creator and not as part of creation, even if some might say that the creating painter is always also part of the work of art - creation is almost an expression of the creator. There is a panentheistic interpretation that says that God is present in everything without being reduced to creation. This idea can be found in many Christian schools of thought, especially among church fathers, mystics and modern theologians.

There are many passages in the Bible that suggest a deep unity between God and creation: These could be interpreted as echoes of a panentheistic view. A central biblical passage is Psalm 139:7-8, which states: *"Where could I go before your Spirit, where could I flee from your presence? If I go up to heaven, you are there; if I lie down in the underworld, you are there."* This passage indicates that God does not only exist in a specific place, but is present everywhere and in everything. Romans 1:20 also picks up on this idea: *"For his invisible nature, his eternal power and Godhead, have been perceived by reason from the creation of the world through the works of creation."* This reveals a pantheistic idea in that God is recognized through nature, it is an expression of his essence. This idea is taken further in Acts 17:28: *"For in him we live and weave and are."* This passage, which Paul takes from the Greek poet Aratos, could be interpreted panentheistically, as all being is contained in God without God being identical with the world.

In Ephesians 4:6, God is also described as an all-pervading principle: *"One is God and Father of all, who is above all and through all and in all."* This formulation is very much in line with pantheistic ideas. Psalm 19:2 formulates it similarly: *"The heavens declare the glory of God, and the firmament proclaims the work of his hands."* Here, nature itself is described as revealing divine truth, which harmonizes with a pantheistic idea.

These echoes have inspired various currents in Christian theology. Earlier church fathers and mystics developed similar ideas. In the 4th century, Gregory of Nyssa spoke of *God as an infinite presence that permeates everything.* Meister Eckhart (13th/14th century) taught that *God exists in everything* and that the knowledge of God is an inner experience that lies beyond all concepts. Johannes Scotus Eriugena (9th century) *saw the whole of creation as an appearance of God.*

There are also pantheistic approaches in modern theology. Teilhard de Chardin, a Catholic priest and theologian, developed the concept of a *"cosmic Christ"*, in which Christ is seen as the driving force of evolution. In *Laudato si'*, Pope Francis talks about a deeper connection between God and creation and emphasizes that God is present in everything.

The Catholic Church could further deepen the panentheistic aspects by recognizing that God works in everything, even outside the Christian tradition. A stronger emphasis on nature as sacred would contribute to a more conscious perception of spiritual connectedness with creation - similar to what is taught in indigenous or Far Eastern religions. In addition, the image of God could be expanded so that God is not only understood as a personal being, but also as a universal force that can be experienced both transcendentally and immanently. A greater openness to mysticism and contemplative traditions could ultimately lead to the unity between God and the world being recognized as a deeper spiritual reality.

In this way, Christianity could develop a more inclusive image of God that is compatible with both biblical traditions and modern spiritual experiences. A pantheistic spirituality could enrich the church by making it possible to experience the divine presence not only in fixed beliefs, but in the whole of creation.

---

d) Epistemological and biological perspectives

---

165 • What role does interreligious dialog play in the future of religions?

Karen Armstrong, a respected religious scholar, emphasizes the central importance of interfaith dialogue for the future of religions. She argues that a deep understanding and respect for different faiths is essential to promote peace and harmony in a globalized world. Armstrong emphasizes that the study of different religions and the practice of compassion are ways to recognize shared values and reduce conflicts. Through *interfaith dialog*, prejudices can be broken down and a deeper understanding of the spiritual needs and expressions of other cultures can be developed. This not only contributes to personal enrichment, but also strengthens social cohesion and promotes more peaceful coexistence.

Armstrong's commitment to interfaith dialog is also reflected in her *Charter for Compassion* initiative, which aims to place compassion as a universal value at the heart of human action. It emphasizes that the practice of compassion, as taught in all major religions, is a key to overcoming conflict and promoting global peace. Through such initiatives, it becomes clear that interfaith dialog is not merely academic in nature, but has practical implications for daily life and relations between different communities.

In a world increasingly characterized by secularization and religious diversity, Armstrong sees interfaith dialogue as a way to preserve the relevance and positive influence of religions. She is convinced that through mutual understanding and cooperation, religions can work together to contribute to a more just and compassionate society. This approach not only promotes peace, but also enables religions to evolve and respond to the needs of the modern world.

Karen Armstrong therefore considers **interreligious dialog to be indispensable for the future of religions**. Through exchange and mutual understanding, religions can emphasize their common values and work together to solve global challenges, ultimately leading to a more peaceful and just world.

Appendix

Draft agenda for Council for the reform of central dogmas and doctrines of the Catholic Church

Agenda: Draft agenda for a council to reform central dogmas and doctrines of the Catholic Church

📍 **Place:** Vatican, Synod Hall
📅 **Date:** recurring
Topic: "Renewal in the spirit of the Gospel - dogmas and doctrines put to the test"

◆ Morning session: Fundamental theological issues and the need for reform

08:30 - 09:00 | Opening and prayer

- Pope's address on the urgency of ecclesial renewal
- Introduction to the methodological approach of theological examination

09:00 - 10:30 | Infallibility of the Pope and its limits

- Historical development of dogmas using the example of the dogma of papal infallibility (1870, First Vatican Council)
- Critical reflection: Infallibility as an obstacle to theological development?
- Proposal: Stronger synodal decision-making structures instead of the sole authority of the Pope and revision of other dogmas

10:30 - 10:45 | Coffee break

10:45 - 12:30 | Compulsory celibacy - an outdated practice?

- Theological justification and historical development of celibacy
- Practical experience: psychological stress and a shortage of priests
- Discussion about an early **abolition of compulsory celibacy**
- Reports from the Eastern churches and Protestant traditions as a comparison
- Decision formulations

12:30 - 14:00 | Lunch break and informal discussions

◆ Afternoon session: Social and moral theological issues

14:00 - 15:30 | Gender equality - Women in church offices

- Theological arguments for and against women's ordination
- Effects of a gender-equitable church on credibility and membership figures
- Legal adjustments
- Historical role of deaconesses and today's expansion to include women as clergy in local churches
- Decision formulations

15:30 - 15:45 | Coffee break

15:45 - 17:00 | Sexual ethics and LGBTQIA+ - Overdue corrections to church moral teaching

- Critical analysis of Catholic sexual morality and its effect on the faithful
- Possibilities for a theological reassessment of same-sex partnerships

- Discussion and decision formulation: Recognition and church blessing of same-sex couples

17:00 - 18:00 | Discussion panel - Increasing the employer brand attractiveness of the Catholic Church through employer branding measures

18:00 - 19:00 | Closing plenary session and adoption of the Reform Charter

- Presentation of the main results of the working groups
- Adoption of the **"Charter of the Church's Readiness to Reform"**
- Joint prayer for wisdom for the future implementation of the resolutions

19:30 | Reception to strengthen networks within the reform-oriented church

20:00| Dinner together

Draft of a possible protocol of a council for the reform of Catholic dogmas and doctrines

Today was characterized by intensive theological, canonical and social debates on the need to revise or at least critically reflect on central dogmas of the Catholic Church and to formulate and jointly decide on corresponding draft decisions. It became clear that many doctrines are historically conditioned and in some cases no longer correspond to the lived realities of the faithful. **The participants agreed** that a renewal in the spirit of the Gospel is essential in order to preserve the credibility of the church in modern society.

1. dogmas such as the "infallibility of the Pope" - obstacles to reform

The discussion revealed that the dogma of papal infallibility, which was defined at the First Vatican Council in 1870**, hinders theological debates and makes it difficult to critically reflect on church teachings**.

- Unanimous opinion: Infallibility must be redefined or restricted, as it **blocks a genuine synodal church**.
- Proposal: Introduction of a **collegial decision-making process** in which the Pope acts only as **primus inter pares (first among equals).**
- Further consideration: **More power for bishops' conferences** to take better account of regional contexts.

2. compulsory celibacy - an outdated relic

The debate on compulsory celibacy led to a broad consensus **that the Church urgently needs to find new ways to combat the shortage of priests** and avoid exposing priests to unnecessary psychological stress.

- Historical analysis has shown that celibacy is not a theological dogma, but a **canonical discipline** that can be changed.
- Unanimous recommendation: **celibacy for priests** only after an approval process.
- The report by pastors showed that **an open priesthood could not only increase vocations, but also make spiritual guidance more authentic**.

3. women in the priesthood - a decisive step for the credibility of the church

The question of **ordaining women as priests** was discussed controversially, but with a view to the future of the Church.

- **Historical retrospectives show** that women **held important spiritual offices in** the early church, including deaconesses and possibly also leaders of house churches.
- **Theological arguments against the ordination of women**, in particular the idea of the "male nature" of Christ as a justification for a purely male priesthood, were refuted as **not compelling and historically grown, but not theologically irrefutable**.
- **Majority recommendation:** Direct steps should be taken to introduce the priesthood of women. Corresponding posts should be made available via quotas.
- **There was widespread agreement that the current exclusion of women from ordained ministries also massively damages the credibility of the church.** In view of social developments and the ever-increasing questioning of previous teaching, it was urgently necessary to include women in the sacramental ministry - anything else would be gender-discriminatory and no longer meet today's standards.

Image26 : Image from the Vatican Council in Rome (illustration) designed above, where priests - women and men - sit together with joyful, open faces radiating an atmosphere of hope, equality and dialog - in a classical-historical style with a touch of reform spirit.

The debate showed that the ordination of women is **not only a question of justice,** but also one of theological consistency and the future viability of the church.

4. reform of sexual ethics and LGBTQIA+ inclusion

Traditional Catholic sexual morals were seen as **outdated and unrealistic**.

- Discussion about the **church's rejection of homosexuality**: The majority of theologians argued that this attitude has **no basis in the Gospels**.
- Proposal: **Blessing of same-sex couples as an official pastoral act**.
- Recommendation: **Theological reassessment** of the concept of marriage as a sacrament.
- Decision: The draft decision was adopted.

The final debate led to the adoption of the **"Charter of the Church's Readiness to Reform"**, which is intended to serve as a basis for future reforms. It emphasizes the priority of **pastoral practice over rigid dogma**, the adaptability of the Church to social developments and the need not to block dialogue with the faithful through dogmatic rigidity.

To-do list for the coming period

- ✓ **Theological commission** convened **to restrict papal infallibility** in order to strengthen synodal structures.
- ✓ Convene **theological commissions** to update church doctrines.
- ✓ Conduct **a study on the possibility of a married priesthood** in pilot dioceses.
- ✓ **Theological commission for the reassessment of the priesthood of women with official revision of *Ordinatio Sacerdotalis*** to lift the ban on the ordination of women.
- ✓ **Establish pilot dioceses** to test and document the first ordinations of women.
- ✓ **Establishment of an international network for Catholic women theologians** in order to integrate feminist theology into church teaching.
- ✓ **Official development of an LGBTQIA+-friendly pastoral strategy** based on the latest developments in the German church.
- ✓ **The International Synod on Sexual Ethics has been convened** to re-evaluate Catholic sexual morality.
- ✓ **Creation of internal reform committees in each bishops' conference** to accompany the implementation of these resolutions.

This Council was a decisive and necessary step towards a renewed, life-oriented Church that is ready to face the challenges of the 21st century. The coming period will be decisive in advancing these reforms and not only freeing the Catholic Church from its dogmatic rigidity, but also increasing its attractiveness as **an** employer brand.

A strong employer branding strategy for the Catholic Church today must go far beyond traditional ideals of vocation and provide answers to the expectations of a value-conscious, diversity-oriented and future-oriented working world. The central challenge is to credibly communicate **why it makes sense to be part of this organization today** and how work in the church can be combined with personal conviction, development and social relevance.

Here are key employer branding points for a **positive employer brand strategy for the Catholic Church**:

🌱 1. meaning and social relevance

- **Core message:** Those who work here shape the way we live together, support people in times of change, and are committed to justice, education and care.
- **Added value:** work in the church means meaning, not just function - a strong motive for many.

👥 2. diversity of occupational fields

- From pastoral care to social services, education, IT, administration, communication and environmental work - the church is a diverse employer.
- Employer branding should make this broad spectrum visible: **not just priests or religious**, but specialists in all areas.

---

3. values-based corporate culture

- **Credibility through practiced values**: solidarity, compassion, sustainability, human dignity.
- Important: Don't just preach values, but bring them to life in leadership behavior, dealings with employees and in decision-making processes.

---

4. personal and spiritual development

- Offers of supervision, spiritual guidance, ethical reflection, further training.
- **Employer branding pitch:** "Not just a job - a space for personal development."

---

5 Diversity and inclusion - with a willingness to change

- The church can show that it is changing, it is listening, it is opening up.
- **Important signal:** addressing grievances, working towards equality (e.. management positions for women, critical examination of celibacy), welcoming diversity.

---

6. compatibility of work and private life

- Many church organizations are already well positioned in terms of **part-time models, parental leave, sabbaticals and job sharing** - this should be communicated proactively.

---

7 Authentic communication and storytelling

- Let people tell us why they like working in the church - not PR, but real voices.

- Formats: Video interviews, Insta campaigns, portraits on websites, "A day as..."

The Catholic Church has great potential as an employer - **if it manages to communicate its strengths honestly, in a modern way and with a willingness to change.** Employer branding here does not mean whitewashing, but the courage to be transparent: yes, there are breaks, but also the will to renew. This can be very attractive - especially for young people looking for meaning.

Draft: Documentation of an address by the Pope at the Council on the reform of central dogmas and doctrines of the Catholic Church

"Get to work – otherwise the AI will do it"

On the effects of demographic change in the Catholic Church and the urgency of church renewal

Demographic change poses profound challenges for the Catholic Church, especially when more and more older clergy are dying or are no longer in office and at the same time it is becoming increasingly difficult to find suitable young people. In many countries, the number of ordinations to the priesthood is falling drastically, while the number of parishioners is also declining or becoming alienated from the church. At the same time, technological and social change is progressing so rapidly that traditional church structures are increasingly out of step with the reality of people's lives.

A key factor is the upcoming generation, which has grown up in a world that is heavily influenced by digitalization, artificial intelligence and a globalized media landscape. If, in future, clergymen come from this so-called "cell phone generation" and even a future pope has grown up with social media, gaming culture and modern forms of communication for the first time, the understanding of how faith is communicated will change effectively. Traditional sermon formats and dogmatic preaching will become less important, while interactive, dialog-oriented and multimedia formats will become increasingly important.

The church's personnel problem is being exacerbated by demographic change. While older generations often joined the church out of a sense of duty, younger people are opting for a spiritual career much more consciously and out of individual convictions. However, it is precisely these convictions that are increasingly diverging from the rigid doctrines of the church. Modern young clergy often bring with them an open-minded attitude to issues such as equal rights, sexuality, diversity and democracy - values that were previously fought against or only hesitantly acknowledged in many Catholic structures.

In order to meet people in their reality, the church must continue to develop its content. Young people expect authenticity, transparency and a theology that keeps pace with the challenges of the 21st century. Rigid moral concepts that, for example, exclude LGBTQIA+ people, keep women away from ordained ministries or view sexuality as a problem are met with rejection by the young generation. A church that does not provide relevant answers to such questions is increasingly losing importance.

Change in content is inevitable if the church still wants to reach the next generation. While for centuries change was seen as a danger, today it could be the only survival strategy. Theological issues need to be more closely aligned with the realities of believers' lives instead of insisting on abstract dogmas. A digitally networked society calls for open dialog, participatory processes and a church that communicates at eye level.

So if a new generation of clergy, bishops and perhaps even popes grows up in the near future, who have grown up with smartphones, AI, social media and a more democratic worldview, the Catholic Church could be facing the biggest upheaval in centuries. The crucial question will be whether it will actively shape this change or continue to insist on outdated structures and thus lose more and more of its relevance.

The urgency of an ecclesial renewal arises from several profound developments that are putting the Catholic Church under increasing pressure. Demographic change, the dwindling number of believers and clergy, the rapid social changes brought about by digitalization and social media and the growing gap between church doctrine and modern values make it clear that our rethinking is inevitable

In detail:

1. shrinking membership figures and loss of credibility

More and more people are leaving the church or distancing themselves from it because they no longer feel represented by its teachings. In Western societies in particular, the church is increasingly perceived as no longer being up to date. Sexual abuse scandals, the treatment of women, LGBTQIA+ people and moral double standards have severely damaged trust in the institution . Without fundamental reforms, this process will continue to accelerate.

2. lack of new blood in the clergy and outdated structures

The number of ordinations to the priesthood is decreasing worldwide, especially in Europe and North America. Many clergy are already of retirement age or are taking on several parishes at the same time because there are no successors. At the same time, the Church is denying women access to the priesthood, thereby depriving itself of the opportunity to recruit urgently needed pastors. Compulsory celibacy also deters many potential applicants. Without structural reforms in personnel policy, there will soon no longer be enough clergy to maintain pastoral care across the board.

3. cultural and technological change accelerates alienation

Modern society is characterized by social media, artificial intelligence, science and individual self-determination. While young people are looking for dialog, transparency and participation, the church often clings to hierarchical, authoritarian structures. Many young believers experience church teachings as unrealistic, dogmatic and morally outdated. If the church does not learn to communicate at eye level, make meaningful use of digital platforms and adapt its teachings to the challenges of today, it will ultimately become irrelevant for the younger generation.

4. incompatibility with modern ethical standards

On many moral and social issues, there is a huge gap between the church's position and the convictions of the majority of believers. While issues such as equal rights, sexual diversity, reproductive self-determination and social justice are considered core values in modern democracies, the church clings to centuries-old norms. The refusal to ordain women, the continued opposition to same-sex partnerships and the dogmatic control over sexual morality are examples of this discrepancy. Without an adjustment of these positions, the church will continue to lose social relevance.

5. risk of complete marginalization

If the church does not reform its structures and content, it risks becoming a marginal phenomenon in society in the long term. Even today, many Western countries have a highly secularized population in which the Christian faith hardly plays a role. Instead of being perceived as a moral authority, the church is increasingly seen as outdated, rigid and backward-looking. Without a profound renewal, it risks not only losing members, but also its influence on social and ethical debates.

Conclusion: "Dance or Die" - No future without change

We as the Catholic Church are at a crossroads. Either it opens up to reform, modernizes its teachings and structures and responds to the reality of people's lives, or it becomes increasingly irrelevant. A church that serves people instead of patronizing them, that does not block ethical debates but helps to shape them, and that recognizes diversity instead of fighting it, would have the potential to become a relevant and credible institution again. The urgency of this renewal arises from the fact that it is not just a question of adapting to the spirit of the times, but of the fundamental question of its ability to survive.

List of illustrations

DEUS EX MACHINA has also independently identified topics and sections for which it makes sense to generate illustrations based on the self-created structure. The following images are generated by artificial intelligence and inserted in the text. The content of the topics, the illustration and interpretation of the image elements as well as the descriptive texts - and thus also their focus - are selected, prioritized and generated entirely by AI:

The image of the curator at the imprint was processed using AI filters and algorithms.

Selected literature: Further readings

1. Church sexual morality between tradition and renewal

- **Bogner, Daniel** - *Love cannot fail. What sexual morality does the 21st century need? (2024):* Innovative approach to sexual morality that takes the human experience of love as its starting point and considers a radical reform of traditional doctrine to be necessary.
- **Breitsameter, Christof & Goertz, Stephan** - *Vom Vorrang der Liebe - Zeitenwende für die katholische Sexualmoral (2020):* Critically analyzes the normative logic of previous sexual doctrine and argues for a revision in favor of the priority of love.
- **Farley, Margaret A.** - *Just Love: A Framework for Christian Sexual Ethics (2006):* Feminist-influenced sexual ethics that puts justice and love at the center.
- **Keenan, James F. (ed.)** - *Catholic Sexual Theology and Adolescent Girls (2006):* Collection of modern perspectives (theological, pastoral, sociological) on the treatment of sexual morality and female adolescence, as an example of modern discourses.
- **Lintner, Martin M.** - *Christian relational ethics (2018):* Comprehensive study of the history and biblical foundations of Catholic sexual morality with the aim of a renewal in the dialog between the magisterium and moral theology.
- **Mahoney, John** - *The Making of Moral Theology (1987):* Classic historical review of the development of Catholic moral teaching, which helps to understand today's conflicts (for example in sexual ethics) in the light of history.
- **Moore, Gareth** - *A Question of Truth: Christianity and Homosexuality* (2003): Careful analysis of the biblical and theological arguments against homosexuality, showing what a theologically sound counter-position might look like.
- **Salzman, Todd A. & Lawler, Michael G.** - *The Sexual Person: Toward a Renewed Catholic Anthropology (2008):* Overview of Catholic sexual ethics over the past 50 years with the goal of a renewed anthropology.
- **Schockenhoff, Eberhard** - *The art of loving: Towards a new sexual ethic* (2021): Posthumously published standard work by a moral theologian that

combines tradition and reform and calls for a paradigm shift in church teaching.

- **Sipe, A.W. Richard** - *Sex, Priests, and Power: Anatomy of a Crisis* (1995): Sociological-psychological examination of the church's handling of sexuality (celibacy, abuse, image of women) and call for honest discussion, as unresolved problems of the system are recognized.

2. Power dynamics and control in the church

- **Coco, Angela** - *Catholics, Conflicts and Choices: An Exploration of Power Relations in the Catholic Church (2013):* Sociological study with interviews (laity, priests, religious) that analyzes gender-differentiated experiences of power in the church structure. It shows that, despite many challenges, hardly any change is possible as long as established power relations are not confronted.
- **Doyle, Tom et al** - *Sexual Abuse in the Catholic Church: A Decade of Crisis (2006):* Uses the abuse crisis to document how opaque power structures and authoritarian control in the church contributed to the cover-up of crimes, and discusses necessary changes in church leadership and accountability.
- **Haslinger, Herbert** - *Macht in der Kirche: Wo wir sie finden - Wer sie ausübt - Wie wir sie überwinden* (2022): Extensive analysis of power structures in the church using social science theories of power; explicitly deals with the connection between sexuality, ordained ministry and the exclusion of women.
- **Iten, Karin** - *A toxic coupling of power and spirituality (Interview, 2021):* Church prevention officer describes how the church's long role of domination has led to a "toxic coupling of power and spirituality"; as long as the institution clings to power of definition, genuine spiritual self-determination remains an illusion.
- **Kopp, Stefan (ed.)** - *Macht und Ohnmacht in der Kirche: Wege aus der Krise (2020):* Anthology (Synodal Path), which self-critically analyzes patterns of thought and action in the church after the abuse crisis and loss of trust and points out paths for reform.
- **Machiavelli, Niccolò** - *Il Principe* (1532): Machiavelli was a political thinker of the Renaissance, who in this work reflects on rule in a sober and power-strategic way. *The Prince* is still considered a key text for analyzing political power today.
- **Reisinger, Doris** - *Spiritual abuse in the Catholic Church (2019):* Theological and autobiographical reappraisal showing how spiritual abuse is facilitated by power structures and calling for reforms to prevent abuse of power against women and religious.

- **Robinson, Bishop Geoffrey** - *Confronting Power and Sex in the Catholic Church: Reclaiming the Spirit of Jesus (2008):* Criticizes the church's exercise of power "from pope to preacher" and proposes a new model of authority that includes all believers as responsible adults.

- **Wilson, George B.** - *Clericalism: The Death of Priesthood (2008):* Examines "clerical culture" as a breeding ground for abuse of power. Emphasizes that all church members share responsibility for this culture and its change. Analyzes underlying attitudes that create destructive clergy-laity relationships and calls for transformation of this culture.

- **Zagano, Phyllis** - *Women: Icons of Christ (2020):* Examines the systemic exclusion of women from ordained ministries as a power problem and argues for women in diaconal ministries as a step towards breaking down clerical monopolies of power.

3. Reflections on dogmatism and church teachings

- **Darwin, Charles** - *On the Origin of Species* (1859): Darwin founded the theory of evolution with this work. His scientific view radically challenged the Christian-biblical understanding of creation.
- **Dawkins, Richard** - *The God Delusion* (2006):n Dawkins is an evolutionary biologist and a prominent representative of the New Atheism. *In The God Delusion* he attacks religious belief as irrational and harmful to society.

- **Haight, Roger** - *Jesus Symbol of God (1999):* Attempts to interpret Christological dogmas in today's language. However, the book was criticized by the Vatican because of deviations from classical formulas - a current example of tensions between innovative theology and the dogma guardian mentality.

- **Harris, Sam** - *The End of Faith* (2004): Harris is a neuroscientist and critic of religion. He argues that faith without evidence is dangerous and that religious dogma hinders moral progress.

- **Küng, Hans** - *Infallible? An inquiry (1970):* Küng's critical questioning of the dogma of papal infallibility. The book caused great controversy - Küng lost his church teaching license for it in 1979 - and is exemplary of the conflict between free theology and dogmatism.

- **Lindbeck, George** - *The Nature of Doctrine (1984):* Establishes the understanding of doctrine not as immutable propositions of truth but as a cultural-linguistic *set of rules*. His approach helped to overcome dogmatism by seeing doctrines as *"simultaneously true and in need of reform"* in an ecclesial language game.

- **Massa, Mark S.** - *The Structure of Theological Revolutions* (2018): Uses the example of the 1968 encyclical *Humanae Vitae* to analyze the rupture between the Church's doctrinal development and the modern world. Shows that many theologians at the time perceived the rigid sexual doctrine as *"rigid, ahistorical and alien to life"* and expected a paradigm shift - the non-opening in *Humanae Vitae* was seen as a reactionary step. Massa uses Thomas Kuhn's concept of paradigm to make such phases of theological upheaval understandable.

- **Metz, Johann Baptist** - *Faith in History and Society (1977):* Political theology that criticizes ossified dogmatism. Metz emphasizes that church doctrine should always be formulated anew from the dangerous memory of Jesus' practice of solidarity with the suffering, rather than in timeless sentences far removed from reality.

- **Ratzinger, Joseph** - *Introduction to Christianity (1968):* Not a plea against dogmas, but an understandable exposition of the creed *in the context of modern issues*. Shows indirectly how even a later strictly dogmatic pope previously recognized the interpretation of dogmas according to the times - for example by emphasizing the personal fulfillment of faith behind or before doctrinal formulas.

- **Schüssler Fiorenza, Elisabeth** - *In Memory of Her (1983):* Feminist theological reconstruction of early Christian history. Shows how dogmatic historiography marginalized the decisive contributions of women in the early church. Challenges the *"androcentric"* nature of church doctrinal traditions and calls for a more inclusive memory.

- **Voltaire** - *Dictionnaire philosophique* (1764): Voltaire was a harsh critic of religious dogma and ecclesiastical power. In *his philosophical dictionary*, he takes a satirical and enlightened look at religion, tolerance and reason.

- **Wills, Garry** - *Papal Sin: Structures of Deceit (2000):* Ruthlessly critical examination of how, in modern times, church authorities defend dogmatic positions (e.g. on the priesthood of women or contraception) at all costs through *"structures of deceit"*. Wills describes a church that denies historical truths and blocks reforms for fear of losing authority.

4. Matters of interpretation: Bible, upbringing & education in dialog

- **Achilles, Oliver** - *Who loves his child, beats it?* (Blog, 2020): A biblical-hermeneutical re-evaluation of *Prov 13:24*. Achilles shows that even ancient translators understood the *"rod"* as an educational metaphor - "love means to educate, not to beat" - and opposes any biblical justification of violence in child rearing.

- **Bible in just language (2006):** German Bible translation based on inclusive language. A practical testimony to the dialog between the Bible and modern understanding: it uses female metaphors of God, for example, and aims to raise awareness of linguistic images in *education and teaching*.

- **Bunge, Marcia J. (ed.)** - *The Child in the Bible (2008):* An anthology of 19 exegetes that examines *biblical perspectives on children and childhood.* The contributions examine, for example, education and discipline in Proverbs, the image of man as God's child, etc. - and invite us to reconsider the role of children in religious communities

- **Descartes, René** - *Meditationes de prima philosophia* (1641): Descartes is considered the father of modern rationalism. In the *Meditations*, he develops his famous principle "I think, therefore I am" and establishes a new method of doubt.
- **Diderot, Denis** - *Encyclopédie* (1751-72): Diderot was co-founder of the *Encyclopédie*, which collected the knowledge of the Enlightenment. It was a revolutionary project to liberate thought from ecclesiastical and absolutist control.
- **Feuerbach, Ludwig** - *The nature of Christianity* (1841): Feuerbach was a critic of religion who argued that God was a projection of human nature. His work was groundbreaking for the later criticism of religion by Marx, Nietzsche and Freud.

- **Groome, Thomas H.** - *Christian Religious Education (1980):* Establishes the method of *Shared Christian Praxis*. Groome shows how religious education can function as a dialog: Christian stories (Bible, tradition) are brought into critical dialog with the life stories of the learners so that faith takes shape in life. This dialogical practice combines biblical interpretation and education in an exemplary way.

- **Hume, David** - *A Treatise of Human Nature* (1739-40): Hume analyzes human thought as a psychological process and doubts the existence of objective causality. He is considered a radical skeptic and pioneer of the Enlightenment.

- **Jeanrond, Werner G.** - *Understanding the Bible (1994):* Introduction to biblical hermeneutics, which also touches on didactic issues. Shows that every interpretation of the Bible must take into account contexts (such as educational situations) and that understanding is always a dialog between text and reader - which is directly applicable to Bible teaching in schools and churches.

- **Jensen, David H.** - *Graced Vulnerability: A Theology of Childhood (2005):* Theological reflection on childhood in dialog with biblical theology. Helps to understand upbringing as participation in God's grace and to view children theologically not as *"unfinished adults"* but as independent subjects.

- **Klein, Stephanie** - *Girls' images of God (2000):* Empirical study in religious education. Illuminates how girls perceive biblical stories and which images of

God arise from this. Provides valuable insights for coordinating biblical interpretation and educational goals in a gender-sensitive way.

- **Laplace, Pierre-Simon** - *Essai philosophique sur les probabilités* (1814): Laplace was a mathematician and Enlightenment philosopher who combined the deterministic view of the world with the theory of probability in this work. He did not see God as a necessary hypothesis for explaining nature.
- **Locke, John** - *An Essay Concerning Human Understanding* (1690): Locke was a central representative of empiricism. In his *essay*, he argues that all human knowledge comes from experience - a counter-model to rationalist thinking.
- **Saramago, José** - *The Gospel according to Jesus Christ* (1991): Saramago was a Portuguese writer and Nobel Prize winner. In his gospel, he focuses on a human, doubting Jesus figure and criticizes institutionalized religion.
- **Schmidt, Tanja** - *The Bible as a medium of religious education (2008):* Religious education study that rethinks classical Bible didactics. She emphasizes that the Bible must be rediscovered in a *"post-traditional"* context. Schmidt shows how the Bible serves as an indispensable resource for identity formation and argues in favor of anchoring Bible lessons centrally in the school curriculum.

5. Women in the church and religion: historical developments and feminist perspectives

- **Boff, Leonardo & Boff, Clodovis** - *Women - Church - Ministry (German, 1982):* The liberation theologians Boff show from a Latin American perspective that the oppression of women in the church is incompatible with the option for the poor. They argue theologically for the complete equality of women in the church and ministry.
- **Cahill, Lisa Sowle** - *Women and Sexuality in Christian Tradition (1996):* Sociological and ethical analysis of the eventful history of church teachings on women (from early Christian communities through the Middle Ages to the present day). Cahill shows continuities and breaks and develops a contemporary feminist sexual ethic within the tradition.
- **Daly, Mary** - *The Church and the Second Sex (1968):* Early feminist criticism of the Catholic Church. Daly, herself a theologian, denounces the fact that the Church has spiritually incapacitated women for centuries. The book inspired an entire generation of Catholic women to demand equal rights and paved the way for Daly's more radical works (e.g. *Beyond God the Father*).
- **de Beauvoir, Simone** - *Le Deuxième Sexe (The Other Sex, 1949):* Beauvoir is considered a co-founder of modern feminism. In *The Other Sex*, she analyzes how religion and philosophy push women into a subordinate role.

- **Heine, Susanne** - *Women and Early Christianity: Are the Feminist Scholars Right? (1987):* Factually examines the theses of feminist exegesis. Heine confirms many unique insights (e.g. a new view of women's roles in the New Testament), but also calls for *an irenic* reconciliation with tradition. An important work in the German-speaking world that reflects the international debate.

- **Küng, Hans** - *Die Frau im Christentum (2001):* Historical overview from the early church to the present day. Küng vividly shows that women *in early Christianity* were naturally companions of the apostles, disciples and prophets. It was not until the Middle Ages that women were ousted from leadership positions - this historical finding forms the basis for today's demands for reform.

- **Mulack, Christa** - *Maria, die geheime Göttin im Christentum* (1983): Cultural-historical study of the repressed female aspects of the Christian concept of God. Mulack interprets Mary as a *"hidden divine feminine"* and criticizes how the church has marginalized female spirituality.

- **Radford Ruether, Rosemary** - *Sexism and God-Talk (1983):* Basic text on feminist theology. Ruether analyzes the Christian tradition for patriarchal distortions (e.g. exclusively male images of God) and drafts guidelines for a renewed, non-sexist theology. Particularly important is her historical section on female figures such as *Macrina, Paula and Marcella*, who assumed spiritual leadership in the early church.

- **Ranke-Heinemann, Uta** - *Eunuchs for the Kingdom of Heaven: Women, Sexuality and the Catholic Church (1988):* Classic of church criticism. With biting irony, Ranke-Heinemann leads *"feminist accusations"* against church fathers and popes from Augustine to John Paul II. She documents how women were treated as second-class Christians and how their sexuality was demonized. A central theme is the church's hostility towards lust, which distorts marriage, motherhood and femininity.

- **Schüssler Fiorenza, Elisabeth** - *In Memory of Her (1983):* Pioneering work of feminist biblical scholarship. Reconstructs the actual role of women in the early church and reveals how established theology has forgotten these contributions. Her approach - *"making women's memory visible"* - became fundamental for later feminist theologies.

6. Queer Jesus: searching for, finding and interpreting his sexual identity

- **Althaus-Reid, Marcella** - *The Queer God (2003):* The Argentinian theologian does not develop a historical thesis on Jesus' sexuality, but she *"queers"* the entire doctrine of God. In doing so, she also raises questions about Jesus' physicality and sexuality. Her "indecent theology" encourages us to look for hidden, possibly queer facets of Jesus instead of depicting him as desexualized.

- **Bauer, J. Edgar** - *Was Jesus married? (2003):* Popular scientific reappraisal of the speculation surrounding Jesus' relationship life (Mary Magdalene, John). Although Bauer does not draw a clear conclusion, he collects historical hypotheses that question the heteronormativity of the images of Jesus.

- **Benny Liew, Tat-siong** - *Queer Biblical Hermeneutics on the Gospel of John (article, 2009):* Reads the Gospel of John from an Asian-American queer perspective. He interprets, for example, the *washing of the feet* and the intimate *breast situation at the Last Supper* as conscious queer codes in the text. Helps to see the figure of Jesus beyond heteronormative clichés.

- **Brinkschröder, Michael** - *Sodom as a symptom (2006):* Queer-theological analysis of the traditional rejection of homosexuals. Not directly about Jesus' sexuality, but Brinkschröder applies queer-theoretical critique to biblical texts (such as Gen 19) and argues that "repressed queer perspectives" should also be applied to Jesus instead of viewing him exclusively in heteronormative terms.

- **Cheng, Patrick S.** - *Radical Love: An Introduction to Queer Theology (2011):* Introduction, which also outlines a *"queer Christology"*. Cheng interprets Christ as the incarnation of radical divine love that transcends all sexual and gender boundaries. In the chapter "Queer Christ", he theologically links Jesus' identity with the experience of queer people (rejection, coming out, liberation).

- **Goss, Robert E.** - *Jesus Acted Up: A Gay and Lesbian Manifesto (1993):* An early queer theological manifesto. Goss, himself a theologian and former priest, portrays Jesus as a solidary *"outcast"* who rebelled against religious and sexual exclusion. He calls on LGBT Christians to radically reclaim Jesus' inclusive message for themselves.

- **Jennings Jr, Theodore W.** - *The Man Jesus Loved: Homoerotic Narratives from the New Testament (2003):* A provocative thesis by an evangelical theologian: Jennings reads the Gospel of John *in a gay-affirmative way* and asks about the *"Beloved Disciple"* relationship. He thoroughly examines the scenes with the "disciple whom Jesus loved" in order to reveal the intimacy of this relationship - without flatly claiming "Jesus was gay", but rather to take the biblical allusions seriously.

- **Werner, Gunda (ed.)** - *Queer Theology (2021):* Anthology with a contribution *"Queer Jesus?"*, which explains how Jesus can be read as an identifying figure for LGBTQIA+. Biblical science, psychology and personal spirituality come together here.

7. Queer community: perspectives in church and theology through LGBTQIA+

- **#OutInChurch** - *For a church without fear (2022, ed. Brinkschröder et al.):* Collection of testimonials from Catholic employees who came out as queer in 2022. Priests, teachers and members of religious orders describe their stories authentically: *"As a lesbian religious education teacher, can I be myself openly? Does the church accept me as I am?"*. Accompanied by specialist contributions (psychology, moral theology), the book ends with an urgent appeal for a *"church without fear"* in which everyone can live their identity honestly.

- **Alison, James** - *Faith Beyond Resentment: Fragments Catholic and Gay (2001):* Theological essays by a gay Catholic theologian. Alison reflects first-hand on faith *between belonging and marginalization*. He shows ways in which LGBTQ Christians can live their faith without despair, while providing subtle criticism of church homophobia.

- **Amaladoss, Michael** - *Inclusive Community: A Gospel Model (1990):* From an Indian perspective, the author develops the vision of an *"inclusive church"*. Not specifically LGBTQ, but the concept of a community that welcomes all identities can be applied to queer believers - an important contribution to the theological foundation of diversity in the church.

- **Boswell, John** - *Christianity, Social Tolerance, and Homosexuality (1980): "Groundbreaking"* historical study of the church's treatment of homosexuality from antiquity to the Middle Ages. Boswell shows that there were phases of relative acceptance in the early church - e.g. homosexual clerics and even saints. His meticulous research refutes the assumption that the condemnation of homosexuals has always been the church's standard.

- **Catholic Youth Commission DBK** - *Blessings for all lovers? (Recommendation 2022):* Impulse text from the youth bishops, which advocates the church's recognition of same-sex couples. Exemplifies the change in perspective within the church in favor of the LGBTQIA+ community.

- **Luciani, Rafael** - *Pueblo de Dios, pueblo diverso* (2021): Spanish-language theology that shows how the Latin American Church is striving to do justice to the diversity of God's people. Includes voices of LGBT Catholics and pleads for *pastoral conversion* in favor of the marginalized.

- **Pope Francis** - *"Who am I to judge him?" (uttered in 2013):* Not a book, but a historically important moment: Francis' publicly stated attitude towards a gay priest (*"Who am I to judge him when he seeks the Lord?"*) marked a turning point in the Church's tone towards LGBTQ people. It is often cited as the beginning of a more open dialog.

- **Zagano, Phyllis / Macy, Gary / et al** - *Women Deacons: Past, Present, Future (2011):* This work focuses on women, but has overlaps with LGBTQ inclusion: it argues that the exclusion of groups (such as women from ministry) contradicts the inclusivity of the gospel. Based on historical research, the authors call for church structures to be opened up to all baptized people. Such reforms would also benefit LGBTQ people as they strengthen a *culture of welcome*.

8. Images of God and gender diversity: deconstructing traditional ideas

- ***Bible in fair language*** - *Addressing "God" (2006):* This Bible translation experiments with addressing God in a gender-equitable way (e.g. "God the Father and Mother"). It reflects the attempt to deconstruct traditional one-sided images of . An example from Hos 11:9: *"For I am God, and not a man"* - emphasizes God's transcendence beyond male concepts.

- **Daly, Mary** - *Beyond God the Father (1973):* Radical feminist standard work. Daly exposes the identification of God as male as a fundamental problem: *"If God is male, then male is God."* - "If God is male, then male is God". She calls for the "depatrification" of the concept of God in order to free women from spiritual subordination.

- **Dinkelaker, Veit** - *The Gender God (Essay, 2019):* Summarizes current considerations: Gender diversity is also reflected in images of God. "Gender diversity and the gender question have always existed", including in biblical metaphors of God. Dinkelaker argues that a contemporary image of God must transcend binarity in order to do justice to God's greatness.

- **Hofmann, Siegfried (ed.)** - *Gott weiblich - Gottesbilder von Frauen (1994):* Essays on female images of God in the Bible, history and the present. Shows, among other things, biblical *"God as mother"* motifs (e.g. Isaiah) and documents how women have repeatedly emphasized God's maternal side in the history of spirituality.

- **Johnson, Elizabeth A.** - *She Who Is: The Mystery of God in Feminist Theological Discourse (1992): A* milestone in feminist theology. Johnson argues for the equal use of female metaphors of God. God has *no concrete gender,* but all our images (paternal and maternal) are inadequate - but only in combination do justice to the infinite mystery. She shows that purely masculine discourse about God draws *false boundaries* around the transcendent God.

- **Catholic Youth Association KjG** - *Proposal "God" (2021):* The youth association discussed writing God with the gender star "God*" in future. This *sensitization* arose because *"more and more believers are alienated by the* *image of a male-patriarchal, white God"*. The initiative is a practical example of how young believers are questioning traditional concepts of God and want to formulate them in a more inclusive way.

- **Moltmann, Jürgen** - *The crucified God (1972):* Questions triumphalist images of God. Although not a gender book, Moltmann emphasizes God's solidarity in suffering. He indirectly deconstructs the overly masculine, monarchical image of God and opens up for a compassionate, *"feminine"* connotated image of God in pain.

- **Seitl, Gertrud** - *God's images - our images (1995):* Religious education study on how children absorb different images of God (paternal, maternal, creative). Shows that diverse images of God can be conveyed from an early age in order to avoid restrictive ideas (e.g. "old man with beard") - such complaints can even be heard from bishops: God is "not an old man with a long white beard".

9. Paths to an inclusive church: Reforms for a contemporary Christian ethic

- **Resolutions of the Synodal Path** *(Germany, 2022):* E.g. the orientation text on church doctrinal development emphasizes that *"Reforms are an integral part of tradition: worship changes; doctrine develops"*. Tradition must not become a *"corset"* - it is alive and must continue to develop **"with the changing times".** This principle supports all reforms towards inclusivity (e.g. new ethics in sexual morality, participation of all the baptized).

- **de Chardin, Pierre Teilhard** - *The Future of the Church (Writings, 1950s):* Forward-looking thoughts of a Jesuit who outlines a dynamic, *inclusive-evolutionary* ecclesiology. Teilhard predicted that the Church would only remain sustainable if it adapted to the growing unity of humanity (keyword *"Point Omega"*) - an indirect vision of inclusion as part of the divine plan.

- **Lay initiative *We are Church*** (since 1995): Citizens' movement calling for reforms (celibacy optional, women's ministries, new sexual morals). Their published catalogs of demands and studies prove that inclusivity in the church is a concern of broad sections of the faithful - and they have developed theologically sound reasons for what a *"church of participation"* could look like.

- **Mann, Gerald** - *Evolution of dogma (2020):* Uses church history (such as the development of social doctrine, religious freedom) to show that the church has always learned to renew ethics and doctrine. From this, Mann deduces that current reforms - from the *inclusion of all genders* to the re-evaluation of modern lifestyles - are legitimate continuations of this tradition.

- **Mertes, Klaus** - *Wounded Church (2019):* The Jesuit Mertes (known as an investigator of abuse) pleads for *humility and a willingness to reform* the church. He sees coming to terms with abuse of power and injustice as a spiritual path to inclusion: only a church that acknowledges its wounds can be **credibly inclusive today**.

- **Pope Francis** - *Amoris Laetitia (2016):* Opens up paths to more mercy and individual justice in questions of family ethics (e.g. dealing with remarried divorcees). This document is exemplary of a new ethical approach that places inclusivity above rigid rules and further develops doctrine.
- **Pope Francis** - *Apostolic Exhortation Evangelii Gaudium (2013):* Programmatic vision of a missionary open church. Francis calls for an end to *"compartmentalization"* and calls for pastoral creativity. In *EG* 47-49 in particular, he shows ways in which a *"Church on the move"* should leave no one behind on the margins.
- **Zagano, Phyllis et al** - *Women Deacons: Past, Present, Future (2011):* Examines the history of women deacons and argues for their reinstatement today. The book thoroughly documents that there were female deacons in the past and that the church needs such ministries *today* - *"in a changing world"*. Opening up ministries to women would be an important step towards a more inclusive church.

10. Self-determination & liberation theology: social and spiritual perspectives

- **Boff, Leonardo** - *Church: Charisma and Power (1981):* Boff is fundamentally critical of clerical power, which often runs counter to the message of freedom. He develops visions of a *grassroots-oriented church* in which the charisms of all are effective - a concept that promotes the self-determination of congregations and aims to structurally anchor the "option for the poor" idea. Boff thus combines inner church reform with social liberation.
- **Cone, James H.** - *God of the Oppressed (1975):* Founder of black theology in the USA. Cone emphasizes that God is on the side of the oppressed (in his context, African Americans). His theology combines biblical exodus and the civil rights movement and calls on the church to actively fight against racism and social sins. An example of how liberation theology has different faces depending on the social context (in this case racism).
- **de Montaigne, Michel** - *Essais* (1580): Montaigne was a French humanist who first made the personal self a philosophical subject in his *Essais*. His skepticism towards absolute truths still shapes modern subjectivity today.
- **de Spinoza, Baruch** - *Ethica* (1677): Spinoza developed a pantheistic view of God and understood God and nature to be identical. *Ethics* is a systematic work that combines logic and metaphysics.

- **Freire, Paulo** - *Pedagogy of the Oppressed (1970):* Key work on education as a path to self-determination. Freire explains: *"Education either serves to integrate the younger generation into the logic of the system - or it becomes the practice of freedom"*. His method of raising awareness (*conscientização*) inspired liberation theologians to combine faith with political education so that the oppressed could stand up for justice in a self-determined way.

- **Gutiérrez, Gustavo** - *A Theology of Liberation (1971):* Founding text of liberation theology. Gutiérrez combines salvation and liberation and calls for *revolutionary changes instead of reform cosmetics: "We therefore speak of social revolution, not reform; of liberation, not development"*. Theology must become a *"critical reflection"* that does not justify the status quo in religious terms, but liberates society from the absolute setting of temporal orders. For him, poverty is a *"scandalous state against the will of God"*.

- **Kairos document (South Africa, 1985):** A *"moment of truth"* for the churches in the struggle against apartheid. In it, South African theologians called on the churches to actively side with the oppressed - if necessary even to engage *in civil disobedience* against the unjust regime. This document is a practical example of liberation theology: faith here directly commits to the fight against social inequality (racial segregation).

- **McKenna, Megan** - *Luke 4:18 - A Spirituality of Liberation (1989):* Biblical spiritual reflection on Jesus' programmatic discourse "The Spirit of the Lord... he has sent me to proclaim liberation to the captives. McKenna shows how this verse can serve as a spiritual center for Christian engagement in the world: true piety always aims at justice and liberation, never just inward.

- **Sobrino, Jon** - *Jesus the Liberator (1991; tr. 1998):* Christology from a Salvadoran perspective. Sobrino portrays Jesus as the one who *liberates holistically* - from sin and from unjust structures. His emphasis that following Jesus today means working for the poor inextricably links spirituality and social perspective.

- **Sölle, Dorothee** - *Leiden (1973) & Stellvertretung (1965):* The German liberation theologian Sölle calls for individual and collective *"self-liberation"*. In *Stellvertretung*, she develops the idea that Christians must not passively accept suffering and injustice, but must stand up for others (political witness). Her works combine mysticism and resistance - for Sölle, self-determination also means emancipating oneself from false authorities (including church authorities).

11. Faith between social justice and social inequality

- **"Kairos for Creation"** - *Ecumenical Declaration (2020):* Combines social justice with environmental justice. The statement *"Climate change hits the poorest hardest"* emphasizes that commitment to God's creation is also commitment to the world's poor. This broad ecumenical consensus shows a broader understanding of justice in which faith motivates the preservation of all creation.

- **"Preferential Option for the Poor"** - *resolution of the Medellín Bishops' Conference (1968):* Latin American bishops declared that the Church must give priority to the poor. This principle - the "option for the poor" - has been at the heart of the Church's social teaching ever since and inextricably links faith with a commitment to justice. It means that church action must be measured by its contribution to reducing inequality.

- **Compendium of the Social Doctrine of the Church (2004):** Overview work by the Vatican that sets out the principles of social justice from a biblical-theological perspective - human dignity, common good, solidarity, subsidiarity. It shows how faith and justice are connected: *"Love without justice is sentimentality, justice without love is legalism."* The numerous quotations (Council texts, encyclicals) illustrate the church's growing consensus against social inequality.

- **Francis, Pope** - *Evangelii Gaudium §53 (2013):* Clear indictment of global injustice: *"An economy like this kills."* Francis asks: *"How can it be that the death of a homeless old man is not newsworthy, but a fall in the stock market is?"*. He denounces indifference towards the poor as the *"globalization of indifference"* and calls for the economy and society to be geared towards people rather than profit.

- **Hitchens, Christopher** - *God Is Not Great* (2007): Hitchens was a controversial journalist and intellectual. In his book, he criticizes religion as a source of violence, oppression and intellectual stagnation.

- **John Paul II** - *Encyclical Centesimus Annus (1991):* On the 100th anniversary of *Rerum Novarum*, the Pope reaffirms the Church's commitment to social justice. He praises free enterprise, but warns: *"A society in which the laws of the market rule absolutely runs the risk of sacrificing the weak."* This doctrinal letter mediates Catholic social teaching between capitalism and socialism and updates the mission of solidarity.

- **Kant, Immanuel** - *Critique of Pure Reason* (1781): Kant attempted to reconcile rationalism and empiricism. His critique is a foundation of modern epistemology and had a lasting influence on theology and ethics.

- **King Jr, Martin Luther** - *Letter from Birmingham Jail (1963):* The Baptist pastor argues biblically and morally against racial inequality: *"Injustice anywhere* *threatens justice everywhere."* This letter - also addressed to moderate church leaders - appeals to the Christian conscience not to remain neutral. It illustrates the tension between personal faith and social responsibility.

- **Onfray, Michel** - *Traité d'athéologie* (2005): Onfray is a French philosopher who advocates secular ethics without God. In his *treatise on atheology*, he polemicizes against the three monotheistic religions.

- **Romero, Oscar A.** - *The voice of the voiceless (collection of sermons, 1977-80):* The Salvadoran archbishop repeatedly denounced social inequality in his sermons: *"The church becomes the voice of those who have no voice."* His words show lived faith in the midst of injustice - and how prophetic advocacy for the poor can ultimately lead to martyrdom. Romero personifies faith in a God of justice.

- **Rousseau, Jean-Jacques** - *Du contrat social* (1762): Rousseau outlines a political philosophy based on popular sovereignty. The *social contract* was central to modern ideas of democracy.

- **Central Committee of German Catholics (ZdK)** - *Social Word (2003):* Joint statement from the Catholic and Protestant sides on the economic and social situation. It calls for a sustainable fight against unemployment and poverty in Germany. An example of how churches accompany concrete political developments and call for the dignity of every human being to be respected in economic life.

12. Interreligious perspectives through dialog and comparisons

- **Declaration *Nostra Aetate* (Vatican II, 1965):** fundamental text of interreligious dialog. Key sentence: *"The Catholic Church rejects nothing that is true and holy in these religions."* It regards with sincere respect the ways of acting and living of other faiths, which *"often reveal a ray of that truth"* which enlightens all people. This new self-understanding opened the door to respectful dialog after centuries of opposition.

- **Eck, Diana L.** - *Encountering God: A Spiritual Journey from Bozeman to Banaras (1993):* The religious studies scholar describes her personal spiritual enrichment through her encounter with Hinduism in India. She illustrates *a "double sense of belonging"* - how a Christian can rediscover her own faith through dialog with Hindu traditions. Such testimonials show the fruit of interfaith comparisons on an individual level.

- **Francis & Grand Imam al-Tayyeb** - *Document on the brotherhood of all people* (Abu Dhabi, 2019): Joint declaration by Pope and Cairo Grand Imam emphasizing brotherhood, peace and freedom as God's will for all people. It condemns extremism in the name of religion. This document is historic because it shows how direct dialogues between the highest representatives of different religions can lead to common moral appeals - a tangible step forward in interfaith understanding.

- **Küng, Hans** - *Global Ethic Project (1990) & Parliament of the World's Religions (Chicago 1993):* Küng's guiding principle *"No peace among nations without peace among religions. No peace among religions without dialog among religions."* became programmatic. The *Declaration on a Global Ethic* (1993) formulated ethical principles common to all religions (Golden Rule, justice, truthfulness, renunciation of violence). This shows how comparisons of traditions can lead to a consensus on basic values, without uniting differences, but enabling cooperation.

- **Kuschel, Karl-Josef** - *Jesus im Dialog der Religionen (1994):* Examines how other religions (Islam, Hinduism, Buddhism) see Jesus, and how Christians in turn can deal with Buddha, Mohammed & Co. Kuschel advocates a **"comparative theological dialogue"**: learning from each other's experiences of God in order to deepen one's own faith instead of relativizing it.

- **Maimonides / von Aquin, Thomas** - *Comparison of the doctrines of God (12th/13th century):* As early as the Middle Ages, Jewish and Christian scholars entered into indirect dialog through texts. Maimonides' *Guide to the Indecisive* and Aquinas' *Summa contra Gentiles* compare philosophical concepts of God. This gave rise to *negative theology*, for example, which influenced Jews, Christians and later Muslims - an example of how comparisons contribute to deeper mutual understanding.

- **Scriptural Reasoning (since around 2002):** A new method of dialog in which Jews, Christians and Muslims read and discuss their Holy Scriptures together. It originated at the University of Cambridge and spread worldwide. This joint *comparison of scriptures* has shown that it is possible to learn together before God in dialog, even with different theologies - parallel narratives (e.g. Abraham) are often compared, which allows surprising insights into all three traditions.

- **Swidler, Leonard** - *The Dialogue Decalogue (1983):* Ten principles for interreligious dialog, including: *"Dialogue requires mutual learning"* and *"Stay rooted in your identity while opening up."* Swidler's rules are widely used in religious studies and serve as a practical guide for successful encounters at eye level.